PENNSYLVANIA
❖DUTCH❖
& Other Essays

Phebe Earle Gibbons

Introduction by Don Yoder

STACKPOLE
BOOKS

Originally published in 1882 by J. B. Lippincott & Co.
Introduction copyright ©2001 by Don Yoder

Published in 2001 by
STACKPOLE BOOKS
5067 Ritter Road
Mechanicsburg, PA 17055
www.stackpolebooks.com

Printed in the United States of America
10 9 8 7 6 5 4 3 2 1
FIRST STACKPOLE BOOKS EDITION

Cover design by Wendy A. Reynolds

Library of Congress Cataloging-in-Publication Data

Gibbons, Phebe, Earle, b. 1821
   [Pennsylvania Dutch and other essays]
   Pennsylvania Dutch & other essays / Phebe Earle Gibbons ; introduction by Don Yoder.—1st ed.
    p. cm.
   Originally published: Pennsylvania Dutch and other essays. 3rd ed.,
rev. and enl. Philadelphia : J.B. Lippincott, 1882.
   Includes bibliographical references.
   ISBN 0-8117-2902-8
   1. Pennsylvania Dutch. 2. Ethnology—Pennsylvania. 3. Pennsylvania—Ethnic relations. 4. Pennsylvania—Social life and customs.
5. Country life—Pennsylvania. 6. Church of the Brethren. Middle Pennsylvania District. 7. Moravians—Pennsylvania. 8. Schwenkfelders—
Pennsylvania. 9. Immigrants—Pennsylvania. I. Title.

F160.G3 G43 2001
305.8'009748—dc21

                             2001034418

INTRODUCTION

by Don Yoder

LIVING IN the midst of the Mennonite and Amish Plain Dutch country of Lancaster County, Phebe Earle Gibbons fulfilled her role as a Quaker farmwife, mother, and neighbor. With her plain Quaker costume and plain language, and her immense sympathy and understanding for the human condition wherever she found it, Phebe developed a strong rapport with her plain neighbors. She visited them frequently, quilted with them, and attended their snitzing parties and applebutter boilings.

Being good at languages, she knew German, and despite her protests to the contrary, she managed to understand much of the spoken Pennsylvania Dutch that was the everyday language of the neighborhood. In fact, she had a good ear for dialect, particularly the "Dutchified" English that came forth when her Dutch neighbors spoke what they thought was English. Many examples of these quaint locutions are reproduced, sympathetically and without malice, in her book. She did the same in her chapters on the farmers of Ireland and England and on the miners of Scranton, with which she rounded out this third edition of her book.

Not only did Phebe absorb the face and look of the Pennsylvania Dutch plain culture of her country neighbors, but she also informed herself on their ways of worship and their religious usages and beliefs by frankly questioning them in person, reading their ponderous German history books, and attending their worship services.

In all this reportage, we can call her, in the sense of Margaret Mead's anthropological approach to the non-Western world, a "participant observer," living in a culture and growing into an understanding of another way of life. She was, indeed, in the best sense of the word, an ethnographer. Among the chapters that illustrate this go-to-meeting-with-them approach are "An Amish Meeting," "The

Dunker Love-Feast," "Ephrata," "Bethlehem and the Moravians," and "Schwenkfelders."

Typical of her ethnographic gift of description is her visit to the Dunker love-feast, where she records joining in the worship services, sharing the love-feast meal, sleeping overnight amid the primitive conditions of the meetinghouse loft, and conversing with and questioning some of the participants about the meaning of it all. Phebe's account of this visit is certainly one of the most finished of her ethnographic reports. It is full of description and conversation with attendees, preachers, men, women, and children. With her splendid gifts of observation and her ready pen, she produced here one of the best accounts of a Plain Dutch religious service that we have from the nineteenth century.

Phebe's book grew by accretion, since she added new chapters and enlarged others in succeeding editions. Three editions of the book appeared: one in 1872, another in 1874, and the last in 1882. All of these were published in Philadelphia by the Quaker firm of J. B. Lippincott and Company. The book grew out of the leading chapter, which had been published anonymously in the *Atlantic Monthly* for October 1869. The book's first edition was also anonymous, although the preface, dated April 1872, was signed "G.," and the telltale initials "PEG" appeared in a fashionable Victorian monogram in gold on the green front cover. The second edition acquired a new preface, dated December 1873, and was signed P. E. Gibbons. In 1882, Phebe used her full name on the title page, adding under it "Author of *French and Belgians*."

The 1872 edition contained a modest 207 pages, plus 8 pages of advertisements for Lippincott books. The 1874 edition was increased to 318 pages, with two new essays ("Bethlehem and the Moravians" and "Schwenkfelders") and a supplement of three lengthy notes. The first of these dealt with the Pennsylvania Dutch dialect, its history and peculiarities; the second was made up of miscellany, including references to the Lutheran and Reformed majorities in counties other than Lancaster, such as Berks and Schuylkill; and the third gave materials on the Russian Mennonites who had emigrated to the Plains States in the 1870s. The section on the Lutheran and Reformed majority probably was inserted to counter the criticism by a Reformed Church editor that the book was weighted too heavily toward the Plain element, but that is what Phebe had to work with and react to in Lancaster County.

The 1882 edition was further revised and enlarged to 427 pages, with three new chapters: "The Miners of Scranton," dealing with Irish and Welsh immigrants of the nineteenth century in Pennsylvania's anthracite region; "Irish Farmers," based on her notebooks kept on her 1881 European travels; and "English," again based on her 1881 trip, this time concentrating on the life and problems of English farmers in Huntingdonshire. In this edition, the notes have become the appendix and are also enlarged very readably. Phebe ends her third-edition preface with the statement: "From personal observation I have been able to revise a considerable part of this volume, which contains more than double the amount of matter comprised in the first edition."

Much of the material in the appendix came, if not from Phebe's personal observation, from her wide reading, as well as from her correspondence with persons who evidently had enjoyed her book and sent her additional materials. These extremely readable excerpts are among my favorites in the entire work, like the description by a Schuylkill County schoolteacher of keeping warm between two featherbeds in the farmhouses where he boarded, and his account of a dance and sleigh ride where the driver, to add to the fun, upset the sleighing party into the snow (pp. 423–24). The account of Pennsylvania Dutch country dances in Berks County is equally good, and I appreciate the list of fiddle tunes that provided the music for these lusty evenings (pp. 424–25).

PHEBE'S FAMILY AND ANCESTRY

To understand Phebe's approach to the human condition, it is necessary to consider the influence of the Quaker concerns of her forefathers and -mothers.

Phebe Earle Gibbons was born in Philadelphia on August 9, 1821, or in Quaker dating, Eighth Month 9th, 1821. She was the first of four children born to Thomas and Mary (Hussey) Earle, both natives of Massachusetts. The spelling "Phebe" is the plain Quaker version of the New Testament name Phoebe (Romans 16: 1–2), which Friends evidently considered too classical and worldly. The other children, in order of birth, were George H. (b. 1823), a Philadelphia lawyer whose grandson, Phebe's great-nephew George H. Earle III (1890–1974), served as governor of the commonwealth of Pennsylvania, 1935–1939; Henry (1829–74); and Caroline (b. 1833), who married Richard P. White, also a lawyer in Philadelphia.

These siblings were all, like Phebe, liberal, reform-minded Hicksite Quakers who aided many of the progressive movements of the day. Phebe's sister Caroline, for example, served for many years as president of the Women's Branch of the Pennsylvania Society for the Prevention of Cruelty to Animals (SPCA). She is remembered for her carefully prepared annual reports and her able writings in the opposition to the common practice of vivisection.

THE EARLE FAMILY OF MASSACHUSETTS AND PENNSYLVANIA

Thomas Earle (1796–1849), Phebe's father, was born in Leicester, Massachusetts, the son of Pliny and Patience (Buffum) Earle and a descendant of Ralph Earle, an emigrant colonist from England who arrived in Massachusetts in the 1600s. In 1820, Thomas Earle married Mary Hussey (1798–1886), daughter of Uriah and Phebe (Folger) Hussey of Nantucket Island.

After his education in the common schools and academy at Leicester, Thomas Earle moved in 1817 to Philadelphia, where, like many urban Quakers, he went into business as a commission merchant. He was never really successful, however, and was actually "disowned," as Quakers termed it, by the Arch Street Meeting, for business failure. He continued attending meeting the rest of his life, and after the Orthodox-Hicksite division of 1827, his family joined the Hicksite branch. Having given up business, he turned, as his biographer, Pliny Earle, put it, "to literary, professional, and philanthropic pursuits." He began the study of law in 1824, was admitted to the Philadelphia bar, and practiced his profession until his relatively early death in 1849.

With his strong antislavery interest, Thomas Earle became publisher and editor of several newspapers, among them *The Pennsylvanian*, the leading antislavery paper of the time in the state. He soon got into Pennsylvania politics and, through his journalism, advocated reforming the state constitution. At the convention in 1837, which did reform the constitution, many of his ideas were adopted by the majority, except his strong proposal that Pennsylvania's many free blacks should be allowed to vote. He also lost out on limiting the terms of judges and transferring their appointment to the people.

In 1840, the newly formed Liberty, or Free Soil, Party chose Thomas Earle as its candidate for vice president, as running mate to James G. Birney. He was also an advocate of railroads and in 1830 had published a pioneering book on the subject in the United States, *A Treatise on Railroads and Internal Communication.* He also wrote textbooks for the public schools, a biography of the antislavery leader Benjamin Lundy, and a translation into English of Sismondi's *Italian Republics.* It is easy to see, from this brief rundown of his many talents and contributions, where his daughter Phebe received much of her inspiration and encouragement for her own reforming and literary work.

Thomas Earle's father, Pliny, a favorite Earle name, was a noted Yankee inventor who developed the carding machines used in Slater's woolen mills, thus aiding in the first stage of the Industrial Revolution in New England. Clever, hard-working, and innovative, the Massachusetts Earles had a strong intellectual direction. Through the Earles, Phebe had two distinguished first cousins, Thomas Chase (1827–92) and Pliny Earle Chase (1820–86), both of whom served as presidents of Haverford College.

THE NANTUCKET HERITAGE

The island of Nantucket, Phebe Gibbons's heritage on the maternal side of her ancestry, lies in the Atlantic Ocean off the coast of Cape Cod in Massachusetts. A barren, windswept land, it was colonized in 1671 by twenty-seven proprietors, all Quakers, many of whom became seafaring men in the whaling and other maritime interests.

A charming and perceptive description of the island, its people, and their customs appears in the book *Letters from an American Farmer* (London, 1782), by J. Hector St. John de Crevecoeur. In this work, the author remarked that the majority of the present inhabitants were the descendants of the twenty-seven proprietors, who patented the island, hence "they are all in some degree related to each other; you must not be surprised therefore when I tell you, that they always call each other cousin, uncle or aunt; which are become such common appellations, that no other are made use of in their daily intercourse." This custom depicts a community that viewed itself as one large family.

Many Nantucket clans bear recognizable Quaker surnames: Hussey, Folger, Coffin, Starbuck, Macy, Trueblood, and others that have spread widely throughout the United States. Phebe's mother was Mary (Hussey) Earle, and Mary's mother was a Folger, a sister of Lucretia Mott's mother. Thus Lucretia and Phebe were cousins. Through the Husseys, Phebe was related to the Quaker Husseys of Newcastle County, Delaware; North Carolina; and York County, Pennsylvania. Nathan Hussey of York was one of the commissioners who laid out York County in 1749, when it was set off from Lancaster County. He also gave the land for the Friends Meetinghouse on Philadelphia Street in York and helped erect the plain, dignified brick structure that today is the oldest church building in the city. Among the Midwestern Husseys was Obed Hussey, one of the inventors of the mowing machine. Interested in history and heritage as she was, Phebe was aware of these relationships and kept in touch with many of her cousins by visit and letter.

For those interested in pursuing this genealogy further, Thomas Allen Glenn, in his two-volume work *Welsh Founders of Pennsylvania* (Oxford, 1911), included an elaborate fan chart of the ancestry of Phebe's nephew, George H. Earle Jr. This gives the lineage of both of Phebe's parents, Thomas Earle and Mary Hussey Earle, back through six generations, ramifying into many distinguished pioneer families of Massachusetts, Rhode Island, New Hampshire, and Nantucket. Glenn's acknowledgments for the book mention first "George H. Earle, Jr., Esq., of Philadelphia, to whom the inception of this volume is solely due, to whom it is dedicated, and whose editorial advice and personal interest has been untiring."

QUAKERISM IN ANTEBELLUM PENNSYLVANIA

In the first half of the nineteenth century, Philadelphia was the nerve center of American Quakerism. It was the vibrant hub of Quaker journalism and opinion making. It was also the storm center of the most disastrous division in Quaker history. Phebe was a young girl in Quaker school when, in 1827–28, the Philadelphia Yearly Meeting was divided into two opposing branches of the Society of Friends—Orthodox and Hicksite. Whereas the majority of Philadelphia's wealthy Quaker merchants took the Orthodox side, the Earles and Motts aligned themselves with Elias Hicks (1748–1830) and his followers.

It is difficult to summarize the differences between the two positions, but the Orthodox party in general, with their merchant connections with England, were influenced by the British Evangelical Movement, with its theological content of the Trinity, Divinity of Christ, and other orthodox dogmas. The Hicksites were the radicals, who preferred the Quaker doctrine of the Inner Light to the forensic Christ on the cross, and progressive revelation to the supposed finality of God's word in the Bible.

Radical Hicksites, such as Lucretia Mott, opposed all formalities in religion, even Sabbath keeping. They were strongly antislavery, many even abolitionist, pro women's rights, temperance minded, and were close to the Unitarians in theology. Lucretia Mott's interests, as revealed in her sermons and writings, and Phebe Gibbons's, as judged from her extensive writings, were all assuredly Hicksite in character.

Unfortunately, this serious division, which spread to other yearly meetings, considerably weakened the impact that Quaker ideas and ideals might have had on the United States in the nineteenth century. The schism was not healed formally until 1955, when the two rival Philadelphia yearly meetings officially rejoined, amid universal Quaker rejoicing.

PHEBE'S HUSBAND AND FAMILY LIFE

In the autumn of 1845, Phebe Hussey Earle married Dr. Joseph Gibbons (1818–83) of Bird-in-Hand, Lancaster County, Pennsylvania. A letter from Lucretia Mott's daughter, Martha Mott Lord, to Eliza Wright Osborne, dated Philadelphia, October 4, 1845, furnishes a brief report on Phebe's wedding:

> Phebe Earle was married last Monday evening. She had as large a wedding as their rooms would accommodate, about sixty. Her dress was white silk. Marianna and Lib wore their wedding dresses. Joseph and Phebe started off the next morning for Boston and Nantucket—to be gone about three weeks.

Dr. Gibbons was the son of a distinguished Quaker abolitionist, Daniel Gibbons (1775–1853), and his wife, Hannah (Wierman) Gibbons. The Wiermans, a Pennsylvania Dutch family from Adams County, had become Quakers. The Daniel Gibbons farm is remembered in Pennsylvania history as the first station on the Underground Railroad in Lancaster County east of Columbia and, according to R. C. Smedley's history of the movement, "the most important in Lancaster County."

The doctor was a farmer and rural physician, although he conducted an active medical practice for only five years. It appears that many of his friends and neighbors were opposed to his belief that slavery should be extinguished by political action, and some also objected to his strong temperance stance.

On the farm at Bird-in-Hand, Phebe and Joseph had five children: Marianna (1846–1929), who aided her father in producing and editing *The Journal*, his important venture into Quaker journalism; Caroline (b. 1848), who married William G. Gibbons (1832–86) of the Wilmington branch of the family; Hannah C. (1851–60); Frances (b. 1852), who married Alfred Pusey; and Daniel (1860–1929), who had a career as a lawyer and editor.

The Gibbonses were members of Sadsbury Monthly Meeting in eastern Lancaster County, one of whose branches, or preparative meetings, as Friends called them, was Lampeter Meeting at Bird-in-Hand, near the Gibbons homestead farm. The diminutive brick meetinghouse where Phebe and her family worshiped on First-Day (Sunday), and probably at weekday meetings as well, still stands along Route 340 at the west end of Bird-in-Hand. It is one of the smallest meetinghouses in the territory of Philadelphia Yearly Meeting and is no longer used for worship meetings.

The major and compelling problem faced by Americans before the Civil War was slavery and what to do with it. Quakers were normally antislavery, and some, (like the Earles, Motts, and Gibbonses, were activist abolitionists. The so-called Underground Railroad was a code name before the Civil War for the elaborate network of routes, from the slave states of Delaware, Maryland, and Virginia up through the Quaker settlements of Pennsylvania, to enable fugitive slaves to escape northward and eventually reach a safe haven in Canada. Not all the operators were Quakers, although the majority were.

Dr. R. C. Smedley's vivid record, *History of the Underground Railroad in Chester and Neighboring Counties of Pennsylvania,* was published at Lancaster in 1883, at the office of the Gibbons periodical, *The Journal.* Phebe's daughter Marianna Gibbons, with Robert Purvis, signed the editors' preface. The book consists of biographies of the major operators, including the Gibbonses, based on firsthand accounts and interviews, in some cases with the fugitive slaves themselves.

The book tells us that Joseph Gibbons's parents, Daniel and Hannah (Wierman) Gibbons, operated an important station that housed, fed, and sent on to the next operators about twelve hundred fugitive slaves. As a teenager, Joseph Gibbons began to assist his father with exciting midnight runs of fugitives, and as late as 1856, long after the passage of the Fugitive Slave Law (1850), which made all this Quakerly activity technically illegal, he was still aiding fugitives.

Like his father-in-law, Thomas Earle, Dr. Gibbons strongly believed that the ultimate goal of the abolitionists should be influencing the political sector to abolish slavery by national law.

Hence, in 1844, he joined the Liberty, or Free Soil, Party, of which Thomas Earle had been a founder in 1840, and in 1854, he became one of the founders in Pennsylvania of the Republican Party—then the liberal and progressive party. In 1856, he campaigned enthusiastically in Lancaster County for John C. Fremont for president, who lost out to another Lancaster Countian, James Buchanan. During the campaign, the doctor distributed thousands of antislavery pamphlets and rode night and day attending political meetings.

Joseph's biographer, Dr. R. C. Smedley, summed up some obviously strict, even puritanical, aspects of his personality:

> It may interest some to learn that, brought up by parents who were both elders in the Society of Friends, and with warm social feelings and no tinge of asceticism, he has never drunk a glass of ardent spirits, never used tobacco in any form, never been within the walls of a theatre (even when a medical student and in four years of public office in Philadelphia), never played a game of cards and never read a novel.

Obviously the good doctor's interests were centered on morality and justice. Though his wife shared many of these abstentions, she did read novels.

CONTRIBUTIONS TO QUAKER JOURNALISM

An important chapter in Phebe Earle Gibbons's busy life in Lancaster County was the publication of her husband's influential Quaker periodical, *The Journal: A Paper Devoted to the Interests of the Society of Friends.* For twelve years (1873–85), it joined the ranks of other Quaker journals, including the widely read Hicksite organ, the *Friends Intelligencer,* and its Orthodox competitor, *The Friend,* both edited and published in Philadelphia.

Judging from the correspondence published in *The Journal* from all parts of the American Quaker world—the opinions, editorials, and articles entitled "For the Journal"—the new paper struck sympathetic ground and filled a definite need in shaping Quaker policy after the Civil War. It was a weekly published in tabloid format, four columns to a page, and ran into twelve huge volumes, until 1885, when, two years after Dr. Gibbons's death, after changing its title to *The Friends Journal,* it was merged with the *Friends Intelligencer,* which accordingly changed its title to *Friends Intelligencer and Journal*. The Philadelphia Quaker periodical of today, called simply *Friends Journal*, reflects this long history and pays its own implicit tribute to the work of Dr. Joseph Gibbons and to his capable daughter Marianna, who edited the journal during and after her father's incapacitation and continued it for two years (volumes XI and XII, 1883–85) after his death.

The first number appeared in Philadelphia on "Third-Day, 1st Mo., 15th 1873," bearing under the masthead George Fox's motto: "Friends, mind the Light." The editors added a disclaimer: "Desiring to be liberal in the admission of articles, we wish it distinctly understood that we are not responsible for anything which may appear except editorials, or such articles as may be particularly endorsed." And its editorial relationship to official Quakerism was made clear in the following statement: "The Society of Friends, as such, is not responsible for anything which may appear in this paper, except when published by its order and signed by its officers."

But the new venture was a Quaker journal nevertheless, reflecting all the liberal and reform tendencies of the editors' Hicksite Quakerism, including temperance, plainness or simplicity, Quaker education including First Day Schools, antivivisection and protection of the animal world, abolition of capital punishment, easing the plight of America's Indian nations, Quaker preaching, detailed reports of Quarterly and Yearly Meetings, education of the freedmen, defense of and advancement of public school education, health, women's rights, reports of scientific discoveries, biblical criticism, and of course, Quaker history and biography. Through it all went a plea for breadth of viewpoint and openness to new scientific and spiritual currents. "The old hedges must be broken down, we must have air and light . . . "

And for this journal, Phebe wrote many articles, signed or unsigned.

TRAVELS ABROAD

Phebe's travels in Europe provided much grist to her epistolary and literary mill, resulting in numerous articles published in the

Lancaster and Philadelphia press, as well as *The Journal,* along
with her second book, *French and Belgians.* Her first European
jaunt took place in 1878, the second in 1881. On May 27, 1881, the
Lancaster Examiner reported that "Mrs. Phebe E. Gibbons, wife of
Dr. Joseph Gibbons, of Bird-in-Hand, this county, sailed for Europe
from Philadelphia yesterday, May 26th, on the steamship *British
Queen* of the American line. We understand that she intends travel-
ing pretty extensively in Great Britain and Ireland, and perhaps
through Germany and Switzerland, with a view to writing a book of
travels. She will probably be gone five or six months, and will corre-
spond with THE JOURNAL, the Friends' paper, of which her husband is editor."

The traveler lost no time in providing copy for *The Journal.* In
the issue for June 22, her first "Letter by the Way" appeared, written on shipboard and sent back from Queenstown, Ireland. It
describes in her inimitable way the varied passengers she shared
the voyage with, all sorted out according to their religious adher-
ences. The second letter appeared in the July 20th number, dated
from Cork on June 20th, describing her visits to Irish farmers and
their homes. The third epistle is dated Manchester, England, and
appeared in the August 17th issue. It describes the decline of the
plain language among British Friends and the use of dialect speech
in England. Letter No. 4 appeared September 7th, dated from London. She had evidently toured Sussex in southeastern England, for
she comments on the similarity of Sussex farmers' speech patterns
to those in Pennsylvania, "he seen it" and "he done it" being cited
as two examples that her Pennsylvania readers would recognize.

In London, Phebe visited Devonshire House, the Quaker "vati-
can" in the city, and apparently was leaving for the Continent to
attend, in Cologne, the Congress for Reforming and Codifying the
Laws of Nations. In Germany, she visited Crefeld, whence the first
settlers of Germantown had emigrated in 1683. Moving south into
the Rhenish Palatinate, she visited Mennonite families and their
farms near Speyer, and an Amish family near Zweibrücken headed
by Jacob Stalter. The Stalter household consisted typically of the
parents, six children, and two maiden aunts. Her host had traveled

to Switzerland, where his ancestors had come from. He brought out to show his guest a copy of the Pirmasens edition (1780) of the Ephrata *Martyr Book* and an old example of their archaic hymnal, the *Ausbund* (still used by the Amish in Lancaster County in the twenty-first century).

In all these sketches, the traveler expressed her friendly talent for communicating with other human beings in her matchless way and with her ever-present sympathy and understanding. And she did thread these Amish and Mennonite sketches from the Palatinate, in abbreviated form, into the 1882 edition of her book.

She also used these well-honed talents, perfected in the Dutch Country of southeastern Pennsylvania, to produce her single European travel book, *French and Belgians,* issued in Philadelphia in 1881 by her longtime publisher, J. B. Lippincott and Company.

Written with her usual verve, the book reports conversations in the farmhouses where she boarded (no grand hotels for her) and offers insights into the political and educational systems of both countries. She was interested in everything, visiting schools and discussing educational theory with the teachers she met. Naturally, she wrote in detail on the status of the Protestant churches, and of the dominant Catholicism as well. And she occasionally compares the rural culture of France and Belgium, particularly such elements as the traditional costume of the farm women, with the plain garb of her Lancaster County Amish and Mennonite neighbors back home. She never forgot Pennsylvania wherever she made her investigative visits.

CORRESPONDENCE

As an ultraliberal, reform-minded Hicksite Quaker, Phebe Gibbons kept in touch with like-minded friends and colleagues through her husband's *Journal* and through her own wide-ranging correspondence. Unfortunately, only bits and pieces of her correspondence appear to have been preserved and archived. One such fragment, in the Haverford College Quaker Collection, is the reply to a letter she wrote to Patrick John Ryan, the Roman Catholic archbishop of Philadelphia. Evidently she had invited him to attend and participate in the Pan-Republican Congress that met in

Philadelphia in the fall of 1891. So it appears that when duty demanded it, Phebe could, like John Woolman and Lucretia Mott, "speak Truth to Power," to admonish and guide those in authority in nation and church.

The few diaries of Phebe's that have been preserved witness how she visited back and forth with her mother's first cousin Lucretia Mott, the most outspoken of the women ministers in the Hicksite fold. They must have shared thoughts and concerns in correspondence, too. The early biography of Lucretia and her husband, *James and Lucretia Mott: Life and Letters* (Boston, 1884), edited by their granddaughter, Anna Davis Hallowell, reveals the interesting fact that one of the very last letters that Lucretia Mott wrote was addressed to Phebe. It deals at large with the career in England of the Quaker preacher Hannah Barnard, who, like Lucretia and Phebe's mother, was a native of Nantucket. While engaged on a ministerial journey in England in 1800, this vocal Public Friend (as ministers were then called) was, as Lucretia put it to Phebe, "unjustly and unwarrantably silenced" by the Quaker authorities in London for "unsound" doctrine. Her "unsound" views were simply the liberal, proto-Hicksite teachings that would become normative in the liberal Hicksite wing of American Quakerism as held by both Lucretia and Phebe. Lucretia's letter is sympathetic to Hannah Barnard in lamenting the bigoted treatment she was given by the London Friends.

Phebe's ideas on education were liberal indeed. She sent her eldest daughter, Marianna, to the state normal school at Millersville in Lancaster County, which had been founded by the Quaker schoolman Dr. James Pyle Wickersham (1825–91), who had attended Jonathan Gause's renowned Quaker school in Chester County with Phebe's husband. Daniel Gibbons (1860–1929), Phebe's son, was sent to Franklin and Marshall College in Lancaster, where he graduated in 1878. In general, Phebe was in favor of public schools, coeducation, and liberal, scientific studies in every discipline.

FINAL YEARS

Phebe spent the last ten years of her life in Philadelphia, where she lived with her sister Caroline White and her family. She took an active part in social work and Friends meeting activities. On First-Days, she attended meeting for worship at the Race Street Meeting House, built by the Hicksite Quakers in 1855. It is still there in central Philadelphia, anchoring the new Friends Center, which surrounds it, and includes the editorial and business offices of the *Friends Journal.* The monthly meeting is now called Central Philadelphia, and the meetinghouse is more frequently called Cherry Street.

Active to the end of her life, Phebe Earle Gibbons died in Philadelphia on June 5, 1893, at the residence of her brother-in-law, lawyer Richard P. White. Obituaries appeared in the *Friends Intelligencer* and the *Philadelphia Public Ledger.* From the columns of the *Intelligencer* we excerpt the following:

Phebe E. Gibbons was not only a frequent contributor to newspapers and periodicals, including occasionally some of the leading magazines, but she was the author of two books of note, "Pennsylvania Dutch," a series of papers on the social life, etc., of the people of German origin in Lancaster county, Pa., and the adjacent region; and a volume descriptive of her travels and brief residence in France and Belgium. Like her sister, C. E. White, President of the Women's Branch of the Society for the Prevention of Cruelty to Animals, she was earnest in efforts against vivisection, and in other measures of a humanitarian nature. Whilst radical in her views and convictions, she was kind and charitable towards those who differed from her, and ever ready to give a helping hand for the encouragement or relief of others.

Of very active and energetic temperament, she had a lively interest in many directions. She was interested in the study of languages, in astronomy, and natural sciences. She belonged to the Linnaean Society in Lancaster. She was also interested in the Society for Organizing Charity in this city, being a visitor in the Eighth Ward. In the procedure of the Yearly Meeting she often took part—as was the case at the late session. Her contributions to this paper, under the caption of "Notes by the Way," were always lively and interesting. The latest one, published Fifth Month 13, was especially suggestive of thought and discussion.

SIGNIFICANCE

It is hard to say what Phebe's attitude would be to the "Amish tourism" that today reigns in Lancaster County, bringing five million tourists each year just "to see the Amish." As their neighbor, who quilted with them and attended their German church services on occasion, Phebe knew their character, was aware of their differences from the "English" population of Lancaster County, and attempted to understand their ways and way of life. In this, judging from her perceptive writings about her plain neighbors, she succeeded. I consider her the nineteenth-century "discoverer" of the Amish, as well as the first writer to bring the Pennsylvania Dutch and their way of life to a national audience.

A significant tribute to Phebe's work in the twentieth century comes from folklife scholar Dr. Alfred L. Shoemaker, internationally known specialist in Pennsylvania Dutch studies. It appeared in *The Pennsylvania Dutchman* for November 1952.

> Phoebe [*sic*] Earle Gibbons was interested in everything and everybody around her. She became a charter member of the Linnaean Society, Lancaster's natural history society. She studied languages, ancient and modern. A portion of the Odyssey, translated by her, was published in the *Ladies' Friend* of Philadelphia. She translated a medical work from the French for Lindsay and Blakiston, which was published in Philadelphia in 1866. She also translated a portion of Goethe's *Herman and Dorothea.* She was a contributor to the *New York Tribune* and the Philadelphia *Public Ledger.* She wrote also for national magazines.

In judging Phebe's masterpiece, *Pennsylvania Dutch and Other Essays,* Dr. Shoemaker wrote:

> I feel no hesitancy in calling it the best thing on the Pennsylvania Dutch up to 1950, the year of the appearance of Fredric Klees' monumental opus, *The Pennsylvania Dutch.* (The interval volumes on the Pennsylvania Dutch were unspeakably dull and lifeless.)
>
> The reason *Pennsylvania Dutch* is so interesting is that its author was a fascinating person, a sort of Eleanor Roosevelt: humanitarian, world traveler, and author. One can unreservedly call Phoebe Earle Gibbons the greatest woman who ever lived in Lancaster County.

Phebe deserved the name she carried throughout her active, outgoing life. She was named for her grandmother, Phebe (Folger)

Hussey (1768–1864) of Nantucket, but ultimately for Phebe of Cenchrea, the New Testament deaconess whom St. Paul in Romans 16: 1–2 recommended to the brethren and sisters of the church in Rome:

> I commend unto you Phebe our sister, which is a servant of the church which is at Cenchrea; that ye receive her in the Lord, as becometh saints, and that ye assist her in whatsoever business she hath need of you; for she hath been a succourer of many, and of myself also.

From my own lifelong fascination with *Pennsylvania Dutch and Other Essays,* I could, with the republication of her ethnographic masterpiece, second St. Paul in commending our Pennsylvania Phebe, with all her winsome talents, to the wider readership she deserves—both locally in the state where she lived and worked, and nationally in the America that she loved and, Quaker liberal that she was, admonished and attempted to reform. In the words of her husband's *Journal,* "The old hedges must be broken down, we must have air and light."

BIBLIOGRAPHY

Bacon, Margaret Hope. *Valiant Friend: The Life of Lucretia Mott.* New York: Walker and Company, 1980.

Bronner, Edwin B. *Thomas Earle as a Reformer.* Philadelphia: International Printing Co., 1948.

"Brubaker, Marianna Gibbons" [Obituary]. *Friends Intelligencer* (Fifth Month 18, 1929): 401–2.

"Earle, George H., Jr." In *Prominent and Progressive Pennsylvanians of the Nineteenth Century.* Leland M. Williamson, ed. vol. 3, 95–98. Philadelphia, 1898.

"Earle, Pliny (1809–92)." *Dictionary of National Biography,* vol. 7, 229–30.

Earle, Pliny. *Ralph Earle and Descendants.* Worcester, Massachusetts: Charles Hamilton, 1888.

"Earle, Thomas (1796–1849)." *Dictionary of National Biography,* vol. 7, 231–32.

Ellis, Franklin, and Samuel Evans. *History of Lancaster County, Pennsylvania, with Biographical Sketches of Many of Its Pioneers and Prominent Men.* Philadelphia: Everts & Peck, 1883.

Gibbons, Daniel. *God in Us: The World Faith of Quakerism.* New York: Macmillan Co., 1928.

"Gibbons, Daniel (1860–1929)" [Obituary]. *Friends Intelligencer* 86 (1929): 881.

"Gibbons, Dr. Joseph" [Obituary]. *Friends Intelligencer.* 40 (1883–84): 714.

"Gibbons, Dr. Joseph" [Obituary]. *The Journal* (Twelfth Month 12, 1883).

"Gibbons, Joseph" [Memorial]. *The Journal* (Twelfth Month 26, 1883, and First Month 2d, 1884.)

[Gibbons, Phebe Earle]. "Pennsylvania Dutch." *The Atlantic Monthly* 24 (1869): 473–87. Translated into Holland Dutch by J. G. deHoop Scheffer as "Churchly and Domestic Life of the Mennonites in This Country and in Pennsylvania [translation]," in *Doopsgezinde Bijdragen*, n.s. 3 (Leeuwarden, 1869): 129–47.

———. *Pennsylvania Dutch and Other Essays.* Philadelphia: J. B. Lippincott & Co., 1872.

———. *Pennsylvania Dutch and Other Essays.* Revised with additions. Philadelphia: J. B. Lippincott & Co., 1874.

———. *Pennsylvania Dutch and Other Essays.* 3rd ed., revised and enlarged. Philadelphia: J. B. Lippincott & Co., 1882.

"Gibbons, Phebe Earle" [Obituary]. *Philadelphia Public Ledger* (June 6, 1893), and (June 7, 1893).

"Gibbons, Phebe Earle" [Obituary (by J. M. T., Jr.)]. *Friends Intelligencer and Journal* 58 (1893): 361–362.

Glenn, Thomas Allen. "Genealogical Chart of Ancestry of George H. Earle, Jr." In *Welsh Founders of Pennsylvania*, vol. 1, between 124–25. Oxford: Fox, Jones and Co., 1911.

Hallowell, Anna Davis, ed. *James and Lucretia Mott: Life and Letters.* Boston: Houghton, Mifflin and Co.; Cambridge: Riverside Press, 1884.

Hamm, Thomas D. *The Transformation of American Quakerism: Orthodox Friends, 1800–1907.* Bloomington: Indiana University Press, 1988.

Hinchman, Lydia S. *Early Settlers on Nantucket: Their Associates and Descendants.* Philadelphia: Ferris and Leach, 1901.

The Journal, later renamed *The Friends Journal*, 1–12 (1873–85).

Myers Collection, Albert Cook. Chester County Historical Society, West Chester, Pennsylvania, Gibbons and Wierman Files.

Ryan, Patrick John, (Roman Catholic archbishop of Philadelphia), letter to Mrs. P. E. Gibbons, dated Philadelphia, October 9, 1891. Roberts Collection, MS 410, Quaker Collection, Haverford College, Haverford, Pennsylvania.

Sanborn, F. B. *Memoirs of Pliny Early, M.D.* Boston: Damrell and Upham, 1898.

Seidensticker, Oswald. "Memoir of Israel Daniel Rupp, the Historian." *The Pennsylvania Magazine of History and Biography* 14 (1890): 403–13.

Shoemaker, Alfred L. "Phoebe Earle Gibbons." *The Pennsylvania Dutchman* 4, no. 7 (November 1952): 5.

Smedley, R. C., MD. *History of the Underground Railroad in Chester and the Neighboring Counties of Pennsylvania.* Lancaster, Pennsylvania: Printed at the office of *The Journal*, 1883.

Taylor, Frances Cloud. *The Trackless Trail: The Story of the Underground Railroad in Kennett Square, Chester County, Pennsylvania, and the Surrounding Community.* Kennett Square, Pennsylvania: KNA Press, 1976.

"PENNSYLVANIA DUTCH."

(PROPERLY GERMAN.)

"PENNSYLVANIA DUTCH,"

AND

OTHER ESSAYS.

BY

PHEBE EARLE GIBBONS,

AUTHOR OF "FRENCH AND BELGIANS."

THIRD EDITION, REVISED AND ENLARGED.

PHILADELPHIA:

J. B. LIPPINCOTT & CO.

1882.

PREFACE.

THE leading article in this collection appeared, as first published, in the *Atlantic Monthly* in October, 1869. After this essay was written I became better acquainted with our plain German sects, and wrote articles describing them, which were published in the first edition of this book. It appeared in 1872.

To the second edition were added "Bethlehem and the Moravians" and "Schwenkfelders," as well as an Appendix, and the edition was published about the opening of 1874.

The present volume contains articles that have never before appeared in book-form, namely, "The Miners of Scranton," "Irish Farmers," and "English." However, the first was published in *Harpers' Magazine* for November, 1877. Another short article appeared earlier in the same periodical; and several other essays were first brought before the public in Philadelphia and New York papers.

From personal observation I have been able to revise a considerable part of this volume, which contains more than double the amount of matter comprised in the first edition.

August, 1882.

CONTENTS.

"PENNSYLVANIA DUTCH."

(PROPERLY GERMAN.)

I HAVE lived for twenty years in the county of Lancaster, where my neighbors on all sides are "Pennsylvania Dutch." In this article I shall try to give, from my own observation and familiar acquaintance, some account of the life of a people who are little known outside of the rural neighborhoods of their own State, who have much that is peculiar in their language, customs, and belief, and of whom I have learned to esteem the native good sense, friendly feeling, and religious character.

LANGUAGE.

The tongue which these people speak is a dialect of the German, but they generally call it and themselves "Dutch."

For the native German who works with them on the farm they entertain some contempt, and the title "Yankee" is with them a synonyme for cheat. As must always be the case where the great majority do not read the tongue which they speak, and live in contact

11

with those who speak another, the language has become mixed and corrupt. Seeing a young neighbor cleaning a buggy, I tried to talk with him by speaking German. "Willst du reiten?" said I (not remembering that *reiten* is to ride on horseback). "Willst du reiten?" All my efforts were vain.

As I was going for cider to the house of a neighboring farmer, I asked his daughter what she would say, under the circumstances, for "Are you going to ride?" "Widdu fawray? Buggy fawray?" was the answer. (Willst du fahren?) Such expressions are heard as "Koock amul to," for "Guck einmal da," or "Just look at that!" and "Haltybissel" for "Halt ein biszchen," or "Wait a little bit." "Gutenobit" is used for "Guten Abend." Apple-butter is "lodwaerrick," from the German *latwerge*, an electuary, or an electuary of prunes. Our "Dutch" is much mixed with English. I once asked a woman what pie-crust is in Dutch. "Pykroosht," she answered.

Those who speak English use uncommon expressions, as,—"That's a werry *lasty* basket" (meaning durable); "I seen him yet a'ready;" "I knew a woman that had a good baby *wunst;*" "The bread is all" (all gone). I have heard the carpenter call his plane *she*, and a housekeeper apply the same pronoun to her home-made soap.

A rich landed proprietor is sometimes called *king*. An old "Dutchman" who was absent from home thus narrated the cause of his journey: "I must go and see old Yoke (Jacob) Beidelman. Te people calls me te kink ov te Manor (township), and tay calls him te kink ov te Octorara. Now, dese kinks must come togeder once." (Accent *together*, and pass quickly over *once*.)

RELIGION.

I called recently on my friend and neighbor, Jacob S., who is a thrifty farmer, of a good mind, and a member of the old Mennist or Mennonite Society. I once accompanied him and his pleasant wife to their religious meeting. The meeting-house is a low brick building, with neat surroundings, and resembles a Friends' meeting-house. The Mennonists in some outward matters very much resemble the Society of Friends (or Quakers), but do not rely, in the especial manner that Friends do, upon the teachings of the Divine Spirit in the secret stillness of the soul.

In the interior of the Mennist meeting a Quaker-like plainness prevails. The men, with broad-brimmed hats and simple dress, sit on benches on one side of the house, and the women, in plain caps and black sun-bonnets, are ranged on the other; while a few gay dresses are worn by the young people who have not yet joined the meeting. The services are almost always conducted in "Dutch," and consist of exhortation and prayer, and singing by the congregation. The singing is without previous training, and is not musical. A pause of about five minutes is allowed for private prayer.

The preachers are not paid, and are chosen in the following manner. When a vacancy occurs, and a new appointment is required, several men go into a small room, chosen for the purpose; and to them, waiting, enter singly the men and women, as many as choose, who tell them the name of the person preferred by each to fill the vacancy. After this, an opportunity is given to any candidate to excuse himself from the service.

Those who are not excused, if, for instance, six in number, are brought before six books. Each candidate takes up a book, and the one within whose book a lot is found is the chosen minister. I asked my friends who gave me some of these details, whether it was claimed or believed that there is any special guidance of the Divine Spirit in thus choosing a minister. From the reply, I did not learn that any such guidance is claimed, though they spoke of a man who *was led* to pass his hand over all the other books, and who selected the last one, but he did not get the lot after all. He was thought to be ambitious of a place in the ministry.

The three prominent sects of Mennonites all claim to be non-resistants, or *wehrlos*. The Old Mennists, who are the most numerous and least rigid, vote at elections, and are allowed to hold such public offices as school director and road supervisor, but not to be members of the legislature. The ministers are expected not to vote.* The members of this society cannot bring suit against any one ; they can hold mortgages, but not judgment bonds.† Like Quakers, they were not allowed to hold slaves, and they do not take oaths nor deal in spirituous liquors.

My neighbor Jacob and I were once talking of the general use of the word " Yankee" to denote one who is rather unfair in his dealings. They sometimes speak of a " Dutch Yankee ;" and Jacob asked me whether, if going to sell a horse, I should tell the buyer every fault

---

* An acquaintance, who lives in Bucks County, tells me that his father, a Mennonite preacher, voted " pretty much always."

† The rule against judgment bonds is not universal.

that I knew the horse had, as he maintained was the proper course. His brother-in-law, who was at times a horse-dealer, did not agree with him.

Titles do not abound among these plain neighbors of ours. Jacob's little son used to call him "Jake," as he heard the hired men do. Nevertheless, one of our New Mennist acquaintances was quite courtly in his address.

This last-mentioned sect branched off some fifty years ago, and claim to be *reformirt,* or to have returned to an older and more excellent standard. They do not vote at all. Their most striking peculiarity is this: if one of the members is disowned by the church, the other members of his own family who are members of the meeting are not allowed to eat at the same table with him, and his wife withdraws from him. A woman who worked in such a family told me how unpleasant it was to her to see that the father did not take his seat at the table, to which she was invited.

In support of this practice, they refer to the eleventh verse of the fifth chapter of First Corinthians: "But now I have written unto you not to keep company, if any man that is called a brother be a fornicator, or covetous, or an idolater, or a railer, or a drunkard, or an extortioner; with such an one *no not to eat.*"

We have yet another sect among us, called Amish (pronounced Ommish). In former times these Mennists were sometimes known as "beardy men," but of late years the beard is not a distinguishing trait. It is said that a person once asked an Amish man the difference between themselves and another Mennist sect. "Vy, dey vears puttons, and ve vearsh hooks oont eyes;" and this is, in fact, a prime difference. All the Mennist sects retain the ordinances of baptism and the Lord's supper, but most also practise feet-washing, and some sectarians "greet one another with a holy kiss."

On a Sunday morning Amish wagons, covered with yellow oil-cloth, may be seen moving toward the house of that member whose turn it is to have the meeting. Great have been the preparations there beforehand,—the whitewashing, the scrubbing, the polishing of tin and brass. Wooden benches and other seats are provided for the "meeting-folks," and the services resemble those already described. Of course, young mothers do not stay at home, but bring their infants with them. When the meeting is over, the congregation remain to dinner. Bean soup was formerly the principal dish, but, with the progress of luxury, the farmers of a fat soil no longer confine themselves to so simple a diet. Imagine what a time of social intercourse this must be.

The Amish dress is peculiar; and the children are diminutive men and women. The women wear sun-bonnets and closely-fitting dresses, but often their figures look very trim, in brown, with green or other bright handkerchiefs meeting over the breast. I saw a group of Amish at the railroad station the other day,—men, women, and a little boy. One of the young women wore a pasteboard sun-bonnet covered with black, and tied with narrow blue ribbon, among which showed the thick white strings of her Amish cap; a gray shawl, without fringe; a brown stuff dress, and a purple apron. One middle-aged man, inclined to corpulence, had coarse, brown, woollen clothes, and his pantaloons were without suspenders, in the Amish fashion. No buttons were on his coat behind, but down the front were hooks and eyes. One young girl wore a bright brown sun-bonnet, a green dress, and a light blue apron. The choicest figure, however, was the six-year-old, in a jacket, and with pantaloons plentifully plaited into the waistband behind; hair cut straight over the forehead, and hanging to the shoulder; and a round-crowned black wool hat, with an astonishingly wide brim. The little girls, down to two years old, wear the plain cap, and the handkerchief crossed upon the breast.

In Amish houses the love of ornament appears in brightly scoured utensils,—how the brass ladles are made to shine!—and in embroidered towels, one end of the towel showing a quantity of work in colored cottons. When steel or elliptic springs were introduced, so great a novelty was not at first patronized by members of the meeting; but an infirm brother, desiring to visit his friends, directed the blacksmith to put a spring inside his wagon, under the seat, and since that time steel springs have become common. I have even seen a youth with flowing hair (as is common among the Amish), and two trim-bodied damsels, riding in a very plain, uncovered buggy. A. Z. rode in a common buggy; but he became a great backslider, poor man!

It was an Amish man, not well versed in the English language, from whom I bought poultry, who sent me a bill for "chighans."

In mentioning some ludicrous circumstances, far be it from me to ignore the virtues of these primitive people.

HISTORY OF A SECT.

The Mennonites are named from Menno Symons, a reformer, who died in 1561, though it is doubtful whether Menno founded the sect. "The prevailing opinion among church historians, especially those of Holland, is that the origin of the Dutch Baptists may be traced to the Waldenses, and that Menno merely organized the concealed and scattered congregations as a denomination."

Mosheim says, "The true origin of that sect, which acquired the denomination of Anabaptists, by their administering anew the rite of baptism to those who came over to their communion, and derived that of Mennonites from the famous man to whom they owe the greatest part of their present felicity, is hidden in the depths of antiquity, and is of consequence extremely difficult to be ascertained." The "Martyr-Book," or "Martyr's Mirror," in use among our Mennonites, endeavors to prove identity of doctrine between the Waldenses and these Baptists, as regards opposition to infant baptism, to war, and to oaths.

Although the Mennonites are very numerous in the county of Lancaster, yet in the whole State they were estimated, in 1850, to have but ninety-two churches, while the Lutherans and German Reformed together were estimated as having seven hundred.

The freedom of religious opinion which was allowed in Pennsylvania had the effect of drawing hither the continental Europeans, who established themselves in the fertile lands of the western part of the county of Chester, now Lancaster. It was not until the revolution of 1848 that the different German states granted full civil rights to the Mennonites; and in some cases this freedom has since been withdrawn; Hanover, in 1858, annulled the election of a representative to the second chamber, because he was a Mennonite. Much of this opposition probably is because the sect refuse to take oaths. With such opposing circumstances in the Old World, it is not remarkable that the number of Mennonites in the United States has been reported to exceed that in all the rest of the world put together.* The Amish are named from Jacob Amen, a Swiss Mennonite preacher of the seventeenth century.

As I understand the Mennonites, they endeavor in church government literally to carry out the injunction of Jesus, " Moreover if thy brother shall trespass against thee, go and tell him his fault between thee and him alone; if he shall hear thee, thou hast gained thy brother. But if he will not hear thee, then take with thee one or two more, that in the mouth of two or three witnesses every word may be established. And if he shall neglect to hear them, tell it unto the church; but if he neglect to hear the church, let him be unto thee as an heathen man and a publican."

Besides these sectaries, we have among us Dunkers (German *tunken*, to dip), from whom sprang the Seventh-Day Baptists of Ephratah, with their brother- and sister-houses of celibates.

Also at Litiz we have the Moravian church and Gottesacker (or churchyard), and a Moravian church at Lancaster. Here, according to custom, a love-feast was

---

* For another estimate, see Appendix.

held recently, when a cup of coffee and a rusk (sweet biscuit) were handed to each person present.

We have, too, a number of "Dutch Methodists," or *Albrechtsleute* (followers of Albrecht), to whom is given the name Evangelical Association. These are full of zeal or activity in church, like the early Methodists; and I saw a young man fall apparently into a trance at a camp-meeting, lying upon the ground, to the satisfaction of his wife, who probably thought he was "happy."

POLITICS.

As our county was represented in Congress by Thaddeus Stevens, you have some idea of what our politics are. We have returned about five or six thousand majority for the Whig, Anti-Masonic, and Republican ticket, and the adjoining very "Dutch" county of Berks invariably as great a majority for the Democratic. So striking a difference has furnished much ground for speculation. The Hon. John Strohm says that Berks is Democratic because so many Hessians settled there after the Revolution. "No," says the Hon. Mr. B., "I attribute it to the fact that the people are not taught by unpaid ministers, as with us, but are Lutherans and German Reformed, and can be led by their preachers." "Why is Berks Democratic?" I once asked our Democratic postmaster. "I do not know," said he; "but the people here are ignorant; they do not read a paper on the other side." A former postmaster tells me that he has heard that the people of Berks were greatly in favor of liberty in the time of the elder Adams; that they put up liberty-poles, and Adams sent soldiers among them and had the liberty-poles cut down; and "ever since they have been opposed to that political party, under its different names."

A gentleman of Reading has told me that he heard James Buchanan express, in the latter part of his life, a similar opinion to one given before. Mr. Buchanan said, in effect, that while peace sects prevailed in Lancaster County, in Berks were found many Lutherans and German Reformed, who were more liberal (according, of course, to Mr. Buchanan's interpretation of the word).

The troubles alluded to in Berks seem to have been principally on account of a direct tax, called "the house-tax," imposed during the administration of John Adams.

The people of Berks and Lancaster gave another striking proof of the difference of their political sentiments, on the question of holding the Constitutional Convention of 1874. The vote of Berks was 5269 for a convention, and 10,905 against a convention; the vote of Lancaster was, for a convention 16,862, against the same 116.

A gentleman of Easton, Northampton County, tells me of a German farmer, who lived near that town, who said he did not see any need of so many parties,—the Democrats and Lutherans were enough. On his deathbed he is reported to have said to his son, "I never voted anything but the Democratic ticket, and I want you to stick to the party."

FESTIVALS.

The greatest festive occasion, or the one which calls the greatest number of persons to eat and drink together, is the funeral.

My friends Jacob and Susanna E. have that active benevolence and correct principle which prompt to a care for the sick and dying, and kind offices toward the mourner. Nor are they alone in this. When a death occurs, our "Dutch" neighbors enter the house, and, taking possession, relieve the family as far as possible from the labors and cares of a funeral. Some "redd up" the house, making that which was neglected during the sad presence of a fatal disease again in order for the reception of company. Others visit the kitchen, and help to bake great store of bread, pies, and rusks for the expected gathering. Two young men and two young women generally sit up together overnight to watch in a room adjoining that of the dead.

At funerals occurring on Sunday three hundred carriages have been seen in attendance; and so great at all times is the concourse of people of all stations and all shades of belief, and so many partake of the entertainment liberally provided, that I may be excused for calling funerals the great festivals of the "Dutch." (Weddings are also highly festive occasions, but they are confined to the "freundschaft," and to much smaller numbers.)

The services at funerals are generally conducted in the German language.

An invitation is extended to the persons present to return to eat after the funeral, or the meal is partaken of before leaving for the graveyard: hospitality, in all rural districts, where the guests come from afar, seems to require this. The tables are sometimes set in a barn, or large wagon-house, and relays of guests succeed one another, until all are done. The neighbors wait upon the table. The entertainment generally consists of meat, frequently cold; bread and butter; pickles or sauces, such as apple-butter; pies and rusks; sometimes stewed chickens, mashed potatoes, cheese, etc.; and coffee invariably. All depart after the dish-washing, and the family is left in quiet again.

I have said that persons of all shades of belief attend funerals; but our New Mennists are not permitted to listen to the sermons of other denominations. Memorial stones over the dead are more conspicuous than among Friends; but they are still quite plain, with simple inscriptions. Occasionally family graveyards are seen. One on a farm adjoining ours seems cut out of the side of a field; it stands back from the high-road, and access to it is on foot. To those who are anxious to preserve the remains of their relatives, these graveyards are objectionable, as they will probably not be regarded after the property has passed into another family.

A Lutheran gentleman, living in Berks County, in speaking of the great funerals among the "Dutch," says, "Our Germans look forward all their lives to their funerals, hoping to be able to entertain their friends on that great occasion with the hospitality due to them, and the honor due to the memory of the departed." No spirituous liquors, he added, are *now* used at funerals, the clergy having discouraged their use on these religious occasions. In a mountain valley in Carbon County, about thirty years ago, a bottle of whiskey was handed to a Lutheran minister, and he was asked to take some. " Yes, I'll have some," he answered ; and taking the bottle, he broke it against a tree.

WEDDINGS.

Our farmer had a daughter married lately, and I was invited to see the bride leave home. The groom, in accordance with the early habits of the " Dutch" folks, reached the bride's house about six in the morning, having previously breakfasted and ridden four miles. As he probably fed and harnessed his horse, besides attiring himself for the grand occasion, he must have been up betimes on an October morning.

The bride wore purple mousseline-de-laine and a blue bonnet. As some of the " wedding-folks" were dilatory, the bride and groom did not get off before seven. The bridegroom was a mechanic. The whole party was composed of four couples, who rode to Lancaster in buggies, where two pairs were married by a minister. In the afternoon the newly-married couples went down to Philadelphia for a few days ; and on the evening that they were expected at home we had a reception, or homecoming. Supper consisted of roast turkeys, beef, and stewed chickens, cakes, pies, and coffee of course. We had raisin-pie, which is a great treat in " Dutchland" on festive or solemn occasions. " Nine couples" of the party sat down to supper, and then the remaining spare seats were occupied by the landlord's wife, the bride's uncle, etc. We had a fiddler in the evening. He and the dancing would not have been there had the household " belonged to meeting ;" and, as it was, some young Methodist girls did not dance.

One of my " English" acquaintances was sitting alone on a Sunday evening, when she heard a rap at the door, and a young " Dutchman," a stranger, walked in and sat down, "and there he sot, and sot, and sot." Mrs. G. waited to hear his errand, politely making conversation ; and finally he asked whether her daughter was at home. " Which one?" He did not know. But that did not make much difference, as neither was at home. Mrs. G. afterwards mentioned this circumstance to a worthy " Dutch" neighbor, expressing surprise that a young man should call who had not been introduced. " How then *would* they get acquainted ?" said he. She suggested that she did not think that her daughter knew the young man. " She would not tell you, perhaps, if she did." The daughter, however, when asked, seemed entirely ignorant, and did not know that she had ever seen the young man. He had probably seen her at the railroad station, and had found out her name and residence. It would seem to indicate much confidence on the part of parents, if, when acquaintances are formed in such a manner, the father and mother retire at nine o'clock, and leave their young daughter thus to " keep company" until midnight or later. It is no wonder that one of our German sects has declared against the popular manner of " courting."

I recently attended a New Mennist wedding, which took place in the frame meeting-house. We entered through an adjoining brick dwelling, one room of which served as an ante-room, where the " sisters" left their bonnets and shawls. I was late, for the services had begun about nine on a bitter Sunday morning in December. The meeting-house was crowded, and in front on the left was a plain of book-muslin caps on the heads of the sisters. On shelves and pegs, along the other side, were placed the hats and overcoats of the brethren. The building was extremely simple,—whitewashed without, entirely unpainted within, with whitewashed walls. The preacher stood at a small, unpainted desk, and before it was a table, convenient for the old men " to sit at and lay their books on." Two stoves, a half-dozen hanging tin candlesticks, and the benches completed the furniture. The preacher was speaking extemporaneously in English, for in this meeting-house the services are often performed in this tongue; and he spoke readily and well, though his speech was not free from such expressions as, " It would be wishful for men to do their duty;" " Man cannot separate them together;" and " This, Christ done for us."

He spoke at length upon divorce, which, he said, could not take place between Christians. The preacher spoke especially upon the duty of the wife to submit to the husband whenever differences of sentiment arose; of the duty of the husband to love the wife, and to show his love by his readiness to assist her. He alluded to Paul's saying that it is better to be unmarried than married, and he did not scruple to use plain language touching adultery. His discourse ended, he called upon the pair proposing marriage to come forward; whereupon the man and woman rose from the body of the congregation on either side, and, coming out to the middle aisle, stood together before the minister. They had both passed their early youth, but had very good faces.

The bride wore a mode-colored alpaca, and a black apron; also a clear-starched cap without a border, after the fashion of the sect. The groom wore a dark-green coat, cut "shad-bellied," after the fashion of the brethren.

This was probably the manner of their acquaintance: If, in spite of Paul's encouragement to a single life, a brother sees a sister whom he wishes to marry, he mentions the fact to a minister, who tells it to the sister. If she agrees in sentiment, the acquaintance continues for a year, during which private interviews can be had if desired; but this sect entirely discourages courting as usually practised among the "Dutch."

The year having in this case elapsed, and the pair having now met before the preacher, he propounded to them three questions:

1. I ask of this brother, as the bridegroom, do you believe that this sister in the faith is allotted to you by God as your helpmeet and spouse? And I ask of you, as the bride, do you believe that this your brother is allotted to you by God as your husband and head?

2. Are you free in your affections from all others, and have you them centred alone upon this your brother or sister?

3. Do you receive this person as your lawfully wedded husband [wife], do you promise to be faithful to him [her], to reverence him [to love her], and that nothing but death shall separate you; that, by the help of God, you will, to the best of your ability, fulfil all the duties which God has enjoined on believing husbands and wives?

In answering this last question, I observed the bride to lift her eyes to the preacher's face, as if in fearless trust. Then the preacher, directing them to join hands, pronounced them man and wife, and invoked a blessing upon them. This was followed by a short prayer, after which the wedded pair separated, each again taking a place among the congregation. The occasion was solemn. On resuming his place in the desk, the preacher's eyes were seen to be suffused, and pocket-handkerchiefs were visible on either side (the sisters' white, those of the brethren of colored silk). The audience then knelt, while the preacher prayed, and I heard responses like those of the Methodists, but more subdued. The preacher made a few remarks, to the effect that, although it would be grievous to break the bond now uniting these two, it would be infinitely more grievous to break the tie which unites us to Christ; and then a quaint hymn was sung to a familiar tune. This "church" does not allow wedding-parties, but a few friends may gather at the house after meeting.

At Amish weddings the meeting is not in a church, like the one just spoken of, for their meetings are held in private houses. I hear that none go to this meeting but invited guests, except that the preachers are always present; and after the ceremony the wedded pair with the preachers retire into a private apartment, perhaps for exhortation upon their new duties.

A neighbor tells me that the Amish have great fun at weddings; that they have a table set all night, and that when the weather is pleasant they play in the barn. "Our Pete went once," she continued, "with a lot of the public-school scholars. They let them go in and look on. They twisted a towel for the bloom-sock, and they did hit each other." (Bloom-sock, *plump-sack*, a twisted kerchief,—a clumsy fellow.)

"The bloom-sock" (*oo* short), I hear, "is a handkerchief twisted long, from the two opposite corners. When it is twisted, you double it, and tie the ends with a knot. One in front hunts the handkerchief, and those on the bench are passing it behind them. If they get a chance, they'll hit him with it, and if he sees it he tears it away. Then he goes into the row, and the other goes out to hunt it."

It has also been said that at Amish wedding-parties they have what they call *Glücktrinke*, of wine, etc. Some wedding-parties are called infares. Thus, a neighbor spoke of "Siegfried's wedding, where they had such an infare." The original meaning I suppose to be home-coming.

It must not be inferred from these descriptions that we have no "fashionable" persons among us, of the old German stock. When they have become fashionable, however, they do not desire to be called "Dutch."

QUILTINGS.

There lives in our neighborhood a pleasant, industrious "Aunt Sally," a yellow woman; and one day she had a quilting, for she had long wished to re-cover two quilts. The first who arrived at Aunt Sally's was our neighbor from over the "creek," or mill-stream, Polly M., in her black silk Mennist bonnet, formed like a sunbonnet; and at ten came my dear friend Susanna E., who is tall and fat, and very pleasant; who has Huguenot blood in her veins, and—

> " Whose heart has a look southward, and is open
>   To the great noon of nature."

Aunt Sally had her quilt up in her landlord's east room, for her own house was too small. However, at about eleven she called us over to dinner; for people who have breakfasted at five or six have an appetite at eleven.

We found on the table beefsteaks, boiled pork, sweet potatoes, kohl-slaw,* pickled tomatoes, cucumbers, and *red* beets (thus the " Dutch" accent lies), apple-butter and preserved peaches, pumpkin- and apple-pie, with sponge-cake and coffee.

After dinner came our next neighbors, " the maids," Susy and Katy Groff, who live in single blessedness and great neatness. They wore pretty, clear-starched Mennist caps, very plain. Katy is a sweet-looking woman ; and, although she is more than sixty years old, her forehead is almost unwrinkled, and her fine fair hair is still brown. It was late when the farmer's wife came,— three o'clock ; for she had been to Lancaster. She wore hoops, and was of the " world's people." These women all spoke " Dutch ;" for " the maids," whose ancestor came here probably one hundred and fifty years ago, do not yet speak English with fluency.

The first subject of conversation was the fall house-cleaning ; and I heard mention of " die carpet hinaus an der fence," and " die fenshter und die porch ;" and the exclamation, " My goodness, es war schlimm" (it

---

* Kohl-slaw (*i.e.*, kohl-salat or cabbage-salad) is shredded cabbage, dressed with vinegar, etc. A rich dressing is sometimes made of milk or cream, egg, vinegar, etc. It may be eaten either as warm slaw or cold slaw.

was bad). I quilted faster than Katy Groff, who showed me her hands, and said, " You have not been corn-husking, as I have."

So we quilted and rolled, talked and laughed, got one quilt done, and put in another. The work was not fine; we laid it out by chalking around a small plate. Aunt Sally's desire was rather to get her quilting finished upon this great occasion, than for us to put in a quantity of needlework.

About five o'clock we were called to supper. I need not tell you all the particulars of this plentiful meal. But the stewed chicken was tender, and we had coffee again.

Polly M.'s husband now came over the creek in the boat, to take her home, and he warned her against the evening dampness. The rest of us quilted a while by candle and lamp, and got the second quilt done at about seven.

At this quilting I heard but little gossip, and less scandal. I displayed my new alpaca, and my dyed merino, and the Philadelphia bonnet which exposes the back of my head to the wintry blast. Polly, for her part, preferred her black silk sun-bonnet ; and so we parted, with mutual invitations to visit.

" SINGINGS."

Mary —— tells me that she once attended a " sing-ing" among the Amish. About nightfall, on a Sunday evening in summer, a half-dozen " girls" and a few more " boys" met at the house of one of the members. They talked a while first on common subjects, and then sang hymns from the Amish hymn-book in the German

tongue.   They chanted in the slow manner common in
their religious meetings; but Mary says that some are
now learning to sing by note, and are improving their
manner.   They thus intoned until about ten o'clock,
and then laid aside their hymn-books, and the old folks
went to bed.   Then the young people went out into the
wash-house, or outside kitchen, so as not to wake the
sleepers, and played, " Come, Philander, let's be march-
ing," and

> " The needle's eye we do supply
>   With thread that runs so true;
> And many a lass have I let pass
>   Because I wanted you."

Which game seems to be the same as

> " Open the gates as high as the sky
>   And let King George and his troops go by."

In these kissing plays, and in some little romping among
the young men, the time was spent until about two or
three in the morning, when they separated, two girls
from a distance staying all night.   Mary was able to
sleep until daylight only, for no allowance is made for
those who partake in these gay vigils to make up in the
morning for loss of sleep.

There were no refreshments upon this occasion, but
once at a singing at Christ. Yoder's, it is said that the
party took nearly all the pies out of the cellar, and
the empty plates were found in the wash-house next
morning.

Dancing-parties are not unknown among us, but they
are not popular among the plain people whom I especially describe.

FARMING.

In this fertile limestone district farming is very laborious, being entirely by tillage. Our regular routine is once in five years to plough the sod ground for corn. In the next ensuing year the same ground is sowed with oats; and when the oats come off in August, the industrious "Dutchmen" immediately manure the stubble-land for wheat. I have seen them laying the dark-brown heaps upon the yellow stubble, when, in August, I have ridden some twelve or fourteen miles down to the hill-country for blackberries.

After the ground is carefully prepared, wheat and timothy (grass) seed are put in with a drill, and in the ensuing spring clover is sowed upon the same ground. By July, when the wheat is taken off the ground, the clover and timothy are growing, and will be ready to mow in the next or fourth summer. In the fifth the same grass constitutes a grazing-ground, and then the sod is ready to be broken up again for Indian corn. Potatoes are seldom planted here in great quantities; a part of one of the oat-fields or corn-fields can be put into potatoes, and the ground will be ready by fall to be put into wheat, if it is desired. A successful farmer put more than half of his forty acres into wheat; this being considered the best crop. The average crop of wheat is about twenty bushels, of Indian corn about forty. I have heard of one hundred bushels of corn in the Pequea valley, but this is very rare.

When the wheat and oats are in the barn or stack, enormous eight-horse threshers, whose owners go about the neighborhood from farm to farm, thresh the crop in two or three days; and thus what was once a great job for winter may all be finished by the first of October.

Jacob E. is a model farmer. His buildings and fences are in good order, and his cattle well kept. He is a little past the prime of life; his beautiful head of black hair being touched with silver. His wife is dimpled and smiling, and her weight of nearly two hundred does not prevent her being active, energetic, forehanded, and "thorough-going." During the winter months the two sons go to the public school,—the older one with reluctance; there they learn to read and write and cipher, and possibly they study geography; they speak English at school, and "Dutch" at home. Much education the "Dutch" farmer fears, as productive of laziness; and laziness is a mortal sin here. The E.'s rarely buy a book. I suggested to one of our neighbors that he might advantageously have given a certain son a chance with books. "Don't want no books," was the answer. "There's enough goes to books! Get so lazy after a while they won't farm." The winter is employed partly in preparing material to fertilize the wheat-land during the coming summer. Great droves of cattle and sheep come down our road from the West, and our farmers buy from these, and fatten stock during the winter months for the Philadelphia market. A proper care of his stock will occupy some portion of the farmer's time. A farmer's son told me also of cutting wood and quarrying stone in the winter, adding, "If a person wouldn't work in the winter, they'd be behindhand in the spring."

Besides these, the farmer has generally a great "freundschaft," or family connection, both his and his wife's; and the paying visits within a range of twenty or thirty miles, and receiving visits in return, help to pass away the time. Then Jacob and Susanna are actively benevolent; they are liable to be called upon, summer and winter, to wait on the sick and to help bury the dead. Susanna was formerly renowned as a baker at funerals, where her services were freely given.

This rich level land of ours is highly prized by the "Dutch" for farming purposes, and the great demand has enhanced the price. The farms, too, are small, seventy acres being a fair size. When Seth R., the rich preacher, bought his last farm from an "Englishman," William G. said to him, "Well, Seth, it seems as if you Dutch folks had determined to root us English out; but thee had to pay pretty dear for thy root this time."

There are some superstitious ideas that still hold sway here, regarding the growth of plants. A young girl coming to us for cabbage-plants said that it was a good time to set them out, for "it was in the Wirgin." It is very doubtful whether she knew *what* was in Virgo, but I suppose that it was the moon. So our farmer's wife tells me that the Virgin will do very well for cabbages, but not for any plant like beans, for, though they will flower well, they will not mature the fruit. Fence should be set in the upgoing of the moon; meat butchered in the downgoing will shrink in the pot.

FARMERS' WIVES.

One of my "Dutch" neighbors, who, from a shoe-maker, became the owner of two farms, said to me, "The woman is more than half;" and his own very laborious wife (with her portion) had indeed been so.

The woman (in common speech, "the old woman") milks, raises the poultry, has charge of the garden,—sometimes digging the ground herself, and planting and hoeing, with the assistance of her daughters and the "maid," when she has one. (German, *magd*.) To be sure, she does not go extensively into vegetable-raising, nor has she a large quantity of strawberries and other small fruits; neither does she plant a great many peas and beans, that are laborious to "stick." She has a quantity of cabbages and of "red beets," of onions and of early potatoes, in her garden, a plenty of cucumbers for winter pickles, and store of string-beans and tomatoes, with some sweet potatoes.

Peter R. told me that in one year, off their small farm, they sold "two hundred dollars' worth of *wedgable* things, not counting the butter." As in that year the clothing for each member of the family probably cost no more than fifteen dollars, the two hundred dollars' worth of vegetable things was of great importance.

Our "Dutch" never make *store*-cheese. At a county fair, only one cheese was exhibited, and that was from Chester County. The farmer's wife boards all the farm-hands, and the mechanics—the carpenter, mason, etc.—who put up the new buildings, and the fence-makers. At times she allows the daughters to go out and husk corn. It was a pretty sight which I saw one fall day,—an Amish man with four sons and daughters, husking in the field. "We do it all ourselves," said he.

(Said a neighbor, "A man told me once that he was at an Amish husking—a husking-match in the kitchen. He said he never saw as much sport in all his life. There they had the bloom-sock. There was one old man, quite gray-headed, and gray-bearded; he laughed till he shook." Said another, "There's not many huskings going on now. The most play now goes on at the infares.")

In winter mornings perhaps the farmer's wife goes out to milk in the stable with a lantern, while her daughters get breakfast; has her house "redd up" about eight o'clock, and is prepared for several hours' sewing before dinner, laying by great piles of shirts for summer. We no longer make linen; but I have heard of one "Dutch" girl who had a good supply of domestic linen made into shirts and trousers for the future spouse whose fair proportions she had not yet seen.

There are, of course, many garments to make in a large family, but there is not much work put upon them. We do not yet patronize the sewing-machine very extensively, but a seamstress or tailoress is sometimes called in. At the spring cleaning the labors of the women folk are increased by whitewashing the picket-fences.

In March we make soap, before the labors of the garden are great. The forests are being obliterated from this fertile tract, and many use what some call *consecrated* lye; formerly, the ash-hopper was filled, and a good lot of egg-bearing lye run off to begin the soap with, while the weaker filled the soft-soap kettle, after the soap had "come." The chemical operation of soap-making often proved difficult, and, of course, much was said about luck. "We had bad luck making soap." A sassafras stick was preferred for stirring, and the soap was stirred always in one direction. In regard to this, and that other chemical operation, making and keeping vinegar, there are certain ideas about the temporary incapacity of some persons,—ideas only to be alluded to here. If the farmer's wife never "has luck" in making soap, she employs some skilful woman to come in and help her. It is not a long operation, for the "Dutch" rush this work speedily. If the lye is well run off, two tubs of hard soap and a barrel of soft can be made in a day. A smart housekeeper can make a barrel of soap in the morning, and go visiting in the afternoon.

Great are the household labors in harvest; but the cooking and baking in the hot weather are cheerfully done for the men, who are toiling in hot suns and stifling barns. Four meals are common at this season, for "a piece" is sent out at nine o'clock. I heard of one "Dutch" girl's making some fifty pies a week in harvest; for if you have four meals a day, and pie at each, many are required. We have great faith in pie.

I have been told of an inexperienced Quaker housewife in the neighboring county of York, who was left in charge of the farm, and during harvest these important labors were performed by John Stein, John Stump, and John Stinger. She also had guests, welcome perhaps as "rain in harvest." To conciliate the Johns was very important, and she waited on them first. "What will thee have, John Stein?" "What shall I give thee, John Stump?" "And thee, John Stinger?" On one memorable occasion there was mutiny in the field, for John Stein declared that he never worked where there were not "kickelin" cakes in harvest, nor would he now. *Küchlein* proved to be cakes fried in fat; and the housewife was ready to appease "Achilles' wrath," as soon as she made this discovery.

We made in one season six barrels of cider into apple-butter, three at a time. Two large copper kettles were hung under the beech-trees, down between the spring-house and smoke-house, and the cider was boiled down the evening before, great stumps of trees being in demand. One hand watched the cider, and the rest of the family gathered in the kitchen and labored diligently in preparing the cut apples, so that in the morning the "schnits" might be ready to go in. (*Schneiden*, to cut, *geschnitten*.)

One bushel and a half of cut apples are said to be enough for a barrel of cider. In a few hours the apples will all be in, and then you will stir, and stir, and stir, for you do not want to have the apple-butter burn at the bottom, and be obliged to dip it out into tubs and scour the kettle. Some time in the afternoon, you will take out a little on a dish, and when you find that the cider no longer "weeps out" round the edges, but all forms a simple heap, you will dip it up into earthen vessels, and when cold take it "on" to the garret to keep company with the hard soap and the bags of dried apples and cherries, perhaps with the hams and shoulders. Soap and apple-butter are usually made in an open fireplace, where hangs the kettle. At one time (about the year 1828) I have heard that there was apple-butter in the Lancaster Museum which dated from Revolutionary times; for we do not expect it to ferment in the summer. It dries away; but water is stirred in to prepare it for the table. Sometimes peach-butter is made, with cider, molasses, or sugar, and, in the present scarcity of apples, cut pumpkin is often put into the apple-butter.

Soon after apple-butter-making comes butchering, for we like an early pig in the fall, when the store of smoked meat has run out. Pork is the staple, and we smoke the flitches, not preserving them in brine like the Yankees. We ourselves use much beef, and do not like smoked flitch, but I speak for the majority. Sausage is a great dish with us, as in Germany.

Butchering is one of the many occasions for the display of friendly feeling, when brother or father steps in to help hang the hogs, or a sister to assist in rendering lard, or in preparing a plentiful meal. An active farmer will have two or three porkers killed, scalded, and hung up by sunrise, and by night the whole operation of sausage and "pudding" making, and lard rendering, will be finished, and the house set in order. The friends who have assisted receive a portion of the sausage, etc., which portion is called the "metzel-sup" (or soop). The metzel-sup is very often sent to poor widows and others.

We make scrapple from the skin, a part of the livers, and heads, with the addition of corn-meal; but, instead, our "Dutch" neighbors make *liverwurst* ("woorsht"), or meat pudding, omitting the meal, and this compound, stuffed into the larger entrails, is very popular in Lancaster market. Some make *pawn-haus* from the liquor in which the pudding-meat was boiled, adding thereto corn-meal. The name is properly *pann-haas*, and signifies, perhaps, panned-rabbit. It is sometimes made of richer material.

These three dishes, just before mentioned, are fried before eating. I have never seen hog's-head cheese in "Dutch" houses. If the boiling-pieces of beef are kept over summer, they are smoked, instead of being preserved in brine. Much smear-case (*schmier-käse*), or cottage cheese, is eaten in these regions. Children, and some grown people too, fancy it upon bread with molasses; which may be considered as an offset to the Yankee pork and molasses.

In some Pennsylvania families smear-case and apple-butter are eaten to save butter, which is a salable article. The true "Dutch" housewife's ambition is to supply the store-goods for the family as far as possible from the sale of the butter and eggs.

We have also Dutch cheese, which may be made by crumbling the dry smear-case, working in butter, salt, and chopped sage, forming it into pats, and setting them away to ripen. The *sieger-käse* is made from sweet milk boiled, with sour milk added and beaten eggs, and then set to drain off the whey. (*Ziegen-käse* is German for goat's milk cheese.)

"Schnits and knep" is said to be made of dried apples, fat pork, and dough-dumplings cooked together.

"Tell them they're good," says one of my "Dutch" acquaintances.

Knep is from the German, *knöpfe*, buttons or knobs. In common speech the word has fallen to nep. The "nep" are sometimes made from pie-crust, or sometimes from a batter of eggs and milk, and may be boiled without the meat; but one of my acquaintances says that the smoke gives a peculiar and appetizing flavor.

Apple-dumplings in "Dutch" are *aepel-dumplins;*

whence I infer that like *pye-kroosht* they are not of German origin.

In the fall our "Dutch" make *sauer-kraut*. I happened to visit the house of my friend Susanna when her husband and son were going to take an hour at noon to help her with the kraut. Two white tubs stood upon the back porch, one with the fair round heads, and the other to receive the cabbage when cut by a knife set in a board (a very convenient thing for cutting kohl-slaw and cucumbers). When cut, the cabbage is packed into a "stand" with a sauer-kraut staff, resembling the pounder with which New Englanders beat clothes in a barrel. Salt is added during the packing. When the cabbage ferments it becomes acid. The kraut-stand remains in the cellar; the contents not being unpalatable when boiled with potatoes and the chines or ribs of pork. But the smell of the boiling kraut is very strong, and that stomach is probably strong which readily digests the meal.

Sometimes "nep" or dumplings are boiled with the salt meat and sour-krout. A young teacher, who was speaking of sour-krout and nep, was asked how he spelt this word. He did not know, and said he did not care, so he got the nep.

"As Dutch as sour-krout," has become a familiar saying here. In Lehigh County, if I mistake not, I heard the common dialect called "sour-krout Dutch."

Our "Dutch" make soup in variety, and pronounce the word short, between *soup* and *sup*. Thus there is Dutch soup, potato soup, etc.; scalded milk and bread is "bread and milk soup," bread crumbed into coffee "coffee   up."

Noodel soup (*nudeln*) is a treat. Noodels may be called domestic macaroni. I have seen a dish in which bits of fried bread were laid upon the piled-up noodels, to me unpalatable from the quantity of eggs in the latter.

Dampf-noodles, or *gedämpfte nudeln*, are boiled, and melted butter is poured over them.

The extremely popular cakes, twisted, sprinkled with salt, and baked crisp and brown, called pretzels (*brezeln*), were known in Pennsylvania long before the cry for "ein lager, zwei brezeln" (a glass of lager and two pretzels), was heard in the land.

One of my "Dutch" neighbors, who visited Western New York, was detained several hours at Elmira. "They hadn't no water-crackers out there," he complained. "Didn't know what you meant when you said water-crackers; and they hain't got pretzels. You can't get no pretzels."

Perhaps not at the railroad stations.

We generally find excellent home-made wheat bread in this limestone region. We make the pot of "sots" (or rising) overnight, with boiled mashed potatoes, scalded flour, and sometimes hops. Friday is baking-day. The "Dutch" housewife is very fond of baking in the brick oven, but the scarcity of wood must gradually accustom us to the great cooking-stove.

One of the heavy labors of the fall is the fruit-drying. Afterward your hostess invites you to partake, thus: "Mary, will you have pie? This is snits, and this is elder" (or dried apples, and dried elderberries). Dried peaches are peach snits.

A laboring woman once, speaking to me of a neighbor, said, "She hain't got many dried apples. If her girl would snits in the .evening, as I did!—but she'd rather keep company and run around than to snits."

The majority keep one fire in winter. This is in the kitchen, which with nice housekeepers is the abode of, neatness, with its rag carpet and brightly polished stove. An adjoining room or building is the wash-house, where butchering, soap-making, etc., are done by the help of a great kettle hung in the fireplace, not set in brick-work.

Adjoining the kitchen, on another side, is a state apartment, also rag-carpeted, and called "the room." The stove-pipe from the kitchen sometimes passes through the ceiling, and tempers the sleeping-room of the parents. These arrangements are not very favor-able to bathing in cold weather; indeed, to wash the whole person is not very common, in summer or in winter.

Will you go up-stairs in a neat Dutch farm-house? Here are rag carpets again. Gay quilts are on the best beds, where green and red calico, perhaps in the form of a basket, are displayed on a white ground; or the beds bear brilliant coverlets of red, white, and blue, as if to "make the rash gazer wipe his eye." The com-mon pillow-cases are sometimes of blue check, or of calico. In winter, people often sleep under feather-covers, not so heavy as a feather-bed. In the spring there is a great washing of bedclothes, and then the blankets are washed, which during winter supplied the place of sheets.

HOLIDAYS.

I was sitting alone, one Christmas time, when the door opened and there entered some half-dozen youths or men, who frightened me so that I slipped out at the door. They, being thus alone, and not intending any harm, at once left. These, I suppose, were Christmas mummers, though I heard them called " bell-schnickel."

At another time, as I was sitting with my little boy, Aunt Sally came in smiling and mysterious, and took her place by the stove. Immediately after, there entered a man in disguise, who very much alarmed my little Dan.

The stranger threw·down nuts and cakes, and, when some one offered to pick them up, struck at him with a rod. This was the real bell-schnickel, personated by the farmer.

It will hardly be supposed that Bell-schnickel and Santa Claus are the same; but the former is Peltz-nickel* or Nicholas dressed in fur. St. Nicholas' day, the 6th of December, is in Advent.

On Christmas morning the cry is, " Christmas-gift!" and not, as elsewhere, " A merry Christmas!" Christmas is a day when people do not work, but go to meeting, when roast turkey and mince-pie are in order, and when the " Dutch" housewife has store of cakes on hand to give to the little folks.

We still hear of barring-out at Christmas. The pupils fasten themselves in the school-house, and keep the teacher out to obtain presents from him.

---

* Some account of Peltz-nickel in Germany will be found in the Appendix.

The first of April (which our neighbors generally call Aprile) is a great occasion. This is the opening of the farming year. The tenant farmers and other "renters" move to their new homes, and interest-money and other debts are due; and so much money changes hands in Lancaster, on the first, that pickpockets are attracted thither, and the unsuspicious "Dutch" farmer sometimes finds himself a loser.

The movings, on or about the first, are made festive occasions; neighbors, young and old, are gathered; some bring wagons to transport farm utensils and furniture, others assist in driving cattle, put furniture in its place, and set up bedsteads; while the women are ready to help prepare the bountiful meal. At this feast I have heard a worthy tenant farmer say, "Now help yourselves, as you did out there" (with the goods).

Whitsuntide Monday is a great holiday with the young "Dutch" folks. It occurs when there is a lull in farmwork, between corn-planting and hay-making. Now the new summer bonnets are all in demand, and the taverns are found full of youths and girls, who sometimes walk the street hand-in-hand, eat cakes and drink beer, or visit the "flying horses." A number of seats are arranged around a central pole, and, a pair taking each seat, the whole revolves by the work of a horse, and you can have a circular ride for six cents.

On the Fourth of July we are generally at work in the harvest-field. Several of the festivals of the church are held here as days of rest, if not of recreation. Such are Good Friday, Ascension-day, etc. On Easter, eggs colored and otherwise ornamented were formerly much in vogue.

Thanksgiving is beginning to be observed here, but the New Englander would miss the family gatherings, the roast turkeys, the pumpkin-pies. Possibly we go to church in the morning, and sit quiet for the rest of the day ; and as for pumpkin-pies, we do not greatly fancy them. Raisin-pie, or mince-pie, we can enjoy.

The last night of October is "Hallow-eve." I was in Lancaster one Hallow-eve, and boys were ringing door-bells, carrying away door-steps, throwing corn at the windows, or running off with an unguarded wagon. I heard of one or two youngsters who had requested an afternoon holiday to go to church, but who had spent their time in going out of town to steal corn for this occasion. In the country, farm-gates are taken from their hinges and removed ; and it was formerly a favorite amusement to take a wagon to pieces, and, after carrying the parts up to the barn-roof, to put it together again, thus obliging the owner to take it apart and bring it down. Such "tricks" as are described by Burns in the poem of "Hallow-e'en" may be heard of occasionally, continued perhaps by the Scotch-Irish element in our population.

PUBLIC SCHOOLS.

Over twenty years ago I was circulating an anti-slavery petition among women. I carried it to the house of a neighboring farmer, who was a miller also, and well to do. His wife signed the petition (*all* women did not in those days), but she signed it with her mark. I have understood that it is about twenty years since the school law was made universal here, and that our township of Upper Leacock wanted to resist by litigation the

establishment of public schools.* It is the school-tax
that is onerous. Within about twenty years a great
impetus has been given to education by the establishment
of the county superintendency, of normal schools,
and of teachers' institutes. I think it is within this
time, however, that the board of directors met, in an
adjoining township, and, being called upon to vote by
ballot, there were afterward found in the box several
different ways of spelling the word "no."

At the last institute, a worthy young man at the blackboard
was telling the teachers how to make their pupils
pronounce the word "did," which they inclined to call
dit; and a young woman told me that she found it
necessary, when teaching in Berks County, to practise
speaking "Dutch," in order to make the pupils understand
their lessons. It must be rather hard to hear and
talk "Dutch" almost constantly, and then to go to a
school where the text-books are English.

There is still an effort made to have German taught
in our public schools. The reading of German is considered
a great accomplishment, and is one required for
a candidate for the ministry among some of our plainer
sects. But the teacher is generally overburdened in the
winter with the necessary branches in a crowded, ungraded
school. Our township generally has school for
seven months in the year; some townships have only
five; and in Berks County I have heard of one having
only four months. About thirty-five dollars a month is
paid to teachers, male and female.

My little boy of seven began to go to public school

---

* Written about 1868.

this fall. For a while I could hear him repeating such expressions as, " Che, double o, t, coot" (meaning good). " P-i-g, pick." " Kreat A, little A, pouncing P." " I don't like chincherpread." Even among our " Dutch" people of more culture, *etch* is heard for *aitch* (h), and *chay* for jay (j), and these are relics of early training.

The standard of our county superintendent is high (1868), and his examinations are severe. His salary is about seventeen hundred dollars. Where there is so much wealth as here, it seems almost impossible that learning should not follow, as soon as the minds of the people are turned toward it; but the great fear of making their children " lazy" operates against sending them to school. Industrious habits will certainly tend more to the pecuniary success of a farmer than the " art of writing and speaking the English language *correctly*."

MANNERS AND CUSTOMS.

My dear old " English" friend, Samuel G., had often been asked to stay and eat with David B., and on one occasion he concluded to accept the invitation. They went to the table, and had a silent pause; then David cut up the meat, and each workman or member of the family put in a fork and helped himself. The guest was discomfited, and, finding that he was likely to lose his dinner otherwise, he followed their example. The invitation to eat had covered the whole. When guests are present, many say, " Now help yourselves;" but they do not use vain repetitions, as the city people do.

Coffee is still drunk three times a day in some families, but frequently without sugar. The sugar-bowl stands on the table, with spoons therein for those who want sugar; but at a late "home-coming" party I believe that I was the only one at the table who took sugar. The dishes of smear-case, molasses, apple-butter, etc., are not always supplied with spoons. *We* dip in our knives, and with the same useful implements convey the food to our mouths. Does the opposite extreme prevail among the farmers of Massachusetts? Do they always eat with their forks, and use napkins?

On many busy farm-occasions, the woman of the house will find it more convenient to let the men eat first,—to get the burden of the harvest-dinner off her mind and her hands, and then sit down with her daughters, her "maid" and little children, to their own repast. But the allowing to the men the constant privilege of eating first has passed away, if indeed it ever prevailed. At funeral feasts the old men and women sit down first, with the mourning family. Then succeed the second, third, and fourth tables.

Among the children of well-to-do parents, the unmarried daughter will sometimes go into the service of the married one, receiving wages regularly, or allowing them to accumulate. An acquaintance of mine in Lancaster had a hired girl living in his family who was worth twelve thousand dollars in cash means, her father having been a rich farmer. Among our plain farmers, such persons are considered more praiseworthy than the reverse.

I lately asked a lawyer in Northampton County why certain persons had allowed the Lutheran and Reformed farmers, men of very little school learning, to outstrip them in the pursuit of wealth. He answered that all the tendency of the education of these last was saving. " In old times," he continued, " when we had no ranges nor cooking-stoves, but a fire on the hearth, I used to hear my mother say to her daughters that they must not let the dish-water boil, or they would not be married for seven years." On the same principle, when a young " English" girl whom I knew told a young " Dutchman" that she was going to make bread, he said, " I'm coming for a handful of your dough-trough scrapings ;" the idea being that there should be no scrapings left.

Mr. S., of Lehigh County, says, " We make money in Pennsylvania by saving; in New York, they make money by paying out."

Mrs. R., of the same county, says, " We Pennsylvanians are brought up to work in the house and to family affairs, but the Eastern girls are brought up more in the factories, and they don't know anything about housework. Many have been married, and lived here in this town (Allentown), of whom I have heard speak, who have not lived happily, because they were not used to keep house in the way that their husbands had been accustomed to. They were very intelligent, but not accustomed to work, and their families would get poor, and stay poor." Mrs. R.'s daughter added, that " the New England men, the Eastern men, milk and do all the outside work."

The writer thinks, nevertheless, that New England women will not be willing to admit that they do not understand housework, and are not eminently " faculized."

We Lancaster " Dutch" are always striving to seize Time's forelock. We rise, even in the winter, about four, feed the stock while the women get breakfast, eat breakfast in the short days by coal-oil lamps, and by daylight are ready for the operations of the day. The English folks and the backsliding " Dutch" are sometimes startled when they hear their neighbors blow the horn or ring the bell for dinner. On a recent pleasant October day the farmer's wife was churning out-of-doors, and cried, " Why, there's the dinner-bells a'ready. Mercy days !" I went in to the clock, and found it at twenty minutes of eleven. The " Dutch" farmers almost invariably keep their time half an hour or more ahead, like that village in Cornwall where it was twelve o'clock when it was but half-past eleven to the rest of the world. Our " Dutch" are never seen running to catch a railroad train.

We are not a total-abstinence people. Before these times of high prices, liquor was often furnished to hands in the harvest-field.

A few years ago a meeting was held in a neighboring school-house to discuss a prohibitory liquor law. After various speeches the question was put to the vote, thus : " All those who want leave to drink whiskey will please to rise." " Now all those who don't want to drink whiskey will rise." The affirmative had a decided majority.

Work is a cardinal virtue with the " Dutchman." " He is lazy," is a very opprobrious remark. At the quilting, when I was trying to take out one of the screws, Katy Groff, who is sixty-five, exclaimed, " How lazy I am, not to be helping you !" (" *Wie ich bin faul.*")

Marriages sometimes take place between the two nationalities; but I do not think the " Dutch" farmers desire English wives for their sons, unless the wives are decidedly rich. On the other hand, I heard of an English farmer's counselling his son to seek a "Dutch" wife. When the son had wooed and won his substantial bride, "Now he will see what good cooking is," said a "Dutch" girl to me. I was surprised at the remark, for his mother was an excellent housekeeper.

The circus is the favorite amusement of our people. Lancaster papers have often complained of the slender attendance which is bestowed upon lectures and the like; even theatrical performances are found "slow," compared with the feats of the ring.

Our "Dutch" use a freedom of language that is not known to the English, and which to them savors of coarseness. "But they mean no harm by it," says one of my English friends. It is difficult to practise reserve where the whole family sit in one heated room. This rich limestone land in which the "Dutch" delight is nearly level to an eye trained among the hills. Do hills make a people more poetical or imaginative?

Perhaps so; but there is vulgarity too among the hills.

———————

The foregoing article was written about fourteen years ago, and appeared (with perhaps some small changes) in the *Atlantic Monthly* for October, 1869. It was published in the first edition of this work in 1872, and in the second edition in 1874. Many of the alterations which were made in one or both of these editions are now removed to the Appendix, where will also be found additional matter on similar subjects.

The passage of over twelve years has considerably changed the neighborhood in which I live. The greatest differences are the rise in the value of land; the division into smaller farms; the general introduction of the culture of tobacco; and the change in the population by the coming in of a larger number of that plainest sect of Mennonites, called Amish.

As regards the rise in the value of land, it is doubtless in part apparent only, from the greater amount of money at this time. I have spoken of one who said, "Well, Seth, it seems as if you Dutch folks had determined to root us English out; but thee had to pay pretty dear for thy root this time." The farm alluded to was sold about 1855, and brought less than one hundred and sixty-three dollars per acre,—there being one hundred and ten acres. It has since been divided, and eighty acres, now a very large farm here, with the newer farm buildings, it is supposed would now bring over two hundred and fifty dollars. Small properties sell much higher in proportion. I hear of twenty acres, with fair farm buildings, having sold last fall for nine thousand dollars.

The division into smaller farms is caused in a great measure by the Amish increasing and dividing properties among their children, so that farms are running as low, in many cases, as from twenty-five down to ten acres. It is rare for the Amish to remain unmarried. The owners of such small properties cannot afford to hire help; the Amish help one another, and are willing to help others also. Many acts of neighborly kindness are exchanged here, even to giving a sick neighbor several days' work in the harvest-field.

Tobacco was cultivated to profit long ago on farms and islands lying on the Susquehanna; but one of the consequences of the civil war was to make the cultivation of the weed more general here, and the immense sums obtained for fine crops have also kept up the value of this land.

The routine of farming described in the foregoing article is now abandoned. The following are the crops raised lately on a farm visible from where I write,—a farm that has been for years under excellent cultivation. It contains sixty-eight acres, of which (in round numbers) twenty-six are in wheat, eighteen in Indian corn, eleven in grass, six in tobacco, three-quarters of an acre in potatoes, and the remainder is occupied by garden, orchard, and buildings. Oats has not been grown on this farm for six years. The ground is so rich that oats lodge or fall, and will not mature the grain. For the last four years wheat has averaged thirty bushels to the acre. During the same time Indian corn has averaged about fifty-five bushels. To speak slang, it is not one of our brag crops. One year the cut-worms took two-thirds of it on the farm mentioned; and this had to be replanted. The greatest crop of corn of which I hear mention on this farm was grown some years ago, and was nine hundred bushels on ten acres.

As regards grass, the owner estimates that for the last four years they have made on an average nearly three tons of hay to the acre; last year they had thirty-six tons on ten acres.

Of the six acres in tobacco this year, they prepare the whole for planting, but only plant two themselves, giving out four to others. The men who take this land plant and cultivate it, and receive one-half of the produce, not being charged for the preparation of the ground, nor for taking the crop to market. One of the advantages of the cultivation of tobacco (I am sensible of its disadvantages, and do not recommend its use) is that it gives the poor laboring man and woman more independence. He or she takes an acre or more, plants, waters, destroys the large tobacco-worm, strips off the suckers, tops it, breaks down the flowering stem, gathers, dries, sorts, and packs, and receives perhaps one hundred dollars per acre in lump, which is very acceptable. They estimate that they make about double wages.

The eight-horse threshers before mentioned are getting out of date; steam threshes now almost entirely, and completes the work on such a farm as just described in two days. The threshing is frequently finished as early as the first of September, so that the farmer can hang tobacco in the barn. Large tobacco-houses have also been erected, in the cellar of which this crop is prepared for sale.

It will be observed that very little attention was paid to potatoes. Last year they brought at the rate of two hundred bushels to the acre. We had a pretty severe drought in 1881, and potatoes have sold this winter at one dollar per bushel, which would make the potato crop superior in value to the tobacco.

The great amount of manure required to keep the land up to such a standard is thus supplied on this farm, which is a model one in the neighborhood. For several months last winter the owner had sixteen horses, five of his own and the rest boarding; he also had twelve head of horned cattle, and fattened nine swine. All the corn, hay, and fodder raised on the farm were fed upon it. (Straw is rarely fed here.)   Besides, the farmer bought five tons of Western mill-feed (the bran and other refuse from wheat flour) and about three hundred bushels of corn.   This spring he has bought two tons of a certain fertilizer for his corn, and applied his own barn-yard manure to the tobacco and wheat.   He has been indemnified in part for the great amount fed, by the money received for boarding horses at twelve dollars apiece by the month.   Horses from Canada and the West are often fattened here for the Eastern market.   This farmer bought two last year, worked them himself on the farm, fattened and groomed them, and sold them so as to make one hundred dollars apiece on them; but this was exceptional.

Besides the fertilizers before mentioned, lime is used in this region, although some have doubted the necessity of applying it to our rich limestone land.   On the farm which I have been describing it is put on about every sixth year, at the rate of six hundred bushels on eleven acres.   It costs ten cents a bushel.

Another change here is that many now buy bread, and several bakers regularly supply the neighborhood. This has caused a great lightening of the labor at funerals.   The bread and rusks (or buns) are bought and the pies dispensed with, which were once considered so necessary.   A jocose youth in a near village used to say, "There will be raisin-pie there," when he wished to express that there was fatal illness; but raisin-pies are no longer so fashionable at funerals.   There is no diminution, however, in the great gatherings.   A wealthy

farmer died lately who was also a Mennonite preacher.
The funeral was on Sunday; the guests heard preaching
at the house, then dined, and the funeral went to the
church, where was preaching again. Four hundred carriages, it is said, were on the ground.

Our school-term in this district is not increased beyond seven months; but the salary has risen, and is
from thirty-five to forty dollars per month, according to
merit.

The Amish in this immediate neighborhood still cling
to the plain customs I have described, except that it has
become quite common for young people to drive in simple buggies. Now the yellow-covered wagons are not
so universal; other colors are also used, and more ele-
gant harness. (They generally keep very good harness.)
Neither do the young men wear their hair to their
shoulders. Many of the Amish now wear suspenders.
One of my friends, who is Amish, says that you cannot
speak of any such rule as regards the church in general,
for every congregation has its own rules in these minor
affairs.

The family graveyard, especially mentioned, has been
removed, and all the bodies that were recovered interred
at the Mennonite church in the neighborhood.

Two or three small changes in this neighborhood are
the following: Sewing-machines are now found here in
great numbers; many houses have large stoves, which
heat at least one room up-stairs; and it is not common
in this immediate neighborhood to sit up with the dead,
in the manner before described.

AN AMISH MEETING.*

It was on a Sunday morning in March, when the air was bleak and the roads were execrable, that I obtained a driver to escort me to the farm-house where an Amish meeting was to be held.

It was a little after nine o'clock when I entered, and, although the hour was so early, I found the congregation nearly all gathered, and the preaching begun.

There were forty men present, as many women, and one infant. Had the weather been less inclement, we should probably have had more little ones, for such plain people do not think it necessary to leave the babies at home.

The rooms in which we sat seemed to have been constructed for these great occasions. They were the kitchen and "the room,"—as our people call the sitting-room, or best room,—and were so arranged as to be made into one by means of two doors.

Our neighbors wore the usual costume of the sect, which is a branch of the Mennonite Society, or nearly allied to it, the men having laid off their round-crowned and remarkably wide-brimmed hats. Their hair is usually cut square across the forehead, and hangs long

* Amish is pronounced *Ommish*, the *a* being very broad, like *aw*. This article was first published some years ago.

behind; their coats are plainer than those of the plainest Quaker, and are fastened, except the overcoat, with hooks and eyes in place of buttons; whence they are sometimes called Hooker or Hook-and-Eye Mennists. The pantaloons are worn without suspenders. Formerly the Amish were often called "beardy men," but since beards have become fashionable theirs are not so conspicuous.

The women, whom I have sometimes seen with a bright purple apron, an orange neckerchief, or some other striking bit of color, were now more soberly arrayed in plain white caps without ruffle or border, and white neckerchiefs, though occasionally a cap or kerchief was black. They wear closely fitting waists, with a little basquine behind, which is probably a relic from the times of the short gown and petticoat. Their gowns were of sober woollen stuff, frequently of flannel; and all wore aprons.

But the most surprising figures among the Amish are the little children, dressed in garments like those of old persons. It has been my lot to see at the house of her parents a tender little dark-eyed Amish maiden of three years, old enough to begin to speak "Dutch," and as yet ignorant of English. Seated upon her father's lap, sick and suffering, with that sweet little face encircled by the plain muslin cap, the little figure dressed in that plain gown, she was one not to be soon forgotten. But the little girl that was at meeting to-day was either no Amish child or a great backslider, for she was hardly to be distinguished in dress from the "world's people."

The floors were bare, but on one of the open doors hung a long white towel, worked at one end with colored figures, such as our mothers or grandmothers put upon samplers. These perhaps were meant for flowers. The congregation sat principally on benches. On the men's side a small shelf of books ran around one corner of the room.

The preacher, who was speaking when I entered, continued for about fifteen minutes. His remarks and the rest of the services were in "Dutch." I have been criticised for applying the epithet to my neighbors, or to their language, but "Dutch" is the title which they generally apply to themselves, speaking of "us Dutch folks and you English folks," and sometimes with a pretty plain hint that some of the "Dutch" ways are discreeter and better, if not more virtuous, than the English. But, though I call them "Dutch," I am fully aware that they are not Hollanders. Most of them are Swiss, of ancient and honorable descent, exiles on account of religious persecution.

I am sorry that I do not understand the language well enough to give a sketch of some of the discourses on this occasion. At times I understood an expression of the first speaker, such as "Let us well reflect and observe," or "Let us well consider," expressions that were often repeated. As he was doubtless a farmer, and was speaking extemporaneously, it is not remarkable that they were so.

When the preacher had taken his seat, the congregation knelt for five minutes in silence. A brother then read aloud from the German Bible, concerning Nicodemus who came to Jesus by night, etc. After this another brother rose and spoke in a tone like that which is so common among Friends, namely, a kind of sing-

4

ing or chanting tone, which he accompanied by a little gesture.

While he was speaking, one or two women went out, and, as I wished to take note of the proceedings, I followed them into the wash-house or outside kitchen, which was quite comfortable. As I passed along, I saw in the yard the wagons which had brought the people to meeting. Most of them were covered with plain yellow oil-cloth. I have been told that there are sometimes a hundred wagons gathered at one farm-house, and that in summer the meetings are often held in barns.

I sat down by the stove in the wash-house, and a very kindly old woman, the host's mother, came and renewed the fire. As she did not talk English, I spoke to her a little in German, and she seemed to understand me. When I wrote, she wondered and laughed at my rapid movements, for writing is slower work with these people than some other kinds of labor. I suppose, indeed, that there are still some of the older women who scarcely know how to write.

I asked her whether after meeting I might look at the German books on the corner shelf,—ancient books with dark leather covers and metallic clasps. She said in reply, " Bleibsht esse ?" (" Shall you stay and eat ?") Yes, I would. " Ya wohl," said she, " kannst." (" Very well, you can.")

A neat young Amish woman, the " maid" or housekeeper, came and put upon the stove a great tin washboiler, shining bright, into which she put water for making coffee and for washing dishes.

I soon returned to the meeting, and found the same

preacher still speaking. I suppose that he had continued during my absence, and, if so, his discourse was an hour and ten minutes in length. This was quite too long to be entertaining to one who only caught the sense of an occasional passage, or of a few texts of Scripture. It was while these monotonous tones continued that I heard a rocking upon the floor overheard. It proceeded, I believe, from the young·mother,—the mother of the little one before spoken of. When the child had become restless before this, or when she was tired, a young man upon the brethren's side of the room had taken it for a while, and now it was doubtless being put to sleep in a room overhead, into which a stove-pipe passed from the apartment where we sat.

My attention was also attracted by an old lady who sat near me, and facing the stove, with her hands crossed in her lap, and a gold or brass ring on each middle finger. She wore a black flannel dress and a brown woollen apron, leather shoes and knit woollen stockings. Her head was bent forward toward her broad bosom, upon which was crossed a white kerchief. With her gray hair, round face, and plain linen cap, her whole figure reminded me of the peasant women of continental Europe or of a Flemish picture.

I have spoken of her wearing rings. Says one of my neighbors of a different Mennist sect, " Were they not brass? She wears them for some sickness, I reckon. She would not wear them for show. One of our preachers wears steel rings on his little fingers for cramps."

When the long sermon was ended, different brethren were called upon, and during a half-hour we had from them several short discourses, one or two of them nearly inaudible. The speakers were, I think, giving their views on what had been said, or perhaps they were by these little efforts preparing themselves to become preachers, or showing their gifts to the congregation.

It is stated in Herzog's Cyclopædia that among the Mennonites in Holland the number of *liebesprediger* has greatly declined, so that some congregations had no preacher. (The word *liebesprediger* I am inclined to translate as voluntary, unpaid preachers, like those among Friends.) I am in doubt, indeed, whether any such are now found in Holland. There seems to be no scarcity in this country of preachers, who are, however, in some, if not all three of the divisions of Mennonites, chosen by lot.

When these smaller efforts were over, the former preacher spoke again for twenty minutes, and several of the women were moved to tears. After this the congregation knelt in vocal prayer. When they rose, the preacher said that the next meeting would be at the house of John Lapp, in two weeks. He pronounced a benediction, ending with the name of Jesus, and the whole congregation, brethren and sisters, curtsied, or made a reverence, as the French express it. This was doubtless in allusion to the text, that at the name of Jesus every knee should bow. Finally, a hymn, or a portion of one, was sung, drawn out in a peculiar manner by dwelling on the words. I obtained a hymn-book, and copied a portion. It seems obscure:

> " Der Schopfer auch der Vater heisst,
> 　Durch Christum, seinen Sohne;
> Da wirket mit der Heilig Geist,
> 　Einiger Gott drey Namen,

Von welchem kommt ein Gotteskind
Gewaschen ganz rein von der Sund,
   Wird geistlich gespeisst und trancket,
Mit Christi Blut, sein Willen thut
Irdisch verschmacht aus ganzen Muth,
   Der Vater sich ihm schenket.''

The book from which I copied these lines was in large German print, and bore the date 1785. In front was this inscription in the German tongue and handwriting: "This song-book belongs to me, Joseph B——. Written in the year of Christ 1791; and I received it from my father." Both father and son have been gathered to their fathers; the book, if I mistake not, was in the house of the grandson, and it may yet outlast several generations of these primitive people.

The services closed at a little after noon. From their having been conducted entirely in German, or in German and the dialect, some persons might suppose that these were recent immigrants to our country. But the B. family just alluded to was one of the first Amish families that came here, having arrived in 1737.

It seems that the language is cherished with care, as a means of preserving their religious and other peculiarities. The public schools, however, which are almost entirely English, must be a powerful means of assimilation.

The services being ended, the women quietly busied themselves (while I wrote) in preparing dinner. In a very short time two tables were spread in the apartment where the meeting had been held. Two tables, I have said,—and there was one for the men to sit at,—but on the women's side the *table* was formed of benches placed together, and of course was quite low. I should have supposed that this was a casual occurrence, had not an acquaintance told me that many years ago, when she attended an Amish meeting, she sat up to two benches.

Before eating there was a silent pause, during which those men who had not yet a place at the table stood uncovered reverentially, holding their hats before their faces. In about fifteen minutes the "first table" had finished eating, and another silent pause was observed in the same manner before they rose.

I was invited to the second table, where I found beautiful white bread, butter, pies, pickles, apple-butter, and refined molasses. I observed that there were no spoons in the molasses and apple-butter. A cup of coffee also was handed to each person who wished it. We were not invited to take more than one.

This meal marks the progress of wealth and luxury, or the decline of asceticism, since the day when bean soup was the principal, if not the only, dish furnished on these occasions. The same neighbor who told me of sitting up to two benches, many years ago, told me that at that time they were served with bean soup in bright dishes, doubtless of pewter or tin. Three or four persons ate out of one dish. It was very unhandy, she said.

But while thus sketching the manners of my simple, plain neighbors, let me not forget to acknowledge that ready hospitality which thus provides a comfortable meal even to strangers visiting the meeting. Besides myself, there were at least two others present who were not members,—two German Catholic women, such as hire out to work.

The silent pause before and after eating was also observed by the second table; and after we rose a third company sat down.

When all had done, I gave a little assistance in clearing the tables, in carrying the butter into the cellar and the other food to the wash-house. The dishes were taken to the roofed porch between the latter and the house, where some of the women-folk washed them. A neat table stood at the foot of the cellar-stairs, and received the valued product of the dairy, the fragments being put away in an orderly manner.

I now had a time of leisure, for my driver had gone to see a friend, and I must await his coming. This gave me an opportunity to talk with several sisters. I inquired of a fine-looking woman when the feet-washing would be held, and when they took the Lord's Supper. When I asked whether they liked those who were not members to attend the feet-washing, I understood her to say that they did not.* (I attended, not a great while after, a great Whitsuntide feet-washing and bread-baking in the meeting-house of the New Mennonites.)

I had now an opportunity to examine the books. Standing upon a bench, I took down a great volume, well printed in the German language, and entitled "The Bloody Theatre; or, The Martyr's Mirror of the Baptists, or Defenceless Christians, who, on Account of the Testimony of Jesus, their Saviour, Suffered and were Put to Death, from the Time of Christ to the Year 1660. Lancaster, 1814." This book was a version from the Dutch (*Holländisch*) of Thielem J. van Bracht,

---

* I learn, 1882, that the Amish feet-washing is public.

and it has also been rendered from German into English. I was not aware, at the time, that I had before me one of the principal sources whence the history of the Mennonites is to be drawn,—a history which is still unwritten.

The books were few in number, and I noticed no other so remarkable as this. Another German one, more modern in appearance, was entitled " Universal Cattle-Doctor Book ; or, The Cures of the old Shepherd Thomas, of Bunzen, in Silesia, for Horses, Cattle, Sheep, Swine, and Goats."

While I was looking over the volumes, a little circumstance occurred, which, although not flattering to myself, is perhaps too characteristic to be omitted. My " Dutch" neighbors are not great readers, and to read German is considered an accomplishment even among those who speak the dialect. To speak " Dutch" is very common, of course, but to read German is a considerable attainment. I have, therefore, sometimes surprised a neighbor by being able to read the language. I am naturally not unwilling to be admired, and, as two or three sisters were standing near while I examined the books, I endeavored in haste to give them a specimen of my attainments. I therefore took a passage quickly from the great " Martyr-Book," and read aloud a sentence like this : " Grace, peace, and joy through God our Heavenly Father ; wisdom, righteousness, and truth, through Jesus Christ his Son, together with the illumining of the Holy Spirit, be with you." Glancing up to see the surprise which my proficiency must produce, I beheld a different expression of countenance, for the attention of some of the thoughtful sisters was attracted by the subject-matter, instead of the reader, and that aroused a sentiment of devotion beautifully expressed.

I asked our host, " Have you no history of your society ?"

" No," he answered ; " we just hand it down."

I have since heard, however, that there are papers or written records in charge of a person who lives at some distance from me. From certain printed records I have been able to trace a streamlet of history from its source in Switzerland, where the Anabaptists suffered persecution in Berne, Zurich, etc. I have read of their exile into Alsace and the Palatinate ; of the aid afforded to them by their fellow-believers, the Mennonites of Holland ; and of their final colonization in Pennsylvania, where they also are called Mennonites. The Amish, however, seem to have been a body of a more rigid rule, with a preacher named Amen, from whom they are called. It has been stated that they took their rise in Alsace in 1693.

Nearly all the congregation had departed when my driver at last arrived. I shook hands with those that were left, and kissed the pleasant mother of our host.

SWISS EXILES.

THE plain people among whom I live, Quaker-like in appearance, and, like the Quakers, opposed to oaths and to war, are to a great extent descendants of Swiss Baptists or Anabaptists, who were banished from their country for refusing to conform to the established Reformed Church.*

Some of the early exiles took refuge in Alsace and the Palatinate, and afterwards came to Pennsylvania, settling in Lancaster County, under the kind patronage of our distinguished first proprietor. William Penn's sympathy for them was doubtless increased by their resembling himself in so many important particulars. Mennonites from Holland were also among the early settlers at Germantown.

If any one inclines to investigate the traditions of these people, let him ask the plain old men of the county whence they originated. I think that a great part of the Amish and other Mennonites will tell him of their Swiss origin.

---

* Our German Baptists are more decidedly non-resistant than the Quakers. Some of them refuse to vote for civil officers.

The term Anabaptist is from the Greek, and signifies one who baptizes again. All Baptists baptize anew those who were baptized in infancy. The term Anabaptist, in the present essay, is used indifferently with Baptist, and, in a degree, with Mennonite.

Nor are very important written records wanting upon the subject of the Swiss persecutions. Two volumes in use among our German Baptists narrate the story. The first is the great Martyr-book, called "The Bloody Theatre; or, Martyr's Mirror of the Defenceless Christians," by Thielem J. van Bracht, published in Dutch, about the year 1660; translated into German, and afterwards into English.

The second printed record, circulating in our county, and describing the sufferings of some of the Swiss Anabaptists, is a hymn-book formerly in use among our Old Mennists, but now, I think, employed only by the Amish. It is a collection of "several beautiful Christian songs," composed in prison at Bassau, in the castle, by the Switzer Brethren, "and by other orthodox (*rechtglaubige*) Christians, here and there."

The first of these works, the Martyr-book, was translated into English by Daniel Rupp, the historian. I have seen no English version of the hymn-book. I met both these volumes in the Rhenish Palatinate in 1881. Bassau, mentioned in the hymn-book as the place where the brethren were imprisoned, I have supposed to be Passau, upon the Danube, in Bavaria. Is it not so written in the Martyr-book?

Near the close of the hymn-book is an account of the afflictions which were endured by the brethren in Switzerland, in the canton of Zurich, on account of the gospel ("*um des Evangeliums willen*").

The first-mentioned work, the great Martyr-book, is a ponderous volume.

The author begins his martyrology with Jesus, John, and Stephen, whom he includes among the Baptist or the defenceless martyrs. I suppose that he includes them among the Baptists on the ground that they were not baptized in infancy, but upon faith. From these the great story comes down in one thousand octavo pages, describing the intense cruelties of the Roman emperors, telling of persecutions by the Saracens, persecutions of the Waldenses and Albigenses, and describing especially the sufferings which the Baptists (in common with other Protestants) endured in Holland under the reigns of Charles V. and Philip II.*

The narrative of the persecution of the Anabaptists of Switzerland by their fellow-Protestants is mostly found at the close of the volume. It comes down to the year 1672, and must therefore be, in part at least, an appendix to the original volume.

Allusions to the severe treatment of the Anabaptists of Switzerland may also be found in Herzog's and Appleton's Cyclopædias.

In the former work we read that Anabaptism, after a public theological disputation, was by the help of the authorities suppressed in Switzerland. And how thoroughly it was suppressed may be inferred from the statement in the latter of the population of Berne. In 1850 the population is given (in round numbers) as 458,000, — of which only 1000 are Baptists, 54,000 are Catholics, and the remainder of the Reformed Church.

In Appleton's Cyclopædia (article Anabaptists), we read that Melanchthon and Zwingle were themselves

---

* Of the heretics executed by Alva in the Spanish Netherlands, a large proportion were Anabaptists.—*Encyclopædia Americana.*

troubled by questions respecting infant baptism, in connection with the personal faith required by Protestantism. Nevertheless, Zwingle himself is said to have pronounced sentence upon Mentz, who had been his friend and fellow-student, in these words : " Whosoever dips (or baptizes) a second time, let him be dipped." "*Qui iterum mergit, mergatur.*" This humorous saying seems to be explained in the Martyr-book, for we read that Felix Mentz was drowned at Zurich for the truth of the gospel in 1526. The persecution of such men is said to have shocked the moderate of all parties.

Upon the authority of Balthazar Hubmor (whom I suppose to be the Hubmeyer of the Cyclopædia), the Martyr-book states that Zwingle, etc., imprisoned at one time twenty persons of both sexes, in a dark tower, never more to see the light of the sun. This early Swiss Protestant persecution occurred, it will be observed, about 1526, and the latest recorded in the Martyr-book in or about 1672, covering a period of nearly one hundred and fifty years.*

At the same time that the Swiss Baptists were suffering at the hands of other Protestants, Anabaptists of the peaceful class were found in Holland in large numbers. The record of their sufferings and martyrs (says Appleton's Cyclopædia) furnishes a touching picture in human history. William of Orange, founder of the Dutch republic, was sustained in the gloomiest hours by

---

* Zschokke, in his History of Switzerland, accuses the Anabaptists of causing great trouble and scandal. Some account of the furious or warlike Anabaptists of Holland may be found in Appleton's Cyclopædia.

their sympathy and aid.* That great prince, however importuned, steadily refused to persecute them.

Menno Symons, born at the close of the fifteenth or the commencement of the sixteenth century, educated for the priesthood of the Roman Catholic church, converted in manhood to the faith of the Anabaptists, became their chief leader. Mennonites and Anabaptists have from his time been interchangeable terms.†

---

* This must not be understood as aid in bearing arms.

† One of Menno's brothers is said to have been connected with the Anabaptists of Münster, those who took up arms, etc. Of these, whose course was so very different from the lives of our pacific Baptists in this country, Menno may have received some, after their defeat, to come under the peaceable rule. There are in the Netherlands, says a recent authority, 40,000 Mennonites. They are a true, pure Netherlandish appearance, which is older than the Reformation, and therefore must not be identified with the Protestantism of the sixteenth century.

Menno does not merit to be called the father of the Netherlandish Mennonites, but rather the first shepherd of the scattered sheep,—the founder of their church community.

The ground-thought from which Menno proceeded was not, as with Luther, justification by faith, or, as with the Swiss Reformers, the absolute dependence of the sinner upon God, in the work of salvation. The holy Christian life, in opposition to worldliness, was the point whence Menno proceeded, and to which he always returned. In the Romish church we see ruling the spirit of Peter; in the Reformed Evangelical the spirit of Paul; in Menno we see arise again James the Just, the brother of the Lord.

See articles *Menno* and *Mennonites*, and *Holland*, in Herzog's "Real-Encyclopädie," Stuttgart and Hamburg, 1858.

Many of the Mennonites of Holland at the present day seem to have wandered far from the teachings of Menno, and to be very different from the simple Mennonite communities of Pennsylvania.

It was about seventeen years after the drowning of Mentz in Switzerland, and while the Catholic persecution was raging in Holland, that in the year 1543 an imperial edict was issued against Menno; for both parties persecuted the Baptists,—the Catholics in the Low Countries, the Protestants in Switzerland. The Martyr-book tells us that a dreadful decree was proclaimed through all West Friesland, containing an offer of general pardon, the favor of the emperor, and a hundred carlgulden to all malefactors and murderers who would deliver Menno into the hands of the executioners. Under pain of death, it was forbidden to harbor him; but God preserved and protected him wonderfully, and he died a natural death, near Lubeck, in the open field, in 1559, aged sixty-six. It is further mentioned that he was buried in his own garden.*

About fourteen years after the death of Menno, or in the year 1573, we read in the Martyr-book that Dordrecht had submitted to the reigning prince, William of Orange, the first not to shed blood on account of faith or belief.

But the toleration which William extended to the Baptists was not imitated by his great compeer, Elizabeth of England. For the Martyr-book tells us that in 1575 "some friends," who had fled to England, having met in the suburbs of London "to hear the word of

---

* The burying of Menno in his garden can be explained by the great secrecy which in times of persecution attended the actions of the persecuted sects. The family graveyards of Lancaster County, located upon farms, may be in some degree traditional, from times of persecution, when Baptists had no churches, but met in secret.

God," were spied out, and the constable took them to prison. Two of these were burnt at Smithfield, in the eighteenth year of Elizabeth. Jan Pieters was one of them, a poor man whose first wife had been burnt at Ghent; he then married a second, whose first husband had been burnt at the same place.

Thus it befell the unfortunate Jan that while his wife was burnt by Catholics, he himself suffered at the hands of English Protestants.*

---

* To the writer it is a question of some interest how far George Fox, the founder of Quakerism, was acquainted with the lives, sufferings, and writings of the Anabaptists.

The common people of England may readily have obtained some knowledge of the Baptists from the number that were cruelly put to death. In 1534, Henry VIII. commanded foreigners who had been baptized in infancy, and had been rebaptized, to leave the realm in twelve days, on pain of death It seems that certain Dutch Baptists braved the threatened punishment; for twenty-six were, in different places, and at different dates, burned within a few years. Under Edward VI., many Baptists suffered extreme punishment, Cranmer and Latimer, Ridley and John Rogers, either approving or actually assisting as inquisitors. See "The Baptists; Who they are, and What they have done," by George B. Taylor, D.D.

The year 1534, in which Henry VIII. issued the proclamation alluded to, was the time of the Anabaptist occupation of Münster. The feelings of Henry towards the Peasants' War and the Münster kingdom doubtless resembled those of his successor, in 1798, towards the French revolutionists,—but George III. did not put any one to death by fire.

Since the above was written has been published Barclay's "Inner Life of the Religious Societies of the Commonwealth," London, 1876. This author speaks of George Fox as having promulgated opinions and founded churches closely approximating to the Mennonite churches in Holland. He further says George Fox tells us that he had an uncle in London who was a Baptist.

The expression "sheep" or "lambs," which is applied to some of the Baptist martyrs, alludes, I suppose, to their non-resistance. Thus, in 1576, Hans Bret, a servant, whose master was about to be apprehended, gave him warning, so that he escaped, but himself, "this innocent follower of Christ, fell into the paws of the wolves. . . . As he stood at the stake, they kindled the fire, and burnt this sheep alive."

The next year after this, William of Orange had occasion to call to order, as it appears, some of his own subjects. The magistrates of Middelburg had announced to the Baptists that they must take an oath of fidelity and arm themselves, or give up their business and shut up their houses. The Baptists had recourse to William, promising to pay levies and taxes, and desiring to be believed on their yea and nay. William granted their request, their yea was to be taken in the place of an oath, and the delinquent was to be punished as for perjury.

In William Penn's Treatise on Oaths it is stated that William of Orange said, "Those men's yea must pass for an oath, and we must not urge this thing any further, or we must confess that the Papists had reason to force us to a religion that was against our conscience."

About nine years after William had thus reproved the magistrates of Middelburg, or in the year 1586, the Baptists came to grief elsewhere. It is stated that those called Anabaptists, who had taken refuge in the Prussian dominions, were ordered by "the prince of the country" to depart from his entire duchy of Prussia, and in the next year from all his dominions. This was because they were said to speak scandalously of infant baptism.

About the close of the century, pleasanter times for the Baptists seem to have followed. " When the north wind of persecution became violent, there were intervals when the pleasant south wind of liberty and repose succeeded."

" But now occurred the greatest mischief in Zurich and Berne, by those who styled themselves Reformed;" but others of the same name, " especially the excellent regents of the United Netherlands," opposed such proceedings.

The Martyr-book says, in substance, " It is a lamentable case that those who boast that they are the followers of the defenceless Lamb do no longer possess the lamb's disposition, but, on the contrary, have the nature of the wolf. It seems as if they could not bear it that any should travel towards heaven in any other way than that which they go themselves, as was exemplified in the case of Hans Landis, who was a minister and teacher of the gospel of Christ. Being taken to Zurich, he refused to desist from preaching and to deny his faith, and was sentenced to death,—the edict of eighty years before not having died of old age. They, however, persuaded the common people that he was not put to death for religion's sake, but for disobedience to the authorities." *

---

* Hans (or John) Landis is the name of the sufferer just spoken of. Several Landises are mentioned in the martyrologies, and the name is very common in Lancaster County at this time. John Landis is remarkably so.

In quoting from the Martyr-book I employ the English version, Martyr's Mirror." I have lately had an opportunity of seeing

After the death of Hans Landis, persecution rested for twenty-one years, when the ancient hatred broke out afresh in Zurich.

The Baptists now asked permission to leave the country with their property, but this was not granted to them. "They might choose," says the Martyrology, "to go with them [the Reformed] to church, or to die in prison. To the first they would not consent; therefore they might expect the second."

This brings us to the era of the persecution described in the hymn-book of which I formerly spoke,—the book now in use among the Amish of our county.

This little volume—little when compared to the ponderous Martyr-book—gives an account of the persecution in Zurich between the years 1635 and 1645. Many of the persons mentioned in the hymn-book as suffering at that time appear to be of families now found in Lancaster County,—not merely from the hymn-book's being preserved here, but especially because some of the surnames are the same as are now found here, or only slightly different. Thus we have Landis, Meylin, Strickler, Bachmann; and Gut, now Good; Müller, now Miller; Baumann, now Bowman.

Mention is made of about eighteen persons who died in prison during this persecution, in the period of nine or ten years. Proclamation was made from the pulpits forbidding the people to afford shelter to the Baptists: even their own children who harbored them were liable

---

an old German copy, from the press of the Brotherhood at Ephrata, about 1750. I find that it is differently arranged from the modern English version, and I suspect there are other variations.

to be fined,—as Hans Müller's wife and children, who were fined forty pounds because "they showed mercy to their dear father."

The hymn-book states that the *Gelehrte* (the learned or the clergy?) accompanied the captors, running day and night with their servants. Many of the persecuted fell into the power of the authorities,—men and women, the pregnant, the nursing mother, the sick.

In the midst of this, the authorities of Amsterdam, themselves Calvinists or Reformed, being moved by the solicitations of the Baptists of Amsterdam, sent a respectful petition to the burgomaster and council of Zurich to mitigate the persecution; but the petition, it is said, excited an unfriendly and irritating answer.

It seems that some of the Baptists, harassed in Zurich, took refuge in Berne; and about the time that the persecution in Zurich came to a close, or about 1645, it is stated that "those of Berne" threatened the Baptists. About four years after, "those of Schaffhausen" issued an edict against the people called Anabaptists.*

Only a few years later, or in 1653, as we read in the Martyr-book, there was another persecution elsewhere. The record says, in substance, "As a lamb in making its escape from the wolf is eventually seized by the bear, so it obtained for several defenceless followers of the meek Jesus, who, persecuted in Switzerland by the Zwinglians, were permitted to live awhile in peace in the Alpine districts, under a Roman Catholic prince,

---

* From Schaffhausen came some of the Stauffer family, as I have read. The Stauffers are numerous in our county. For some family traditions, see the close of this article.

Willem Wolfgang. About this year, however, this prince banished the Anabaptists, so called. But they were received in peace and with joy elsewhere, particularly in Cleves, under the Elector of Brandenburg, and in the Netherlands. ' When they persecute you in one city,' saith the Lord, ' flee ye into another.' " *

About six years after, or in 1659, an edict was issued in Berne, from which extracts are given in the Martyr-book. If the edict in full brings no more serious charges against the Baptists than do these extracts, this paper itself may be regarded as a noble vindication of the Anabaptists of Switzerland at this era.

According to the substance of this Bernese edict the teachers of this people—*i.e.*, the preachers—were to be seized wherever they could be sought out, "and brought to our orphan asylum to receive the treatment necessary to their conversion; or, if they persist in their obstinacy, they are to receive the punishment in such cases belonging. Meantime the officers are to seize their property, and present an inventory of the same.

" To the Baptists in general, who refuse to desist from their error, the punishment of exile shall be announced. It is our will and command that they be escorted to the borders, a solemn promise obtained from them, since they will not swear, and that they be banished entirely from our country till it be proved that they have been converted. Returning unconverted, and refusing to re-

---

* In the duchy of Cleves, the town of Crefeld, some fifty or sixty years later, gave refuge to the Dunkers. It appears also to have harbored some of the French Protestant refugees at the revocation of the Edict of Nantes. See " Ephrata."

cant, they shall be whipped, branded, and again banished, which condign punishment is founded upon the following reasons and motives:

" 1. All subjects should confirm with an oath the allegiance which they owe to the authorities ordained them of God. The Anabaptists, who refuse the oath, cannot be tolerated.

" 2. Subjects should acknowledge that the magistracy is from God, and with God. But the Anabaptists, who declare that the magisterial office cannot exist in the Christian church, are not to be tolerated in the country.

" 3. All subjects are bound to protect and defend their country. But the Anabaptists refuse to bear arms, and cannot be tolerated. . . .

" 5. The magistracy is ordained of God to punish evil-doers, especially murderers, etc. But the Anabaptists refuse to report these to the authorities, and therefore they cannot be tolerated.*

" 6. Those who refuse to submit to the wholesome ordinances of the government, and who act in opposition to it, cannot be tolerated. Now the Anabaptists transgress in the following manner:

" They preach without the calling of the magistracy; baptize without the command of the authorities; . . . and do not attend the meetings of the church.

" We have unanimously resolved that all should inflict banishment and the other penalities against all who belong to this corrupted and extremely dangerous and wicked sect, that they may make no further progress,

---

* They were probably conscientiously opposed to the death penalty.

but that the country may be freed from them; on which, in grace, we rely.

"As regards the estate of the disobedient exiles, or of those who have run away, it shall, after deducting costs, be divided among the wives and children who remain in obedience.

"We command that no person shall lodge nor give dwelling to a Baptist, whether related to him or not, nor afford him the necessaries of life. But every one of our persuasion should be exhorted to report whatever information he can obtain of them to the high bailiff.

"And an especial proclamation of this last article shall be made from the pulpit."

This Bernese edict, being read in all parts, was a source of great distress, and it appeared to the Baptists as if "the beautiful flower of the orthodox Christian church" would be entirely extirpated in those parts.

It was therefore concluded to send certain persons from the cities of Dordrecht, Leyden, Amsterdam, etc., to the Hague, where the puissant States-General were in session, to induce them to send petitions to Berne and Zurich for the relief of the people suffering oppression.

The States-General, as "kind fathers of the poor, the miserable, and the oppressed," took immediate cognizance of the matter.

Letters were written "to the lords of Berne" for the liberation of prisoners, etc., and to the lords of Zurich for the restoration of the property of the imprisoned, deceased, and exiled Baptists. The letter to Berne narrates (in brief) that "the States-General have learned, from persons called in this country Mennonists, that their brethren called Anabaptists suffer great persecution at Berne, being forbidden to live in the country, but not allowed to remove with their families and property. We have likewise learned that some of them have been closely confined; which has moved us to Christian compassion.

"We request you, after the good example of the lords-regent of Schaffhausen, to grant the petitioners time to depart with their families and property wherever they choose. To this end we request you to consider that when, in 1655, the Waldenses were so virulently persecuted by the Romans for the confession of their Reformed religion, and the necessities of the dispersed people could not be relieved but by large collections raised in England, this country, etc., the churches of the Baptists, upon the simple recommendation of their governments, and in Christian love and compassion, contributed with so much benevolence that a remarkably large sum was raised. . . . Farewell, etc. At the Hague, 1660."

The letter of the States-General to Zurich is similar to the foregoing abstract.

Besides these acts of the States-General, several cities of the United Netherlands, being entirely opposed to restraint of conscience, reproved "the members of their society in Switzerland," and exhorted them to gentleness.

Thus, the burgomasters and lords of Rotterdam, speaking in behalf of the elders of the church called Mennonist, whose fellow-believers in Berne are called in derision Anabaptists: "As to ourselves, honorable lords, we are of opinion that these men can be safely tolerated in the commonwealth, and for this judgment we have to thank William, Prince of Orange, of blessed memory, who established, by his bravery, liberty of conscience for us, and could never be induced to deprive the Mennonites of citizenship.

"We have never repented of this, for we have never learned that these people have sought to excite sedition, but, on the contrary, they have cheerfully paid their taxes.

"Although they confess that Christians cannot conscientiously act as officers of government, and are opposed to swearing, yet they do not refuse obedience to the authorities, and, if they are convicted of a violation of truth, are willing to undergo the punishment due to perjury. We indulge the hope that your lordships will either repeal the onerous decree against the Mennonists or at least grant to the poor wanderers sufficient time to make their preparations, and procure residences in other places.

"When this is done, your lordships will have accomplished a measure well pleasing to God, advantageous to the name of the Reformed, and gratifying to us who are connected with your lordships in the close ties of religion. Rotterdam, 1660."

These appeals of the States-General and of the cities of Holland seem to have had very little effect, at least upon the authorities of Berne, for there arose eleven years later, or in 1671, another severe persecution of the Baptists in that canton, which was so virulent that it seemed as if the authorities would not cease until they had expelled that people entirely.

In consequence of this, seven hundred persons, old and young, were constrained to forsake their property,

5

relations, and country, and retire to the Palatinate. Some of them, it seems, took refuge in Alsace, above Strasburg.

An extract from a letter given in the Martyr-book says, "Some follow chopping wood, others labor in the vineyards; hoping, I suppose, that after some time tranquillity will be restored, and they will be able to return to their habitations; but I am afraid that this will not happen soon. . . . The authorities of Berne had six of the prisoners (one of whom was a man that had nine children) put in chains and sold as galley-slaves between Milan and Malta."

(We may infer that this, however, was not the first infliction of this punishment at Berne. A list in the Martyr-book of persons put to death for their faith concludes thus: "Copied from the letter of Hans Loersch, while in prison at Berne, 1667, whence he was taken in chains to sea.")

This severe penalty of being sold as slaves to row the galleys or great sail-boats which traversed the Mediterranean was also impending over other able-bodied prisoners, as it is said, but "a lord of Berne," named Beatus, was excited to compassion, and obtained permission that the prisoners should leave the country upon bail that they would not return without permission.

In the year 1672 the brethren in the United Netherlands (the Mennonites or Baptists) sent some of their members into the Palatinate to inquire into the condition of the refugees, and the latter were comforted and supported by the assistance of the churches and members of the United Netherlands.

There were among the refugees husbands and wives

who had to abandon their consorts, who belonged to the
Reformed Church and could not think of removal.
Among these were two ministers, whose families did not
belong to the church (Baptist), and who had to leave
without finding whether their wives would go with
them, or whether they loved their property more than
their husbands. "Such incidents occasioned the greater
distress, since the authorities granted such persons remaining permission to marry again." *

Alsace and the Palatinate (lying upon the Rhine),
where our Swiss exiles had taken refuge, were soon after
devastated in the great wars of their ambitious neighbor,
Louis XIV., King of France. Turenne, the French
general, put the Palatinate, a fine and fertile country,
full of populous towns and villages, to fire and sword.
The Elector Palatine, from the top of his castle at Mann-
heim, beheld two cities and twenty towns in flames. Turenne, with the same indifference, destroyed the ovens,
and laid waste part of the country of Alsace, to prevent
the enemy from subsisting.†

About fourteen years after, or in the winter of 1688–
89, the Palatinate was again ravaged by the French
king's army. The French generals gave notice to the
towns but lately repaired, and then so flourishing, to the
villages, etc., that their inhabitants must quit their
dwellings, although it was then the dead of winter; for
all was to be destroyed by fire and sword.

"The flames with which Turenne had destroyed two

---

* Martyr's Mirror.

† The troops of the empire of Germany, or of Germany and
Spain combined. See Voltaire's "Age of Louis XIV."

towns and twenty villages of the Palatinate were but sparks in comparison to this last terrible destruction, which all Europe looked upon with horror."*

Between the time of these two great raids there occurred several noteworthy incidents. There came to Holland and Germany, in the year 1677, a man who was then of little note, a man of peace, belonging to a new and persecuted sect, but who has since become better known in history, at least to us who inhabit Pennsylvania, than Marshal Turenne, or the great Louis XIV. himself. It was the colonizer and statesman, the Quaker William Penn.

The Elector Palatine then reigning was a relative of the King of England. Penn failed to see this prince, but he addressed a letter to him, to the "Prince Elector Palatine of Heydelbergh," in which he desires to know "what encouragement a colony of virtuous and industrious families might hope to receive from thee, in case they should transplant themselves into this country, which certainly in itself is very excellent, respecting taxes, oaths, arms, etc."

I know not what encouragement, if any, the Elector

---

* "Age of Louis XIV." The following is testimony for the Mennonites: "In the words of the Dutch embassador (Van Beuning) to Monsieur de Turenne: 'The Mennonites are good people, and the most commodious to a state of any in the world; partly because they do not aspire to places of dignity; partly because they edify the community by the simplicity of their manners, and application to arts and industry; and partly because we fear no rebellion from a sect who make it an article of their faith never to bear arms.' The said industry and frugality they carried with them to Pennsylvania, and thereby are become very wealthy."— MORGAN EDWARDS.

offered to Penn ; but only about four years later Penn's great colony was founded across the Atlantic, a colony which afforded refuge to many " Palatines." *

Of this journey to Germany and Holland, just spoken of, Penn kept a journal, and there is mention made at Amsterdam of Baptists and " Menists," or Mennonites ; but whether he ever met on the Continent any of our Swiss exiles I do not find stated in history. Of his other two journeys to Germany, no journal has been found.

Eight years after Penn's journey there occurred, in the year 1685, a circumstance which may have especially interested our Swiss Baptists and have operated to bring their colony to Pennsylvania; for in June of that year the Elector Palatine dying without issue, the electoral dignity went to a Roman Catholic family.†

The Swiss exiles that first took refuge in Lancaster County came here about thirty-eight years after the severe Bernese persecution of 1671. Rupp, the historian of our county, tells us that in 1706 or 1707 a

---

* Several towns and townships in southeastern Pennsylvania bear record of the Palatinate, etc. In Lancaster County we have Strasburg, doubtless named for that city in Alsace, and both town and township of Manheim. Adjoining counties have Heidelbergs. The Swiss Palatines do not seem to have preserved enough affection for the land of their origin to bestow Swiss names upon our Lancaster County towns. What wonder ?

† "This year of which I am now writing must ever be remembered as the most fatal to the Protestant religion. In February a king of England declared himself a papist. In June, Charles, the Elector Palatine, dying without issue, the electoral dignity went to the house of Newburgh, a most bigoted popish family. In October the King of France recalled and vacated the edict of Nantes."
—*Burnet's History of his Own Time.*

number of the persecuted Swiss Mennonites went to England and made a particular agreement with the honorable proprietor, William Penn, for lands. He further says that several families from the Palatinate, descendants of the distressed Swiss, emigrated to America and settled in Lancaster County in the year 1709.*

The sympathy of the Society of Friends, William Penn's co-religionists, was at this time called out for this people in a substantial manner. Barclay says, "Not only did the leaders of the early Society of Friends take great interest in the Mennonites, but the Yearly Meet-

---

* This was twenty-eight years after the founding of Penn's colony. Several years earlier, or in 1701, some Mennonites bought land in Germantown, and in 1708 built a church (or meeting-house). For this information I am obliged to Dr. Seidensticker, of the University of Pennsylvania.

"In the year 1708 about fifty Palatines, who were Lutherans and were ruined, came over to England. Queen Anne allowed them a shilling a day, and took care to have them transported to the plantations; and from these circumstances there arose a general disposition among all the poor of that country to come over. They came to Holland in great bodies: the Anabaptists there were particularly helpful to them, both in subsisting those in Holland and in transporting them to England. Great numbers of these were sent to Ireland, but most of them to the plantations in North America, where it is believed their industry will quickly turn to a good account."—See Burnet's "Own Time." I am told that of those thus sent to Ireland many afterwards came to America; of such was Philip Embury, who, being converted in Ireland, came to New York, and was the first to introduce Methodism on the continent. He and his family were from the Palatinate.

Mention has just been made of Lutherans going to England from the Palatinate. I infer that many who fled thence were of the Reformed Church. The French Huguenots would in Germany probably join the Reformed Church?

ing of 1709 contributed fifty pounds (a very large sum
at that time) for the Mennonites of the Palatinate who
had fled from the persecution of the Calvinists in Switzerland." *

The next year the commissioners of property had
agreed with Martin Kendig, Hans Herr, etc., "Switzers"
lately arrived in this province, for ten thousand acres of
land twenty miles east of Connystogoe. (This Connystogoe I cannot locate. The Conestoga Creek empties
into the Susquehanna below Lancaster.)

The supplies of the colonists were at first scanty, until
the seed sown in a fertile soil yielded some thirty-, others
forty-fold.† Their nearest mill was at Wilmington, distant, as I estimate, some thirty miles.

One of their number was soon sent to Europe to bring
out other emigrants, and after the accession the colony
numbered about thirty families. They mingled with
the Indians in hunting and fishing. These were hospitable and respectful to the whites.‡

We are told that the early colonists had strong faith
in the fruitfulness and natural advantages of their choice
of lands. "They knew these would prove to them and
their children the home of plenty." Their anticipations
have never failed.§

---

* Barclay's "Religious Societies of the Commonwealth." London, 1876.

  † Rupp.   ‡ Ibid.

§ The question has been discussed, why did the Germans select
the limestone lands, and the Scotch-Irish take those less fruitful?
Different hints upon this subject may be found in Day's Historical Collections of Pennsylvania. Under the head of Lancaster
County he says that a number of Scotch-Irish, in consequence of

The harmony existing between the Indians and these men of peace is very pleasing. Soon after their first settlement here, Lieutenant-Governor Gookin made a journey to Conestogo (1711), and in a speech to the Indians tells them that Governor Penn intends to present five belts of wampum to the Five Nations, "and one to you of Conestogo, and requires your friendship to the Palatines, settled near Pequea." * About seven years after this, William Penn died in England, in the year 1718.

Dr. Seidensticker compares the German emigration hither, in its origin, to the Quaker and Puritan. After the Lutherans and Reformed had succeeded in gaining a recognition, there were sects in Germany who did not agree with the three recognized confessions and who were bitterly persecuted. Against such Christians the indignation of the clergy and the wrath of the civil authorities was directed in almost every German land.

Says Herzog's Cyclopædia:

" When the Baptists were oppressed in Switzerland

---

the limestone land being liable to frost and heavily wooded, seated themselves (1763) along the northern line of the counties of Chester and Lancaster. It seems that the Germans did not fear the labor of clearing off heavy timber.

A gentleman of Lancaster County says that ninety in one hundred of the regular members of the Mennonite churches are farmers, and that they follow the limestone land as the needle follows the pole.

* The Pequea Creek (pronounced Peck'way) waters some of the finest land in the county, if not the very finest. "The Piquaws had their wigwams scattered along the banks of the Pequea."

and the Palatinate, the Mennonites united into one community with the Palatines at Groningen (Holland), and established in 1726 a fund for the needy abroad, to which Baptists of all parties richly contributed. About eighty years after this fund was discontinued, being no longer thought necessary."

Thus active persecution of the Baptists in those regions had ceased, it seems, about the year 1800.

The German or Swiss colony in Lancaster County is said to have caused some alarm, though we can hardly believe it a real fear. Nine years after the death of William Penn, representation was made to Lieutenant-Governor Gordon (1727) that "a large number of Germans, peculiar in their dress, religion, and notions of political government, had settled on Pequea, and were determined not to obey the lawful authority of government; that they had resolved to speak their own language, and to acknowledge no sovereign but the great Creator of the universe."

Rupp, from whom I quote the above passage, adds: "There was perhaps never a people who felt less disposed to disobey the lawful authority of government than the Mennonites against whom these charges were made."

The charges were doubtless dropped, or answered in a satisfactory manner; for two years subsequently, or in 1729, a naturalization act was passed concerning certain Germans who had emigrated into the province between the years 1700 and 1718. Over one hundred persons are naturalized by this act (Martin Meylin, Hans Graaf, etc.); and a great part of the people of the county can find their surnames mentioned therein.* All the names, however, are not necessarily those of Baptist families.

Nearly to the same date as this naturalization act belongs a letter written from Philadelphia, in 1730, by the Rev. Jedediah Andrews.

Mr. Andrews says, in substance, " There are in this province a vast number of Palatines ; those that have come of late years are mostly Reformed. The first-comers, though called Palatines, are mostly Switzers, many of whom are wealthy, having got the best land in the province. They live sixty or seventy miles off, but come frequently to town with their wagons laden with skins belonging to the Indian traders, with butter, flour, etc." †

Mr. Andrews, in his letter, while speaking of the Switzers, continues : " There are many Lutherans and some Reformed mixed among them. . . . Though there

---

* Not always as at present spelled. The present Kendig appears as Kindeck, Breneman as Preniman, Baumgardner as Bumgar-ner, Eby as Abye. These were probably English efforts at spell-ing German names. Rupp says that he was indebted to Abraham Meylin, of West Lampeter Township, for a copy of the act. There appear to have been among the Palatines who came into our county some Huguenot families ; but, from intermarrying with the Germans, and speaking the dialect, they are considered " Dutch." The name of the Bushong family is said to have been Beauchamp.

† This mention of the Switzers' wagons reminds me of the great Conestoga wagons, which, before the construction of railroads, conveyed the produce of the interior to Philadelphia. With their long bodies roofed with white canvas, they went along almost, I might say, like moving houses. They were drawn by six power-ful horses, at times furnished with trappings and bells ; and the wagoner's trade was one of importance.

be so many sorts of religion going on, we don't quarrel about it. We not only live peaceably, but seem to love one another."

This harmony among the multitudinous sects in Pennsylvania must have been the more remarkable to Mr. Andrews from his having been born and educated in Massachusetts, where a very different state of affairs had prevailed; and on this subject Rupp says, "The descendants of the Puritans boast that their ancestors fled from persecution, willing to encounter perils in the wilderness, and perils by the heathen, rather than be deprived of the free exercise of their religion. The descendants of the Swiss Mennonites in Lancaster County claim that while their ancestors sought for the same liberty, they did not persecute others who differed from them in religious opinion." *

The letter of Mr. Andrews, above quoted, bears date 1730. Twelve years after, or in 1742, a respectable number of the Amish (pronounced Ommish) of Lancaster County petitioned the General Assembly that a special law of naturalization might be passed for their benefit. They stated that they had emigrated from Europe by an invitation from the proprietaries; that they had been brought up in and were attached to the Amish doctrine, and were conscientiously scrupulous against taking oaths; "they therefore cannot be naturalized agreeably to the existing law." An act was

---

* A test-oath, or oath of abjuration, seems to have been in force at one time in Pennsylvania, concerning the Roman Catholics. (See Rupp's History of Berks and Lebanon.) Must we not attribute this act to the royal home government rather than to William Penn?

passed in conformity to their request. (I give this statement as I find it, although somewhat surprised if the laws of Pennsylvania did not always allow those to affirm who were conscientiously opposed to oaths.)

The history of our Swiss Exiles is nearly finished. It is chiefly when a nation is in adversity that its history is interesting to us. What is there to tell of a well-to-do farming population, who do not participate in battles, and who live almost entirely secluded from public affairs?*

Under the date 1754 it is noted that Governor Pownall, travelling in Lancaster County, says, "I saw the finest farm one can possibly conceive, in the highest culture; it belongs to a Switzer." Thus Gray's lines (slightly altered) may be said to comprise most of the external history of this people for a century and a half:

> " Oft did the harvest to their sickle yield,
>   Their furrow oft the stubborn glebe hath broke;
> How early did they drive their team a-field,
>   How bowed the woods beneath their sturdy stroke!"

Some difficulty had arisen, however, between the Germans of our county and the "Scotch-Irish." Thus,

---

* "I fear this volume will be deemed a heap of dry records, without a sufficient number of anecdotes to give them a relish; this is owing to the peace and liberty which the Baptists have ever enjoyed in Pennsylvania. In other provinces they have had their troubles, which will make their history interesting to every reader." —MORGAN EDWARDS: Advertisement [or preface] to " Materials towards a History of the Baptists in Pennsylvania, both British and German." 1770.

Day, in his Historical Collections, says, " The Presbyterians from the north of Ireland came in at about the same time with the Germans, and occupied the townships of Donegal and Paxton." (Paxton, now Dauphin County.) " Collisions afterwards occurring between them and the Germans concerning elections, bearing of arms, the treatment of the Indians, etc., the proprietaries instructed their agents in 1755 that the Germans should be encouraged, and in a manner directed to settle along the southern boundary of the province, in Lancaster and York Counties, while the Irish were to be located nearer to the Kittatinny Mountain, in the region now forming Dauphin and Cumberland Counties."*

In the Revolutionary war, the German Mennonites did not early espouse the cause of independence. Some of them doubtless felt bound by their promise of loyalty to the established government, while others were perhaps influenced by the motive lately attributed to them in the correspondence of one of our county papers (*Examiner and Herald,* Lancaster, October 27, 1869). The writer tells us that Lancaster County was settled principally by Mennonites, etc., who are strict non-resistants. They were peculiarly solicitous to manifest their loyalty to the powers that be, because they had been accused by their enemies of having been implicated in rebellion during the unhappy events at Münster, Germany, in 1535. " When our Revolutionary struggle began, these people

---

* Day says that there was policy in the order above given ; that the Irish were warlike, and could defend the frontier. It was not long after the above date (in 1763) that the " Paxton Boys" made a raid down to Lancaster and massacred the remnant of the Conestoga Indians in the jail of this town.

were cautious in resisting the established government."

During the late rebellion, although very few of our Mennonites bore arms, yet some were active in raising funds to pay bounties to persons who did enlist.

It appears to the writer that there can scarcely be a people in our country among whom the ancient practices are more faithfully maintained than among the Amish of Lancaster County.*

Notwithstanding the great falling off from ancient principles and practices which we read of among Holland Mennonites (see Herzog's Cyclopædia and the Encyclopædia Americana), it seems that there are yet left in Europe others of the stricter rule. In Friesland, Holland, where the Mennonites are divided, as here, into three classes, there are found, by comparison, most traces of the old Mennonism.†

And we have lately heard of Amish in France. A letter from that country, published in the *Herald of Truth* (Elkhart, Indiana, July, 1871), alludes to the late European war. The writer says, "The loss we here sustained is indescribable. Many houses have been

---

* The Amish seem to have originated in Europe, about the year 1700, when Jacob Amen, a Swiss preacher, set up, or returned to, the more severe rule, distasteful to brethren in Alsace, etc., and enforced the ban of excommunication upon some or all of those who disagreed with him. Appleton's Cyclopædia calls him Amman, and says that the Amish rose in 1693, in Alsace. A small pamphlet upon this subject has been published at Elkhart, Indiana, and is for sale at the office of the *Herald of Truth.*

† See Herzog.

entirely shattered to pieces by the cannon-balls, and others totally destroyed by fire." He adds, "As you desire to know what kind of Mennonites there are residing here in France, I will briefly state that most of them are Amish Mennonites." He signs himself Isaac Rich, Etupes, par Audincourt, Doubs, France.

This department, Doubs, adjoins Switzerland.

The church history of our Mennonites has not been entirely uneventful. Rupp tells us that they were very numerous about the year 1792, and that Martin Boehm and others made inroads upon them. A considerable number seceded and joined the United Brethren, or *Vereinigte Brüder*.

A society of Dunkers was formed near the Susquehanna, many years ago, by Jacob Engle, who had been a Mennonite. This society is called "The River Brethren," and from it has been formed the society of "Brinser Brethren," popularly so called.

The Rev. John Herr is generally considered the founder of a sect popularly called "New Mennists." They call themselves, however, "Reformed Mennonites," and claim that they have only returned to the ancient purity of doctrine.

In Montgomery County, in 1873, I find the term New Mennonites applied to another sect, while those of whom I have just spoken are called "*Herrelite*," * or followers of Herr. The former are followers or friends of a preacher named Overholtzer,—a man who refused to put on a coat of a peculiar cut when he became a preacher.

---

* The German word *leute*, people, is here pronounced *lite*.

In, or near, the same part of our State certain Mennonites have left the society, desiring to "defend their country," and to join oath-bound societies. They call themselves Trinity Christians.

How far the "Albrechtsleut," or "Dutch Methodists,"—the Evangelical Association, as they call themselves,—have made converts among the Mennonites, I cannot tell.

Mr. Rupp, whose history of Lancaster County is as yet the standard, speaks of the Mennonites as the prevailing religious denomination in 1843, having about forty-five ministers preaching in German, and over thirty-five meeting-houses.

The Amish meet in private houses. (In this year 1882, when preparing my third edition, I hear, however, of their having so far broken through their old custom as to have built at least one meeting-house in this State.)

Although I have never heard that our Mennonites as a religious body passed any rules forbidding slaveholding, as did the Quakers, yet they are in sentiment strongly anti-slavery, having great faith in those who are willing to labor with their own hands. Of this strong anti-slavery sentiment I offer convincing proof in the votes by which they supported in Congress our late highly distinguished representative, Thaddeus Stevens.*

---

* Traditionary stories exist in our county concerning the Swiss origin, etc., of certain families. I have heard one concerning the Engles and one of the Stauffers. A member of the Johns family has also told me of their Swiss origin, and of their name being formerly written Tschantz.

It is probable that other traditionary stories concerning Swiss

In the *Columbian Magazine* for January, 1789, appears an " Account of the Manners of the German Inhabitants of Pennsylvania." The writer, Dr. Rush,

---

families could now be collected, if some one would exert himself to do it before their custodians "fall asleep." But let those who gather these stories beware of the "fine writer," lest he add what he considers embellishments, and make the narratives improbable.

The Stauffer traditions were mentioned to me by a venerable member of the family, one who has kindly lent me his aid and sympathy in some of my records of the " Pennsylvania Dutch." John Stauffer is now a great-grandfather, and he calculates that it was, at the nearest, his own great-great-grandfather who, with his mother and his three brothers, came to this country, his ancestors being of Swiss origin. " The mother," says my neighbor (in substance), " weighed three hundred, and the sons made a wagon, all of wood, and drawed her to the Rhine. When they got to Philadelphia, they put their mother into the wagon and drawed her up here to Warwick township. There they settled on a pretty spring; that is what our people like."

The reader of this little story may remember the " pious Æneas," who " from the flames of Troy, upon his shoulders," the old Anchises bore. [John Stauffer is now dead, 1882.]

The tradition of the Engle family was narrated to me by two of its members. Mr. Henry M. Engle has felt some difficulty in reconciling the tradition with the fact of the family's having been in this country only about one hundred years, and with his idea that the Swiss persecution must have ceased before that period. But we have seen that some Baptist families tarried in the Palatinate, etc., before coming here, and a circumstance like the imprisonment of one of their women would be remembered among them for a long time.

Tradition says that it was the grandmother's mother or grandmother of Henry M. Engle and Jacob M. Engle, who was a prisoner in Switzerland for her faith. The turnkey's wife sympathized with the prisoner, because she knew that Annie had children at home. So she said to her, in the Swiss dialect, " Annie, if I were you, I would go away once." ("Annie, wann i die wär, i det would properly have included Friends in the following passage :

"Perhaps those German sects of Christians among us, who refuse to bear arms for the purpose of shedding human blood, may be preserved by Divine Providence, as the centre of a circle which shall gradually embrace all the nations of the earth in a perpetual treaty of friendship and peace."

Since the first edition of this book was prepared, the public attention has been much attracted to a great body of Russian Mennonites who have come to this country, rather than perform military duty in Russia; some of these are of Swiss origin.*

---

mohl geh." — "Annie, wenn ich dich wäre, ich thut einmal gehen.")

She therefore set Annie to washing clothes, and, turning her back upon her, gave her opportunity to escape.

Annie's husband was not a Baptist; nevertheless, he was so friendly as to prepare a hiding-place for her, into which she could go down, if the persecutors came, by means of a trap-door; and she was never taken prisoner again.

* The *Herald of Truth*, a Mennonite paper of this country, under the date of July, 1873, contains a "Letter of Authority," beginning, "We, the Bishops and Directors of the entire body of the Swiss Mennonites in the colonies of Kotusufka, in the district (county or canton) of Schitomir, state of Volkinien, Russia."

This Letter of Authority concerns the proposed migration above alluded to. Of the six names signed thereto, one at least appears to belong also to this county of Lancaster, where it is now sometimes written Graybill; in the Russian letter Krehbiehl. A similar name is found among the Schwenckfelders, who were of Silesian origin.

One of my neighbors had before spoken to me in very favorable terms of Russian Mennonites, but it did not seem probable that such a body of people were to be found in that empire, and I paid but little attention to the subject.

The account which seems to me most valuable, among newspaper items concerning them, was contained in a St. Petersburg letter in the *New York Tribune* of May 11, 1872.

The writer tells us that about the time of Menno's death there was a large emigration of his flock to East Prussia, where their Dutch neatness and industry soon made those desolate and swampy regions to flourish like a garden. In 1730 and 1732 they were threatened with expatriation for refusing to serve in the army; but the storm passed by, and other colonists came in. Arbitrary measures, however, were still taken from time to time, and in 1789 they were forbidden to purchase landed property.

Catherine II. of Russia, while inviting German colonists, also invited these, and before the year 1800 about three hundred and fifty families of Mennonites had entered Russia, and settled on the lower Dnieper. They came on condition of receiving freedom of worship, " the administration of oaths in their own way" (the writer does not appear to understand their objection to swearing at all), " and exemption forever from military service." They were also to receive one hundred and ninety acres of land for each family, money for their journey, etc.

The privileges were confirmed by the Emperor Paul, and extended to all coming after; and although the laws of Prussia had been altered, there was a continued migration of Mennonites to Russia until 1817. These settled near their brethren, and not far from the town of Berdiansk.

The Mennonites have prospered until they number about forty thousand. They settled on a waste steppe, where the land was rich enough, but suffered much from want of water. They irrigated, and raised agriculture to a higher point than anywhere else in Russia. They had no wood, and they planted trees. The introduction of tree culture on the steppes is entirely owing to them. They have not only large orchards, but productive forest-trees, and plantations of mulberry-trees, by means of which they produce silk. They are also large raisers of stock.

Although originally agriculturists, they have endeavored to supply their own wants in manufactured articles, and in 1854 they had in activity three hundred and fifty mills and factories, including cloth-mills, water- and grist-mills, dyeing and printing works, breweries, distilleries, silk-spinneries, brick and tile works, potteries, etc., and in their villages there were men exercising nearly every known trade.

There is no drunkenness or gambling among them. Crime is exceedingly rare. Besides all this, they are educated. Every child knows how to read and write; and in every village there is a school.

Up to this time they have been loyal subjects to Russia. During the Crimean war they sent large gifts of grain and provender to the besieged army. It is only because the privileges granted to them are infringed, and they will be compelled to enter the army against their conscience, that they now wish to emigrate.

Their success in tree culture on an arid steppe points naturally to the Western prairies as their future home. In their petitions to the American and British governments they asked whether they could obtain land free, or at low prices, for their whole colony; whether they could have exemption for themselves and their descendants from military service of every kind; and whether the government would advance them any money to defray their travelling expenses. Though the colony is prosperous, and some of the members rich, yet there are some who either have no land, or have so little property that a forced sale would leave them almost destitute.

In addition to the above from the *New York Tribune*, I have found an extract concerning the Mennonites of South Russia, from *The Friend* (London), in which it is stated that a deputation was sent to St. Petersburg in hopes of changing the purpose of the government, but only obtained a delay of ten years, which expired in 1881, and also the option of hospital and other non-fighting military service in place of actual soldiership. Many deputations have since followed. The last attempt was by a company of "eldest persons" to the emperor, while he was staying at his country palace in the Crimea. We learn "the emperor did not accept an audience, but kind words by others were spoken plenty." Extracts follow from an original letter, preserving the quaint English: "We greatly see the need of leaving Russia, not only because of military service, but also of the curtailing of religious and other liberties, which clearly shows an intention on the part of the government to take this and our language from us. Formerly, the administration of all laws connected with the colonies was in the hands of the colonists themselves; now they are mixed up with the Russian peasants. The Russ language, hitherto not, or little, wanted, is introduced into the schools, and Russian teachers are given to those schools. Prisons, like as in the Russian villages, are by law commanded to build; before, not at all wanted."

But while the Russian Mennonites are thus preparing to emigrate, it is stated that in Prussia there are only a few churches that are not willing to submit to the new military law.

The editor of the *Herald of Truth,* a Mennonite paper (Elkhart, Indiana), speaks to the Russians nearly as follows: "I believe I understand the sad dilemma in which you are placed. You have homes, the result of honest toil; you love and cherish them; there is a long journey to make into a strange land; it will cost you a great many anxieties and trials; all these things seem almost impossible for you to accomplish, and yet you cherish the principles of your church, you want to abide in the faith of your fathers.

"In the country where you now are you are called to do that which we believe Jesus, the Prince of Peace, forbids. Now here is a dilemma. It will be for you to choose. Shall we stay,—and yield the principles of our religion? or shall we do as the Saviour said, 'If they persecute you in one city, flee into another'?"

———

In 1881 I visited a few Mennonite communities in Germany; the first being in the city of Crefeld, in

Rhenish Prussia. I sought this town especially from what I had learned of it in my own country. Crefeld seems to have been a place of refuge in former times for persecuted religionists. Here, in the seventeenth century, Huguenot refugees introduced the manufacture of silk, for which the town is still distinguished. Here William Penn and others gained adherents to the Quaker doctrine.* And when the Dunkers were persecuted, some of them took refuge in Crefeld, in the duchy of Cleves.

Although Crefeld was so liberal, and although it now belongs to Prussia, it is greatly Catholic. The population is thus estimated: Catholics, 56,000; Evangelicals or United Lutherans and Reformed, 18,000; Jews, 1500; Mennonites, 1000. But the attendance at the Mennonite church which I visited did not indicate so great a number. I cannot express more fully to our own people of Lancaster County how much this church differs from their own simple meetings at home than to tell them that the preacher is paid, that he spoke from a pulpit, wore a black robe, and read a prayer from a book. Yet it is simple compared with the display of Catholic churches.

But what my neighbors will probably consider as a more vital difference between them and the Mennonites of Crefeld is that the latter bear arms. Since 1868 they have not been exempted from military service. They can, however, if they desire, take peaceful positions, such as nurses in military hospitals, or clerks; but while some of their fellow-believers in Prussia avail themselves of

* See the article " Ephrata," in this volume.

this permission, those in Crefeld do not. One not a Mennonite said to me that the positions in the army are more honorable.

Why, then, do they not join the Evangelicals? Two of the chief differences between them are that Mennonites only baptize those of mature years and refuse to swear in a court of justice, making instead nearly the following declaration, " My yes is yes, my no is no, and in testimony thereto I offer my right hand,"—the *handschlag*.

The next Mennonite settlement which I visited was that at Kuhbörnchenhof, not far from Kaiserslautern, in the Rhenish Palatinate. Going among these people with no letters of introduction, I was received with much hospitality in the small rural settlement. Their ancestors came from Switzerland in 1715. The first who came to this place seems to have built himself a log house; the country being nearly covered with wood, with wild animals therein. Others joined him, until the little settlement numbered eight families. Counting all in the country round belonging to this church (or congregation), it is said to number ninety-four baptized persons. They baptize at the age of thirteen. Until lately this settlement had an unpaid ministry; but a few years ago they concluded to employ a minister. However, he is not heavily paid. He preaches by turns in three different settlements, and receives a salary of about one hundred and eighty dollars (having a wife and infant). There are larger communities, which pay as much as two hundred and fifty to four hundred and fifty dollars.

The Rhenish Palatinate belongs to Bavaria. The Mennonites here are no longer allowed to purchase exemption from military service ; all who are drawn must serve.

One more effort I made in Germany to visit the Mennonites. I heard in the city of Speyer that some were living near Zweibrücken, and by perseverance I found an Amish family not far from the town. It proved to be that of a wealthy farmer, living in some respects more plainly than our people here. This farmer, Mr. Stalter, told me that all the Mennonites in the Palatinate came from Switzerland. When they came many of them were weavers, but now they have earned money, and all, or almost all, are farmers. The manner in which the sons of this family avoid protracted military service seems to be by obtaining a higher degree of education. I was told that since 1871 every young man in Germany must perform military service at the age of twenty. If he prefer, he may begin at sixteen. They usually go into barracks for three years. But the three years' service can be shortened to one year, and otherwise lightened, thus: First, the young man must be three years in a common public school,— *Volks-schule.* Then he must go six years to a school of higher grade, a *Real-schule*, where he studies a foreign language (either French or English), chemistry, physics, mathematics, history, and natural history. (At the end of six years, if he cannot pass his examination, he may go back and study another year.) After this he is ready to enter upon the mitigated military service for one year only. If he does not wish to live in garrison, he can take a room elsewhere and board himself, but go through all the military exercises with the other soldiers. In this case he must furnish himself his uniform and other trappings. Of this manner of escaping the three years' service I think that two sons of the Stalter family had already availed themselves.

Close by Mr. Stalter lived another family named Oesch. They had been Amish until 1871, and have now joined the Tunkers (Dunkers), or those who immerse. The Tunkers do not go to war. If they are forced to do so, they go to America. They do go into garrison, but they will not bear arms. They are then taken before a military judge, and sometimes he sends them to prison. When allowed to come out they can work in barracks in bread-baking, the care of horses, etc., but will not take arms, even possibly if they should be threatened with death.

But they are not always sent to prison. When the matter is understood by the authorities other labor than military service is often assigned to them. It was in this family of Oesch that I saw the two volumes which I had before seen in Lancaster County. One was the Martyr-book, which was published in Dutch, turned into German by the brotherhood at Ephrata, and by them printed in 1748;* printed anew by the united brotherhood in Europe. The date, I think, was 1780. The other volume was the old Hymn-Book, still in use among the Amish in my own country. This copy was published at Basle in 1809.

I have before spoken of the congregation that I visited not far from Kaiserslautern, and of its preacher, who re-

---

* See article " Ephrata" in this volume.

ceived a salary of about one hundred and eighty dollars. I met the preacher there and at his own dwelling, and he gave me a list, published in 1881, of the Mennonite congregations in Germany, Galicia, Poland, and Russia. Why those in Holland are not included I do not understand. Others are omitted, for the preface says, " We are sorry that we have not received any information concerning the small congregations found in Switzerland, as well as those in Alsace and Lorraine." As far as my own observation goes, the number of Mennonites in Germany is not large. In Holland the number given in Appleton's Cyclopædia is over forty-four thousand in the year 1869. Of those in Russia, the number mentioned in the list which was presented to me (published in 1881) is about forty thousand. But a private letter from a Mennonite editor estimates that fifteen thousand Russian Mennonites have come to this country, and that, as there were about forty thousand in Russia in 1870, only about twenty-five thousand are left there. The editor mentions that they have settled here in Kansas, Nebraska, Dakota, Minnesota, and Manitoba.

THE DUNKER LOVE-FEAST.

On the morning of the 25th of September, 1871, I took the cars of the Pennsylvania Central Railroad for the borough of Mount Joy, in the northwest part of this county of Lancaster. Finding no public conveyance thence to the village of C., I obtained from my landlord a horse and buggy and an obliging driver, who took me four or five miles, for two dollars. We took a drive round by the new Dunker meeting-house, which is a neat frame building,—brown, picked out with white window-frames. Behind it is a wood, upon which the church-doors open, instead of upon the highway.

We heard here that the meeting would not begin till one o'clock on the next day. Some of the brethren were at the church, however, with their teams, having brought provisions, straw, and bedding. We went into the neat meeting-room, and above into the garret, where straw was being laid down. A partition ran down the middle, and upon the women's side a small room had also been divided from the rest, wherein were one or two bedsteads and the inevitable cradle. The basement had a hard earthen floor, and was divided into dining-room, kitchen, and cellar. Upon spacious shelves in the cellar a brother and sister were placing food. Many large

112

loaves of bread were there. The sister was taking pies from a great basket, and bright coffee-pots stood upon the kitchen-table.

All here seemed to speak " Dutch," but several talked English with me. They seemed surprised that I had come so far as twenty-three miles in order to attend the meeting. One remarked that it was no member that had put the notice of the meeting which I had seen into the paper. Others, however, seemed interested, although by my dress it was very plain that I was not of the brotherhood.

I found C. a neat place of about a dozen houses, and we drove to the only tavern. The landlady was young and pleasant, but she could speak little English. She was quite sociable, however, and thought that she could teach me " Dutch" and I her English. By means of some German on my part, we got along tolerably together. She took me to a good chamber, and began removing from it some of their best clothing. Showing me two sun-bonnets, one of them made of black silk, she said, " It is the fashion." " The fashion?" said I. " Yes ; the fashion for married women." This was, doubtless, the Dunker influence even among those not members.

Being at leisure in the afternoon, I walked to an ancient Moravian church in the neighborhood, with the landlady's little daughter,—a pretty child.

Her mother said, " Geh mit der aunty :" so she went with her adopted relative.

" Do you speak English ?" I said to the little one.

" Na !" she answered.

" Hast du ein Bruder ?" (Have you a brother ?) I continued.

" Na !" she replied, in the dialect.

" Wie alt bist du ?" (How old are you ?) I said afterward.*

" Vaze es net." (I don't know.)

Conversation flagged.

I found the church a small log building that had been covered with boards. Many of the tombstones were in the Moravian fashion, such as I had seen at Litiz,— small square slabs, lying flat in the grass; and some were numbered at the top of the inscription. One of these is said to be one hundred and twenty years old. But the Herrnhüter (as my landlady said) are all gone, and another society now holds meetings in the lowly church.

Although my little guide of six years could not speak English, she was not wanting in good sense. As I was trying to secure the graveyard gate, holding it with one hand, and stooping to roll up the stone that served to keep it fast, the little one, too, put out her hand, unbidden, to hold the gate. I thought that there were some English children that would not have been so helpful, and reflected, as I walked along, upon *unspoken language*, if I may use the expression.

The landlady had a plentiful supper after we returned. I was the only guest, and, as is usual here, the maid sat down with us. We had fried beef, sweet potatoes, pie, very nice apple-butter, canned peaches, barley-coffee, brown sugar, etc. The charge for board was at the rate of one dollar per day.

---

* Our " Dutch"—all of them, I believe—use the singular pronoun " du," *thou.*

In the evening I heard my hostess up-stairs preparing my bed, as I supposed. My surprise was therefore considerable, on turning down the woollen coverlet, to find no sheets upon the feather bed. On lifting this light and downy bed, which was neatly covered with white, I found one sheet, a straw bed, and then a bed-cord in the place of a sacking-bottom. I at once perceived that the feather bed was a feather cover, of which I had often heard, but had never met with one before during my sojourn in Pennsylvania "Dutchland." I should think that this downy covering might be pleasant in cold weather, but now I rolled it off upon the floor, and, with the help of a spare comfortable, was soon at rest. The pillow-cases, which were trimmed with edging, were marked with black silk, in a large running-hand, in this manner: "Henry G. Kreider, 1864."

As I sat the next morning a while with the landlady in her basement kitchen, she remarked, "Here is it as Dutch as Dutchlant." But she said that my Dutch was not like theirs. The neighborhood, however, is not nearly so German as Germany. I was told by an intelligent young man that half the grown men did not speak English; I understand by this, not that they do not speak our language at all, but not habitually and with fluency. Many speak English very well, but the "Dutch" accent is universal. For several years the school-books in the township have all been English. I laughed with the landlady, who herself seemed somewhat amused, at the children having English books and speaking Dutch, or, as she would say, "Die Kinner lerne Englisch und schwetze Deitsch." However, at the Dunker church a pretty girl told me afterward that she had had no difficulty at school the preceding winter, although " we always talk German at home."

At breakfast this morning, among other dishes, we had raisin-pie. Not a great while after this meal was over, the morning having proved wet, a neighbor took me over to the church in his buggy for twenty-five cents. Although the hour was so early, and meeting was fixed to begin at one, I found a considerable number here, which did not surprise me, as I knew the early habits of our " Dutch" people. Taking a seat, I began to read a number of the *Living Age*, when a black-eyed maid before me, in Dunker dress, handed me her neatly-bound hymn-book in English and German. I told her that I could read German, and when I read a verse in that language she said, " But you don't know what it means." Reading German is with us a much rarer accomplishment than speaking the dialect.

Ere long, a stranger came and sat down behind me, and entered into conversation. He was a preacher from a distance, named L., and spoke very good English. We soon found that we had mutual acquaintances in another county, and when dinner was ready he invited me down to partake.

Here the men sat upon one side, and the women on the other, of one of the long tables, upon which was laid a strip of white muslin. We had bowls without spoons, into which was poured by attending brethren very hot coffee, containing milk or cream, but no sugar. We had the fine Lancaster County bread, good and abundant butter, apple-butter, pickles, and pies. The provisions for these meals are contributed by the members at a previous meeting, where each tells what he intends to furnish, how many loaves of bread, etc., while some prefer to give money. To furnish provisions, however, is natural to a people of whom about seventy-five in a hundred are farmers, as is the case with the Dunkers. Whatever food is left over after the four meals are finished is given to the poor, without distinction of sect; " whoever needs it most," as a sister said.

At this dinner, before eating, my new acquaintance, L., gave out, by two lines at a time, the verse,—

" Eternal are thy mercies, Lord."

But few joined in the singing. They would doubtless have preferred German. In that language thanks were returned after eating.

When we went up into the meeting-room again, a young man of an interesting countenance, a preacher, named Z., asked me if I was not the one who had written an article which had lately appeared in one of our county papers. It was very gratifying to be thus recognized among strangers.

An elderly sister, who sat down by me and began to talk, was named Murphy. The name surprised me much, but it was not the only Irish one here. It is probable that some such persons were taken into Dunker families, when young, to be brought up, and thus had been led to join the society.

Having observed that there was a good deal of labor to be performed here in waiting upon so many people, I asked Mrs. Murphy whether there were women hired. She told me, " There's a couple of women that's hired; but the members does a heap, too."

On another occasion, I made a remark to a friendly

sister about the brethren's waiting upon the table, as they did. She answered that it was according to the Testament to help each other; the women cooked, and the men waited upon the table. She did not seem able to give the text. It may be, "Bear ye one another's burdens." I was amused that it should be so kindly applied to the brethren's helping the sisters.

Before meeting began in the afternoon, a lovely aged brother, with silvery hair and beard, and wearing a woollen coat nearly white, showed me how the seats were made, so that, by turning down the backs of some, tables could be formed for the Love-Feast. He told me that the Dunkers number about one hundred thousand,— that they have increased much in the West, but not in the Eastern States. To which I rejoined, smiling, "You Dutch folks do not like poor land, like much of that at the East."

"This is not good land," he said, "we have improved it;" for I had left the rich limestone soil and had come to the gravelly land in the northern part of the county.

When meeting began, as brethren came in, I saw some of these bearded men kissing each other. These holy kisses, as will be seen hereafter, are frequent among the Dunkers, and, as the men shave only the upper lip, it seems strange to us who are unaccustomed to the sight and the sound. The oft-repeated kissing was to me, perhaps, the least agreeable part of the ceremonial.

The afternoon meeting became very crowded, and, as is usual among our "Dutch" people, a number of babies were in attendance. During the sessions their voices sometimes rose high, but the noise did not seem to affect those who were preaching or praying. They felt it perhaps like the wailing and sighing of the wind, which they regard not, and would rather bear the inconvenience of the children than to have the mothers stay away from meeting. This afternoon, during prayer, a little fellow behind me kept saying, " Want to go to pappy ;" but if his father was among the brethren, he was on the other side of the house.

My new acquaintance, L., was the only preacher here who spoke in English. All the other exercises, except a little singing, were in German or in our Pennsylvania dialect. This afternoon L. said, among many remarks more sectarian, or less broad, " Faith is swallowed up in sight; hope, in possession; but charity, or love, is eternal. It came from God, for God is love." The allusion here is to Paul's celebrated panegyric on charity; but how much more charming it is in the German version, " Faith, hope, love; but the greatest of these is love. Love suffereth long and is kind, is not puffed up," etc.

About the middle of the afternoon I perceived a speaker giving some directions, and I asked the women near me what he had said. One answered and said something about " *Wahl halten für prediger,*" by which I perceived that the election for a preacher was now to take place. Both brethren and sisters were to vote; not to select from a certain set of candidates, however; but at random, among the congregation,—or *family*, as it is sometimes called, " for all ye are brethren."

In the room above-stairs were the bishop or elder and an assistant, to receive the votes. This bishop we might call the father of this family, which has four preachers and as many meeting-houses. The bishop is always that preacher who is oldest in the ministry. Meeting is held by turns in the different houses, occurring only once in six weeks in the large new house which we then occupied. These particulars, which I gathered in conversation, are, I believe, substantially correct.

During the interval of the election I sat and read, or looked out from my window at the young people, the gayly-dressed girls mostly grouped together. Some of these were, probably, relatives of the members, while others may have come for the ride and the fun, to see and to be seen,—meetings of this kind being great occasions in the country-side.

The young men stood around on the outside of these groups of girls, some holding their whips and twirling them, with the butts resting upon the ground. Of course the young girls were not conscious of the presence of the beaux.

On the back of the house, or rather the front,—for, as I have said, the main doors open upon the wood instead of upon the roadside,—were more young girls, and plain sisters and brethren.

I asked a nice-looking woman about the election, but she could not tell me, although she wore the plain cap. "Most of the women do around here," she said, and added that Dunker women in meeting had offered to kiss her. "You know they greet each other with a kiss."

After the brethren, the sisters were called up to vote. I laughed, in talking with some of the members, at the women's being allowed to vote, in contrast to the usual custom. Mrs. Murphy reckoned it would be different if the women should undertake to vote for Governor or President.

I said to some of the sisters, " Who do you think will be chosen ?" But they pleasantly informed me that to talk upon this point was against their rules,—it was a matter for internal reflection.

After meeting was over next day, as the bishop was talking with a sister, I ventured to ask him whether a majority was necessary to elect a preacher, or only a plurality. He seemed quite willing to talk, displaying no clerical pride, and answered, "A majority," adding, " Do you speak German ?" I feared that I could not readily understand him on such a subject, and put the case to him thus in English : " Suppose one man has twenty votes, another fifteen, and another ten ?" Then the bishop said that the one having twenty would be elected; whence it seems that a plurality only is required. On this occasion the vote was doubtless much divided, for I afterward heard that the bishop had said to the congregation that it seemed there were a good many there that were thought fit for preachers.

As sunset approached, some of the members began to form tables from the benches for the Love-Feast, which made me wonder when supper was to be ready. I soon found, however, that my ignorance of the language had prevented my observing that while the "family" voted the rest of the congregation were to sup. I was told, however, that if I would go down I could still get something to eat. These meals were free to every one that came. All were received, in the hope that they would obtain some spiritual good.

In the basement I found a number of men sitting at the end of one of the tables, waiting for food, and I also sat down near them. I was invited, however, by a sister to step into the kitchen, where I stood and partook of hot coffee, bread and butter, etc. As we went along through the dining-room, I thought that the sister cast a reproachful glance at a disorderly man seated at the table with his whip, and who was perhaps intoxicated. I wondered that she should have taken me from the table to stand in the kitchen, till I remembered that that was *a men's table.*

In the kitchen, brethren were busily occupied cutting large loaves of bread into quarters for the coming Love-Feast; and when I returned to the room above, active preparations were still going on, which consumed much time. The improvised tables were neatly covered with white cloths, and hanging lamps shed down light upon the scene. Piles of tin pans were placed upon the table, knives, forks, and spoons, and sometimes a bowl. The tables, with their seats, occupied nearly the whole floor of the church, leaving but little room for spectators. I was myself crowded into a corner, where the stairs came up from the basement and went up to the loft; but, though at times I was much pressed for room, I had an excellent place to observe, for I stood at the end of the main table. Here stood, too, a bright and social sister from a neighboring congregation, who did not partake of the feast, and was able and willing to explain the ceremonial to me, in English,—Mrs. R., as I will call her.

Near by at the table, among the older sisters, sat a pair who attracted a great deal of my attention—a young mother and her babe—herself so quiet, and such a quiet babe! They might have been photographed. Once or twice the little six-weeks' child gave a feeble young wail, and I saw the youthful mother modestly give it that nourishment which nature provides.

The brethren came up carrying tubs of meat, which smelt savory, for I had fasted from flesh since the morning. Then came great vessels of soup,—one of them a very large tin wash-boiler. The soup was taken out into the tin pans before mentioned, and the plates of meat were set upon the top, as if to keep both hot. And, now that "at long last" the Love-Feast tables were spread, the fasting family was ready to begin, not the supper, but the feet-washing! This was the more remarkable, because the Testament, their rule of action, relates that "supper being ended," Jesus washed the disciples' feet.

The bishop arose in his place at the table, and, lamp in one hand and book in the other, read in German the account of the feet-washing in John's gospel.

Four men who stood in front of him, watching his words, started when he said "legte seine Kleider ab" ("laid aside his garments"), and, in imitation of Jesus, took off their coats; and, as the Scripture says, "He took a towel and girded himself," they, or two of them, put on long white aprons tied around the waist. Two washed feet and two wiped, and then he who was thus ministered unto was kissed by one or both of the ministering brethren. I was a little surprised that two should perform that office, which Jesus is said to have performed alone: but Mrs. R. told me that, as the church was one body, it was considered that it made no difference to have two persons.

The four who had ministered took their seats, and were served in their turn, four others taking their places, and so on. Upon the sisters' side of the house, on a front bench, the sisters were, in a similar manner, performing the same ordinance.

While the religious services of the evening were going on within, from without there came the sound of voices and laughter,—from where the young people *of the world* were enjoying themselves in the clear, cool moonlight. I doubt not that, by this time, the girls had recognized the presence of the young men.

Once there was a shriek or a yell, and Mrs. R. said, "Oh, the drunken rowdies! there's always some of them here!"

Having heard of the non-resistant or *wehrlos* tenets of the Dunkers, I wondered what they would do should the disturbance without become very great and unpleasant. Mrs. Murphy thought that the other people would interfere in such a case,—that is, that those not members would interest themselves to maintain order. But on this point I afterward received information from a brother, as I shall mention. The services were so long that I told Mrs. R. I thought that the soup would be cold. "Oh, no!" she said, "that won't get cold so soon." So I ventured to put my finger against a pan near me, and it was yet warm. She asked me, during feet-washing, whether I did not think that I should feel happy to be there, partaking of that exercise.

I answered, in a non-committal manner, that if I had been brought up to such things, as she had been, I might feel so, but that all my friends and acquaintances were of a different mind. She rejoined, "But we must follow Christ, and serve God, in spite of the world." Even after the feet were all washed, the fasting family could not yet eat, on account of the protracted exhortations.

At length they broke their fast. From two to four persons, each with a spoon, ate together from one pan of soup, very quietly, fifty feeding like one, so to speak; the absence of sound proceeding in part perhaps from the absence of earthen plates. Then they cut from the meat and from the quarter-loaves, and partook of the butter, this being all the food. There was no salt nor any other condiment. The occasional bowl was for water. I suppose that most persons would think that there had been enough kissing of the kind; but about this time a young bishop, an assistant, stood up at the centre of the main table, and after some remarks shook hands with the sister upon his left and kissed the brother upon his right, and from brother to brother, and from sister to sister, the kiss went around the congregation.

The bishop, and this assistant, went around upon ours, the women's side, superintending this ceremony, as if to see that none failed in this expression of unity, and that it was conducted in an orderly manner. The last sister, who has no one to kiss, goes forward and kisses the first one, with whom the bishop had shaken hands, thus completing the chain of unity. This was doubtless done before the Communion, and showed that brotherly love existed among these brethren, fitting them to partake of the sacrament. I was also told that the latter half of the afternoon meeting had been for self-examination on the same subject.

About this time of the evening Mrs. R. told me that if I would go down I could get some of the soup, as there was plenty left. I was willing to partake, not having had a regular supper, and I got a bowl of good mutton-broth, containing rice or barley, etc.

After the Love-Feast, these "Old Brethren," as they are sometimes called, held the Communion. The bread and wine were placed upon the general or main table—being set before the bishops—and were covered with a white cloth.

Before the celebration of the ordinance there was read in German the passage of Scripture upon which it is founded; and also, as it seemed to me, the narrative of the crucifixion. The hymn now sung was an English one, and the only one in our language that was sung by the whole congregation during the two days' meeting. It was,

" Alas! and did my Saviour bleed?"

Meantime, the assistant bishop divided the bread, or cakes, which were unleavened and sweetened. He directed the members, while eating the bread, to reflect upon the sufferings of the Saviour. His manner was devout and impressive. As he and Bishop D——passed around among the women, distributing the bread, the former repeated several times, in a sonorous voice, these or similar words: "Das Brod das wir brechen ist die Gemeinschaft des Leibes Christi." ("The bread that we break is the communion of the body of Christ.")

The wine, which smelt strong, was the juice of the grape, and was made in the neighborhood. An aged bishop from another congregation made some observations, and while speaking marked the length of something upon his finger. Mrs. R. said that he was showing the size of the thorns in the crown. She added, "They are there yet." I looked at her in much surprise, wondering whether she believed in the preservation of the actual thorns ; whereupon she added, " They grow there still.   Did you never read it in Bausman's book on the Holy Land?—Bausman, the Reformed preacher."   The simplicity of the surroundings upon this occasion were, it seemed to me, in keeping with those of the original supper, at which sat the " carpenter's son" and the fishermen.

When meeting was over, as I did not see my escort to the public-house, and as I had been told that I could stay here, I followed those who went above-stairs, and received a bolster made of a grain-bag filled with hay or straw.   I shared it with Mrs. Murphy.   Our bed was composed of straw laid upon the floor, and covered, or nearly so, with pieces of domestic carpet.   We had a coverlet to lay over us.   I talked with some of the other women who lay beside us, and could not get to sleep immediately ; but at last I slept so sweetly that it was not agreeable to be disturbed at four o'clock, when, by my reckoning, the sisters began to rise.   When some of these had gone down, I should perhaps have slept again, had it not been for a continued talking upon the men's side of the partition, quite audible, as the partition only ran up to a distance of some feet, not nearly so high as the lofty ridge of the building.   The voices appeared to be those of a young man and one or two boys, talking in the dialect.   A woman near me laughed.

" What is it ?" said I.

" It's too mean to tell," she answered.

I surmise that the Dunker brethren had gone down and left these youths.   Although a baby was crying, I lay still until two girls in Dunker caps—one ten years old, the other twelve—came with a candle, looking at us, smiling, and making remarks, perhaps thinking that it was time for us to be up.

I asked the eldest what o'clock it was.

She did not know.

" What made you get up, then ?"

" I got up when the others did."

Then some one explained that there were a good many dishes left unwashed the evening before.

I was surprised to see such young persons members of the meeting, for I supposed that the Dunkers, like the Mennonites, are opposed to infant baptism. The former explained to me, however, that they thought such persons as these old enough to distinguish right from wrong. I was told, too, of one girl, still younger, who had insisted on *wearing the cap.* The Mennonites baptize persons as young as fifteen. Both sects seem to hold peculiar views upon original sin.

A Dunker preacher once said to me,—

" We believe that, after Adam, all were born in sin ; but, after Christ, all were born without sin."

And a Mennist neighbor says,—

" Children have no sin ; the kingdom of heaven is of little children."

I continued to lie still, looking at the rafters and roof, and speculating as to their being so clean, and clear of cobwebs, and whether they had been laboriously swept ; and then, gathering my wardrobe together with some little trouble, I was at last ready to go down. As I went to a window, I saw Orion and Sirius, and the coming day.

Going down to wash at the pump, in the morning gloaming, while the landscape still lay in shade, I found two or three lads at the pump, and one of them pumped for me. I was so ignorant of pump-washing as to wonder why he pumped so small a stream, and to suspect that he was *making fun;* but thus it seems it is proper to do, to avoid wetting the sleeves.

Here I met a pretty young sister, from Cumberland County,—fat and fair,—whose acquaintance I had made the day before. Her cap was of lace, and not so plain as the rest. There was with her at the pump one of the world's people, a young girl in a blue dress.

" Is that your sister ?" I asked.

" It's the daughter of the woman I live with," she replied. " I have no sister. I am hired with her mother."

To my inexperienced eye it was not easy to tell the rich Dunkers from the poor, when all wore so plain a dress. I was afterward much surprised on discovering that this pretty sister did not understand German. Another from Cumberland County told me that I ought to come to their meeting, which was nearly all English.

After washing, I went up into the meeting-house, where the lamps were still burning. A few sisters were sitting here, and two little maidens were making a baby laugh and scream by walking her back and forth along the empty benches. About sunrise the bishop had arrived, and a number of brethren ranged themselves upon the benches and began to sing. Before long, we, who had stayed over-night, had our breakfast, having cold meat at this and the succeeding meal. I think it was at breakfast that my pleasant friend with the silvery hair mentioned that there was still a store of bread and pies.

The great event of the morning meeting was the "making the preacher." At my usual seat, at a distant window, I was so busily occupied with my notes that I did not perceive what was going on at the preachers' table, until I saw a man and woman standing before the table with their backs to the rest of the congregation. I made my way to my former corner of observation, and found that there was another brother standing with them (the sister in the middle), and these were receiving the greetings of the family. The brethren came up, one by one, kissed one of the men, shook hands with the sister, and kissed the other man. This last was the newly-chosen preacher, the former brother, named Z., being a preacher who, by the consent of the members (also given yesterday), was now advanced one degree in the ministry, and was henceforth to have power to marry and to baptize. The sister was his wife. She is expected to support her husband in the ministry, and to be ready to receive those women who, after baptism, come up from the water. This office and that of voting seem to be the only important ones held by women in this society. Herein they differ greatly from another plain sect,—Friends or Quakers, among whom women minister, transact business, etc.*

---

* A friend tells me that he once heard a discourse from a celebrated Dunker preacher, named Sarah Reiter. She was allowed to preach, it seems, by a liberal construction of Paul's celebrated edict, because she was unmarried. Even when afterward married, by a more liberal construction still, the liberty to preach was not forbidden her. Possibly it was assumed that her *husband at home* was not able to answer all her questions upon spiritual matters. She removed to Ohio.

In the Encyclopædia Americana the following are given as

After the brethren were done, the sisters came up, shook hands with Z., kissed his wife, and shook hands with the new preacher, whose wife, I believe, was not present.

The bishop invited the sisters to come forward: " Koomet alle! alle die will. Koomet alle!"

While this salutation was in progress, L., who spoke in English, made some explanatory remarks. He told us that he had read or heard of two men travelling together, of whom one was a doctor of divinity. The latter asked the younger man what he was now doing. He replied that he was studying divinity. He had formerly been studying law, but on looking around he saw no opening in the law, so he was now studying divinity, which course or which change met the approval of the reverend doctor.

" Now," said L., " *we* do not approve of men-made preachers;" a striking remark in a congregation where a preacher had just been elected by a plurality. But he went on to explain that he trusted that there was no brother or sister who had voted for him who had just been chosen for this arm of the church who had not

---

propositions of some of the former Anabaptists: "Impiety prevails everywhere. It is therefore necessary that a new family of holy persons should be founded, enjoying without distinction of sex the gift of prophecy, and skill to interpret divine revelations. Hence they need no learning, for the internal word is more than the outward expression."

At this time, however, while our German Baptists still believe in an unpaid, untaught ministry, none of them, I think, hold to the doctrine that the gift of prophecy or preaching is without distinction of sex. In this respect, George Fox seems to have agreed with the early Anabaptists just mentioned.

prayed God earnestly that they might make such a choice as would be profitable in the church. He went on to explain that the newly-chosen preacher was now receiving from the congregation an expression of unity.

There were various other exercises this morning,— preaching, praying, and singing,—before the final adjournment. At the close we had dinner. I made an estimate of the number who partook of this meal as about five hundred and fifty. One of the men guessed a thousand; but we are prone to exaggerate numbers where our feelings are interested.

Before we parted, I had some conversation with certain brethren, principally upon the non-resistant doctrines of the society. In my own neighborhood, not a great while before, a Dunker had been robbed under peculiar circumstances. Several men had entered his house at night, and, binding him and other members of the family, had forced him to tell where his United States and other bonds were placed, and had carried off property worth four thousand dollars. The brother had gone in pursuit of them, visiting the mayor of our town, and the police in neighboring cities (without recovering his property). I asked these brethren at different times whether his course was in agreement with their rules. They answered that it was not.

On the present occasion I repeated the question as to what they would have done on the previous evening if the disturbance had risen to a great height. One of the brethren, in reply, quoted from the Acts of the Apostles, where it is narrated that forty Jews entered into a conspiracy to kill Paul. But Paul sent his nephew to the chief captain to inform him of the conspiracy. The captain then put Paul under the charge of soldiers, to be brought safe unto Felix the governor.

From this passage the Dunkers feel at liberty to appeal to the police for their protection; but only once: if protection be not then afforded them, they must do without it.

I further mentioned to these brethren a case which had been told to me some time before by a Dunker preacher, of a certain brother who had been sued in the settlement of an estate, and had received a writ from the sheriff. This writ was considered by the Dunkers as a call from the powers that be, to whom they are ordered to be subservient, and the brother therefore went with some brethren to the office of a lawyer, who furnished him with subpœnas to summon witnesses in his defence. But the Dunkers argued among themselves that for him to take these legal papers from his pocket would be to draw the sword. He therefore sent word to his friends, informally, to come to the office of a magistrate; and, the evidence being in his favor, he was released. "This," said my informant, "is the only lawsuit that I have known in our society since I joined the meeting," which was, I believe, a period of about seven years.

In repeating this narrative to the brethren at the Love-Feast, I learned that they are now at liberty to engage in defensive lawsuits. They have, as I understood one to say, no creed and no discipline, although I believe that a certain confession of faith is required. The New Testament, or, as they say, the Testament, they claim to be their creed and their discipline. There is also much independence in the congregations. But in some cases they have resort to a general council, and here it has been decided that a Dunker may defend himself in a lawsuit, but only once. Should an appeal be taken to another court, the Dunker can go no further. This reminds me of Paul's question to the Corinthians, " Why do you not rather suffer loss than go to law ?" * Does it not seem hard to practise such non-resistance, to remain upright and open-minded, and at the same time to acquire much wealth?

The Dunkers do not like to be called by this name ; their chosen title is Brethren.

———

The Love-Feast, above described, was held by the " Old Brethren," who originated in Germany about the year 1708.

It has been said that they originated among the Pietists ; but a very great resemblance will be found among them to our German Baptists of the Mennonite or Anabaptist stock.

I afterward visited other Dunkers, belonging to a division called the " River Brethren." They originated near the Susquehanna River, but they have now spread as far as Ohio, if not farther.

That these are of the old Baptist stock there is no doubt, as Jacob Engle, their founder, was of a Mennonite family,—a family which boasts that one of their ancestors was a prisoner in Switzerland, on account of her faith. (See note, in " Swiss Exiles," page 101.)

In coming to this country, about one hundred years

———

* See the questions in full,—1 Corinthians, chap. vi.

ago, tradition tells us that the Engle family joined with thirty others, who were upon the same vessel, to remain bound together in life and in death. The young infants of these families all died upon the voyage, except Jacob Engle, whereupon an old nurse said, "God has preserved him for an especial purpose." He became a preacher, and this his friends regarded as a fulfilment of the prophecy.

Jacob Engle, or "Yokely Engle," as he was sometimes called, considered that there was not sufficient warmth and zeal among the Mennonites at that time. He became very zealous; experiencing, as he believed, a change of heart.

Before he became a preacher, some joined him in holding prayer-meetings. It was found that some wished to be baptized by immersion, and the rite was thus performed (whereas the Mennonites baptize by pouring).

A common observer would see very little difference between these Brethren and the Old Dunkers. The River Brethren allow all present to partake of the love-feast, or paschal supper. Some of them have said that the paschal supper is an expression of the love of God to all mankind, and love toward all men constrains them to invite all to partake thereof. But from the Lord's Supper they exclude all strangers.

Their meetings are usually held in private houses, or in summer in barns.

Some of their preachers have been heard, upon rising to speak, to declare that they intend to say only what the Spirit teaches them.

One of their most striking peculiarities is their opposition to the use of lightning-rods. A preacher said to me, when talking upon this subject, "If God wishes to preserve the building, he can preserve it without the lightning-rod. If he does not wish to preserve it, I am willing to submit to the result." It has been thought that an acquaintance with the laws of electricity would remove the objection which they feel.

The Brinser Brethren were formed from the River Brethren some years ago. They are popularly thus called, from an able preacher named Matthias Brinser. They erect meeting-houses, in preference, as I understand, to meeting in private houses. Their church has not opposed electrical conductors, though some members feel conscientious in the matter.

The question of erecting meeting-houses seems to have caused considerable trouble among the River Brethren. A gentleman of our county remarked to me that the custom of meeting in private houses is traditional among our people, and dates from times of persecution.

Since the foregoing was published, there has appeared in the *Century* magazine, December, 1881, an article by Dr. Seidensticker on the Ephrata Baptists. In this article the author states that the Dunkers number in the United States (for they have also missions in Europe) about two hundred thousand souls, with nearly two thousand ministers, none of whom receives a salary. They have three collegiate institutions,—one in Pennsylvania, one in Ohio, and one in Illinois.

He states that those who fail in business among the Dunkers are aided to make a new effort, and such assistance may be lent three times [twice?]. After the third failure, they take it to be the will of God that the unfortunate brother shall not succeed. Dr. Seidensticker says, too, that in the holy kiss of the Dunkers, the first kiss among the women is applied by the minister to the first sister's hand, which differs from the statement that I have made of the Love-Feast.

EPHRATA.

THIS quiet village in Lancaster County has been for over a century distinguished as the seat of a Protestant monastic institution, established by the Seventh-Day German Baptists about the year 1738.

Conrad Beissel, the founder of the cloister, was born in Germany, at Oberbach, in the Palatinate, in the year 1691. He was by trade a baker, but, after coming to this country, he worked at weaving with Peter Becker, the Dunker preacher, at Germantown. He is said to have been a Presbyterian, which I interpret to mean a member of the German Reformed Church. According to the inscription upon his tombstone, his "spiritual life" began in 1716, or eight years before he was baptized among the Dunkers.

This may be explained by an article written by the Rev. Christian Endress, who seems to have studied the Ephrata community, in connection with their published writings, more than some others who have endeavored to describe this peculiar people.*

---

* See Hazard's Register, vol. v. C. L. F. Endress, D.D., preached twelve years in Trinity (Lutheran) Church, Lancaster. To the learned Dr. Seidensticker, of Philadelphia, and to Mr. I. D. Rupp, I am indebted for assistance.

Mr. Endress says, "The Tunkers trace their origin from the Pietists near Schwarzenau, in Germany." *

While they yet belonged among the Pietists, there was a society formed at Schwarzenau composed of eight persons, whose spiritual leader was Alexander Mack, a miller of Schriesheim.

The members of this little society are said to have been re-baptized (by immersion), because they considered their infant baptism as unavailing, and to have first assumed the name of *Taeuffer,* or Baptists.†

The Dunkers first appeared in America in 1719, when about twenty families landed in Philadelphia, and dispersed to Germantown, Conestoga, and elsewhere.

Beissel was baptized among them in 1724, in Pequea Creek, a tributary of the Susquehanna. He lived for

---

* A new movement in German theology arose in the second half of the seventeenth century, through Spener, the founder of Pietism. The central principle of Pietism was that Christianity was first of all life, and that the strongest proof of the truth of its doctrines was to be found in the religious experience of the believing subject. The principles of the Pietists were in the main shared by the Moravians. (See American Cyclopædia, article *German Theology.*) Compare this statement of the main principle of Pietism with this of the Anabaptists, whom the mass of our Dunkers so much resemble: "The opinions common to the Anabaptists are founded on the principle that Christ's kingdom on earth, or the church, is a visible society of pious and holy persons, with none of those institutions which human sagacity has devised for the ungodly." (See American Cyclopædia, article *Anabaptists.*)

† They took for themselves the name of Brethren, says an article in Rupp's "Religious Denominations." The Dunkers in our county call themselves Brethren,—"Old Brethren," "River Brethren," etc. Whether the Ephrata Dunkers took the same name, I cannot say.

a while at Mühlbach, or Mill Creek, in Lancaster County. Some time after this baptism, or in 1728, he published a tract upon the Seventh Day as the true Sabbath. This tract caused a disturbance among the brethren at Mill Creek, and Beissel and some with him withdrew from the other Dunkers, and Beissel re-baptized those of his own society.*

Not long after, says Endress, Beissel, who had appointed several elders over his people, withdrew from them, and retired to live a solitary life in a cottage that had been built for a similar purpose, and occupied by a brother called Elimelech. This cottage stood near the place where the convent was afterward built. Here we infer that he lived for several years.

To live the life of cenobites or hermits, says Rupp, was in some measure peculiar to many of the Pietists who had fled from Germany to seek an asylum in Pennsylvania. "On the banks of the Wissahickon, near Philadelphia, several hermits had their cells, some of them men of fine talents and profound erudition."

Of some of these hermits, and of the monastic community afterward settled at Ephrata, it is probable that a ruling idea was the speedy coming of Christ to judge the world. It is stated that after the formation of Beissel's "camp" midnight meetings were held, for some time, to await the coming of judgment. Those who remember the Millerite, or Second Advent, excitement of

---

* Speaking of a certain Seventh-Day Baptist, an "Old Mennonite" writer says that he was "doubtless unaware that the Lord Christ is also Lord of the sabbath, and that in him no day, except for sake of common law, is to be observed above another. See *Der Waffenlose Waechter* (or *Unarmed Watchman*), Jan. 1873.

the year 1843, can appreciate the effect that this idea would have upon the minds of the Dunkers, and how it could stimulate them to suffer many inconveniences for the brief season that they expected to tarry in the world.*

While Beissel was dwelling in his solitary cot, about the year 1730, two married women joined the society, of whom the Ephrata Chronicle tells us that they left their husbands and placed themselves under the lead of the director (or *vorsteher*, the title applied to Beissel in the Chronicle). He received them, although it was against the canon of the new society. One of these was Maria Christiana, wife of Christopher Sower, him who afterward established the celebrated German printing-office at Germantown. She escaped in the year 1730, and was baptized the same fall. In the beginning she dwelt alone in the desert, "and showed by her example that a manly spirit can dwell in a female creature." †

While Beissel was still in his hermitage, discord and

* In the time of the Millerite excitement above alluded to, many prepared ascension robes. One of my acquaintances went to the roof of his house, where, in his robe, he could look for the coming of Christ, and whence he was prepared immediately to ascend. More recently, namely, in August of 1873, I recollect meeting with a person who told me that he writes for Advent papers. He was himself a *Time-ist*, thinking that "the second coming of the Lord will take place this year."

† "Afterward, she held to edification for many years, in the sister-convent, the office of a sub-prioress, under the name of Marcella. Finally, in her age, she was induced by her son to return to her husband,—although another motive was the severe manner of life in the encampment, which she could no longer bear."— *Chronicon Ephratense*, p. 45.

strife arose among the brethren of his society, news of which reached him by some means, for in the year 1733 he cited them to appear at his cottage.

They met, and some of the single brethren agreed to build a second cottage near that occupied by their leader. Besides this, a house was also built for females, and in May, 1733, two single women retired into it.*

In 1734, a third house for male brethren was built and occupied by the brothers Onesimus and Jotham, whose family name was Eckerlin.†

---

* Are thes3 the married women just spoken of, who had become single?

† These remarkable men seem to deserve especial notice. In Rupp's History of Lancaster County it is stated that they were from Germany, and had been brought up Catholics. Israel Eckerlin (Brother Onesimus) became prior of the brother-house at Ephrata. Peter Miller, in an original letter, complains that he obliged them to meddle with worldly things further than their obligations permitted; and that when money came in it was put out at interest, "contrary to our principles."

They could not, however, have been very rich, for when in 1745 a bell arrived in Philadelphia, from England, which had been ordered by Eckerlin, and which cost eighty pounds, they knew not how to pay for it. The name of Onesimus (or Eckerlin) had been placed upon the bell. When the news of its arrival was received, a council was held in the presence of the spiritual father, Beissel, and it was concluded to break the bell to pieces and bury it in the earth. The next morning, however, the father appeared in the council, and said that he had reflected that as the brothers were poor, the bell should be pardoned. It therefore was sold, and was placed upon the Lutheran church in Lancaster, where it was long in use. Afterwards it was sold to a fire company, and is now on the tower of the house of the Washington Company. It bears a Latin inscription with the name of the "reverend man," Onesimus.

Miller says that the prior (Eckerlin) conceived a notion to make

Soon after, says Endress, they all united in the building of a bake-house and a storehouse for the poor. And now the whole was called the camp (*das Lager*).

The early history of the society is quaintly narrated by Morgan Edwards, the Baptist historian. They had, he says, their existence as a society in 1724, when Conrad Beissel and six others were baptized in Pequea River by Rev. Peter Baker. The same day these seven incorporated into a church, and chose Conrad Beissel to be their minister. After this they continued some time at Mill Creek, and then, removing about three miles northward, pitched on the land of Rudolph Neagley, in Earl Township. Here they continued about seven years; and hither resorted many to see them, some of whom joined the society. Here they began their economy, the men living by themselves on the fore-mentioned lands, and the women also by themselves on the adjoining lands of John Moyly.

---

himself independent of Beissel, and was stripped of all his dignities.

The Eckerlins appear to have gone into the wilderness, and encamped on a creek flowing into the Monongahela, in Pennsylvania, to which stream they gave the name of Dunkard Creek, which it still bears. They afterward seem to have removed to Dunkards' Bottom, on Cheat River, which they made their permanent residence. After many vicissitudes, Miller tells us that Eckerlin and his brother were taken prisoners by Mohawks, and sold to Quebec, whence they were transported to France, "where, after our prior had received the tonsure and become a friar of their church, they both died." The Ephrata Chronicle says (chap. xxiii.) that the prior went *out of time* twenty years before Beissel. The latter died in 1768. By the former reckoning, the prior went out of time in 1748, or about three years after the difficulty about the bell at Ephrata.

Here Conrad Beissel appointed two elders and a matron to preside over his church in the wilderness, binding them by a solemn promise (and at the same time giving to each a Testament) to govern according to the rules of that book. Then he withdrew, and made as though they should see him no more. This was done in the year 1732 or 1733. He travelled northward till he came to the spot where Ephrata or Tunkerstown now stands, and with his hoe planted Indian corn and roots for his subsistence. But he had not been long in the place before the society found him out, and repaired to his little cot, the brethren settling with him on the west bank of Cocalico, and the sisters on the east, all in sight of one another, with the river running between them. The next year they set about building their village, beginning with a place of worship.

Endress tells us that about the time of the formation of the camp there was a revival in Falconer Swamp, in consequence of which many families took up land round about the camp, and moved upon it. Another revival on the banks of the Schuylkill drove many more into the neighborhood; by it the sister establishment gained accessions; but only two, Drusilla and Basilla, remained steadfast. "A further revival in Tolpehoccon," 1735, brought many to the society. Hereupon they built a meeting-house, with rooms attached to it for the purpose of holding [preparing?] love-feasts, and called it Kedar. About the same time, a revival in Germantown sent additional brothers and sisters to the camp.*

---

* The reader is referred to an article alluded to in the preceding essay, namely, Dr. Seidensticker's " A Colonial Monastery," in *The*

It was in 1735, during the revival at Tulpehocken, that Peter Miller was baptized * or rebaptized. Miller, in one of his letters (see Hazard's Register, vol. xvi.), speaks of several persons who, as it appears, were baptized with him; namely, the schoolmaster, three *elderlings* (one of them Conrad Weyser), five families, and some single persons. This, he says, raised such a fermentation in that church (by which I suppose he means the Reformed Church, which they left), that a persecution might have followed had the magistrates consented with the generality.

Peter Miller, whom we are now quoting, was one of the most remarkable men that joined the Ephrata Baptists. He was born in the Palatinate, and is said to have been educated at Heidelberg. He came to this country when about twenty years old. He is mentioned, it seems, in an interesting letter of the Rev. Jedediah Andrews, under date of Philadelphia, 1730, which letter may be found in Hazard's Register. He says that there are "in this province a vast number of Palatines. Those that have come of late years are mostly Presbyterian, or, as they call themselves, Reformed, the Palatines being about three-fifths of that sort of people."

Mr. Andrews says, in substance, "There is lately come over a Palatine candidate for the ministry, who applied to us at the Synod for ordination. He is an extraordinary person for sense and learning. His name is John

---

Century magazine for December, 1881. Dr. S. is a professor in the University of Pennsylvania.

* The Tulpehocken Creek is a tributary of the Schuylkill, which rises in Lebanon County, and empties at Reading, in Berks County.

Peter Miller,* and he speaks Latin as readily as we do our vernacular tongue." †

Peter Miller, in one of his letters, speaks of his baptism (or re-baptism) in the year 1735. He says at that time the solitary brethren and sisters lived dispersed " in the wilderness of Canestogues, each for himself, as hermits, and I following that same way did set up my hermitage in Dulpehakin [Tulpehocken], at the foot of a mountain, on a limpid spring; the house is still extant [1790], with an old orchard. There did I lay the foundation of solitary life.‡

" However," he continues, " I had not lived there half a year, when a great change happened ; for a camp was laid out for all solitary persons, at the very spot where now Ephrata stands, and where at that same time

---

* In Rupp's " Thirty Thousand Names" of immigrants to Pennsylvania will be found, under date of August 29, 1730, the names of Palatines with their families, imported in the ship " Thistle" of Glasgow, from Rotterdam, last from Cowes. Among these occurs Peter Müller, whom by a note Rupp connects with the Peter Miller of the text. As to the name John Peter, as given by Andrews, it is surprising to see how many of these immigrants bear the names of John, Hans, Johan, Johann, and Johannes, prefixed to other names. I count twenty in a column of thirty-four.

† Mr. Andrews, from whom I quote, was a graduate of Harvard, who seems to have come to Philadelphia in 1698, and to have preached in an Independent or Presbyterian church, or in both.

‡ The Conestogas were a small tribe . . . consisting in all of some dozen or twenty families, who dwelt a few miles below Lancaster. They sent messengers with corn, venison, and skins, to welcome William Penn. When the whites began to settle around them, Penn assigned them a residence on the manor of Conestoga. (Day's Historical Collections.)

the president [Beissel] lived with some hermits. And now, when all hermits were called in, I also quitted my solitude, and changed the same for a monastic life; which was judged to be more inservient to sanctification than the life of a hermit, where many under a pretence of holiness did nothing but nourish their own selfishness. . . . We were now, by necessity, compelled to learn obedience. . . . At that time, works of charity hath been our chief occupation.*

"Canestogues was then a great wilderness, and began to be settled by poor Germans, which desired our assistance in building houses for them; which not only kept us employed several summers in hard carpenter's work, but also increased our poverty so much that we wanted even things necessary for life."

He also says, "When we settled here, our number was forty brethren, and about so many sisters, all in the vigor and prime of their ages, never before wearied of social life, but were compelled, . . . with reluctance of our nature, to select this life."†

---

* When this letter was written, Miller was about eighty years old. He doubtless spoke German during the sixty years that he lived at Ephrata, as well as before that time. It will be observed that he does not write English elegantly.

† In the year 1740, says Fahnestock, there were thirty-six single brethren in the cloisters, and thirty-five sisters; and at one time the society, including the members living in the neighborhood, numbered nearly three hundred.

Rev. C. Endress says that some were anxious to retain the solitary life, and some (it appears) were opposed to giving to Beissel the title of Father. Sangmeister left the society and retired to Virginia (whence, however, he returned to Ephrata). "His book," says the same writer, "is much tainted with bitterness,

It was, it seems, about the same time that Miller was baptized that the midnight meetings were held at the camp, "for the purpose of awaiting the coming of judgment."

Not long after the building of the meeting-house called Kedar (says Endress), a widower, Sigmund Lambert, having joined the camp, built out of his own means an addition to the meeting-house and a dwelling for Beissel. Another gave all his property to the society, and now Kedar was transformed into a sister-convent, and a new meeting-house was erected.

Soon after 1738 a large house for the brethren was built, called Zion, and the whole camp was named Ephrata.* The solitary life was changed into the conventual one ; Zion was called a kloster, or convent, and put under monastic rules. Onesimus (Eckerlin) was appointed prior, and Conrad Beissel named father. (His general title appears to be *vorsteher*, superintendent or principal.)

It was probably about this time, or earlier, that the constable entered the camp, according to Miller, and demanded the single man's tax. Some paid, but some refused. Miller says that some claimed personal immunity on the ground that they were not inferior to the monks and hermits in the Eastern country, who supplied the prisons in Alexandria with bread, and who were

---

and undertakes to cast a dark shade upon the whole establishment."

* Larger accommodations were afterward built in the meadow below ; a sister-house, called Saron, a brother-house, named Bethania, etc. Most of these are still standing, I believe, in 1882; but the former buildings on the hill long since disappeared.

declared free of taxes by Theodosius the Great and other emperors. But these Ephrata brethren were not to be thus exempted. Six lay in prison at Lancaster ten days, when they were released on bail of a "venerable old justice of peace." When the brethren appeared before the board of assessment, the gentlemen who were their judges saw six men who in the prime of their ages had been reduced to skeletons by penitential works. The gentlemen granted them their freedom on condition that they should be taxed as one family for their real estate, " which is still in force (1790), although these things happened fifty years ago." (See Miller's letters in Hazard's Register.)

A monastic dress was adopted by the brethren and sisters, resembling that of the Capuchins.*

The Chronicle, published in 1786, speaks of the sisters as having carefully maintained the dress of the order for nearly fifty years. About the same date we read of Miller in his cowl.

It appears from the Chronicle that the other members of the society at one time adopted a similar dress, but

---

* The Ephrata Chronicle speaks nearly in this manner of that of the sisters :

Their dress was ordered, like that of the brethren, so that little was to be seen of the disagreeable human figure (*von dem verdriesslichen Bild das durch die Sünd ist offenbar worden*). They wore caps like the brethren, but not pointed ones. While at work these caps or cowls hung down their backs ; but when they saw anybody, they drew them over their heads, so that but little could be seen of their faces. But the principal token of their spiritual betrothal was a great veil, which in front covered them altogether, and behind down to the girdle. Roman Catholics who saw this garment said that it resembled the habit of the scapular.

that the celibates (*die Einsamen*) appeared at worship in white dresses, and the other members (*die Hausstände*) in gray ones. The secular members, however, "saddled themselves again" and conformed to the world in clothing and in other things.

In an article upon Ephrata in Hazard's Register, vol. v., 1830, will be found the statement that, thirty or forty years before, the Dunkers were occasionally noticed in Philadelphia (when they came down with produce), with long beards and Capuchin habiliments; but this statement does not seem to agree in date with that of the Chronicle, if these were secular brethren.

Among the austerities practised at Ephrata formerly, was sleeping upon a bench with a block of wood for a pillow.*

The late Dr. William Fahnestock tells us that these and other austerities were not intended for penance, but were undertaken from economy. Their circumstances were very restricted, and their undertaking was great. They studied the strictest simplicity and economy. For the Communion they used wooden flagons, goblets, and trays. The plates from which they ate were thin octagonal pieces of poplar board, their forks and candlesticks were of wood, and every article that could be made of that substance was used by the whole community.

Rupp says that the chimneys, which remain in use to

---

* The Chronicle tells us that once, in Beissel's absence, a costly feather bed was brought into his sleeping-room. He made use of it one night, but sent it away afterward,—and not even in dying could be brought to give up the sleeping-bench (*die Schlafbanck*).

this day (1844), are of wood; and the attention of the present writer was called in 1872 to wooden door-hinges.

Rupp says also that they all observed great abstemiousness in their diet; they were vegetarians, and submitted to many privations and to a rigid discipline exerted over them by a somewhat austere spiritual father. Peter Miller himself says that he stood under Beissel's direction for thirty years, and that it was as severe as any related in the Romish Church (but this sounds exaggerated).

In the brother- and sister-houses, it has been stated that six dormitories surrounded a common room in which the members of each subdivision pursued their respective employments. "Each dormitory was hardly large enough to contain a cot, a closet, and an hour-glass." *

Of the industries established at Ephrata, one of Peter Miller's letters gives us a good idea. He complains, as before mentioned, of Eckerlin's obliging them to interfere so far in worldly things, and that money was put out at interest. He adds that they erected a grist-mill, with three pairs of stones; a saw-mill, paper-mill, oil-mill,

---

* In "Carey's Museum" for 1789, will be found a letter from a British officer to the editor of the *Edinburgh Magazine*, whence it appears that at that time, 1786, a rug was laid upon the sleeping-bench. The writer says that each brother had a cell, with a closet adjoining; that the smallness of the rooms was very disagreeable, and that they were not clean. The churches were clean and neat, but perfectly unadorned, except by some German texts. The house "occupied by the nuns" was uniformly clean, and the cells were in excellent order. (Some of the statements of this writer appear very loose.)

and fulling-mill; had besides three wagons with proper teams, a printing-office, and sundry other trades.

He adds, "Our president [by whom he means Beissel] never meddled with temporal things."

Mr. Rupp (who cites the Life of Rittenhouse) says that the women were employed in spinning, knitting, sewing, making paper lanterns and other toys. A room was set apart for ornamental writing, called "Das Schreibzimmer," and "several sisters," it has been said, devoted their whole attention to this labor, as well as to transcribing the writings of the founder of the society; thus multiplying copies before they had a press. But the press appears to have been early established, and it was the second German one in our State. It has been stated that Miller was at one time the printer.*

Among the books published at Ephrata were some of Beissel's, who had adopted the name of Peaceful (*Friedsam*). One of their publications was a collection of hymns, and was entitled "The Song of the Solitary and Abandoned Turtle Dove, namely, the Christian Church, . . . by a Peaceful Pilgrim travelling towards Quiet Eternity." Ephrata, from the press of the Fraternity, 1747. 500 pages, quarto.†

---

* At Ephrata, in the winter of 1872, I was told that Miller was once met, as he was taking a load of paper from the mill to the press, by a certain man named Widman. This Widman, according to tradition, had been a vestryman in Miller's former church. " Is this the way they treat you," said Widman, "harnessing you up to a wheelbarrow ?" and he spat in Miller's face.

Allusion will be made hereafter to the traditionary tale of Miller and Widman.

† Of one of the collections of hymns published at Ephrata, Fahnestock says that four hundred and forty-one were written

Beissel also wrote a dissertation on man's fall, of which Miller says (1790), "When, in the late war, a marquis from Milan, in Italy, lodged a night in our convent, I presented to him the said dissertation, and desired him to publish it at home, and dedicate it to his Holiness."

In 1748, a stupendous book was published by the society at Ephrata. It is the Martyr's Mirror, in folio, of which copies may be seen at the libraries of the Pennsylvania Historical Society, and of the German Society, in Philadelphia.

The Chronicon Ephratense, or Ephrata Chronicle, so often alluded to in this article, was also from their press, but was published thirty-eight years later. It contains the life of Beissel, under the title of the venerable "Father in Christ, Peaceful Godright (*Friedsam Gott-recht*), late founder and *vorsteher* of the Spiritual Order of the Solitary (*Einsamen*) in Ephrata, collected by Brothers Lamech and Agrippa." I have heard of several copies being still extant,—one in Lancaster County, one in Montgomery, and one in the library of the Historical Society at Philadelphia. The last I have been allowed to consult.

In speaking of the occupations practised at Ephrata, it may be permitted to include music. Beissel is said to have been an excellent musician and composer. "There was another transcribing-room," says Fahnestock, "appropriated to copying music. Hundreds of volumes,

by Beissel, seventy-three by the brethren in the cloister, one hundred by the single sisters, and one hundred and twelve by the out-door members. Endress speaks in unfavorable terms of the literary merits of some of the Ephrata hymns.

each containing five or six hundred pieces, were transferred from book to book, with as much accuracy, and almost as much neatness, as if done with the graver." In composing music, Beissel is said to have taken his style from nature. "The singing is the Æolian harp harmonized. . . . Their music is set in four, six, and eight parts."

Morgan Edwards* (as cited in Day's Historical Collections) says, "Their singing is charming,—partly owing to the pleasantness of their voices, the variety of parts they carry on together, and the devout manner of performance." This style of singing is said by Rupp (1844) to be entirely lost at Ephrata, but to be preserved in a measure at Snow Hill, in Franklin County. Fahnestock, who was himself a Seventh-Day Baptist (or *Siebtaeger*), gives a very enthusiastic account of the singing at Snow Hill. It may be found in Day's Historical Collections, article "Franklin County."†

In addition to the various industries which claimed the attention of the community, there must not be forgotten the care of their landed estate. It has been said that they bought about two hundred and fifty acres of land.‡

---

* "Materials towards a History of the American Baptists." 1770.

· † Dr. Fahnestock resided for a while in the latter part of his life in the sister-house, at Ephrata. Here Mr. Rupp, the historian, visited him. Rev. Mr. Shrigley, librarian of the Pennsylvania Historical Society, who visited Ephrata, has spoken to me of Fahnestock's venerable appearance.

‡ In after-years they seem to have been much troubled by litigation. Dr. Fahnestock says that they considered contention with arms, and at law, unchristian ; but that they unfortunately had to defend themselves often in courts of justice. To set an example of

A very large tract was once offered to them by one of the Penns, but they refused it. I was told at Ephrata that they were " afraid they would get too vain."

Count Zinzendorf, the celebrated Moravian bishop, came to Pennsylvania in 1741. At one time he visited Ephrata, and was entertained in the convent, where his friendly behavior was very agreeable to the brothers. (We may suppose that Miller, and Eckerlin, who was not yet deposed, were men fit to entertain him.) He also expressed a wish to see Beissel. This was made known to the latter, who answered, after a little reflection, that Zinzendorf was no wonder to him, but if he himself were a wonder to Zinzendorf, he must come to him (or as it seems, to Beissel's own house). Zinzendorf was now in doubt what to do, but he turned away and left without seeing the father (*vorsteher*). The Chronicle adds that thus did two great lights of the church meet as on the threshold, and yet neither ever saw the other in his life.

The Moravians also erected brother- and sister-houses, but they were not monastic institutions.*

---

forbearance and Christian meekness, they suffered themselves for a long time to be plundered, until forbearance was no longer a virtue. He says (Hazard's Register, 1835) that the society is just escaping from heavy embarrassments which they incurred in defending themselves from the aggressions of their neighbors. The British officer, whose statement was published as. early as 1789, speaks of Peter Miller as often engaged in litigation.

In a recent work (Belcher's History of Religious Denominations, 1854), the Seventh-Day Baptists at Ephrata are said to possess about one hundred and forty acres.

* Morgan Edwards, in speaking of the recluses at Ephrata, says that they took the vow of celibacy. But, as so many of our Ger-

Dissension arose at one time between some of the brethren of the Ephrata Society and Count Zinzendorf, at a conference held by the latter at Oley, now in Berks County. Zinzendorf seems to have desired to unite some of the sects with which Pennsylvania was so abundantly supplied. But the solitary brethren (of Ephrata) were so suspicious of the thing that they would no longer unite with it. They had prepared a writing upon marriage, how far it is from God, and that it was only a praiseworthy ordinance of nature. This they presented, whereupon there arose a violent conflict in words.

The ordinarius (Zinzendorf) said that he was by no means pleased with this paper; his marriage had not such a beginning; his marriage stood higher than the solitary life in Ephrata. The Ephrata delegates strove to make all right again, and spoke of families in their society who had many children.*

But Zinzendorf left his seat as chairman, . . . and at last the conference came to an end, all present being displeased.†

---

man Baptists are opposed to oaths, I presume that they did not. "Teach, by example, that a promise is truly an oath," says a late Pennsylvania paper.

* Somewhat altered from the original.

† A writer in the Chronicle speaks of being at one of the count's conferences, where there were Mennonites, Separatists, and Baptists. But when he came home, he told the *vorsteher* that he regarded the count's conference as a snare to bring simple awakened souls again into infant-baptism and church-going. Then they held a council, and resolved to have a yearly conference of their own.

The above expression—infant-baptism and church-going—

About this date (or about 1740) took place the formation of the Sabbath-school, by Ludwig Hoecker, called Brother Obed.* He was a teacher in the secular school at Ephrata,—a school which seems to have enjoyed considerable reputation. The Sabbath-school (held on Saturday afternoon) is said to have been kept up over thirty years. This was begun long before the present Sunday-school system was introduced by Robert Raikes. (American Cyclopædia, article *Dunkers*.)

Not long after the visit of Zinzendorf, or about 1745, occurred the deposition of Eckerlin, the prior Onesimus. In one of his letters, Miller says (1790), " Remember, we have lost our first prior and the sisters their first mother . . . because they stood in self-elevation, and did govern despotically ;" and adds, " the desire to govern is the last thing which dies within a man." (It seems probable that Eckerlin has not received sufficient credit, however, for the pecuniary success of the infant community.)

Some ten years after his deposition (or in 1755), began the old French and Indian war. Fahnestock tells us that the doors of the cloister, including the

---

sounds so much like the account of the Baptist or Anabaptist persecutions narrated in the Martyr-book, that we might almost conclude that the Dunkers had a direct connection with the Anabaptists, instead of originating among the Pietists. But it will be remembered that the Ephrata Dunkers had printed an edition of the great Martyr-book, and it is most probable that some of them were familiar with it. Still, there may have been among the Pietists some who were or had been Baptists.

* Near the close of this sketch mention is made of " Hoeckers a Creveld." Perhaps Ludwig belonged to the same family.

chapels, etc., were opened as a refuge for the inhabitants of Tulpehocken and Paxton * settlements, which were then the frontiers, to protect the people from the incursions of the hostile Indians. He adds that all these refugees were received and kept by the society during the period of alarm and danger. Upon hearing of which, a company of infantry was despatched by the royal government from Philadelphia to protect Ephrata.†

But why, we might ask, did these people seek refuge in a communion of non-combatants? The question bears on the controversy, as to whether the men of peace or the men of war were nearer right in their dealings with the savages.‡

---

* Paxton township is now in Dauphin County. The Paxton church was three miles east of Harrisburg.

† The Ephrata Chronicle says that, as the enemy approached (the Indians came within thirteen miles of Ephrata), many persons sought refuge in the cloister, with those who were themselves in need of protection. As reports of murders reached Ephrata day after day, the celibates (*Einsamen*) became despondent, and even the leader turned pale,—a thing that had never been witnessed before. When danger was so imminent, the fathers proposed to take the sisters away on wagons to a safer place. It was then that Beissel received by night a divine revelation to the effect that no *Einsamer* should perish by the hands of the Indians.

Accordingly they remained at their station, and it really turned out as Beissel had predicted. The people who took refuge in the monastery probably stayed at Ephrata, not with a view of finding protection behind the wooden walls of the cloister, but for the sake of shelter and support. The statement that the government sent a company of soldiers for the protection of Ephrata seems to be verified by the mention in the Chronicle of *Rothröcke* or Redcoats.

‡ The Mennonites and Quakers were peaceably disposed towards the Indians, but the Presbyterians from the north of Ireland, who

Beissel died in the year 1768, or about thirty years after the establishment of the cloister. Upon his tombstone was placed, in German, this inscription :

" Here rests a Birth of the love of God, Peaceful, a Solitary, but who afterward became a Superintendent of the Solitary Community of Christ in and around Ephrata : born in Oberbach in the Palatinate, and named Conrad Beissel.

" He fell asleep the 6th of July, A.D. 1768 : of his spiritual life 52, but of his natural one, 77 years and 4 months."

Endress says, " He appears to me to have been a man possessed of a considerable degree of the spirit of rule ; his mind bent from the beginning upon the acquirement of authority, power, and ascendency." For ourselves, we have just seen how he received Count Zinzendorf, who had crossed the ocean, and come, as it were, to his threshold.

Mr. Endress further says, " Beissel, good or bad, lived and died the master-spirit of the brotherhood. With him it sank into decay."

The British officer who wrote in 1786 (?), eighteen years after Beissel's death, gives the number of the cel-

---

had settled at Paxton, felt a deadly animosity against them, and, as Day says, against the peaceful Moravians and Quakers, who wished to protect the Indians, at the expense, as the Paxton men thought, of the lives of the settlers. The Paxton rangers were commanded by the Presbyterian minister, the Rev. Colonel Elder, who seems to have opposed the massacre of the Indians at Lancaster by the " Paxton boys." Day says that no historian ought to excuse or justify the murders at Lancaster and Conestoga, and adds that they must ever remain dark and bloody spots in our provincial history.

ibates as seven men and five women. I do not consider him good authority; but if the numbers were so much reduced from those of 1740, it seems probable that they had begun to decline before the decease of Beissel.*

Eighteen years after Beissel's death, was published at Ephrata the Chronicle of which I have so often spoken, giving an account of his life. He was succeeded by Peter Miller. Miller was sixty-five years old when our Revolutionary war broke out, and had been the leader at Ephrata seven years.

Fahnestock says that after the battle of Brandywine "the whole establishment was opened to receive the wounded Americans, great numbers of whom (Rupp says four or five hundred) were brought here in wagons a distance of more than forty miles, and one hundred and fifty of whom died and are buried on Mount Zion."†

It is also narrated that before the battle of Germantown a quantity of unbound books were seized at Ephrata by some of our soldiers, in order to make cartridges. "An embargo," says Miller, "was laid on all our printed paper, so that for a time we could not sell any printed book."

A story has appeared in print, and not always in the same manner, about Miller's going to General Washington and receiving from him a pardon for his old enemy Widman, who was condemned to die.

This story Mr. Rupp thinks is based upon tradition;

---

* See Carey's "American Museum."

† An insignificant hill overlooking the meadow where the brother- and sister-houses now stand.

one version has been told in a glowing manner, and is attributed to Dr. Fahnestock. It runs thus: On the breaking out of the Revolution, committees of safety were formed in different districts to support our cause. At the head of the Lancaster County Committee was Michael Widman, who kept a public house, and who had been a vestryman in the Reformed Church. This church Miller had left when he joined the Baptists. He persecuted Miller to a shameful extent, even spitting in his face when he met him.

Widman was at first bold and active in the cause of independence, but he became discouraged, and resolved to go to Philadelphia and conciliate General Howe, the British commander, who then held that city. Howe, however, declined his services,* but gave orders to see him safely beyond the British outposts. His treasonable intentions having become known to the Americans, he was arrested and taken to the nearest block-house, at the Turk's Head, now West Chester; was tried by court-martial, and sentenced to be hung. Peter Miller, hearing of his arrest, went to General Washington and pleaded for mercy towards him. The general answered that the state of public affairs was such as to make it necessary that renegades should suffer, "otherwise I should most cheerfully release your friend."

"Friend!" exclaimed Miller: "he is my worst enemy,—my incessant reviler." †

Said the general, "My dear friend, I thank you for this example of Christian charity!" and he granted Miller's petition.

---

* A remarkable statement.

† Compare this inflated language with Miller's letter, as quoted.

It is not necessary for me to go further, and describe the scene of Miller's arriving upon the ground with the pardon just as Widman was to be hung, nor the subsequent proceedings there, for I am quite sure that they did not take place. Evidence to this effect is found in the Pennsylvania Archives, vol. ix., where Peter Miller writes to Secretary Matlack, interceding (apparently) for a man named Rein. Miller says, " I have thought his case was similar to Michael Wittman's, who received pardon without a previous trial."

The secretary replies (1781), " Witman did not receive a pardon previous to a surrender."

Thus it seems that the story of Widman's trial by court-martial is also wrong. That his property was confiscated, as I was lately told at Ephrata, I have no reason to doubt, as the Colonial Records, vol. xii., show that in council, in 1779, it was resolved that the agents for forfeited estates should sell that of Michael Wittman, subject to a certain claim.*

At Ephrata, during the past winter, I stood in the loft of the brother-house beside a great chimney of wood and clay, and was told that here Widman had been hidden. Whether he actually concealed himself in the brother-house, as has been narrated, I do not find that history declares.

At a subsequent date, 1783, we find in the Pennsylvania Archives, vol. ix., that Miller intercedes for certain Mennonites who had been fined for not apprehend-

---

* The different modes of spelling what appears to be the same name will not surprise those who are familiar with our Pennsylvania German names.

ing British deserters; the Mennonites not being permitted by their principles to do so. Does this mean deserters from ourselves to the British,—who were, as deserters, liable to the punishment of death? a punishment which the Mennonites, as non-resistants, could not inflict.

Certain letters of Peter Miller, published in Hazard's Register, and of which I have made considerable use, were written at an advanced age,—eighty or thereabout. He says in one of them (December, 1790), "Age, infirmity, and defect in sight are causes that the letter wants more perspicuity, for which I beg pardon."

He died about six years after, having lived some sixty years a member of the community at Ephrata. Upon his tombstone was placed this inscription in German:

"Here lies buried Peter Miller, born in Oberampt Lautern, in the Palatinate (Chur-Pfalz); came as a Reformed preacher to America in the year 1730; was baptized by the Community at Ephrata in the year 1735, and named Brother Jaebez; also he was afterward a preacher (*Lehrer*) until his end. He fell asleep the 25th of September, 1796, at the age of eighty-six years and nine months."

In the plain upon the banks of the Cocalico still stand the brother- and sister-houses (although not the buildings first erected). But the society is feeble in numbers, and the buildings are going to decay. They are still, however, occupied, or partly so. I found several women living here in 1872. Some of these were never married, but the majority are widows; and not all of them members of the Baptist congregation. Nor are the voices of children wanting.

The last celibate brother died some forty years ago.

One, indeed, has been here since, but, as I was told, "he did not like it," and went to the more flourishing community of Snow Hill, in Franklin County.

The little Ephrata association (which still owns a farm), instead of supporting its unmarried members, now furnishes to them only house-rent, fuel, and flour. The printing-press long since ceased from its labors, and many of the other industrial pursuits have declined.

No longer do the unmarried or celibate members own all the property, but it is now vested in all who belong to the meeting, single and married, and is in the hands of trustees. The income is, I presume, but small.

The unmarried members wear our usual dress, and none are strictly recluse.

Formerly a large room or chapel was connected with the brother-house. It was furnished with galleries, where sat the sisters, while the brethren occupied the floor below. (This building, I am told, is not standing.) In the smaller room or chapel (*saal*) connected with the sister-house, about twenty people now meet on the Seventh day for public worship. But among all these changes the German language still remains! All the services that I heard, while attending here in February of 1872, were in that tongue, except two hymns at the close. We must not suppose that this language is employed because the members are natives of Germany. One or two may be, but the preacher's father or grandfather came to this country when a boy.

Around the meeting-room are hung charts or sheets of grayish paper, containing German verses in ornamental writing, the ancient labors of the celibates, or perhaps of the sisters alone. One small chart here is said to represent the three heavens, and to contain three hundred figures in Capuchin dress, with harps in their hands, and two hundred archangels. Perhaps this and their celibate doctrine are drawn, at least in part, from the opening of chapter xiv. of the book called the Revelation of John.

But for these old labors in pen and ink, the chapel is as plain as a Quaker meeting-house. It is kept beautifully clean.* Opening out of it is a kitchen, furnished with the apparatus for cooking and serving the simple repasts of the love-feasts. Among these Baptists, love-feasts are held not only, as I understand, in a similar manner to the other Dunkers, but upon funeral occasions, —a short period after the interment of a brother or sister. Rupp speaks of their eating lamb and mutton at their paschal feasts. In the old monastic time, it was only at love-feasts that the celibate brothers and sisters met.

Here I was shown a wooden goblet made by the brethren for the Communion. It has been said that they preferred to use such, even after more costly ones had been given to them.

After attending the religious services in the chapel, three or four of us—strangers—were supplied with dinner in the brother-house, at a neat and well-filled table.†

---

* It may be observed how nearly this description of the chapel agrees with that given by the British officer of the one he visited here some eighty-five years ago.

† Fahnestock says that, like some dilapidated castles, Ephrata yet contains many habitable and comfortable apartments. The brother- and sister-houses, etc., form but a small part of the modern village of Ephrata. He wrote some time ago.

I afterward sat for an hour in the neat and comfortable apartment of Sister Sarah in the sister-house. Here she has lived twenty-two years, and, though now much advanced in life, has not that appearance. She seemed lovely, and, I was told, had not been unsought. One of her brothers has been thirty-three years at the Snow Hill community.

Sister Sarah produced for me a white cotton over-dress, such as was formerly worn by the sisters. It was a cap or cowl, with long pieces hanging down in front and behind nearly to the feet; and, if I remember it right, not of the pattern described in the Chronicle. But fashions change in fifty to a hundred years.

She also showed me some verses recently written by one of the brethren at Snow Hill. They were in German, of which I offer an unrhymed version:

> " Oh divine life, ornament of virginity !
>   How art thou despised by all men here below !
>   And yet art a branch from the heavenly throne,
>   And borne by the virgin Son of God."

I was surprised to find such prominence given to the idea of the merits of celibacy, for I had not then seen the *Chronicon Ephratense.*

One object which especially attracted my attention was an upright clock, which stood in the room of Sister Sarah, and which was kept in very good order. It was somewhat smaller than the high clocks that were common forty or fifty years ago.

All that I heard of its history was that it had come from Germany. It had four weights suspended on chains. Above the dial-plate hovered two little angels, apparently made of lead, one on either side of a small disk, which bore the inscription " Hoeckers a Creveld," —as I interpret, made by the Hoeckers at Crefeld. Crefeld,—historic town! Here then was a relic of it, and standing quite disregarded,—it was only an old German clock!

When the Dunkers were persecuted in Europe, soon after their establishment, some of them took refuge in Crefeld, in the duchy of Cleves; and I have lately read that in Crefeld, Mühlheim, etc., William Penn and others gained adherents to the doctrine of the Quakers.*

We also find in the American Cyclopædia that at Crefeld (Ger. *Krefeld*), a colony of Huguenot refugees in the seventeenth century introduced the manufacture of silk—Dunkers and Quakers; perhaps also Huguenots fleeing from France when Louis XIV. revoked that edict of Nantes which had so long protected them. (Crefeld is now in Rhenish Prussia.)

Who were the Hoeckers, or who was the Hoecker that made this old clock?† Who bought it in historic Crefeld? Who brought it from Europe, got it up into Lancaster County, and lodged it in the monastery or nunnery at Ephrata? What, if anything, had Ludwig Hoecker or Brother Obed to do with it—he who taught the early Sabbath-school? What tales could it not tell! But it is well cared for in the comfortable apartment of the kindly sister.

The Snow Hill settlement, I presume, is named from

---

* See article " Francis Daniel Pastorius," by Dr. Seidensticker, in the *Penn Monthly*, January and February, 1872.

† The name Hacker, still heard at Ephrata, is doubtless the same as the above.

the family of Snowberger,* one of whom endowed the society. It is situated on the Antietam, in Franklin County, Pennsylvania; where a large farm belongs to "the nunnery" (an expression that I heard at Ephrata). There were, until lately, five sisters and four brothers at Antietam, but one of the brethren has died.

The brethren have sufficient occupation in taking care of their property; the sisters keep house, eating in the same apartment at the same time with the brothers. Under these circumstances I could imagine the comfort and order of the establishment, and think of the brothers and sisters meeting in a cool and shaded dining-room. What question then should I be likely to ask? This one: "Do they never marry?"

I was told that marriages of the brothers and sisters (celibates) are not unknown; but I also understood that such a thing is considered backsliding. Persons thus married remain members of the church, but must leave the community, and find support elsewhere.†

In an article by Redmond Conyngham (Hazard's Register, vol. v.) will be found the statement that the

---

* *Schneeberger*, or people of Snow Hill?

† Mr. Endress tells us that with many of the single brethren and sisters at Ephrata, the mystical idea of the union with Christ was evidently used to gratify one of the strongest natural affections of the human heart. "The Redeemer was their bridegroom or bride. . . . He was the little infant they carried under their hearts, the dear little lamb they dandled on their laps."

He adds that this at least was found much more among the single than among those whose affections were consecrated in a conjugal life. "The powers of human nature would evince their authority." "According to Sangmeister, some sank under the unceasing struggle." See Hazard's Register, 1830.

" President of the Dunkers" says, " We deny eternal punishment; those souls who become sensible of God's great goodness and clemency, and acknowledge his lawful authority, . . . and that Christ is the only true Son of God, are received into happiness; but those who continue obstinate are kept in darkness until the great day, when light will make all happy." According to Dr. Fahnestock, however, the idea of a universal restoration, which existed in the early days, is not now publicly taught.

The observance of the Seventh day as a sabbath must always be onerous, in a community like ours. Hired people are not required by the Siebentaeger (or Seventh-Day men) to work on Saturday; and, unless of their own persuasion, will not work on Sunday.

It has been said that the customs at Ephrata resembled the Judaic ones; and Endress says that they consider baptism similar to purification in the Mosaic law,—as a rite which may be repeated from time to time when the believer has become defiled by the world, and would again renew his union with Christ. But Miller says (1790), " Our standard is the New Testament." *

Fahnestock says that they do not approve of paying their ministers; and it seems that the women, or at least the single sisters, are at liberty to speak in religious meetings.

In the correspondence of one of our Lancaster papers of 1871, there was given the following account: " Ephrata, May 21.—The Society of the Seventh-Day Baptists

---

* Upon this subject of the New Testament as a creed, etc., all or nearly all our German Baptist sects seem to unite.

held their semi-annual love-feast yesterday, when one new member was added to the society by immersion. In the evening the solemn feast of the Lord's Supper was celebrated, the occasion attracting a large concourse of people,—only about half of whom could obtain seats. The conduct of a number of persons on the outside was a disgrace to an intelligent community."

The article also mentions preachers as present from Bedford, Franklin, and Somerset Counties. However, the whole number of the Seventh-Day German Baptists, in our State, is very small.

The foregoing article is published nearly as it appeared in the second edition of this volume. In the present year, 1882, Mr. Adam Konigmacher Fahnestock, of Harrisburg, Pennsylvania, has lent me a little memorial which he had prepared of his own family. A passage in it seems to elucidate the history of the clock at Ephrata, which bears on its face " Hoeckers a Creveld." On St. John's day, November 13, 1753, Diedrich Fanestuck writes to his brother in Prussia. (The letter is said to have been written near Ephrata.) He writes that his son, who is going to Europe, will stop at Crefeld, " where he is to have some clocks made for us." He adds, " I pray you to write again. You may send the letters to Crefeld, there are three brothers living there, Wilhelmus, Christophorus, and Lucas Heckers, to them you might send them."

In a foot-note A. K. Fahnestock says, 1878, October 17 : " I had the pleasure this day of seeing one of those clocks (seven feet high), still showing the time of day. It is in the 'sister-house' at Ephrata." (The preposition *a* on the clock, Hoeckers a Creveld, would seem to indicate that the Hoeckers were French refugees. Perhaps with a translated name.)

In this year, 1882, the writer of this volume again visited Ephrata. One of her acquaintance spoke to her of the community at Snow Hill, on the Antietam. She said, "It's a large nunnery, and the rooms are all empty; there's hardly any one there." She added, however, that there are a good many married Seventh-Day Baptists at Snow Hill.

The old buildings at Ephrata, the brother- and sister-house, are still kept in sufficient repair to make inmates comfortable, and are occupied by unmarried women, widows, and families; not all Seventh-Day Baptists. The farm belonging to the Baptists contains about eighty acres.

As I drew near one of these buildings on Sunday, I saw washed clothes hanging out. Saturday is the Sabbath of these Baptists, and like the rest of the world it appears that such begin their week with washing.

The little community at the time of my visit was grievously exercised over a lawsuit among the members. The matter had been referred to a master in chancery, who thus speaks of them in his report: "At the time of the commencement of the differences from which has sprung the present controversy, and for some years previously, the members of the society in regular attendance at its meetings, and habitually observant of its religious ordinances, were in number about thirty, of whom not less than three-fourths appear to have been women. They seem to be an uneducated or but slightly educated people, in narrow circumstances as to property, the male members being in general mechanics and laboring men, resident in and about the village of Ephrata, in this county, and a considerable proportion of all the members, male as well as female, being dependent for subsistence either wholly or partially upon the funds of the society. They do not appear to have formulated specifically articles of faith or rules of discipline, but profess to take for their guidance simply the Bible and New Testament, and the distinctive features of their practice are, their observance of the seventh day of the week instead of the first as the Sabbath; the administration of the rite of baptism by trine immersion, with forward action, in a stream of flowing water; and by the love-feasts held annually at their communion, and lasting from Friday evening until Sunday morning, at which food is provided for all members, as well as all strangers who may choose to attend the meeting; and by the washing of each other's feet by the members, previously to the breaking of bread at the communion. . . . The church at Ephrata, it should be mentioned, is one of four branches, as they are called, of the society of [German?] Seventh-Day Baptists. The other three being established, respectively, at Snow Hill, Bedford, and Alleghany, in this State."

BETHLEHEM AND THE MORAVIANS.

On August 22, 1873, as I stood upon the tower of Packer Hall, Lehigh University, I saw spread out before me the whole of Bethlehem, with furnaces, railroads, bridges, churches, schools; and the rolling country and cultivated fields of Northampton and Lehigh Counties. Pointing to a wooded hill, my little guide said, " That is Iron Hill, where iron ore comes from."*

In the first house built at Bethlehem, on the 24th of December, 1741, Zinzendorf and his companions celebrated their first Christmas Eve in America. I saw in the town a picture, by Grünewald, of the house in which they met,—a long, one-story log house, with overhanging eaves, the unbroken forest behind admirably expressing the loneliness of the situation. In the beginning, one end of this building was for cattle, as in Switzerland and other parts of South Germany.

When this first house was newly erected, Zinzendorf visited it, and on Christmas Eve he went with others into the stable and sang,—

> " Nicht aus Jerusalem, sondern Bethlehem
> Aus dem kommt, was mir frommt."

or, in prose,

---

* This article now appears nearly as it was published in the second edition of this work, issued several years ago.

"That which is profitable to me comes not from Jerusalem, but from Bethlehem,"—

and thus the new-born *town* was named Bethlehem.

" The material treasures of the Lehigh valley," says a Moravian bishop, " the national rage of hastening to be rich, will, I fear, too much overgrow the spiritual interests of the people."

Since Zinzendorf entered the log cabin of Bethlehem one hundred and thirty years have passed by, and four or five generations of mortal men. Other changes too have befallen the Moravians. For twenty years they lived in an *economie,* or associated like one family. That strict rule, which afterwards kept the unmarried in brother- and sister-houses, has since been annulled, and no vestige of it remains here but in the custom of sitting in church, the brethren on one side, and the sisters on the other. And this is not universal: families sit together.

In like manner has disappeared here the custom of appealing to the lot, which formerly prevailed even in matters so solemn as marriage.*

The plainness of apparel which distinguished the Moravians has disappeared also. Once even the young ladies who studied at the boarding-school were obliged to wear the peculiar Moravian dress.

In the Historical Collection at Nazareth are preserved thick muslin caps, such as the women once wore, with

---

* The general use of the lot was abrogated in 1817. Although marriage by lot is no longer obligatory, yet a Moravian gentleman has told me that this manner of decision is still resorted to,— and frequently in Europe. Bishops are usually appointed by lot.

peculiar pieces, like a scallop shell, to cover the ears. Those tasteful little caps now worn by the young women in the choir, and the neat ones worn by the sisters who serve at the love-feasts, can scarcely keep up the memory of those of olden time.

Once the Moravians did not take oaths, but obeyed literally the command, " Swear not at all;" but now judicial oaths are permitted.

Formerly, the bulk of the real estate belonged to the church, and none could buy who were not members; but this rule has been broken, and *foreigners* have been allowed to buy land in Bethlehem and other Moravian towns.*

One trait, which has hitherto remarkably distinguished them, still exists, namely, a great missionary zeal. In 1873 a gentleman gave the numbers of the Moravians at seventy thousand baptized missionary converts, to twenty-three thousand home members in Europe and America. On this estimate the missionary converts are more than three to each of the members in the other lands.†

---

* The *lease system*, so called, was abolished in 1844. The Moravian communities abroad, especially upon the continent of Europe, are close communities, no one being allowed to buy of their lands who is not a member of the Moravian Church. They retain more plainness of dress in Saxony and Prussia, and even in Great Britain, than prevails in America. There the women all wear caps in religious services.

† The heavy expense entailed by enterprises so great does not fall entirely upon the Church. The Mission Report of 1872, in speaking of Australia, mentions that the missionaries are cheered by the sympathy and aid of Christians of different denominations; and adds that the mission has sustained a loss in the death of the

At Bethlehem a considerable landed estate belongs to the Church, whence is drawn an income of about eighteen thousand dollars. All the institutions of learning here, including the Young Ladies' Boarding-School, belong to the Church, and the teachers are its salaried officers.

The different provinces of the Church, the American, English, and German, are like separate States of our Union, their general head meeting or residing in Saxony. This general synod still, in some respects, gives rules to our Pennsylvania Moravians; and one of the bishops says that the Moravian is the only Protestant Church which is a unity throughout the world.

FESTIVALS.

My first visit to Bethlehem occurred at Whitsuntide, —Whitsunday or Pentecost falling upon June 1. As early as half-past seven there was music from the steeple of the large Moravian church, from a choir of trombone players. This instrument, which is of the trumpet kind, is much in use among the Moravians for church music,* the choir generally consisting of four pieces.

In the morning I went to the large church, in which English services are held. In this church there were no pews, or rather, there were " open pews" without doors.

Rev. Mr. Mackie, of the Presbyterian Church, in Melbourne. The *Moravian Manual* also speaks of missions that are self-supporting, and of missionaries who labor, like Paul, for their own support.

* Its use is taught it seems even to barbarians, for the Mission Report, in speaking of an Esquimaux church, says, "The corner-stone was solemnly laid, when the native trombone players discoursed sweet music."

Soon after the opening of the services, passages of Scripture were read alternately, a verse by the preacher, and one by the congregation. Afterwards the Apostles' Creed was repeated in concert. Also a litany was read; for the Moravians, if in some things they resembled Quakers, were very far from them in discarding outward forms.*

There was in the morning no public extemporaneous prayer, nor any prayer in the printed service, except the litanies.

Notice was given that the anniversary of the Female Missionary Society would be celebrated in the afternoon by a love-feast, and that the Communion would be held in the afternoon in the German language, and in the evening in the English.

The love-feasts of the church, which are numerous,—fifteen in the course of the year,—are religious meetings accompanied by a simple refection of coffee, and rusks or buns. They are founded, it seems, upon a passage in Jude, and are intended to set forth by a simple meal, of which all partake in common, that there is no respect of persons before the Lord.

The religious services upon the present occasion consisted of singing and prayer, and some remarks were made by a gentleman who had formerly been a missionary in Jamaica. In a calm manner, mothers were urged to devote their children to the missionary service, rather than to active business (worldly) employments.

---

* In the following from the litany, I observed an inconvenience:
Preacher.—" By thy glorious resurrection and ascension,
        By thy sitting at the right hand of God."
Congregation.—" Bless and comfort us, gracious Lord and God."

The love-feast coffee is celebrated. As it was brought in, diffusing its odor through the church, there was singing in the German language. It was handed in white mugs by one of the brethren, and the rusks, which were light and good, were presented in a basket by a sister.

After the address was over, neatly dressed sisters, as well as brethren, passed among the congregation and collected the coffee mugs upon wooden trays.*

In a manner similar to this just described, the Moravians celebrate upon the 25th of June the anniversary of the founding of Bethlehem.

The services on Easter morning are described in a familiar manner by Mr. Grider, in his "Historical Notes on Music in Bethlehem."†

About three in the morning the band of trombone players begins to pass through the streets, to awaken the members of the congregation. The spacious church is usually filled at an early hour, and the Easter morning litany, which embraces the creed of the Church, is repeated. At the passage, "Glory unto him, who is the resurrection and the life," the minister announces that the rest of the litany will be repeated on the burial-ground. A procession is formed, and it is so timed that as it enters the grounds it is met by the glorious beams of the rising sun, an emblem of resurrection.

---

* The frequent repetition of the word love-feast has caused it to be often shortened in conversation, it being pronounced by some as if written *luff-east.*

† To the Rev. W. C. Reichel, author of several historical works, I am indebted for a correction in the article "The Dunker Love-feast."

The services are continued in the open air, the singing being led by the instrumental performers. It is said that on a fair morning "about two thousand persons usually attend this really grand and impressive service;" the grounds, which are always kept neat, being especially attended to before Easter.* Their first service on Easter Sunday took place at Herrnhut, Saxony, in the year 1732. The "Young Men's Class" repaired before dawn to the graveyard, and spent an hour and a half in singing and prayer.†

The same manner of observing Easter seems to be world-wide. From the Mission Report, we learn that Brother A. Gericke, writing from Fredericksthal, Greenland, says, "At Easter it was so beautifully mild that we could read the Church litany, according to the custom at home, in the burial-ground."

The celebration of Christmas Eve is spoken of by Mr. Grider, who says, "The services last about two hours, during which the Rev. J. F. F. Hagen's 'Morning Star, the darkness break!' is sung alternately by the choir in the gallery and the children in the body of the

---

* Tombstones are placed on the newly-made graves, old tombstones are cleaned, etc. These stones are "breast-stones," not of large size, and lie flat upon the graves,—in the Moravian manner.

† I am quite at a loss to know why the colored eggs, purple, red, and yellow, in use among the Moravians (as among other Germans), should here have been called rabbits' eggs, and the idea been held out that the eggs were of different colors because different rabbits brought them.

(This note was published in the second edition. Other remarks on the subject of the Easter rabbit and eggs will be found in the Appendix.)

church. This anthem," he says, "although simple, and intended for children only, has taken deep root in the hearts of the congregation, who seem never to tire of its performance."

Other musical compositions are performed, such as,—

> "For unto us a child is born" (*Handel*).
> "Sey willkommen" (Welcome) (*Haydn*).
> "Lift up your heads, O ye gates!" (*Handel*).
> "Gloria," 12th Mass (*Mozart*).

Mr. G. tells us that at this time the church choir numbers sixteen female and eight male singers. The accompaniment consists of the organ, two first and two second violins, viola, violoncello, double bass, two French horns, two trumpets, trombone, and flute. This is certainly a remarkable variety of instruments in a church choir.

A lady of Nazareth tells me that Christmas Eve is celebrated among the Moravians by a love-feast in the church. After the cakes and coffee, little wax-candles, lighted, are brought in upon trays, and distributed to the children, while verses are sung. "This," says she, " is to give them an impression of the Sun of Righteousness." The following lines were sung for several years (and may still be in use):

> "Geh' auf mit hellem Schein,
>   Und leucht ins Herz hinein,
>   Leucht über Gross und Klein !
>   Du Sonne der Gerechtigkeit !
>   Verbreite Wonn' und Seligkeit,
>   Und flamme jedermann

Yetzt und fortan
Zu brünst'ger Liebe an."

Of which I offer the following version :

"Rise with clear lustre,
And shine within the heart,
Shine over great and small,
Thou Sun of Righteousness !
Spread joy and blessedness !
And kindle every one,
Henceforth as well as now,
To warmest love."

A lady of Bethlehem says that the Moravians there follow the German fashion, not of having a Christmas-tree merely, but a *Putz*, or decoration ; in which they usually represent a manger with cattle, the infant Jesus and his mother, and the three wise men. At the young ladies' seminary she says that the *Putzes* are often very fine. The people go around to see the decorations. Christmas is a great festival.

The New Year is thus celebrated. At half-past eleven, on New Year's Eve, the congregation assemble for "watch meeting." I condense Mr. Grider's description : "After the officiating minister enters, the choir sing Bishop Gregor's solemn composition, 'Lord, Lord God,' and then the congregation sing ; after which the text for that day is read from the Text-Book, and is the subject of the discourse which follows. Meanwhile the musicians in the choir watch the progress of the night, and assemble before the organ ; and the organist sits with his feet poised, ready to begin. When the

9

year expires, the new one is welcomed by a loud crash
of melody from the organ, and a double choir of trombone players. The congregation rise and join in singing, followed by prayer, etc." These services are always
largely attended.

I have just spoken of the text for the day. A friend
says, "These texts for the day are published in a little
annual volume, 'Doctrinal Texts of the Unitas Fratrum,' prepared in Saxony and sent to the Moravians the
world over,—in Africa, Asia, Australia, and America.
The first text is selected by lot, the remainder by a committee at Herrnhut. This is a relic of the old times,
when the Moravians used the lot in many religious
ceremonies,—even in marriage."

Another says, "The Text-Book consists of a selec-
tion of verses from the Bible, for each day, with appropriate collects taken from the Hymn-Book. It has been
issued since 1731. The first verse, or 'daily word,' contains a short sentence of prayer, exhortation, or promise.
The second, or 'doctrinal text,' is intended to enforce
some doctrinal truth or practical duty. The Text-Book
is printed in English, German, French, Dutch, Swedish,
Danish, Esquimaux, and in the Negro-English of Suri-
nam, S. A."

Birthdays were formerly celebrated among the Moravians, and still are in some families, as a citizen of Bethlehem tells me, by little home parties, called *vespers*,
where the friends of the family are bidden between two
and three P.M., and where they partake of coffee and
sugar-cake; a cake used not only among the Moravians
here, but by the people of Northern Germany. Birthdays were formerly celebrated by serenades. Record

was also kept of the birthdays of friends, of distinguished members of the church, etc.

The Birthday-Book and Text-Book, says Mr. Grider, were placed on the breakfast-table each morning. After the text was read, and while the family were being served, the record was generally consulted to see whose birthday it was. This custom served as a bond which held the inhabitants in social union.*

When a death occurs in the Moravian congregation at Bethlehem, the choir of trombonists plays several tunes from the steeple of the large church. Any Moravian can tell from the tunes played to which choir or band the deceased belonged, whether to the married men's or married women's, to the young men's or young women's, to the children's, or to any other of the bands into which the congregation is divided,—divisions which were formerly of more importance than now.

At funerals the same choir of trombones heads the procession.

THE GRAVEYARD.

Walking in the street at Bethlehem, I saw a large, shaded, and grassy enclosure with seats in it, and a number of girls and children, children's carriages, etc. I said to a working man, "What do you call this,—a square?"

---

* A lady in Bethlehem told me that she had expected a man to help her put down carpet, who had failed to appear. About nine the next morning she met him upon the street somewhat intoxicated and friendly and communicative. "Oh, Mrs. ——," said he, "I couldn't come yesterday. It was my *bursday.*" Whence we may infer that the celebration of birthdays has spread in the community.

It was the graveyard or old burial-place, but there were no monuments visible, from the Moravian custom of laying stones, called breast-stones, flat upon spots of interment.

If you enter this yard from the northwest corner, from Market Street, you come immediately upon the graves of three bishops, in no way more conspicuous than the others which bear breast-stones. One says, " Johannes Etwein, Episcopus Fratrum (or Bishop of the Brethren); born June 29th, 1721, at Freudenstadt in Germany, departed Jan. 2d, 1802.

" Here he rests in peace."

The graves of the Indians and negroes, who were buried here, are not in an especial corner or division, but are indiscriminately mingled with those of the other Moravians. But on the outer edge are buried some persons of disreputable life.

One stone bears the following inscription :

" In memory of Tschoop, a Mohican Indian, who in holy baptism, Ap. 16, 1742, received the name of John : one of the first fruits of the mission at Shekomeko, N. Y., and a remarkable instance of the power of Divine Grace, whereby he became a distinguished teacher among his nation. He departed this life in full assurance of faith at Bethlehem, Aug. 27, 1746.

" There shall be one fold, and one Shepherd.—John x. 6."

About sixty-two Indians are buried here. A daughter of Heckewelder (the distinguished missionary) furnished new grave-stones for some of these Indian remains.

The largest stone in the enclosure rests upon the grave

of one of mixed blood, not a Moravian, and I may be allowed to give a portion of the inscription as it is:

" In Memory to my dearest Son, James McDonald Ross, eldest son of John Ross, principal Chief of the Cherokee Nation . . . died in St. Louis, Nov. 9th, 1864. His Corps transported by Adams Express to Bethlehem, and interred at this sacred spot Nov. 22d, 1864, aged 50 years 29 days."

One of the stones bears the name Traugott Leinbach, which may be translated Trust-God Flaxbrook, but which does not seem peculiar to those familiar with it.

At some of the graves there were bright, freshly-cut flowers.

At Nazareth I visited an enclosure which had once been a graveyard, but which had been neglected, and the stones in it had been moved by one who had become owner. This neglect has lately been atoned for by erecting a monument inscribed with the names of those buried here. The list was obtained by consulting the full and accurate accounts, which it is the duty of all Moravian ministers to keep. In looking at the names on the monument, I observed one Beata, an Indian, who died in 1746, and two others, Beatus Schultz and Beata Böhmer. These were names assigned to infants dead before christening; Beatus, Beata, meaning Blessed.

OLD RECOLLECTIONS.

I met, at Bethlehem, a member of the Moravian Historical Society, who was born in that town in 1796, and was educated there. He was taught German, and could scarcely speak English at all at eighteen.

He learned his trade as clock- and watch-maker in the brethren's house. He was also employed until lately as teacher of vocal music in the parochial school.

When he was in the brethren's house—he began to learn his trade in 1810—there were about twenty brethren domiciled there,—though some of these had their shops elsewhere. They were all mechanics; there being a baker, shoemaker, tinsmith, etc. The cook was also an unmarried brother, all these household services being performed by the brethren themselves. My informant (he was the youngest boy) had to prepare breakfast for his employer.

When the morning bell sounded aloud (*Morgen Glocke zum Aufstehen*) the boys sprang up, and when one story down, went into the prayer-hall, where the *vorsteher* or superintendent directed the services; first they "sang a verse," and then the *vorsteher* read the text for the day. When the boys got down to the lower floor (the four boys who then lodged in the building), they swept out the rooms that were used for shops, ground their coffee, ran down to the cook in the cellar-kitchen and set their pots upon the coals, preparing a simple breakfast of bread, butter, and coffee, of which each boy partook with his employer in the shop. Then they made their cot-beds or threw the blankets back upon them; the brethren made their own.

Mr. W.'s mother did not admire her son's manner of performing these domestic services. When she came down to bring fresh bedclothes and to look after matters, she said, "If I had wax, I'd take a mould of your body here from your bed." "Why, what a crust you have inside of your coffee-pot!"

Breakfast, in Mr. W.'s time, was thus eaten separately, but before that, when all the property was in common, "*eine economische Haushaltung,*" or economical household,—"every one was poor in that early day," —all the meals were eaten at a common table.

After breakfast, the boys washed the dishes and went to their work.

At a quarter before twelve the chapel bell rang for dinner, a custom which continued until about 1870. "I missed it," said Mr. W., "when it stopped, for I had heard it all my life."*

I inquired of Mr. W. whether they kept their time a half-hour or more ahead, like other Pennsylvania Germans. He replied that one of the brethren kept his clock by the sun-dial.

Mr. W. did not dine or sup at the brother-house, but went home for these meals. At the age of twelve, according to the usual custom, he left the children's choir, and became a member of the great boys' choir. The little boys and girls held their festivals together.

At eighteen he joined the young men's choir. About this time the brethren's house was given up to the female seminary or boarding-school, and the few remaining brethren scattered through the town.†

There had been little or no intercourse between these unmarried brethren and the sisters, but some staid, el-

---

* The bell upon Nazareth Hall is still rung at a quarter before twelve, daily.

† The brethren's house was thus given up in 1812, some time before the date above assigned.

derly sister was appointed to visit the brother-house and see whether all the surroundings were clean.

"I remember," Mr. —— said, "when marriages were made by lot, but that drove off a great many of the young people. The marriage by lot was more suited to missionaries who had not time for a two years' courtship. Dr. Franklin, when in Bethlehem, asked Bishop Spangenberg whether this practice did not make unhappy marriages, but the bishop replied, 'Are all marriages happy that are made after long courtship?' We did not have divorces, anyhow," said Mr. W.*

This was the manner of the marriage by lot.

If a young missionary came home, and met his friends, they would say, "Well, you've come home to get married?"

He would answer, "Yes; do you know of any one suitable?"

"Yes; there's Sister Gretchen" (or Peggy).

Another might say, "There's Sister Liddy;" and thus a half-dozen names would perhaps be gathered. He had the privilege of arranging the order of this list himself. Then, after prayer, the elders drew lots, taking the first name; one ballot being *Ja* and the other *Nein* (Yes and No).

The idea was of an especial Providence, by which he should find out whether it was the Lord's will that he

---

* An enthusiastic friend says, "It is a well-known and abundantly substantiated fact that fewer unhappy marriages were known among the Moravians than among the same number of people in any other denomination of Christians while the lot was in practice." If so, let us burn our romances.

should have the first. If the first lot should prove *Ja*, the result was communicated to the sister, and time was allowed her to reflect whether to accept or refuse.

In the course of our conversation, Mr. W. rose and went into the next room; and, returning, brought two vest-buttons of crystal, set in silver, of which he gave the following account:

" My grandfather was a clothmaker, at Basle, in Switzerland. Zinzendorf being there* called upon the young man, who was about leaving for America, to join the Bethlehem and Nazareth settlements.

" Zinzendorf said to him, ' Matthias, we won't meet any more in this world, but hope to meet in a better.' He put his hand into his vest-pocket, and said, ' I'm sorry I have nothing to leave you to remember me by.'

" Young Matthias answered, striking his breast, ' As long as this heart shall beat, I'll not forget you.'

" With a glance, Zinzendorf seized the shears from the clothmaker's table, and quickly cut off two of his vest-buttons. ' Take these,' he said, ' they're nearest the heart.'"

It was the grandson of the clothmaker, himself a great-grandfather, who narrated the story, which he had received traditionally.

" I think," said he, " that this exhibits the quickness of thought of Count Zinzendorf. He was a great recruiting sergeant. On meeting a young man whom he took a fancy to, he would say, ' I have a place for you; I want you to go to Greenland, or (perhaps) to the Cape

---

* This perhaps occurred during Zinzendorf's banishment from Saxony. See note at close of this article.

of Good Hope.' The young man, astonished, would wonder what this conspicuous nobleman meant by this. He generally succeeded, however, in charming the young man, and the matter ended by his going upon the mission."

A few recollections of old times were also given to me by a citizen of Nazareth, aged eighty-two, whom I call Mr. P. He himself was born in Bethlehem, but his father in Connecticut; his grandfather having migrated and bought a farm at Gnadenhütten, a Moravian settlement, near Mauch Chunk.

Mr. P.'s mother was a Miksch. She was placed at the age of four years at the building at Nazareth, called Ephrata, to enable her mother to work.* She did not like the treatment that she received here. "Her mother worked in the house (her house), and in the field, I think," said Mr. P. "The women now do not work much in the fields," he added. "They're afraid they might spoil their fingers. They're brought up altogether too proud. I don't know what will become of the next generation.

"My father moved to Bethlehem, and worked at his carpenter's trade. When he was married he went to the ferry (at Bethlehem), and kept it for ten years. There were no bridges then. He saw hard times in cold weather and high water. After that he moved to the saw-mill and distillery, which belonged to the Moravian

---

* This building, Ephrata, was once a "nursery," where as many as fifty-six young children were placed at one time. Some were removed from their mothers at as early an age as eighteen months, and placed under the common charge. See Transactions of Moravian Historical Society, 1857–58.

Society. I think he got all he made in the distillery, but worked for wages in the saw-mill."

"The Moravians distilled liquor, then?" said I.

"Yes; they commonly drinked a little too, about nine o'clock.

"When I was between thirteen and fourteen, I went to my trade. I was put into the brothers' house to sleep. My trade was a blacksmith's, and a pretty hard one too. I served my trade seven years and seven months. When I was in the brother-house, I spent my evenings and Sundays there. I had liberty to go home to my parents, but not to be running, like they do nowadays, and do mischief.

"My wife was not a member of the church,—we were married fifty-five years ago. Brother Seidel, the Moravian preacher, married us. They were not so strict then as they had been, in turning all those out of meeting that married out."

Mr. P. has a strong German accent. He said, "I never talked much English, only when I lived nine years and a half at Quakertown. I now speak German altogether in my family. The young people here now all try to speak English. They're throwing the German away too much."

At Nazareth, in 1874, I met Mr. M., eighty-six years old, who said that he was married in 1812. "I thought," said he, "that my wife and I were the last couple married by lot; but I have heard that there was one since."

Mr. M. said that the young men and women had some opportunity to see each other, for although the young men were not allowed to visit the young women at their own houses, yet they would sometimes meet in visiting; but they were not allowed to speak to each other more than "a couple of times."

Mr. M. and I did not agree in sentiment with a Moravian woman who had told me that young men and young women were not allowed to keep company, and *they did not think about it.*

Sometimes there would be young persons attached to each other for a couple of years, and the lot being unfavorable, they would go away and leave the congregation. "Well, it was a pretty hard thing," said the old man, "for a pair of young people who loved each other dearly to have the lot go against them." He continued nearly thus: "There was one of the boys who was with me in the brother-house who, I think, left the congregation to be married to a member. It was generally the case, then, that after a couple of years they would ask pardon, and be taken back. We used to say, 'You'll have to take your hat under your arm and ask pardon.'"

Mr. M. told me, concerning the Moravians formerly, that the *verlobung*, or betrothal, lasted sometimes only about a week. "When I was married we had a kind of love-feast after the marriage. Some were picked out to stay, and we had wine or coffee and cake in the church. That was the old custom."

I suggested to Mr. M. that as there were meetings held every evening the young people could see each other there. "There were meetings nearly every evening," he answered. "I remember when I worked at my trade breaking off work and going to church. We went in our every-day clothes, just putting on our coats. Most every evening it was, when I was young. My trade was a blacksmith, and I was seven years an apprentice with my father. He was a pretty strict master, and I had to get up, winter or summer, at five o'clock, and now I wake at that hour although eighty-six."

Recollections of a people would be imperfect without those of the women.

I saw at Nazareth Mrs. B., who was born at the Moravian town of Litiz, in Lancaster County, and who was in her eightieth year.

"When I was a child," said she, "we had Christmas dialogues, about the birth of Christ, his sufferings and death, which were repeated by the children. The dialogues were in the school on Christmas-day, but were repeated several times, so that all might hear, and we never got tired of it.* Christmas-trees were put up then, as they are now. The Christmas *Putzes* or decorations were left standing until after New Year.

"On Easter morning we meet in the church at five in the morning, and the first tune they sing is:

> " ' Der Herr ist aufershtanden,
> Er ist wahrhaftig aufershtanden,' †

> " ' The Lord has arisen,
> He has indeed arisen.'

"At a certain place where the litany speaks of those

---

* A friend adds: "These Christmas dialogues are still to be heard in Moravian towns, in their parochial schools."

† The tendency to pronounce *s* like *sh* will be observed.

who are buried in the churchyard, and of their rising again, we walk out into the churchyard, and the trombone players accompany the hymns that are sung. If the weather is stormy that we cannot go out, this is always a disappointment.

"When I was young, if a child was born in the morning, it was taken to church in the evening to be christened. Religious meetings were held every evening; sometimes a prayer-meeting, sometimes a *sing-meeting*.

"I recollect marriages by lot very well, because they continued until about 1818. All marriages were by lot. Young men and young women were not allowed to keep company, and they did not think about it."

"They hardly dared to look at each other," said another person present.

Mrs. B. continued: "If a young man wanted to marry,—of course he had his eye on some one he would like,—he told it to the *Brüder-Pfleger* (Caretaker of the Brothers), who told it to the minister, and the minister to the *Schwester-Pfleger* (Caretaker of the Sisters). The name that the young man chose was taken into the lot, and if the lot was favorable he might proceed, but if not he must look out for another. If the lot was favorable it was told to the young woman by the *Schwester-Pfleger*, and if the young woman was willing this sister told the minister. There was a *Brüder-Pfleger* in each brother-house, and a *Schwester-Pfleger* in each sister-house.

"Betrothals took place after the young woman had given her consent, in the presence of the conference, composed of the ministers and their wives, and the marriage would generally take place within a week, in the church. The wedding was public, but those who were invited stayed to the *Schmaus* (feast),* which was cake and wine in the church. Thus the ceremony was completed.

" Moravians then dressed with great plainness, much like the Quakers."

As the Moravians were so very strict about the intercourse of the sexes, they could not have allowed two young men and two young women to sit up together with the unburied dead, as has been the custom among some of our Pennsylvania people.

I spoke upon this point to Mrs. B., who said, " Women always sat up with women, and men with men. However, in old times, as soon as there was a death, the trombones sounded, as they do now, and the body was taken when dressed, immediately to a small stone building called the corpse-house, and here remained until the funeral." †

Mrs. —— said that she lost her parents before she was three years old, and was taken into the sister-house, and her brothers into the brother-house. Even those who had parents living sometimes preferred to live in these buildings.

Some simple details of home-life were given to me by Mrs. C., of Bethlehem.

In their own family, in her youth, they rose about five, and breakfasted at six, usually on bread, butter, and

---

* A friend says, " Schmaus" is a vulgar term,—use " Fest."

† The corpse is sent to the corpse-house by some families, to this day.

coffee, perhaps with the addition of molasses. At nine they had a lunch of cold meat, pie, and bread and butter; and at a quarter before twelve came the dinner of meat and vegetables. Often they had soup. There was soup every day at the sister-house, and I was told that in cases of sickness it could be bought there.

"We always had pie for dinner. At two we had coffee and bread and butter. This was called vesper. At six was our supper of cold meat, bread and butter, and pickles. We always had pickles, and every day in the year we had apple-butter."

Mrs. C.'s father was a miller, and perhaps lived more "full and plenty" than some of his neighbors.

She continued: "Every Saturday, we baked bread, pies, and sugar-cake. We made a great many dough-nuts, or *Fast-nacht gucke*." (Shrove-Tuesday pancakes, as we may say.) "We made crullers, and called them *Schtrumpf-bänder*" ("garters," doubtless from their form). "Nearly all our cakes were made from raised dough. One we called *Bäbe*. 'Snow-balls' were made with plenty of eggs, milk, flour, and a little sugar, and were fried in fat.

"At Christmas we always had turkeys; and then we baked a great supply of cakes, from four quarts of molasses and four pounds of sugar, and these lasted all winter. Then every evening before we went to bed we had Christmas cakes, sweet cider, and apples.

"The two o'clock vesper has generally fallen out of use, but if any one comes to town now that I want to invite, and it is not convenient to have them to dinner or supper, I say, 'Come to vesper.' Then we have coffee, and always sugar-cake."

" It would not be a vesper without the sugar-cake," said Mrs. C.'s daughter.

For a vesper-party for guests, Mrs. C. sets a table, and adds smoked beef, preserves, or anything that she chooses.

She further told me that her parents were married by lot, and lived very happily, and she added that as far as we hear, and have seen, most of the pairs thus married lived happily. But the young people were dissatisfied with these marriages. Although the young man had the privilege of putting in the names of several whom he would like, yet if none of these were drawn he became discontented.

"Should a name be chosen that did not please the young man, I believe he had liberty to withdraw.*

"In those times of strict rule, there was no opportunity for the young people of both sexes to become acquainted. This rule originated at Herrnhut. It was on account of it that an unmarried brother who worked in our mill was not allowed to sleep in our house, but must go every night to the brother-house to lodge until the rule was given up, about sixty years ago, and the brother was then allowed to sleep in the mill."

While Mrs. C. was talking, her husband remarked that if he could find a town such as Bethlehem was in 1822 (when, if I remember aright, he had come to the place a stranger), he would go thousands of miles to get his family there to live. The whole town, he said, was

---

* Another person says, that if a man had no proposal to make, he left it to the authorities to suggest a woman ; but the authorities never forced a woman upon him against his will.

composed of Moravians, and was like one family, living well, all in comfort, plain in their dress, happy and contented with their lot.

OLD BUILDINGS.

The sister-house, the *Gemein-haus*, and the widow-house are still standing at Bethlehem, solid stone buildings with great roofs and dormer-windows. One of them has immense stone buttresses, and all are fitted to withstand the effects of time. Their appearance, indeed, is becoming peculiar. The brother-house is still standing, but has disappeared from view as a separate structure, having been incorporated, as I have mentioned, in the young ladies' seminary.

The sister-house is owned by the Board of Elders of the Northern Diocese of the Church of the United Brethren (Unitas Fratrum) in the United States, and apartments are furnished to the widows and daughters of servants of the church, rent free. Any unmarried Moravian woman (or widow) may also have rooms here, but not free of charge.

The corner-stone of the widow-house was laid in 1767. This conspicuous building has recently been purchased by a friend of the church. The apartments will be appropriated free of rent to the widows and unmarried daughters of missionaries, ministers, and other servants of the church, including teachers in the seminaries.*

---

* A lady whom I met at Nazareth spoke of the visits that she used to make in the widow-house, when they went at one, had vesper of coffee and sugar-cake at two, and left at five.

The *Gemein-haus* (congregation-house) was used for the ministers' families, sometimes three or four, who resided in Bethlehem. It is no longer occupied by these, but by other members of the society. It adjoins the old chapel, where the preaching is in German. These old buildings, especially the widow-house, are in good repair.

One of the most striking circumstances connected with some of the old buildings at Nazareth is the account of the numbers of persons whom they are said to have once sheltered. The sister-house is a large structure, but the brother-house is so inconspicuous upon the street of the quiet little town, being, indeed, occupied as a store and dwelling, and probably sheltering not more than two families, that it is quite wonderful to hear tell of fifty persons having once had their homes in it.*

Of one of the most noteworthy buildings at Nazareth I have already made mention. It was called Ephrata.† The foundations were laid by Whitefield, the celebrated preacher, who bought five thousand acres in the forks of the Delaware, or where the Lehigh empties into that stream. This tract was afterwards bought by the Moravians. In 1744, thirty-three married couples from Bethlehem moved into this house.‡ In 1749, the "nursery," of which I have before spoken, was removed here from Bethlehem. Recently this old build-

---

* Upon this passage, a friend makes the following remark : "Not regular occupants, but Moravian missionaries or strangers who might arrive in large bodies; twenty, I think, would be a large number."

† *Ayfrahtaw* I heard this word pronounced.

‡ There were two log houses, says a friend.

ing has been completely renovated, and the upper floor contains the collection and library of the Moravian Historical Society. The building is called the White-field-house, but it might still be called Ephrata, or a place of rest, for the lower part is a dwelling for retired missionary families. Only one family was there at the time of my visit, a widow with children. Little people were running about and laughing below, quite at home.

The "sustentation fund" of the Moravian Church supports the "resting ministers" (such as the Methodists call superannuated ministers) the widows and children of missionaries, etc.

MISCELLANEOUS REMARKS.

An acquaintance said to me in Lancaster, "The people of Bethlehem are not Pennsylvania Dutch. They speak the high German." I think, however, that the younger people have acquired the Pennsylvania dialect. An elderly gentleman of Bethlehem, to whom mention was made of a work upon the "Pennsylvania Dutch," etc., replied in this manner (with a German accent): "We don't want to know anything about the Pennsylvania Dutch. We know enough about them already. We see enough of them on our farms."

It may be inferred from what has been said that the Moravians are persons of very considerable culture. I may go further, and speak of the thoughtful, spiritual expression of many faces.

As agriculture may be called the vocation of the Pennsylvania Germans in general, so education may be called the vocation of the Moravians. To the support of the parochial school at Bethlehem I heard that about nine thousand dollars are annually appropriated from the income of the church property there. This enables those who have charge to put the terms of instruction very low. These are four dollars, or four to six, annually, for Moravian children.

The daughters of Moravian preachers are entitled to four years' tuition in one of the young ladies' schools, either at the celebrated one at Bethlehem, that at Litiz, Pennsylvania, at Salem, North Carolina, or at Hope, Indiana.* Besides these institutions, there is a flourishing boys' school at Nazareth, and a college and divinity school at Bethlehem.

Very few of the Moravians here are engaged in agriculture. They have remained in towns, as it seems, and rarely or never become large and wealthy farmers; a circumstance that I do not comprehend. That religious scruples against the acquisition of wealth, or of individual property, have influenced their actions, I have not been able to discover.

I have not in my reports of aged citizens repeated some of the " orthodox" expressions which they used.

" The distinguishing feature of Moravian theology," says Appleton's Cyclopædia, " is the prominence given to the person and atonement of Christ."

I noticed at Bethlehem a sweet simplicity in speaking to or of the preachers.

---

* They not only receive tuition here, but board and clothing, and a similar privilege is extended to the sons of preachers.

A young man told me that Brother W. had sent him, and one of the sisters unaffectedly addressed a venerable bishop as Brother S.   One of these gentlemen said to a person, not a member of his church, "Call me brother."

———

I have never heard Moravians call themselves Herrn-hutters.   The favorite name of their churchmen for their organization is Unitas Fratrum, or Unity of Brethren.   A venerable preacher tells me that they have been called the *Johannische Gemein*, or community like St. John; or their view the *Johannische Auffassung*, or John-like expression, of the spirit of the gospel, especially as we read in the seventeenth chapter of John the prayer of Christ, "That they, Father, may be one, as we are one." *

———

I conclude this sketch with an abridged passage from the Mission Report of 1872, an extract which may be interesting to thoughtful minds:

"The celebration of the centenary of the Labrador mission took place at all the six stations on the 5th and 6th of January, 1871.   Some of the people assisted in decorating the chapels by fetching fir-tree branches and making festoons.   A number of welcome jubilee presents from the Ladies' Association in London, and other sisters, were distributed, and the services closed with the

---

* During the period of the anti-slavery agitation, preceding the war, the Moravians as a body did not take an anti-slavery stand. Their members were allowed to hold slaves, like those of almost all the other sects in this country.   Their European brethren did not agree with them on this subject.

celebration of the Lord's Supper; a love-feast, at which printed odes were used; and a thanksgiving service. The brethren of Okak remark, 'Stillness, not unusually a feature of festive seasons in Labrador, prevailed in a striking degree, and was to our minds more valuable as a proof of spiritual blessings enjoyed than the finest words could have been, especially as the Esquimaux have great readiness in using religious phrases.' "

Note.—Christianity was introduced into Bohemia and Moravia in the ninth century. It is claimed that the people of these countries, for several centuries, manifested in matters of faith the spirit of what was afterwards Protestantism. The most celebrated of their reformers was John Huss, who was burned, by order of the Council of Constance, in 1415. The Hussites separated into two parties, of whom the Taborites were defeated by the Calixtines in 1434, and the latter became the national church of Bohemia. A party among the remnant of the Taborites, dissatisfied with what they thought corrupt practices in this church, removed more and more from the Calixtine communion, and at length were permitted to settle on the barony of Lititz. It is claimed that some, if not all, of these were men of God, who had not taken up arms during the war. They afterwards adopted the name *Unitas Fratrum*, or *Unity of the Brethren*. Their pastors were Calixtine priests who had joined the society. Such was the beginning of the Moravian Church. They obtained the episcopal succession from a colony of Waldenses, on the confines of Bohemia and Austria. Toward the year 1500 they had more than two hundred churches in Moravia and Bohemia, and had published a Bohemian Bible and several confessions of faith.

Their numbers and influence increased very much, and gradually the *Unitas Fratrum* was composed of three provinces, the Bohemian, Moravian, and Polish. But, in 1621, Ferdinand II. began a series of persecutions of all the Protestant denominations in Bohemia and Moravia, known as the anti-reformation. Protestantism was totally overthrown here, more than fifty thousand of the inhabitants having emigrated. In Poland, the Brethren's Church became united with the Reformed, and the *Unitas Fratrum* disappeared from the eyes of men, and remained as a "hidden seed" for ninety-four years. In Moravia many families remained, who secretly entertained the views of their fathers, and among these an awakening took place in the early part of the eighteenth century, through the instrumentality of a Moravian exile named Christian David. The desire to live in a Protestant country was felt more and more, and two families escaped in the night, and after eleven days safely reached Berthelsdorf, an estate in Saxony belonging to Count Zinzendorf, a pious young nobleman, who had offered them a refuge. Other Moravians joined them, and in a few years a colony of three hundred persons lived on Count Zinzendorf's estate. He himself soon relinquished all worldly honors, became a bishop of the brethren, and devoted himself entirely to their service.

Nicolaus Ludwig, Count of Zinzendorf and Pottendorf, descended from a noble Austrian family, was born in Dresden in 1700. His father dying soon after his birth, his education was confided to his grandmother, the Baroness de Gersdorf, who had adopted the idea of Spener, the founder of the Pietists, of *little churches within the church*, having for their aim the promotion of piety and the purifying and sanctifying of the whole church.

The mind of Zinzendorf, when he was a mere child, took an enthusiastic direction, and he used to write letters to the Saviour and throw them out of the window, hoping that the Saviour might find them. At the university of Wittenberg, he applied himself, without direction or aid, to the study of theology, fully resolved to become a minister of the gospel. In 1722 he married, and about the same time gave some emigrant Moravian brethren permission to settle upon his estate of Berthelsdorf. In connection with some others, he labored to instruct them and their children. But it would seem, from subsequent circumstances, that he himself became, in some degree, their pupil.

They were not all agreed in religious opinions, and, with a view to unity, he formed statutes for their government. He was also appointed a warden of the congregation. In 1734 he went, under an assumed name, to Stralsund, and passed an examination as a theological candidate. The same year he received holy orders at

Tübingen. On returning from Switzerland, in 1736, he met an edict forbidding his return to his native country, and repaired to Berlin, where, under sanction of the King of Prussia, he was consecrated bishop of the Moravian congregation, and from that time was always called the Ordinary of the Brethren. The order of banishment was repealed after eleven years.

Within this period he visited the islands of St. Thomas and St. Croix, where the Brethren had already established missions He also came to Pennsylvania in 1741. He remained in this country two years, during which he was very diligently and successfully occupied. He also made several visits to Holland and England. He spent his latter years at Herrnhut, where he died. His remains were borne to the grave by thirty-two preachers and missionaries whom he had reared, from Holland, England, Ireland, and North America, including Greenland. He wrote more than one hundred books. His son, who was an elder of the single brethren, died before his father. His son-in-law, the Baron de Watteville, was a bishop of the Moravian Church.

On the continent of Europe the Moravian system of the time of Zinzendorf is kept up in every respect. The governing board for the whole "Unity," or whole Moravian Church, meets at Berthelsdorf, in Saxony, in the castle once inhabited by Count Zinzendorf, who devoted his entire property to the good of the church.

A community of goods never existed at any time in a Moravian institution. The *Economie,* or *Economische Haushaltung* (Economical Household, or Common Housekeeping), seems to have existed for about twenty years, during the Indian wars, when the settlements of the Brethren at Bethlehem, etc., were feeble and exposed to attack.

The numerical force of the Moravians is not great. The number of communicants—home-communicants, if I may call them so—is 12,947 (estimate of 1859?), and over 53,000 mission converts, including baptized children. There are also, as I understand, 80,000 "Diaspora members" on the continent of Europe; for which remarkable movement see the article *Moravians,* in Appleton's Cyclopædia. See, also, the *Moravian Manual.* This historical sketch is drawn principally from these sources, and from the articles *Zinzendorf* and *German Theology* of the same Cyclopædia.

10

SCHWENKFELDERS.

I HAD before seen the Schwenkfelders mentioned as a people who, like the Mennonites, Quakers, etc., are opposed to war, but I never became personally acquainted with them until the spring of 1873. At that time, a gentleman of West Chester advised me to inform myself concerning them, speaking of them as a delightful people. On arriving at Norristown, I therefore made inquiry about them from citizens of that borough, and was kindly furnished with several letters of introduction to members of the Schwenkfelder community living about seven miles north of the town.*

It was about noon when the stage left me at the house of one who had formerly been a preacher in the society. Here I dined, conversed with my host about his people, and looked at various large old volumes which he showed to me. Then, having been supplied with an escort, I went to a house in the same neighborhood, the

---

* A recent writer tells us that the upper, middle, and lower parts of Montgomery County, the lower end of Berks, and the south corner of Lehigh contain the only settlement of Schwenkfelders in the wide world. He adds that it is no misnomer to call these people the Pennsylvania German Quakers. It will be seen, however, that they are more ancient than George Fox.

dwelling of an elderly brother, who had learned my errand, and had expressed a wish to meet me.

Under his hospitable care, I remained until Sunday evening; he taking me to the meeting-house and other places. Through him I also received a present of several books, giving the history and doctrines of the society.

On Sunday evening he took me to the house of another member, whose kindly care did not cease until he had conveyed me — on Monday morning — again to the borough of Norristown.

MEETING-HOUSE AND GRAVEYARD.

The church which I visited is in Towamensing Township, Montgomery County, and is one of six in Eastern Pennsylvania which hold all the Schwenkfelders now living. I was surprised to find the church in neat order and in good preservation, thus indicating no lack of vitality in this small religious body, which, like a transplanted tree, has thrown out so few roots into adjoining soil. The plain meeting-house stood upon the edge of a wood; the graveyard was neat, and was enlivened by the blossoms of the mountain pink,* and the bright sunshine and tender green of May animated the scene.

Among the monumental stones was a rough one bearing this inscription only: " A. R. W. 1745." And this was, I believe, the oldest here. Of nine years' later date was a gravestone, still unhewn and irregular in shape, but with a longer inscription: " Psal. 90 v. 7. Baltzer Anders, Gestorben 1754, 56." The passage cited from

---

* *Phlox subulata.*

the Psalms is the text of the funeral sermon. The rest we may translate: "Balthazar Anders. Died 1754, at the age of 56."

At the date 1762 we find a carved marble head-stone, but no showy monuments have been erected here. One of the more modern stones says, "Rosina Kribelin, geb. Hübnerin, alt 27 Yahr 5 monat,"—or "Rosina Kribel, born Hübner, aged twenty-seven years and five months;" the feminine termination *in* being added to both the names.*

Inscriptions older than these may be found at the meeting-house in Lower Salford Township, and one of them goes to a somewhat greater length in honor of him for whom it was erected. Translated it reads thus: "In memory of George Weiss, was born in Silesia, and first teacher of the Schwenkfelder community in Pennsylvania; died the 11th of March 1740, 53 years old."

(The word teacher means preacher.)

Within the meeting-house there were enclosed benches or open pews; the pulpit and the ends of these benches upon the aisle being painted white. The men sat upon one side of the house, the women upon the other; the women removing their bonnets and wearing caps. These caps were not severely plain, like those of the Mennonites, etc., but were trimmed with white satin ribbon.†

---

* This feminine termination has not disappeared from the dialect. Mr. Rauch speaks of "de olt Lawbucksy," which is rendered, old Mrs. Lawbucks.

† The decline in the severity of the cap seems to have reached its lowest point among the Moravians, where but few women in this country wear caps in church. See "Bethlehem and the Moravians."

The Schwenkfelder women bent the knee at the name of Jesus, but this observance has fallen into disuse among the men.

Before the morning service there is school, in which the children are taught from the Catechism and Testament; the Catechism containing the Apostles' Creed. On Sunday afternoon, a school is held in which the children are taught to read the German language, in which tongue the church exercises are conducted.* The Schwenkfelders claim to have been among the earliest to establish Sabbath-schools, but their school is of later date than that of Ludwig Hoecker.†

During service, the pulpit or desk was occupied by three preachers. The oldest had a fine countenance, forehead, and coronal region of the head. The youngest, a very solid-looking, fair-haired man, read a portion of Scripture, and *read* a prayer.‡ Singing accompanied these exercises, and then a few extemporaneous remarks were made by the youngest preacher; the open Bible lying before him, upon which his eyes were cast. The oldest preacher spoke at length, and was followed by the third, who wore a heavy black beard.

The ministers of the Schwenkfelders, like those of our similar sects, are unsalaried and without special theological training.

---

* At Flourtown, or Chestnut Hill, the English language is used, and there is no instruction in German.

† See article "Ephrata."

‡ It appears that there was also extemporaneous prayer during the exercises.

BOOKS.

I have mentioned that he whom I first visited brought out a number of large books for me to examine. They were all in the German language.

The first bore title, "The first part of the Christian, orthodox book, of the man noble, dear, and highly favored by God, Caspar Schwenckfeldt." The volume was a folio; the place of printing not given; the date 1564. It is embellished by a large plate, which apparently represents Christ with Death and Satan under his feet. Below, upon the left, is a man in a furred robe kneeling, with the motto, "Caspar Schwenckfeldt von Ossing. Nil Christo triste recepto" (or, "If I have Christ, nothing makes me sad"). On the right is a troop of similar appearance, with the motto, "And the fellow-believers of the glories and truth of Jesus Christ."*

Another ancient folio, bound in parchment, with brazen clasps, tips, and bosses, was said to be a volume of Schwenkfeld's letters. There is no place of printing; the date is 1570. The same plate as the preceding. These epistles, says my host, are upon the popish doctrine and faith.

The third folio was of the same date, 1570, and was in a splendid state of preservation. This contains letters upon the Lutheran doctrine, with which Schwenkfeld did not agree.

Two of the folios brought out by my host were manuscripts, bound in leather, with brazen clasps. One of

---

* Why is not Schwenkfeld spoken of by the title *von Ossing?* We read of Ulrich von Hütten, German scholar and reformer.

them had the great number of thirteen hundred and three pages, very neatly written in the German hand. It contained the sermons, " *Postilla*," of Michael Hiller, preacher at Zobten, in Silesia, who " disappeared in God" in 1554 ; written and collected by Nicholas Detschke, 1564, and now written anew, 1747. I did not find the name of the copyist.

Although my host told me he that he had never been in Quaker meeting in his life, yet I found among his books a history of the rise, etc., of the Christian people called Quakers, originally written in Dutch by William Sewel, and by himself translated into English, from English translated into German (*Hochdeutsch*), 1742. This is Sewel's History, one of the most celebrated of the Quaker books.

At the second house which I visited there lay in the window-seat several books in German. One was a large copy of the Scriptures, a clasped volume, with many plates. Lying loose in it were two plates of Caspar Schwenkfeld, in his furred robe, with beard descending upon his breast, and his motto (already given) in German : " *Wenn ich Christum habe, so bin ich nicht traurig*" ; or, " If I have Christ, I am not sorrowful." In selecting this motto, he may have had reference to his exiled condition.

(There seems to be among the Schwenkfelders much more regard than among most of our plain Pennsylvania Germans for the pictures, the " counterfeit presentments," of men.*)

---

* In using the name Schwenkfeld, I have abbreviated it a little, giving it as it is in the New American Cyclopædia, which calls

The volumes given to myself, while among these people, are:

1. Schwenkfeld's *Erläuterung,* or Explanation, concerning many points in history and theology. Not written by their leader himself, but composed by several of the "godly exiles from Silesia to Pennsylvania." An appendix contains, among other matter, a sketch of the life of Schwenkfeld, and an account of the journey of the Silesian emigrants from Altenau to this State. Of this volume I have made much use.*

2. Questions on the Christian Doctrine of Faith, for Instructing Youth in the First Principles of Religion. By the Rev. Christopher Schultz, Sen. My copy is a translation.

3. Constitution of the Schwenkfelder Society, subscribed in 1782, etc.

HISTORY.

In the year 1490, seven years after the birth of Luther, two years before the discovery of America by Columbus, and one hundred and thirty-four before the birth of George Fox, was born in Silesia,† in the German or Austrian empire, Caspar Schwenkfeld von Ossing, of a

---

him, however, Von Schwenkfeld. The Cyclopædia, in speaking of his writings, some ninety treatises, says that they are regarded as one of the most valuable sources of the history of the Reformation.

* A copy of this volume has been deposited for reference in the library of the German Society, Philadelphia.

† That portion of Silesia which was the home of the Schwenkfelders lies east of Saxony, the home of Count Zinzendorf. It, or the greater part of it, was conquered by Frederick the Great, and added to Prussia.

very old and noble extraction. His brother-in-law is mentioned as Conrad Thumb von Neuburg, hereditary marshal of the principality of Würtemberg. Caspar Schwenkfeld was a person of very handsome mien, dignified behavior, remarkable modesty, courtesy, and gentleness, accompanied by godliness, and fervency in prayer, and was of a Christian, pure, and temperate life. It is added that thus much even his bitter enemies must acknowledge, "as the clergy know."* In his youth he studied two years at Cologne, and lived several years at other universities. He at length became well read in the writings of the Greek and Latin fathers. He was also many years in the confidential service of his liege lord, the Prince of Liegnitz (the Duke of Liegnitz?). Afterwards " God touched his heart," and he turned away from his life at court, and became a teacher at St. John's Church, in Liegnitz. He diligently read the writings of Luther and of others who were leaving the papacy, and he afterwards remarked that he had been as good a Lutheran as any. With the fiery reformer he, however, differed greatly afterwards ; the first cause of difference being, as it appears, Luther's views upon the Supper. Schwenkfeld says that the Lord Jesus had shown to him that he was not a bodily bread, but a spiritual and heavenly one.

Schwenkfeld also wrote a little work upon the misuse of the sacraments, which, without his knowledge, was printed in Switzerland. Hereupon Dr. Faber, bishop at Vienna, represented to the emperor, Ferdinand, that Schwenkfeld held false doctrines concerning the sacra-

---

* The clergy, *die Gelehrten.*

10*

ment of the Supper, etc.; and Ferdinand was himself angry because his enemies had published the book. The emperor (or, as he is called, the king) wrote to the duke at Liegnitz to punish Schwenkfeld, but as his innocence was known to the duke, this prince thought it well that Schwenkfeld should ride away for a while.*

He did ride away in 1529, but, although he lived for thirty-three years after, he never rode back again.

He travelled to many places in Germany, and was prized and heard at many noble courts. Many times he stopped in cities of the empire, and suffered much opposition from the preachers.

A letter of pardon was sent to him by the emperor, Ferdinand, saying that if he would recall his opinion, and act differently, he should receive his knightly possessions; but, as already stated, he never returned to Silesia.

During his life he published ninety-two treatises, and after his death many of his books were published by his fellow-believers. All his writings were forbidden to be printed by the Papists and Lutherans, and in different places his writings were burnt, "nevertheless God has given means for several of these books to be published four or five times." †

Many years after the publication of his little work,

---

* *Erläuterung.*—Schwenkfeld appears to have abstained from the sacraments for a great part of his life,—from the outward forms, at least, if we may add the expression.

† The three folios before spoken of in this article were published within ten years after his death, and it seems possible that the place of printing was omitted on account of the opposition to his works.

before spoken of, upon the misuse of the sacraments, Schwenkfeld sent to Luther a number of his own works, and called Luther's attention to one of his favorite doctrines, " the glory of the manhood of Jesus Christ." To the noble messenger who bore the letter, etc., Luther returned an answer, speaking in severe and ignominious terms of the author, reproaching him with having kindled a fire in Silesia against the holy sacrament, and with his Eutychianism, as Luther calls Schwenkfeld's doctrine that the manhood of Jesus Christ is no creature.*

It was not the desire of Schwenkfeld to build up a sect of his own, nor did he judge any congregation already collected, but he exhorted all to pray in spirit and in truth in all places. He is said to have directed men only to Christ and his power, and to have filled, until his death, the office of a true evangelical preacher.

Before he departed, we read that he heard a voice, " Up, up into heaven!" which voice he had heard also before he rode out of his fatherland, saying, " Up, up out of the fire!" (His hearing had failed nearly forty years before his death.)

Not long before dying he said, " Now home; home into the true fatherland."

" He died in God, and went home to his rest," in the city of Ulm, in 1562.†

---

* In the New American Cyclopædia Schwenkfeld is said to have differed from Luther and others upon the deification of the body Christ. In the latter part of this essay this point is spoken of again.

† Ulm, a town in Würtemberg, on the left bank of the Danube. It was long an imperial free city.

He was buried in a cellar. (It may be remembered that Menno was buried in a garden.)

Nearly three hundred years after the birth of Caspar Schwenkfeld von Ossing, the first Schwenkfeld congregation was organized; he was born in 1490, it was formed in 1782. It was upon the new continent discovered by Columbus, in the English colony of Pennsylvania, that a little band of exiled Schwenkfelders formed this society after they had sojourned here nearly fifty years. How were they able to continue Schwenkfelders, during the period of more than two hundred years between the death of their founder and their organization here?*

In Silesia the ruling church was Roman Catholic, but the Lutherans were generally tolerated. The Lutheran preachers, coming into contact with the Schwenkfelders, were often hostile and unfriendly to them ; but the final self-banishment of the Pennsylvania colony was owing to the rigorous measures taken by the Jesuits for their conversion.†

---

* This title was probably not in former times their chosen name. In a little inartistic aria, near the close of the *Erläuterung*, they are twice called *die Stillen*, or the quiet ones. Looking in a German dictionary for this word, I find "*die Stillen*" is rendered Quakers. In the same aria they are called *die Friedlichen*, or the peaceful ones. One of Schwenkfeld's volumes, a collection, states that they were gathered and put in order by *the fellow-confessors and lovers of the glories and truth of Jesus Christ.*

† As in the principality of Lower Silesia Lutheran preachers had been installed in nearly all the offices, many of the common people who had accepted Schwenkfeld's teachings stood back in stillness, not being able conscientiously to agree with these teachers. This was very offensive to the parsons, and they soon made use of their high dignity against tender consciences to force such

In one of the persecutions of earlier times, we read of a certain Anthony Oelssner, who was called to strengthen the scattered faithful, about the year 1580; in which call he showed great diligence in prayer and preaching, until he was seized and lay imprisoned a while at Liegnitz. Afterward he was imprisoned at Löwenberg, in the tower, where he suffered almost the same strong temptations of Satan as we read in the lives of the fathers that old Anthony did, from which he was happily set free, as he writes in a long letter. One of his letters is from the lowest dungeon at Vienna, where he lay among thieves and malefactors.

He was also dragged about in the trenches and galleys,* all which he bore without a murmur, and met his persecutors with cheerfulness, encouraging the faithful by letters when he did not lie in dungeons too dark, or when ink, paper, etc., were not denied him. Of these writings a great part is still extant.

Certain of the Schwenkfelder prisoners, it seems, were sent upon the galleys to the Turkish war. "In taking the castle Gran, in 1593, they were obliged to go before the soldiers, through a narrow street; but they never killed a Turk, nor stained their hands with the blood of men (as is proper for the soldiers of Christ)." †

---

persons to their means of grace,—to make them come to the baptismal font, to the pulpit, and the altar.—*Schwenkfeld's Erläuterung*, chap. iv. The Schwenkfelders express the opinion that the action of the Lutheran clergy, in calling attention to them, frequently caused their persecution by the Catholic authorities.

* Digging trenches for military defence, and working the galleys or great boats of the Mediterranean.

† They do not seem to have been very profitable as soldiers.

Another sufferer, old Martin John, tells how, when he lived at Kaufig, he beheld the lives of the priests, how they loaded themselves with eating and drinking, avarice and gaming, dancing and debauchery, and produced uproar in the beer-houses, and made a nine-pin alley, and played together in the parsonage yard. "And I thought that I could not any longer approve their godlessness. I was thus induced to stay at home, and read to my wife and children, and call them to repentance. Then the priest ran to my landlord,* and complained of me, but he would not listen, and I was left in peace for a year. Then my old master died, and his son, to please the godless preacher, drove me from my paternal inheritance." The priest was named George M., and this was in 1584.

Martin John also says that the priest made jest of the Holy Ghost, saying, "Thou wilt have to wait long before the Holy Ghost will come and teach thee."

Martin tells further, that he found a property cheap at Armenruh ; but there he saw the same manner of life. "I did not have to go far, but heard in. my own yard how the priest fiddled, and the rest danced and cried out, and found it much worse than in my own (former) home. So I stayed at home, and read, prayed, and sang, and other people came to hear. Then the priests ran to our landlords, and we were put into prison, where I was kept over four years, and the others over a year, and to these nothing was given to eat nor to drink."

One man can lead a horse to water, but several cannot make him drink.

* *Herrschaft.* The narrative is condensed from the *Erläuterung*, or Explanation.

These cases of persecution all took place within fifty years after the death of Schwenkfeld, and seem to have befallen those who lived around the Spitzberg, in Lower Silesia; but in Upper Silesia, and in the district of Glatz, there was repose; and toward the end of the sixteenth century persecution appears to have declined, for *we do not find that any one writes letters from prison.*

During the Thirty Years' War the Schwenkfelders, like others who opposed the Romish Church, did not remain undisturbed. Once during this period complaint was made of them to the prince at Liegnitz, but they sent to him one of Caspar Schwenkfeld's books, which he graciously received, and permitted them to hold meetings in their houses. Meetings in the open air were forbidden by the emperor.*

At the close of the war they were again persecuted, the preachers complaining of them to the nobility. But the prince at Liegnitz set them all free, and allowed them to worship again in their houses.

Simple religious services, formerly held among the Schwenkfelders, are thus described. †

If any one had books and read on Sunday, the others went and listened. But this was the order: in the morning, after each prayed when he rose, they came together. (Elsewhere it is stated that they were generally fasting.) They sang morning songs standing;

---

* Mention is made of the time when the destroyer came upon the destroyer because his measure was full,—namely, the Thirty Years' War, and the banishment of the Lutherans from the imperial dominions.

† See *Erläuterung,* or Explanation. The passage is slightly abridged.

afterward prayed out of a prayer-book; then all, standing, sang prayer-songs, especially to the Holy Spirit; they also sang sitting, and prayed, and then read several sermons; then prayed again and sang a couple of songs; then ate dinner. Afterward prayed again standing, and sang prayer-songs; afterward read till toward evening; then standing prayed and sang. That was the order on Sunday.

And if, in week-time, the people came together at a spinning (*beym spinnen*), then there was almost always singing, and when they would go home they knelt down together and prayed.

In coming down to the year 1730, we read that there being no longer any great persecution, the zeal of most began to be extinguished; the young people liked to go to church, especially at Harpersdorf, where there was beautiful music. Some dreaded contempt; some, it is said, found freedom to live in sin, for if they only went to the Supper they might live as they pleased, and receive a beautiful funeral sermon; many left on account of a marriage. Thus the Schwenkfelders greatly declined.*

---

* Hence we may infer that the Schwenkfelders forbade marriages with those not of their own persuasion. During the period of their troubles it seems that marriage by the church was at times refused them, no doubt from their refusing the sacrament. Maimed funeral rites were also among the persecutions of which they complained. In speaking thus of their decline, they may, however, overestimate their numbers in former times.

The following characteristic sketch may be introduced here nearly in the words of the original: The two pastors in Harpersdorf having been called to a new church, there came as pastor Herr John Samuel Neander (the pastor Neander who died in July

It was somewhat before the date above given, or in the year 1719, that the celebrated Jesuit mission came among the Schwenkfelders; that is, by imperial decree, there arrived two missionary priests. In 1721, the Schwenkfelders sent delegates to the emperor, craving further indulgence.

While the missionaries were trying to make them Catholic, the Lutherans offered protection to those who should join them; but a few ("a little heap") remained true, without falling off on either side. Of the delegates sent to the emperor, two remained in Vienna five years, and found him not ungracious. He ordered that time should be taken for further consideration.

During this time the mission was taking severe measures, with fine and imprisonment. No Schwenkfelder was to be buried in the churchyard, but upon the cattle-paths (highways?), and none should accompany them to burial (but this they could not prevent).* None should

---

1759). He was by nature a very fiery man, so that he hardly knew how to govern his passions; by birth a Brandenburger, from Frankfort on the Oder. When he was installed, the Herr Superintendent in Liegnitz brought before him that he was a stranger, and therefore he might not know how it was in Harpersdorf, that there was a people there, who had already lived there about two hundred years, called Schwenkfelders. Therefore he would give him good advice, that he should leave these people in peace; preceding pastors had tried it enough, and had accomplished nothing by force. But if he thought he could not endure these people, he should say so, and another would be put into the place.

But Herr Neander promised everything good, and did not keep to it. For soon after entering upon his office he gave out that he had sworn to bury none of the Schwenkfelders as before practised, and this he began to carry out. See *Erläuterung*, chap. v.

* The aria already alluded to says,—

be married who did not promise their offspring to the Catholics, which none would do ; therefore many marriages were postponed for long years. On the contrary, when the new Lutherans (converts) were buried there was a great parade and procession, and a great throng at weddings. At length, in 1725, a severe edict was issued to oblige old and young to attend the mission teachings, and the Schwenkfelders were threatened with being fastened to wheelbarrows (*Schübkarren*), and with having their children taken away.

Now when affairs had come to an extremity, they heard that they might flee for a while to an honorable senator in Gorlitz, and also to his excellency Louis, Count of Zinzendorf, and Lord of Berthelsdorf ;* and in 1726, and afterward, several families broke off by night, and in great danger, leaving their estates and property behind. More followed, and as they could better earn a living in the villages,† the greater part went to Berthelsdorf, and enjoyed protection there for eight years. But while living here in all stillness, in 1733, Zinzendorf informed them unexpectedly that they

---

" Throw their dead away, like foul corruption,
  The cow-path is too good ; don't tread upon the grass ;
  The father shall not follow the body of his child,
  Nor the wife accompany her husband to the house of death."

The word that I have translated cattle-path, etc., is *viehweg*. A note upon this verse of the aria says, " 1722. Three hundred persons lie upon the cow-paths at Harpersdorf and Langendorff." If so many were buried during the time of the Catholic mission, these people must have been numerous.

* Zinzendorf's estate of Berthelsdorf was, it seems, near the town of Gorlitz.

† By agriculture? rather than in the town of Gorlitz.

were no longer to be tolerated in Saxony. In this matter they suspected the influence of the Jesuits with the elector. (Zinzendorf himself was banished from 1736 to 1747.*)

One year was allowed them before removing, and, after looking elsewhere, they concluded to come to Pennsylvania. In 1733 a couple of Schwenkfelder families had come hither,—and, as they say, "Our faithful friends in Holland advised us strongly to go." About forty families, therefore, began the journey in the latter part of April, 1734, and cast anchor at Philadelphia on the 22d of September. "There, by the praiseworthy constitution of the country, we were made citizens, and partakers of all civil and religious freedom."

After this flight the missionaries continued their efforts in Silesia, and several more families fled and came to Pennsylvania. In 1740 an imperial command was issued, that the Schwenkfelder heresy must out. Now were they greatly urged to join the Lutherans for their protection; and now, in houses, two were against three, and three against two, and a man's foes were those of his own household. At last, the greater part went over to the Lutheran Church. However, in the following autumn, the emperor died, and Silesia was soon after conquered for Prussia by Frederick the Great.

All the Roman Catholic offices were then vacated, and Pater Regent, one of the mission, "retreated after us into Saxony; and other instruments sought shelter out of the country. The books of which we were robbed by the doctors and their followers were, we heard, taken to

---

* See " Bethlehem and the Moravians."

Liegnitz; and as for the homes and goods we had left behind, they had helped themselves to them, which is all one to us. We hope their enjoyment of them will be as profitable to them as the abandoning of them has been to us."

In 1742, or eight years after the principal migration to Pennsylvania, the King of Prussia published an edict in favor of freedom of conscience, inviting the exiled Schwenkfelders to return to his duchy of Lower Silesia, or to dwell in any other part of his possessions. No further persecution afflicted these people, but they have become extinct in Europe, the last having died in 1826.

THE JOURNEY TO AMERICA.

When these wandering people no longer found a place of refuge in Saxony, in April of 1734 about forty families began that journey to Pennsylvania already spoken of. This was completed in September, in a period of about five months. An account of this long voyage is given at the close of the book already often referred to, the *Erläuterung*, or Explanation.

In Altona (near Hamburg), during a stay of eleven days, they received great hospitalities from the Herren v. Smissen, father and son.

On arriving at Haarlem (from some of whose citizens they had received contributions while still in Saxony), they could not enough admire the common joy and proofs of love with which they were received. The brothers Abraham, Isaac, and Jann v. Byuschanse were especially kind, entertaining them with flesh, fish, all kinds of vegetables, beer, coffee, and tea, and besides the children were daily presented with all kinds of baked gingerbread and such things.*

As regarded the journey of the exiles to America, the Herren v. Byuschanse had made an agreement with the captain at their own expense.

Two days' journey from Holland, Gregory Meschter was presented with a healthy little son. Fifteen days they lay at Haarlem, and at Rotterdam, on the 21st of June, they went on board the English ship "St. Andrew," Captain Stedman commander. While they lay still one week on board this vessel, "God gave David Schubert a young son."

On the 28th they left Rotterdam. On the 16th of July, six Palatinate women and two men fought each other, and she who began it received her deserts.†

At Plymouth, England, which they left on the 29th,

---

* The word translated gingerbread is *Pfeffer-kuchen,* or pepper-cakes. Pepper-nuts are now made in Lancaster County,—a delicate cake, as I have seen them, somewhat resembling jumbles. If plainer they would be like the New England cookies. Cooky comes from the German *kuchen?*

In Allentown, a young gentleman tells me that the people of Lehigh County, all through, eat Schwenkfelder-cake. "Our mothers made them for us. They are a kind of vesper-cake, or rusk baked in a loaf." In Allentown the name is sometimes pronounced Schwinkfelder.

† No one should confound these emigrants from the Palatinate with the Palatines for whom William Penn desires the friendship of the Indians. See "Swiss Exiles," in this volume. The numerous refugees from the Palatinate probably came from different motives; some for religious freedom, and some to earn their bread. Many German emigrants were redemptionists,—*i.e.,* they sold their time to pay for their voyage. Of this class, we learn, was an ancestor of the late John Covode.

a rich woman gave the whole ship's company one hundred and twenty-five shillings, and when it was divided each person received four and a half stivers, English. (The stiver is a Dutch coin of the value of one English penny, or two cents in our money.)

On the 9th of August a Palatinate mother and daughter fought each other. On the 10th a great fish was seen, which spurted water on high powerfully, as if out of pipes. (Our inland Silesians were not familiar with whales.)

A number of children and several grown persons died upon the sea. On September 22d, "God be forever thanked," the anchor was happily cast before Philadelphia, and guns were fired. On the 23d, all males over sixteen had to go to the court-house to take the oath of fidelity to the King of Great Britain. "We Silesians, as on account of conscience we could not swear, were readily excused, and were allowed to promise faith by giving the hand" (*mit einem Handschlage*).

THE ANNIVERSARY OR YEARLY MEETING.

I asked a Schwenkfelder, "What are the exercises of your commemorative festival?" He answered, "It is a day of thanksgiving to God, that we live under a free government, where we can serve him according to our conscience."

An animated description of the day has been given by the Rev. C. Z. Weiser, in the *Mercersburg Review*. This article, although apparently not quite true to history, and though written in a peculiar style, has a sprightliness which interests the reader.*

---

* Mr. Weiser tells us, in speaking of the Schwenkfelders, that

Mr. Weiser tells us, that whoever is not providentially prevented is bound to attend their yearly reunion. Nor has it been found necessary thus far to enter an urging statute to secure the presence of the fraternity. The " seeding" is done, the corn stands in shocks, and the farm-work of September is timely put aside, in order that all may participate in the memorial ceremonies of the 24th with a light, gay, and thankful heart.* It is on the day and day before that you may feast your eyes on many a well-laden carriage, the horses all in good condition, moving on toward one of the Schwenkfelder meeting-houses, selected in rotation, and one whole year in advance. The aged and infirm of both sexes stay not behind. The young men and women are largely and promptly there. The fathers are similarly enough clad to be considered uniformed. So too are the mothers arrayed in a manner very like to one another, with snow-white caps and bonnets that never vary. The sons and

---

on a late occasion, having heard that the tombs of their ancestors, near Liegnitz and Gorlitz, were fast being desecrated, and the earth, with their very dust, carried away for road-making purposes, their Pennsylvania posterity collected a handsome sum and forwarded it to the authorities, with a view of purchasing the grounds, and having them set apart and enclosed as the burying-ground of the Silesian Schwenkfelders. It is not believed, however, he adds, that their moneys were appropriated to the laudable end which they had in view.

This narrative might apply to those Silesians who were buried upon the cow-paths (Mr. Weiser says, taken to the carrion pit or bone commons), but does it apply to them after they had taken refuge at Gorlitz?

* It has been estimated that ninety-five in one hundred of the Schwenkfelders are farmers.

daughters do indeed not love the habits of their elders any the less, yet only the wicked world's a little more.*

The morning service opens at nine o'clock, and is filled out with singing, praying, and recitals of portions of their ancestral history. All is gone through with in the Pennsylvania German dialect, but withal reverentially, solemnly, and earnestly, just as though it were newly and for the first time done.†

At twelve o'clock, the noonday feast is set. This is the feature of the day. It consists of light and newly-baked rye bread, sweet and handsomely printed butter, and the choicest apple-butter.‡ Nothing beyond these is set, but these are of the first water. The bare benches, but lately occupied by devout worshippers, serve as tables,

---

* In the Rules and Ordinances of the Schwenkfelder community may be found this passage: "Yet a Christian places no holiness in wearing the oldest fashioned clothes; he also takes care not quickly to ape all new fashions, much less does he make it his business to bring up new ones."

† Mr. Weiser speaks as if the singing was in the dialect. The following is a copy of some lines which were sung at their meeting-house when I attended, from which the student of German may observe the quality of the language, and the theologian may notice, as it seems to me, two or three of their peculiar doctrines:

> "Jehovah, Vater, Sohn, und Geist!
> O Segens Bronn, der ewig fleuszt!
> Durchfleusz Herz, Sinn, und Wandel wohl;
> Mach uns dein's Lob's und Segens voll!"

Jehovah, Father, Son, and Spirit! Oh, spring of blessing, forever flowing! Flow through heart, thought, and life; make us full of thy praise and blessing!

‡ Wheat bread is now used. At a Schwenkfelder house I ate apple-butter, sweet, because made from sweet apples, and seasoned with fennel, of which the taste resembles anise.

along which the guests are lined out. Not in silence, nor in sullenness, do they eat their simple meal, but spicing it with cheerful talk, they dine with hearts full of joy. Still, you need fear no profane utterance or silly jest. They are mindful of the spirit of the occasion, of the place in which they congregate, and of the feast itself, which the singing of some familiar hymn has consecrated. If any one thirst, let him drink cold water.

And now think not that they feign simply to eat and drink,—that the meal from first to last is but a poor pretence. A full and hearty dinner is " made out" there. It is a bona fide eating and drinking that is done in the meeting-house of the Schwenkfelders on their *Gedächtniss Tag* (Remembrance Day). They are all hard-working men and women,—farmers and farmers' wives and farmers' children. They are sunburnt, healthy, and hungry besides. And why should they not relish the sweet bread, with their sweet butter and apple-butter, then? Even strangers who attend and are hospitably entertained by the society show that one can make a full hand, even at such a table.

At two o'clock the tables become pews again, and the afternoon exercises are conducted according to the programme of the morning. These concluded, a general invitation is again extended to partake of the baskets of fragments gathered up and stored away in the rear of the meeting-house. A fraternal hand-shaking closes the anniversary for the year. The reflection that many part now who may never meet again on earth causes tears to trickle down some furrowed cheek, which generally prove more or less contagious, as is always the case in a company of hearts, when those tears flow in

11

sincere channels. Hence, though all were happy all day long, they now feel sad.

To appreciate the meaning and spirit of this apparently homely scene, it is necessary to know that it is a memorial service all through. It was on this very 24th of September, 1734, that some seventy [forty] families of Schwenkfelders, who had landed on the 22d, and declared their allegiance on the 23d, held their thanksgiving service, in gratitude to God for a safe deliverance to the colony of Pennsylvania. They had arrived in the ship "St. Andrew," at Philadelphia, as fugitives from Silesia.

Poor, but feeling rich in view of their long-sought liberty, they blessed God in an open assembly. We may judge their store and fare to have been scant and lean indeed; and to perpetuate the original service of their forefathers from generation to generation, they statedly celebrate their *Gedächtniss Tag.*

The poor fare before them is finely designed to impress the sore fact of their ancestors' poverty indelibly upon their minds, memories, and hearts. They eat and drink in remembrance of former days,—the days of small things. They join thereto at the same time a gladsome worship, in thankfulness for the asylum opened up for them from their former house of bondage, and which proved so fair a heritage to their people ever since.*

CUSTOMS.

A lawyer of Norristown tells me that he taught a subscription school among the Schwenkfelders, some

---

* It may be observed that I have used Mr. Weiser's language.

thirty years ago, and a day or two before the school closed he sent out his bills by the scholars. Every cent of the money due was paid in on the next morning,— and as he was then poor this was a delightful and memorable circumstance.*

Further, I find it laid down as a rule of their community that members must see to it that their debts are paid without legal proceedings.

Another instance of exactness in money matters is given in their history, namely, that while they were sojourning with or near Zinzendorf, some of their well-wishers in Holland sent to them a considerable contribution in money, of which they knew nothing until the merchants of Gorlitz announced and paid it to them. By their diligence in labor, and their skilful use of this money, they were able to supply the pressing wants of their poor, and to pay the expenses of the same to Altona. On their arrival at Haarlem, a little that remained was laid at the feet of their noble benefactors.†

I met with a young Dunker woman, in the neighborhood of the Schwenkfelder community, who said, " The poor always find their way to the Schwenkfelders ;" and on my mentioning this subject at one of the houses which I visited, my host told me of persons having come to his house asking " how far they had to the Schwenkfelder *Thal*" (or valley).

The language spoken at two of the houses which I visited was almost entirely the Pennsylvania German ;

---

* Before public-schools were established the Schwenkfelders had a fund for the education of their poorer members.

† " Which these ordered back into our fund, to supply the wants of the poor, when we should arrive at Philadelphia."

but my ignorance of the dialect forbids my knowing whether these Silesian emigrants speak it differently from the South German Palatines.

My power of talking German was perhaps never more exercised in the same length of time than during my visit here; the women and children in the houses alluded to speaking no English. In the second, the mother, who was in delicate health, had been reading German books, but was unable to read English. A like circumstance is certainly very uncommon, if not unknown, among the "Dutch" of my own county.

Neither does there appear to be the same objection to education there that exists among some of our people here. One of the Schwenkfelders said to me that he told his boys to learn as much as they can; "I'd not seen a man yet that had been too wise; and the girls may do the same." He also told me that they do not neglect to teach the children in their family to read and write German, a custom which tends to preserve the purity of the language. But the Schwenkfelders find it difficult to preserve a knowledge of German, since the language is no longer taught in the public schools in their neighborhoods.

Like Quakers, Dunkers, etc., the Schwenkfelders have an unpaid ministry. One whom I met, who had been a preacher, cultivated fourteen acres of ground, and joined to this labor the mechanical occupations of making brooms and cigar boxes. I said to one of the society, "You do not pay your ministers?"

"No," he answered, "but they are excused from all church expenses, such as the treasury for the poor, and building and keeping in repair our meeting-houses.

Then, as one minister will be a farmer and another a mechanic, and one is called upon to leave his shop and the other his farm to attend funerals, we generally make such a one a present.

" It has been at times the case that presents have been offered to men in good circumstances, who would answer, thanking the giver, but they had no need of the gift; if at any other time it should be necessary they would accept it."

Candidates for the ministry are elected by ballot; the votes being collected in a hat. Women do not vote, and of course they do not preach. If the candidates when elected prove to be " men of able tongues," they are confirmed. Formerly the Schwenkfelders did not vote for preachers, but it seemed to them that the right kind did not come forward, and those who did come forward were not always desirable persons.

The sacraments of baptism and the supper have never been held among them.* A modern custom, originating in this country, and established in 1823, has thus been described: After the birth of a child, it is brought by the parents into church, and a preacher prays for the happiness and prosperity of the child, and admonishes the parents to bring it up in the nurture and admonition of the Lord, according to the will of God. Then there is prayer, and the singing of some appropriate verses. If the child or mother is delicate, this service is sometimes performed at their house.†

---

* It is probable that baptism will be introduced, but only optionally.

† Mr. Weiser tells us that a mother whose adult daughter entered the Reformed Church, by baptism, earnestly protested against

Not only are the Schwenkfelders forbidden to become soldiers, but also to train in military exercises. Upon this point, however, the late rebellion seems to have tried some of their members, as it did some Quakers.

"Do you bring lawsuits?" said I to a member.

"Not if we can help it. I never brought a lawsuit, nor had one brought against me, and hope I never shall."

DOCTRINES.

In plainness of speech, behavior, and apparel, in opposition to war, to oaths, and to a paid ministry, in a belief in the teachings of the Divine Spirit and in the inferiority of the written word to the indwelling Spirit, in discarding religious forms, in opposition to priest-craft or a hierarchy, and, although not practising silent worship, yet in their desire to live "in the stillness," the Schwenkfelders resemble Quakers. We might almost say that they are Quakers of an older type (Quakers it may be of whom George Fox had never heard). They differ from Quakers in employing stated prayers, in electing preachers, in not acknowledging the spiritual equality of women, and in their peculiar doctrine of the "glory of the manhood of Jesus Christ,—how it is no creature." *

---

the performing of the sacrament over her, on the ground that "prayers were had for their child in the meeting-house."

* All Quakers do not teach the inferiority of the written word. Mr. Weiser says, "In general terms it may be said that Caspar Schwenkfeld has been the George Fox of Silesia, or the veritable George Fox, perhaps somewhat educated and sublimated."

Although some of the doctrines taught by George Fox seem to

We give from the *Erläuterung*, or Explanation, some striking extracts upon some of these points. Upon the word of God, Schwenkfeld and Illyricus had a violent contest. Schwenkfeld holds that the tables upon which God writes, and the book or paper upon which man writes, are entirely two kinds of thing : between all printed and written books in the world and the true word of God a fundamental difference is to be maintained. The word is a living, internal, spiritual word, and can only be contained in the book of the believing heart.* Faith existed many hundred years before the Scripture. It proceeded from the eternal Word or Son of God, Jesus Christ, and from God, the All-powerful.†

Against what are called " the means of grace" Schwenkfeld preached. (Spiritual things, it is said, come not through canals.) Schwenkfeld maintained that Christ is only to be sought above with the Father, and thence we must all draw that which will make us upright and blessed. This was also recognized by the

---

have been given before him by Schwenkfeld, yet were these not previously taught among the Anabaptists, and possibly among the Waldenses ?

It has been said that the better classes of Anabaptists claimed a descent from the Waldenses, the Wickliffites, and the Hussites, who had struggled for a church separated from the world and distinguished by the holiness of its members.

* A note says, " No one can deny that at last all books must perish, but the word of the Lord endureth forever."

† On his death-bed Schwenkfeld declared that he believed that all in the Old and New Testament was profitable for salvation to the elect; that he was certain that his own writings, if read impartially, and after prayer, agreed with Holy Scripture, but he must acknowledge to the praise of God that they proceeded more from gracious revelation.

leaders who came out from the papacy; but there came a time when they taught that Christ and salvation were to be found below in external works and worship. But Schwenkfeld neither could nor would admit that Christ and the Holy Spirit were in outward works of preaching and hearing and in elements of this earthly existence, in water, bread, and wine. *

On baptism we find the following: The first and most eminent work of the sacrament of baptism is, the internal grace of inworking faith in the love of God, which moves, glows, and lives through the outpouring of the heavenly waters which flow from the Word of God, which is Christ. The other point is the external word and water which is outwardly poured upon and washes the body outwardly as the internal does the soul.

John the Baptist says, "I baptize with water to repentance, but he who comes after me will baptize you with the Holy Ghost and with fire." Here he distinguishes the work of the minister from the office of the Lord, and the visible water from the Holy Spirit.

Ambrose says, "Peter has not purified, nor Ambrose, nor Gregory, for ours is the ministry, but thine, Lord, are the sacraments. It is not the work of man to give divine things, thine is it, Lord, and the Father's, who says through the prophets [prophet,] I will pour out my Spirit upon all flesh."

That the subject of the Holy Supper is especially weighty may be judged by the agitations on account of it, and by the fact that on this account many thous-

---

* See the *Erläuterung*, or Explanation, chap. x. These passages in general are greatly abbreviated, or are picked out, I may say.

ands in many lands have been killed and burnt. And this was the article upon which the Reformers, with their gloriously begun work, fell to pieces. Upon this article Luther renounced his friendship to Schwenkfeld, and they publicly differed.*

Schwenkfeld thought that when they came out from the papacy they should preach the gospel in its purity, instruct old and young in the catechism, and earnestly pray until they could come to the right use of the sacrament. . . . Whereby whole parishes, towns, and countries should not at once be taken up, as if fit for the table of the Lord. But it should be held with those who received the word, and in whom there were tokens of amendment, whether these were only Caleb and Joshua. Schwenkfeld declared that he had no command to establish the sacraments, but his command had been to spread the gospel and point every man to Jesus Christ. " But we are comforted that we are instructed by God and from the Holy Scripture that our soul's salvation is necessarily placed on no outward thing, but that one thing is needful." (Luke x.) " But we pray the Lord Jesus Christ that he will reveal a right use of the sacraments, and himself establish them. We strive, moreover, to hold his supper daily with the Lord Christ, in the spirit of faith." (Rev. iii.†) But though Schwenk-feld did not feel called upon to establish the sacraments,

---

* *Erläuterung*, chap. xi.

† The passage alluded to is doubtless this: " Behold, I stand at the door, and knock : if any man hear my voice, and open the door, I will come in to him, and will sup with him, and he with me."

there is nothing in the catechism of the society opposed
to the external rites.

The twelfth chapter of the Explanation, containing
nearly eighty pages, is devoted to Schwenkfeld's peculiar
doctrine, of which I shall content myself with the head-
ing of the chapter, as follows: "Of the divine Sonship
and glory of the Manhood of Jesus Christ, that the
same is no creature, but extinguished in the Transfig-
uration, and changed into the Godhead."

To one passage in the Catechism I would like to call
attention:

Question.—How did God reveal himself in an external manner?

Answer.—First, when God, by his almighty word,
framed the universe, by which he has shown how great,
almighty, wise, and good he is.*

And now may we not also rest our souls upon these
expressions from the constitution of the Schwenkfelder
society, translated almost literally?

In the nature of God, we first perceive love as that
noble and outflowing power which binds God and

---

* The thoughtful reader may perhaps find something in this answer to contrast with these passages from the decrees of the late
Ecumenical Council at Rome:

"If any one shall say that human sciences ought to be pursued
in such a spirit of freedom that any one may be allowed to hold
as true their assertions, even when opposed to revealed doctrine,
and that such assertions may not be condemned by the church, let
him be *anathema.* If any one shall say that at any time it may
come to pass, in the progress of science, that the doctrines set forth
by the church must be taken in another sense than that in which
the church has ever received and yet receives them, let him be
anathema." Quoted from a report of a dogmatic decree on Catholic faith, confirmed 1870.

men together. . . . If the society build upon this fundamental part of the divine nature, namely, love, then their only immovable aim will be, first, the glory of God, and second, the promotion of the common weal of every member."

The preceding article is published nearly as it appeared in the second edition of this work, which was issued late in 1873, with the date 1874. Almost as soon as the edition appeared, I learned that baptism had been introduced among the Schwenkfelders at a meeting held a few months before; and that perhaps in two cases it had also been administered at the approach of death.

In the spring of the present year, 1882, I visited a Schwenkfelder settlement in the upper part of Montgomery County, and was hospitably entertained at the house of one of their preachers. German or the Pennsylvania dialect was the language of the family. On Sunday I attended church, where, as before in another locality, the services were in German, as were nearly all the proceedings in the Sunday-school. Here I learned that the rite of the Supper has also been introduced among the Schwenkfelders, though not without opposition. I inquired on what grounds the opposition was brought, but received no satisfactory reply.

At the house of my entertainer I was shown a volume, published in 1879, containing a genealogical record of the descendants of the Schwenkfelders in this country, to which is prefixed a historical sketch by C. Heydrick, a lawyer of Franklin, Pennsylvania.

Herein it is stated that Schwenkfeld differed with Luther on several points; chiefly on the eucharist, the efficacy of the divine word, the human nature of Christ, and baptism.

Schwenkfeld held, says the writer, that the penitent believer partakes of the bread and the body of the Lord, not only at the sacramental altar, but elsewhere.

On the second point Schwenkfeld denied that the external word in the Scriptures has the power of healing and renewing the mind, but ascribed this power to the internal word, Christ himself. He regretted that Luther, who at first agreed with him, saw fit afterward to ascribe to the written or preached word the efficacy which is only in Christ, the eternal word.

Further, Schwenkfeld rejected infant baptism, and held that baptism and the Supper were not intended as means by which the unregenerate partaker can obtain salvation.

Two other volumes on these subjects have very lately come within my notice. One in German, by a pastor named Kadelbach, published about 1860, at Lauban, which is within forty miles of the city of Liegnitz, where Schwenkfeld was canon in a church. As early as 1846, in composing a history of the village of Probsthayn (where some of the Schwenkfelders formerly lived), he added to it some material concerning these people.

As this subject attracted attention, he endeavored to obtain material for a history of them, in which matter he met with much difficulty. It came to pass, however, that the Schwenkfelders in America sent an inquiry to the burgomaster of Probsthayn, asking whether there were still Schwenkfelder communities (*Gemienden*) there. This inquiry came, in 1855, into the hands of Kadelbach, who was very glad to communicate with the Schwenkfelders in America, as he had never before been able to do. His volume is called "Complete History of Kaspar von Schwenkfeld and of the Schwenkfelders in Silesia, Upper Lusatia, and America." * A copy has been placed in the archives of the German Society's library in Philadelphia.

We may infer that the attention of the author was attracted to his subject by certain local objects or remains. He tells us that the Catholic chapel at Harpersdorf, and the graves on the cow-path (*viehweg*), are the last memorials that testify of the existence there, and of the persecution of the Schwenkfelders. The Catholic chapel was built for one of the missionaries who was striving to convert them. As to the graves on the cow-paths, the statement has before been quoted (in a note on page 222), that three hundred persons lay upon the cow-paths at Harpersdorf and Langenneudorff (or Langendorff).

The other volume in which the Schwenkfelders are especially noticed is Barclay's Inner Life of the Religious Societies of the Commonwealth. London, 1876. Barclay finds that on several points the teaching of Schwenkfeld was identical with that of George Fox, the first Quaker. Barclay gives a passage from Schwenkfeld, in which he says that the true knowledge of Christ, that which is according to the Holy Ghost must be ex-

---

* Ausführliche Geschichte Kaspar v. Schwenkfelds, etc.

pected, not alone out of the Scriptures, but much more from the gifts of grace revealed by the Father, yet so that this revelation should always be in unison with the witness of the Scriptures.*

Struck with the similarity between the Schwenkfelders and Quakers, Barclay appears to have written to the former, and to have received an answer, from which the following passages are taken:

To Robert Barclay, England:

. . . "Judging from the brief notices of the teachings of George Fox in our possession, we have reason to believe that they did not differ materially from those of Schwenkfeld, and among the followers of both, here in America, there is a striking similarity in the almost total absence of formalities and ceremonies in their religious practices. Both are discarding judicial oaths, carnal weapons, and are unostentatious in dress.

"Notwithstanding the fact that the Friends are of English descent, having their books, worship, and conversation in the English language, and the followers of Schwenkfeld here all of it in German, yet there always existed a lively sympathy, love, and esteem between the parties. . . . It is, however, proper to mention the fact that neither in Europe nor here have the followers of

---

* Kadelbach tells us of George Mattern, a teacher in Silesia, who inclined to the opinions of Schwenkfeld, and who migrated to Holland, and afterward to England, where he joined the Quakers. He wrote a letter with this expression: "Dear father, thou must not be surprised that I thee and thou thee. *Dich. dutze.*"

Schwenkfeld at any time administered baptism and the Lord's Supper.*

"Owing to the persecutions which prevailed from 1630 to 1640, the religious practices of our ancestors in Germany about that period were chiefly confined to meeting in private houses for prayer and admonition, and in endeavors in the daily work of life to imitate as much as possible the example of the heavenly Master.

"In the love of Christ, sincerely your friends,

> "GEORGE MESCHTER.
> "WILLIAM SCHULTZ.
> "JACOB MESCHTER.
> "Per DAN. S. SHULTZ.

"December 17th, 1875   COLEBROOKDALE, PENNA."

---

* This letter is dated 1875. It was late in 1873 that I heard of baptism as having been administered among them.

A FRIEND.

About twenty miles from the line that divides Maryland and Pennsylvania, there stands, in the latter State, a retired farm-house, which was erected more than fifty years ago by Samuel Wilson, a Quaker of Quakers.

His was a character so rare in its quaintness and its nobility, that it might serve as a theme for a pen more practised and more skilful than the one that now essays to portray it.

Samuel Wilson was by nature romantic. When comparatively young, he made a pedestrian tour to the Falls of Niagara, stopping upon his return journey, and hiring with a farmer to recruit his exhausted funds; and when he had passed his grand climacteric, the enthusiasm of his friendship for the young, fair, and virtuous, still showed the poetic side of his character.

Veneration induced him to cherish the relics of his ancestry,—not only the genealogical tree, which traced the Wilsons back to the time of William Penn, and the marriage certificates of his father and grandfather, according to the regular order of the Society of Friends; but such more humble and familiar heirlooms as the tall eight-day clock, and the high bookcase upon a desk and chest of drawers, that had been his father's, as well as

244

the strong kitchen-chairs and extremely heavy fire-irons of his grandfather.

To this day there stands beside the Wilson farm-house a stone taken from one of the buildings erected by Samuel's father, and preserved as an heirloom. Upon it the great-grandchildren read nearly the following inscription:

"James Wilson, ejus manus scripsit. [His hand wrote.] Deborah Wilson, 5 mo. 23d, 1757."

Samuel Wilson, having been trained from his earliest years to that plainness of speech in which the Discipline requires that Friends bring up those under their care, not only discarded in speaking the simple titles in use in common conversation, but did not himself desire to be addressed as Mr. Wilson.

A colored woman, the wife of one of his tenants, said that he refused to answer her when she thus spoke to him.

A pleasant euphemism was generally employed by these people in addressing him. He and his wife were "Uncle Samuel" and "Aunt Anna" to their numerous dependents.

The apparel of Samuel and Anna was of the strict pattern of their own religious sect. To employ a figure of speech, it was the "wedding-garment," without which, at that time and place, they would not have become elders in their society, and thus been entitled to sit with ministers, etc., upon the rising seats that faced the rest of the meeting.

But the plainness of Uncle Samuel was not limited to the fashion of his own garments. When Aunt Anna had made for her son a suit of domestic cloth, dyed brown with the hulls of the black walnut, and had arrayed him in his new clothes, of which the trousers were made roomy behind,—or, as the humorist says, " baggy in the reverse,"—she looked upon him with maternal pride and fondness, and exclaimed, " There's my son !"

For this ejaculation she was not only reproved at the time by her husband, but in after-years, whenever he heard her, as he thought, thus fostering in the mind of their dear and only child pride in external appearance, he repeated the expression, "There's my son !" which saying conveyed a volume of reproof.

From this and other circumstances of the kind, it may be supposed that Friend Wilson was a cold or bitter ascetic. But he possessed a vein of humor, and could be gently and pleasantly rallied when he seemed to run into extremes. But, though his intellect was good, the moral sentiments predominated in his character. His head was lofty and arched. His wants were very few ; he possessed an ample competence, and he had no ambition to enter upon the fatiguing chase after riches. He disliked acquisitive men as much as the latter despised him. " I want so little for myself," he said, " I think that I might be allowed to give something away."

Sometimes—but rarely—a little abruptness was seen in his behavior. He had the manners of a gentleman by birth,—tender and true, open to melting charity, thinking humbly of himself, and respecting others.

The vein of humor to which I have alluded prompted the reply which he made on a certain occasion to a mechanic or laboring man employed in his own family. In this section of Lancaster County the farming population is composed principally of a laborious and in some respects a humble-minded people, who sit at table and eat with their hired people of both sexes.

The same custom was pursued by Samuel and Anna; but, as their hired people were mostly colored, they sometimes offended the prejudices or tastes of many who were not accustomed to this equality of treatment, which was maintained by several families of Friends. The white hired man to whom I have alluded, when he perceived who were seated at the table, hesitated or refused to sit down among them. As soon as Samuel was conscious of the difficulty, for which indeed his mind was not unprepared, he thus spoke aloud to his wife: "Anna, will thee set a plate at that other table for this stranger? He does not want to sit down with us." And his request was quietly obeyed. The man who was thus set apart probably became tired of this peculiar seclusion, for he did not stay long at the Quaker homestead.

I think that Samuel was also in a humorous mood when he called that unpretending instrument, the accordion,—from which his daughter-in-law was striving one evening to draw forth musical sounds,—"Mary's fiddle." But, indeed, he left the house and went to call upon a neighbor, so greatly did he partake of that prejudice which was felt by most Friends against music.

The Discipline asks whether Friends are punctual to their promises; and (to quote a very different work) Fielding tells us that Squire Allworthy was not only careful to keep his greater engagements, but remembered also his promises to visit his friends.

Anna Wilson on one occasion having thoughtlessly made such a promise,—as, indeed, those in society frequently do when their friends say, "Come and see us,"—

was often reminded of it in after-years by her husband. When he heard her lightly accepting such invitations, he would reprove her by saying in private, "When is thee going to see Benjamin Smith?"—the neighbor to whom the ancient promise was still unfulfilled.

The hospitality which the Scriptures enjoin was practised to a remarkable degree by Samuel and Anna. It has always been customary in their religious society to entertain Friends who come from a distance to attend meetings, and those travelling as preachers, etc. But the Wilson homestead was a place of rest and entertainment for many more than these. It stood not far from the great highway laid out by William Penn from Philadelphia westward, and here called the "Old Road." Friends travelling westward in their own conveyance would stop and refresh themselves and their horses at the hospitable mansion, and would further say to their own friends, "Thee'd better stop at Samuel Wilson's. Tell him I told thee to stop." A further and greater extent of hospitality I shall mention hereafter.

The Discipline asks whether Friends are careful to keep those under their charge from pernicious books and from the corrupt conversation of the world; and I have heard that Samuel Wilson was grieved when his son began to go to the post-office and take out newspapers. Hitherto the principal periodical that came to the house was *The Genius of Universal Emancipation*, a little paper issued by that pioneer, Benjamin Lundy, who was born and reared in the Society of Friends. It does not appear, however, that the class of publications brought from the little village post-office to the retired farm-house were of the class usually called pernicious.

They were *The Liberator*, *The Emancipator*, and others of the same order.

Samuel himself became interested in them, but never to the exclusion of the " Friends' Miscellany," a little set of volumes containing religious anecdotes of Friends. These volumes were by him highly prized and frequently read.

It has been said that he was a humorist; and perhaps he was partly jesting when he suggested that his infant granddaughter should be named Tabitha. The mother of the little one, on her part, suggested Helen.

" He-len !" the grandfather broke out in reply; "does thee know who *she* was?" thus expressing his antipathy to the character of the notorious beauty of Greece. He did not insist, however, on endowing the precious newly-born infant with that peculiar name which is by interpretation Dorcas, the name of her who, in apostolic times, was full of good works and alms-deeds.

Friend Wilson shared the Quaker disregard for the great holidays of the church. To the colored people around him, who had been brought up at the South, where Christmas is so great a festival,—where it was so great a holiday for them especially,—it must have been a sombre change to live in a family where the day passed nearly like other working-days. One of the colored men, however, who had started at the time of the great festival to *take Christmas*, was seen, before long, coming back ; " for," said he, " Massa Wilson don't 'prove on't nohow."

Among the lesser peculiarities of Samuel Wilson was his objection to having his picture taken,—an objection, however, which is felt to this day by some strict people belonging to other religious societies, but probably on somewhat different grounds.

One who warmly loved and greatly respected Friend Wilson took him once to the rooms of an eminent daguerreotypist, hoping that while he engaged the venerable man in looking at the objects around the room, the artist might be able to catch a likeness. But Samuel suspected some artifice, and no picture was taken. Some time after, however, the perseverance of his friend was rewarded by obtaining an excellent oil-painting of the aged man, from whom a reluctant consent to sit for his likeness had at length been obtained. It was remarked, however, that the expression of the face in the painting was sorrowful, as if the honorable man was grieved at complying with a custom which he had long stigmatized as idolatrous,—as idolatry of the perishing body.

Although at the time of the great division in the Society of Friends Samuel Wilson had decidedly taken the part of Elias Hicks, yet was he seldom or never heard to discuss those questions of dogmatic theology which some have thought were involved in that contest.

Samuel probably held, with many others of his Society, that the highest and surest guide which man possesses here is that Light which has been said to illumine every man that comes into the world ; that next in importance is a rightly inspired gospel ministry, and afterward the Scriptures of truth. One evening, when certain mechanics in his employ were resting from their labors in the old-fashioned kitchen, he fell into conversation with them on matters of religion, and shocked one of his family, as he entered the sitting-room, by a sudden declaration of opinion. It was probably the uncommon warmth of his manner which produced this effect, quite as much as or more than the words that he spoke, which were nearly as follows: " There's no use talking about it; the only religion in the world that's worth anything is what makes men do what is right and leave off doing what is wrong."

As far as was possible for one with so much fearless independence of thought and action, Samuel Wilson maintained the testimony of Friends against war. Not only did he suffer his corn to be seized in the field rather than voluntarily to pay the military taxes of the last war with Great Britain, but he went to what may appear to some a laughable extreme, in forbidding his young son's going to the turnpike to see the grand procession which was passing near their house, escorting General Lafayette on his last visit to this country. He was not, however, alone in this. I have heard of other decided Friends who declined to swell the ovation to a man who was especially distinguished as a military hero. But we shall see hereafter that Friend Wilson met with circumstances which tried his non-resistant opinions further than they would bear.

The distinctive trait of his character, however,—that trait which made him exceptional,—was his attachment to the people of color. It was in entertaining fugitives from slavery that he showed the wide hospitality already referred to ; and in this active benevolence he was excelled by few in our country. He inherited from his father this love of man ; but I have imagined that the hostility to slavery was made broad and deep in his soul by removing, with the rest of his family, in his youth, from Pennsylvania into Delaware, and seeing the bondage which was suffered by colored people in the latter State contrasted with what he had seen in the former. Be that as it may, no sooner was he a house-holder than his door was ever open to those who were escaping from the South, coming by stealth and in dark-ness, having travelled in the slave States from the house of one free negro to another, and in Pennsylvania from Quaker to Quaker, until in later times the hostility to slavery increased in our community so far that others became agents of this underground railroad, and other routes were opened.

When the Wilson family came down in the morning, they saw around them these strange sable or yellow travellers ("strangers," they were called in the family), who, having arrived during the night, had been received by some wakeful member of the household.

What feelings filled the hearts of the exiles! Alone, at times, having left all that they had ever loved of per-sons or of places, fearful, tired, foot-sore, throwing them-selves upon the charity and the honor of a man unknown to them save by name and the direction which they had received to him, as one trustworthy.

Sometimes they came clothed in the undyed woollen cloth that showed so plainly to one experienced in the matter, the region of its manufacture; the heavy, strong cloth which had delighted the wearer's heart when he received the annual Christmas suit with which his master furnished him, but which was now too peculiar and striking for him safely to wear. Women and children came too, and sometimes in considerable numbers.

When they had eaten and partaken of the necessary

repose, they would communicate to Friend Wilson, in a secure situation, some particulars of their former history, especially the names and residences of the masters from whom they had escaped.

Some years after he had begun to entertain these strangers, Friend Wilson commenced a written record of those who came to him, and whence and from whom they had escaped. This list is estimated to have finally contained between five and six hundred names.

The next care was to bestow new titles upon the fugitives, that they might never be known by their former names to the pursuer and the betrayer.

From what has been already said, it may be supposed that these names were not always selected for their euphony or æsthetic associations. One tall, finely-built yellow man, who trembled when he was questioned in the sitting-room, lest his conversation about his old home and the free wife whom he longed to have brought to him should be overheard in the kitchen, expressed to me his dissatisfaction with his new name— Simon. "I never knowed anybody named that," he said. His beautiful bright wife—bright in the *colored* sense,—that is, bright-colored, or nearly white,—was secretly and safely brought to him, and nursed him through that fatal disease which made him of no value in the man-market,—the market which had been the great horror of his life. The particulars Friend Wilson collected concerning his humble charge the venerable man entered in his day-book, in a place especially assigned to them. If this record were still existing, I should, perhaps, be able to tell what name the fortunate and unfortunate Simon had been obliged to renounce. This record, however, is lost, as I shall mention hereafter. If the services of any of these fugitives were needed, within-doors or without, and the master's pursuit was not supposed to be imminent, they were detained for a while, or perhaps became permanent residents in the neighborhood; otherwise, they were forwarded at night to Friends living nearer Philadelphia. Of these, two other families willing to receive the poor exiles lived about twelve miles farther on.

The house and farm were generally pretty well stocked with colored people, who were a wonder to the neighbors of the Wilson family; for these were in a great measure " Pennsylvania Dutch,"—a people anxious to do as much work with their own hands and by the hands of their own family as possible, in order to avoid expense. It is a remarkable circumstance that, although Samuel Wilson during thirty years or more entertained the humble strangers, and although he received so large a number, only one of them was seized upon his " plantation" and taken back to slavery. This was owing partly to the secluded situation of his house, and partly to the prudence and discretion that he exercised. "He was crafty," it has been said.

Neither did he suffer any legal expenses, such as lawsuits, from the slaveholders who came in pursuit of their fleeing bondmen. Two friends who lived not far from him, and who prosecuted kidnappers, had their barns burned, and others, of whom he had knowledge, suffered great pecuniary loss in consequence of their assisting runaway slaves. He, however, limited his care to receiving, entertaining, and forwarding those who came to him in person, and never undertook any measures of offence,—any border raids, so to speak,—such as sending secretly into Maryland and Virginia for the relatives and friends of fugitives who were still living in those States as slaves. The one person of whom I have spoken, who was recaptured from the Wilson farm, was a young girl of fifteen or sixteen. Samuel and Anna were absent from home at the time, gone on a little journey, such as they frequently took, to attend their own monthly and quarterly meetings; assisting to preserve the discipline and order of the Society of Friends. The men who came in pursuit of the young girl told her that her friends, who had run away too, had concluded to go back South again; and the poor child, under these circumstances, could hardly do anything but go with the beguilers; not, however, to find the friends whom she expected.

There was also a man who was very near being taken, —a man who had "come away," to use the brief euphemism sometimes employed in the Wilson family in speaking of fugitives from slavery. He escaped by having gone down the creek or adjacent mill-stream to set his muskrat-traps. This creek where it ran by the house was well wooded; therefore the colored man, looking up to the house, could see the white strangers without being seen himself. With what trembling did he see that they were persons whom he "knowed in Murrland," as he expressed it! However, the friendly woods sheltered him, while Samuel at the house was talking with the slaveholder or his agents,—kidnappers, as the Wilsons called them.

The men told Samuel that they had come after a runaway nigger,—black, five feet ten inches high, lost one of his front teeth, etc. To this description Friend Wilson listened in silence. I do not know what he would have done had he been directly questioned by them, for the different items suited him of the muskrats,—the man who had gone to the woods. But during Samuel's continued silence they went on to say, "He's a very ornary nigger; no dependence to be placed on him nohow." "There is no man here," rejoined Samuel, greatly relieved, "that answers the description." "We've very good reason to think he came here," said one; "we got word very direct; reckon he's lyin' around here. Hain't there been no strange nigger here?"

"There was a colored man here, but he has gone away; I don't know as he will ever come back again." For, from the man's protracted absence, he doubtless had some idea of his having seen his pursuers, and having sought shelter.

"Tell him that his master says that if he will only come back again, down to Baltimore County, he sha'n't be whipped, nor sold, nor nuthin', but everything shall be looked over."

"I'll tell him what you say," said Samuel, "if ever I see him again; but," he added, regaining his accustomed independence, "I'll tell him, too, that if I was in his place I'd never go back to you again."

The men left, and under cover of the friendly night the fugitive sought a more secure hiding-place.

There was one heroic black man in whom Samuel Wilson felt an abiding interest. When Jimmy Franklin told the tale of his perilous escapes and recaptures in the States of Maryland, North and South Carolina, Georgia, and Florida,—when he showed the shot still remaining in his legs—shot that had been fired at him as he ran, and, working through to the front, were perceived through the skin, like warts upon his legs,—the lads of the family looking and listening had their sympathies enkindled in such a manner as could never entirely die out. One of them, in after-years, was asked:

"How does thee account for that man's persistent love of freedom? What traits of character did he possess that would account for his doing so much more than others to escape from the far South?"

"I don't know," was the reply, in the freedom of familiar conversation. "What was the reason that Fulton invented his steamboat? or that Bacon wrote his System? or that Napier invented logarithms?

"This man was a genius,—a greater man in his way than those I spoke of. If he had had education, and had been placed in circumstances to draw him out, he would have been the leader in some great movement among men."

The narrative of James Franklin was written by a dear friend of him whom I call Samuel Wilson, but is supposed to have been burned when the mob destroyed Pennsylvania Hall.

It was in relation to these fugitives that Samuel sometimes forgot for a while his strictly peaceful principles; for there were to be found among the men of color those who could be induced to betray to the pursuers their fugitive brethren, giving such information as would lead to their recapture; or, if they should escape this, to their being obliged to abandon their resting-places and to flee again for safety.

It was in talking of some such betrayer that Samuel

Wilson said to his colored friends, "What would you do with that man, if you had him on Mill-Creek bridge?" (a lofty structure by which the railroad crossed the adjacent stream,) thus hinting at a swift mode of punishment, and one that might possibly have been a fatal one.

Though with an unskilled pen, yet have I endeavored to describe that quiet family among whom the fugitive-slave law of 1850 fell like a blow. Samuel Wilson had ample opportunity to study its provisions and its peculiarities from the newspapers of which I have before spoken, and from the conversation which these journals called forth.

This horrible act gave the commissioner before whom the colored man was tried five dollars only if the man went free from the tribunal, but ten dollars if he was sent into slavery. Hitherto, men had suffered in assisting the fugitive *to escape;* now it was made a penal offence to refuse to lend active assistance in apprehending him.

Friend Wilson had read much of fines and imprisonment, having studied the sufferings of the people called Quakers. (Even a lady of so high a standing as she who became the wife of George Fox was not exempt from many years' imprisonment, nor from persecution at the hands of her own son.) Friend Wilson was about seventy-five years old when the fugitive-slave bill was passed. In spite of his advanced years, however, after sorrowful reflection upon it, he said to one of his household, "I have made up my mind to go to jail."

That hospitality and charity which had so long been the rule of his life he was not now prepared to forego through fear of any penalties which the law would inflict upon him.

It was while suffering from the infirmities of advanced years, and from the solicitude which this abominable enactment had called forth, that Samuel destroyed the record which he had kept for so many years of the slaves that had taken refuge with him. This record was contained in about forty pages of his day-book, and these he cut out and burned. How would they now be prized had they not thus been lost!

Samuel Wilson saw, with the prophetic eye of faith and hope, what he did not live to behold in the flesh,— the abolition of slavery. His mortal remains repose beside the Quaker meeting-house where he so long ministered as an elder. No monumental stone marks that humble resting-place; but these simple lines of mine, that portray a character so rare, may serve for an affectionate memorial.

COUSIN JEMIMA.

"WELL, Phebe, I guess thee did not expect me this afternoon. Don't get up. I will just lay my bonnet in the bedroom myself. Dinah Paddock told me thy quilt was in; so I came up as soon as I could. Laid out in orange-peel! I always did like orange-peel. Dinah's was herring-bone; and thine is filled with wool, and plims up, and shows the works, as mother used to say. I'll help thee roll before I sit down. Now then. Days are long, and we'll try to do a stroke of work, for thee's a branch quilter, I've heard say.

"Jethro Mitchell stopped to see me this morning. They got home from Ohio last week, and he says that Cousin Jemima Osborne's very bad with typhoid fever. Poor Jemima! It had been pretty much through the family, and after nursing the rest, she was taken down. I almost know she has no one fit to take care of her,— only Samuel and the three boys, and maybe some hired girl that has all the housework to do. The neighbors will be very kind, to be sure, sitting up nights; but there's been so much sickness in that country lately.

"Jemima was Uncle Brown Coffin's daughter, thee knows, who used to live down at Sandwich, on the Cape, when thee and I were girls. She always came to

Nantucket to Quarterly Meeting with Uncle Brown and Aunt Judith; and folks used to say she wasn't a bit of a coof, if she *was* born on the Cape. When Samuel and she were married, they asked me and Gorham Hussey to stand up with them. Jemima looked very pretty in her lavender silk and round rosy cheeks. When meeting was over, she whispered to me that there was a wasp or bee under her neck-handkerchief that had stung her while she was saying the ceremony. But I don't think anybody perceived it, she was so quiet. Poor dear! I seem to see her now on a sick-bed and a rolling pillow.

"After my Edward died, I was so much alone that I thought I couldn't bear it any longer, and I must just get up and go to Ohio, as Samuel and 'Mima had often asked me to. I stopped on the way at Mary Cooper's at Beaver, and Mary's son was joking a little about Cousin Samuel's farming, and said he didn't quite remember whether it was two or three fences that they had to climb going from the house to the barn-yard. I told him that Samuel wasn't brought up to farming; he bought land when he moved out West.

"I found Jemima a good deal altered, now that she had a grown family; but we just began where we left off,—the same friendliness and kindness. When I was in Ohio was just when the English Friends, Jonathan and Hannah Purley, were in the country. We met them at Marlborough Quarterly Meeting. We were all together at William Smith's house,—one of the neatest of places,—everything like waxwork, with three such daughters at home. How they worked to entertain Friends!

" First-day a great many world's people were at meeting on account of the strange Friends. Meeting was very full,—nearly as many out in the yard as in the house. Very weighty remarks were made by Jonathan and Hannah. She spoke to my own state:—' Leave thy widows and let thy fatherless children trust in Me.' The meeting was disturbed some by the young babies; but we could hardly expect the mothers to stay away.

" Second-day was Quarterly Meeting. Of course the English Friends, being at William Smith's, drew a great many others. We had forty to dinner. One of William's daughters stayed in the kitchen, one waited on the table, and one sat down midway, where she could pass everything and wait on the Friends. It was in the Eighth Month, and we had a bountiful table of all the good things of that time of year,—vegetables and fruit too. William was a nurseryman.

" There was a little disturbance at breakfast, William's son—a rather wild young man—making the young people laugh. We had fish,—mackerel, and little fresh fish out of the mill-dam. I sat near the middle, and heard Friend Smith at one end say to each, ' Will thee have some of the mackerel, or some of these little dam-fish ?' Then young William, at the other end, spoke low to his friends: ' Will thee have some of the mackerel, or some of these dam little fish ?' But most of the young women kept pretty serious countenances. When Quarterly Meeting was over, the English Friends went out to Indiana, visiting meetings and Friends' families, and I went back with Cousin Samuel's.

" I was dreadfully disappointed once. One evening Samuel and 'Mima and the rest of us were sitting round the table, and Samuel put his hand into his coat-pocket and drew out the paper and two or three letters. As he read, I noticed that one of the letters had not been opened, and caught sight of my name—Priscilla Gardner; so I put out my hand and took it. It was from sister Mary, —just as James and she were starting for California. She told me that they should stay in Pittsburg over one night, and she hoped I should be able to meet them there and bid them a long farewell. But when I looked again at the date of the letter, and glanced at the paper that Samuel was reading, I found that my letter was ten days old. The time had gone by. Oh, dear! I walked out into the kitchen and stood by the stove, in the dark, and cried. Some one came up behind me. Of course it was Jemima. She kissed me, and waited for me to speak. I gave her the letter, and in about ten minutes I felt able to go back to the sitting-room. When I sat down, Samuel said, ' 'Mima tells me, Priscilla, that thee is very much disappointed about thy letter. I had on this coat when I went to the post-office a week ago, and I didn't put it on again till to-day. I hope thee'll excuse me. Thomas, my son, will thee bring us some red-streaks? I feel as if I could eat a few apples.'

"I felt sorrowful for some time about my sister; but my mind was diverted when we got word that the English Friends were coming to our Monthly Meeting on their way back from Indiana; and as we lived very near the meeting-house, of course they would be at Samuel's. As the time came near, Jemima and I were a good deal interested to have things nice. They were going to be at William Smith's again, where everything was so neat, and I felt very anxious to make everything in-doors, at Jemima's, as nice as we could.

"In the sitting-room was one empty corner, where the great rocking-chair ought to stand. It was broken, and put away in the bedroom. I wanted very much to have it mended; but it seemed as if we could not get it to Salem. One time the load would be too large, another the chair would be forgotten. At last one day it was put in the back of the covered wagon, and fairly started. When Samuel got home it was rather late in the evening, and I heard him say to 'Mima, 'Only think of my forgetting thy large chair. I was late starting from home, thee knows; and when I got to Salem there was a good deal of talk about the war; and when I got half-way home I remembered the big chair in the back of the wagon. It can go in next week.' We did send it again, but it did not get home before Monthly Meeting.

"Jemima had a very neat home-made carpet on the sitting-room: she had a great taste for carpets. As there had been some yards left, she let me cover the front entry too, and her youngest son Edward, a nice lad, helped me put it down. A little colored girl, near by, rubbed up the brass andirons for us, and Edward built up a pile of wood ready to kindle the fire when it was wanted. A good many panes of glass had been broken, and as we had just had an equinoctial storm, some old coats, and so on, had been stuffed in at several places; but we managed to get most of the glass put in before Monthly Meeting.

"When we had done all we could to the house, of course we began to think of the cooking. Jemima said, 'I sha'n't be able to get Mary Pearson to come and cook : she is nursing. I wonder whether I hadn't better heat the oven on meeting-day. I can get the dinner in before I go; and then between meetings I can run over and see to it. I shall hardly be missed. I can slip in at the side-door of the meeting-house before Mary Ann has done reading the Minutes.'—'Then thee will heat the oven ?' said I.—'I reckon,' she said; 'but it is only a mud oven. Samuel has been talking for a good while about having a brick oven. This one is not very safe.' —'Suppose I make a little sponge-cake, and put it in too,' said I. 'I'll send for some sugar, if thee is willing. Polly Evans used to call me a dabster at sponge-cake.'

"Jemima was willing, and we began to get ready to go to the store. Edward and the little colored girl hunted the barn and the straw-shed, and brought in a quantity of eggs. All could not be sent, because we needed some at home, and some had been set on, and some had lain too long. Then Jemima sent to the garret for brooms and rags, and spared a little butter too for the store,—not much, to be sure, when Monthly Meeting was coming. I thought I might as well ride over with Edward; and when we had got coffee, and tea, and so on, and were just starting home, I caught sight of some lemons. I bought a few, and when I got home asked Jemima if she would not like some lemon-puddings. 'Thy apple-pies and rice-puddings are nice, dear,' I said; 'but Hannah Purley and Jonathan are such strangers, we might go a little out of the common way.' Jemima smiled at my being so anxious, but agreed, as she generally did.

"Fourth-day morning we were up very early. Jemima

was going to roast some fowls and a loin of veal. Edward and the little colored girl helped me to beat eggs, grate lemons, and roll sugar; and everything was ready for the oven before the Friends came in from a distance, who always stopped before meeting to get a cup of tea.

" We had a nice little table for them, of course,—dried beef, preserves, and so on; and one woman Friend, a single woman, asked for a warm flat-iron to press out her cap and handkerchief. At last we were ready to start. Jemima had set everything into the oven, which stood out in the yard. She put the meats back, and the cakes and puddings near the door, where it was not so hot. ' The door isn't very safe,' said she, 'and I propped a stick against it to keep it up. Don't let the dog knock it down, Susan, while we are gone.'

" The day was beautiful; all signs of the storm over, except the roads a little muddy; and as we stepped over to the meeting-house Jemima whispered, ' I am glad I told Susan to set both tables. I think we shall have a good many to dinner. I wanted cole-slaw, like Pennsylvania folks, but the cows broke in last night and ate all the solid cabbage.' She did not talk of these things generally going into meeting; but our minds were very full.

" First meeting was rather long, for several Friends spoke besides the strangers. When it broke, Jemima stepped out, and I quietly followed her. We walked over to the house, and round into the side-yard, going toward the oven. But just as we had got into the yard we saw the old sow. She had broken out of the barn-yard, and had been wallowing in a pond of brown water near the fence. Now she had knocked down Jemima's stick, and as the door fell I guess she smelt our good things, for she had her fore-feet upon the oven floor. We ran and screamed, but she did not turn. She made a jump up to the oven, over my cakes and puddings, the veal and chickens, and carried the oven roof off with her. Oh, dear! oh, dear! poor Jemima! I could laugh too, if it wasn't so dreadful."

Reader.—And what did they do then?

Writer.—The best that they could. I do wonder at Jemima, poor thing, to undertake so much on Monthly Meeting day.

THE MINERS OF SCRANTON.

A FEW years ago I visited Hyde Park,—a mining division of the youthful city of Scranton. Besides boarding in the family of an operative, I talked with citizens, from miners to ministers, and took notes of these conversations. Upon the information thus obtained the following article is founded.

There hangs in our house a large map of the State of Pennsylvania of the year 1851. Scranton is not marked upon it. A little village named Providence is, indeed, to be found, which is now an inconsiderable part of consolidated Scranton. Nine years after the date of this map, by the census of 1860, the population of Scranton is given at nine thousand, and in 1870 at thirty-five thousand. This very rapid increase was caused by the working of the immense coal-beds which underlie the narrow valley of the Lackawanna, in which the city is situated.

Forty-five per cent. of the population is given as foreign, or fifteen thousand eight hundred and eighty-seven. The miners are almost all of foreign birth, the Irish being the most numerous, next the Welsh, then the Germans, and lastly the English and Scotch. Among the Welsh-speaking population there are, however, natives of Monmouthshire, not now a portion of Wales, but belonging to England. Among the miners there are some Pennsylvania Germans. With the exception of these, there is scarcely to be found at Scranton a native of this country working underground, either as miner or laborer.

Gaelic is extensively spoken by the Irish here, there being women, I am told, newly come over, who do not speak English. The Welsh language is more extensively employed. There are seven churches of which the services are in that language, a Welsh newspaper, and a literary or scientific society.* But as the Pennsylvania German employs many English words in speaking "Dutch," so does the Welshman introduce many into his vernacular, as "all right," "exactly," "you know," "twenty per cent.," "mortgage," "explosion," "universe." In speaking English, those from South Wales treat the letter *h* as the English do, and speak of Mr. 'Iggins, and of picking 'uckleberries, or say, "That's a hodd name," "I have a hell kitchen to my house." The Welshman frequently emphasizes a statement, as, "Yes, sure," "Yes indeed, man." He says, "Dear to goodness!" "I 'on't do it, whatever," etc., etc.

The Welsh have been accused of bearing malice, and of being clannish, or of "keeping together." "I think," says a Scotchman, "that that is why they keep up the Welsh language." For themselves they claim that they were never subjugated. They are Republicans almost to a man, and equally Protestant; lovers of liberty, stubborn and enduring, not fickle. The Welsh churches at

---

* I believe the paper is discontinued, 1882.

Scranton belong to the three following sects: Independent or Congregational, Baptist, and Calvinistic Methodist.

The Welshman is an experienced miner in his own rugged country. We are informed that the coal-field of Glamorganshire, in Wales, is one of the most important mineral districts in the world, and that in this small district more iron is manufactured than in all the United States. The Welsh here work more exclusively at mining than do the Irish and Germans. The Welshman is the miner, who blasts and takes down the coal, while the Irishman loads it upon the cars, a certain number of car-loads forming his daily task.

The Irish are more volatile. They do not practise much domestic economy; their motto is more, "Come day, go day." On a long strike they have generally nothing laid by for the emergency. A Catholic clergyman says, "The Irish are not fit for *bossing;* they are kept in too much subjection at home." But the rule is not without exceptions. I visited a mine of which the inside foreman was an Irishman, and from Connaught too, that wild western district. Besides having attained to this position, he was a landed proprietor, the owner of a farm. He was more interested in politics than my Welsh acquaintances, saying that a friend of his, a miner, could speak as well as any politician.

The Irish are inclined to superstition. An Irishman tells me that some years ago a man having been killed in a mine by the falling of the roof, the story afterward got round that if persons would go on a moonlight night to a certain spot—a back road at Scranton—the fairies might be met there, and the lost man with them; then by throwing something, his friends could get him back all right. Some went there in fun, and some in earnest.

This is like the idea in "the old country" when a a child dies, that the fairies have changed him, leaving another in his place, and that he might by some means be recovered. "Some tell it for a fact that they used to do so in Ireland."

A Scotchman tells me that if a child, a cow, or a pig suddenly begins to decline in health, or a cow in milk, the Irish accuse some one of "looking over it." They say that such persons do not know when they do it. This is doubtless "the evil-eye."

An Irishwoman was telling us of her son's losing a leg, the result of an accident when mule-driving in a mine. When she learned that the person hurt was her "Jamesey," "Oh!" said she, "it was to be. I dreamed it a year ago." She told us her dream, but it was very unlike the circumstance.

Germans, especially Catholics, are said to retain some of the superstitions of their native country, and to find "spooks" or spirits. A harmless superstition, if there be any such, is mentioned of them. They generally have gardens, and plant things "by the signs." Beans planted in the decline of the moon they do not think will take to the poles.

A German foreman says, "I have sat and listened to the miners of different nations telling of spooks and ghosts seen in the mines and other places, but, if one questions them closely, it is a brother or an uncle who saw it, and not the man himself."

The Welsh were formerly very superstitious, but they

are not so now. Says one, " We do not believe in signs
or omens, or that any flesh can see spirits." Another
tells me that the belief in hobgoblins, ghosts, witches,
fairies, and all kinds of signs and omens prevailed in
Wales in his childhood, until about thirty years ago a
very eminent Baptist minister, Robert Ellis, brought out
a work called *Ofergoelion y Cymry* (or Superstitions of
the Welsh), which attracted a great deal of attention,
and had great effect upon the minds of the people in
banishing all these ideas.

In spite of the efforts of their clergy the Irish still
keep up wakes at funerals, watching the body of the
dead. I am told that the friends of the family do not
feel like sleeping, being sorrowful. In the old country
neighbors would gather whether invited or not, and
games would be introduced to keep them awake, but
this custom is not followed here.

A Scotchman says that he thinks the Irish attend
"buryings" better than any other nationality. At
Scranton they impoverish themselves by the train of
carriages hired to attend funerals. " It was a funeral of
fifty carriages ;" thus they estimate the honor and glory
of the occasion. But that number was exceeded at the
funeral of a poor Irishwoman at Scranton, when there
were about one hundred and forty " rigs,"—the name
given here to turnouts.

The Welsh do not make such display. A prominent
Welsh citizen, a man of means, apparently wishing to
set an example, hired only one carriage when burying
his son, and walked himself in the funeral procession.

The chief hardship of the miner is the insecurity of

his life. He is liable to accidents at any moment, either in blasting the coal, or from the falling of the roof in the passages and chambers of the mine, or from the explosion of fire-damp,—carburetted hydrogen gas,—an extremely explosive substance generated in the mine.

By an awful accident which occurred in the Avondale mine, more than one hundred men were suffocated below. At Scranton are interred the remains of about sixty of these sufferers. The fatal accident is supposed to have occurred thus. Over each of the mining shafts is erected a breaker or cracker,—an immense wooden structure,— to the top of which the loaded cars are drawn up and then "dumped," the coal in its gradual downward progress being sorted, the greater part of it broken, sifted, and delivered into the cars beneath. The mine at Avondale was ventilated by means of a furnace or great fire, causing a draught. From this it is generally supposed that the breaker took fire, and this in turn set to burning a great body of coal; and as there was at the Avondale mine only one way of egress,—that is, up the shaft, —the men perished below.

At Scranton I saw a sad though simple ballad upon this disaster :

> "But all in vain. There was no hope
>   One single life to save,
> For there is no second outlet
>   From the subterraneous cave.
> No pen can write the awful fright
>   And horror that did prevail
> Among those dying victims
>   In the mines of Avondale."

The Ventilation Act passed by the Legislature of

Pennsylvania after this great disaster forbids the working of any mine without two outlets. In one that I visited, instead of a furnace for ventilation, there was employed an immense fan, worked by a steam-engine, and supplying sixty thousand feet of pure air per minute.

Great precautions are also taken to prevent the explosion of fire-damp. Nevertheless, accidents do still occur from this cause, and, as we have said, from the falling of the roof, and this although one-third of the coal is left in for support for the rock above. Some companies will not insure the lives of miners, and when they do insure they demand a very high rate,—about like that charged for those engaged in the manufacture of gunpowder.

Besides the more fearful sufferings to which the miner is liable, it is not uncommon to see him working in water, perhaps up to his knees, and at the same time water may be dropping upon him from above. Sometimes, on account of powder-smoke from blasting, he must feel his way rather than see it. Yet it is a general impression that the miner's health is good.

It must be accounted one of his hardships that he has not regular employment. At the time of my visit more than half the mines were not working at all, and the rest only on half time.

The miner's luxuries are those of other poor men,— his pipe and glass of ale or beer,—though I must acknowledge that the Irishman has not dispensed with whiskey. " I do not think," says Father ——, " that he drinks more than the Welshman, but perhaps he is more frequently seen intoxicated in public." The Welshman, it has been said, does not drink so much here as at home, for he has bidden his native land farewell with the intention of making money. The use of malt liquors is very common in this region, and beer is abundant in the hardest times.

The Irish are fond of singing, dancing, and carousing. The saloons on Lackawanna Avenue have two rooms, the front one for drinking, the back for dancing and general amusement. On the contrary, dancing is generally considered a heinous sin among the Welsh. Says a friend, " The ministers denounce balls and dancing parties as they would manslaughter or murder."

The German is fond of hunting. He has a gun and dog, and on a Sunday or other holiday, or when there is a breakdown in the mine, he goes hunting on the mountain, and brings home partridges, rabbits, or perchance a deer. Nor does he have to go far to find his hunting-ground. The valley of the Lackawanna is only about two miles wide, and lies in the Moosic Mountains, a part of the Alleghanies. The Germans are fond, too, of fishing. Their picnics and musical festivals generally begin on Saturday afternoon and conclude on Sunday evening. About two-thirds of the Germans go to church on Sunday morning, and many visit the beer gardens in the afternoon with their wives and children. They observe the church holidays, Good-Friday and Easter-Monday.

No Irish miners will work on St. Patrick's Day. They generally go to church in the morning, and immediately after service, or about half-past nine, organize and form processions composed of their various beneficial societies,—the Father Mathew, St. Mary's, St. Joseph's, Young Men's Beneficial, etc. They do not have a ball on St. Patrick's Day, considering it to be somewhat a desecration. On the parade day of the Miners' Union the different branches frequently have balls in the evening, and often with a charitable object, as for the relief of a poor woman whose husband or son has been killed in the mine. But since the unsatisfactory termination of the great strike in 1871 the parade day of the Miners' Union, August 1, is not generally observed.

Our national holiday, July 4, is kept with great zeal by the Irish. It is an outlet for the expression of their animosity to England. In 1874 there was a great parade of several thousand persons, about two-thirds of whom were foreigners.

The Welsh have only one national holiday,—St. David's Day, March 1. On this day, in Wales, they form processions and carry the leek, the national emblem. I saw it growing at Scranton, very much like the onion when standing. On this day in Wales they also have meetings for literary pursuits and for vocal music, being a great singing nation. St. David's Day is still observed in some American cities, but among the people at large the celebration has died out here. Christmas is a great day among the Welsh, and is observed by meetings of the *Eisteddfod*, a very ancient national gathering, which can be traced back for nine hundred years. The word means an assembly, and is pronounced *Ice-teth-vod*, the *dd* being like *th* in *thee*.

These gatherings are literary and musical. At Hyde Park it is announced in the Welsh paper, in the spring of the year, that the Philosophical Society will, at the ensuing Christmas, give prizes for the best essay or the best poem on given subjects, and the best piece of original music for given words, also for singing and recitation. But although, as I have stated, these meetings are generally held on Christmas, yet sometimes a neighboring town may prefer to fix upon New Year, thus enabling parties to attend both; and St. David's Day is sometimes celebrated by an eisteddfod. From the exercises of these gatherings women are not excluded. The eisteddfods are very generally attended by the Welsh, and are held in some large public hall, the greater part of the performances being in the Welsh language. Some of the observances are described to me in simple language by one who has been a miner. He says that church choirs attend the eisteddfods, and some very difficult piece is selected for them to sing, the prize being about sixty to eighty dollars. Then there are singers alone, and in parties of three. " They get their poets there; they meet on Christmas morning about ten, and adjourn about twelve, and then give out subjects for the poets,—likely the Lackawanna River, or some subject they had never thought of before. At two o'clock these poets will be called upon to recite their verses,—two, perhaps,—and a small prize is given (about a dollar), principally for amusement. Again, they call for compositions in music on some given subject. They must be sent in beforehand, about two weeks before the eisteddfod, with the proper name under a seal, the judges being allowed only to see the fictitious name. Also they read, and the best reader gets a small prize, the piece being given out at the meeting where it is read. Another thing causes a good deal of laughter,—they ask who will volunteer to sing a musical composition from the notes; some half-dozen will throw in their names (fictitious), and then one

13

will be called out,—perhaps 'Greenhorn;' the other five will retire from the room, while he picks up the difficult piece, and begins to clear his throat and show his embarrassment, which is a subject of amusement to the spectators; then the second comes on, perhaps equally unskilful; and when all have finished, the remarks of the judge upon each performance are also very amusing, the prize being only about fifty cents. In order to avoid the singers being previously acquainted with the piece, sometimes a person may be sent out half an hour beforehand to compose one. The piece chosen is generally one very difficult to sing. They hold these eisteddfods in Wales. The Welsh bards have for centuries back been accustomed to poetry, and so forth. In London they invited, I think, nearly all the musicians in Europe to sing on a certain day, all nationalities, for a prize of one thousand pounds,—a silver cup. There came a choir of singers from Wales to compete with the best talent they had in England. The lords and members of Parliament were there. The English selected some of their most cultivated people, and the Welsh singers were miners and men of very little education, and they had to go from their own country; but they won the prize by a great distance, and then sang through different towns and cities in England. There was money raised here in Hyde Park to support them while they were training, and to take them up to London."

A minister at the Welsh Congregational Church in Hyde Park gave me some explanation of this subject. He said that a company of musical persons connected with the Crystal Palace offered a prize for competition for vocal choirs, the reward being a silver cup worth one thousand pounds. In 1872 a choir of five hundred persons from South Wales, called the South Wales Choral Union, men, women, and children, principally miners and their children, appeared, and took the prize without competition. The next year, 1873, a trained band of English musicians, three hundred and fifty in number, appeared to compete for the prize, but without success, for the Welsh won it again. The English were from London, and were called the Tonic Sol Fa Association.

I heard nothing at Scranton, however, of the harp, once thought indispensable to the bards, two men on the street at Hyde Park, with pipe and bagpipe, being the only peculiar instrumental performers that I remember.

It might be supposed that so dangerous a pursuit as mining, with the horror of beholding accidents sometimes mortal, the uncertainty of obtaining regular employment, and, more than any of these, the working so far from the excellent light of the sun, would repress the buoyant spirits of the Irishman; but, says my Connaught acquaintance, " Working in the mines does not dull an Irishman's spirits,—not a bit of it."

A German also says that he does not think that working in the mines makes the Irish and others less fond of jokes, for they get together more. The mine is cool in summer and warm in winter, and if there is a lull, from want of cars or other cause, the men will squat down, miner fashion, and tell stories and crack jokes.

On a like occasion the little blackened slate-pickers swarm out of the cracker, like children let loose from school or like bees from the hive, and play at boyish games. Sometimes they get hold of an empty truck car, and ride down grade full speed, having the labor afterward of getting the car up again. When a loaded car is coming up the shaft, they can hear the warning whistle of the steam-engine, for soon the coal will be running down the chutes, and their labors recommence.

When the circus comes to town there is danger of a stampede among the boys who drive mules and perform like labors. They will come to the mine in the morning and gather together, and unless the "boss" is on the watch, they may be off in a body, and all work be at an end for the day, as the men cannot get on without them. On the contrary, if they are separated and started at their work, they will stay. But even the little fellows lately spoken of, "the boys in the cracker," who pick the slaty refuse from the coal, have been known thus to stop mining operations.

The Welsh are not a humorous and jocose people like the Irish, though I am told that they are inclined to mirth when speaking together in their own language. A faint smile was caused at the Congregational church by a remark of the preacher. Translated, it amounts to this : "Some men drink a quantity of beer, which does not affect the brain, as they have so little brains ;" and the application seems to have been that in a like manner the trials and vicissitudes of life affect some men little, as they have but little sensibility.

I am told that among the works of the Welsh poets are many epigrammatic stanzas. Of one of these, an epitaph, I received the following prose version : " In this life she told all the untruth that she could. Be careful not to wake her: if you do, she will say that she has been to heaven."

The late hours which have been kept by our "Pennsylvania Dutch" when *Fanny has a beau once* do not prevail among the Welsh at Scranton. A gentleman who leads a large church choir, of which all the men are miners, and not half of these church members, tells me that the young men wait upon the young women home before nine, chat a while on the front porch or steps, and generally leave at ten.

A physician says that most of the courtship of the Welsh is begun, and often finished, while walking the streets after church. "This street is thronged," says he, "on Sunday nights in summer. At first the young men walk behind, but after a while one step is quickened or the other slackened, or both, and they come together, and form lively parties, until ten or after. Courtships are brief, and the marriages early and happy."

I asked a Welsh acquaintance whether his son married young. "No, he didn't marry young; he was twenty-three." Says another, "Young women among the Welsh miners marry from eighteen to twenty-two. At the latter age they are joked about being old maids."

Miners' wives generally hold the purse. As soon as he gets his pay and his fill of beer, the miner hands his wages to his wife, who acts as treasurer with much discretion, making all the purchases of the house and transacting the business of the family. A miner's wife said to me, "My husband is a good workman. He never lost any time by drinking or anything like that. I nearly supported the family by my own sewing and by taking boarders. Ever since I have been married I tried to keep our own table, and could generally do it unless I was sick. I 'most always had a good deal of my own way, but I always consulted him. He always gave me his wages. I think when a man gives his wife his wages she feels more interest. I'd kick up a big fuss if he did not give me his wages. Whenever he was going away, I'd remind him, ' Charley, haven't you got any money in your pocket?' He knew where the money was, you know? We always had one purse. My purse was his, and his was mine. We have always lived in good unity together.

" This is not always the way with miners. We have a neighbor who must always go to the office on pay-day to get her husband's money. He'll go and take the pay, and hand it over to her. She says he always gives it to her. If she did not go and get it, he'd go to the saloon and spend it. It looks to me as if a man was so weak-minded, to do the like of that !"

The Welsh boys, too, hand their wages over to their mother. Germans, on the contrary, do not give their pay to the feminine head of the family; and, alas! a physician says that Germans are the best pay.

The Welsh woman is ambitious for her husband's shoes to shine, and on every Saturday evening she blacks the shoes of the family (all set in a row), until the girls are old enough to relieve her. Another corrects this statement, saying that by the old Welsh rule Monday is the day for cleaning and putting away the Sunday's shoes.

Mrs. —— says that she sets a tub of warm water for her son when he comes home from picking slate at the mine, and gives him soap and a woollen cloth, that he may "wash all over." To bathe in this manner is almost a universal rule with the men on leaving the mine, and a physician says that he considers the daily bath beneficial to their health. Says an acquaintance, "Many think, 'I would not have miners to sleep in my beds, they look so black and dirty.' But there is scarcely one in five hundred that does not wash all over when he comes home from his work; the general rule is, before he eats his supper. He washes his head, and puts on his clean clothes, and looks more like a clerk in a store than a miner."

When first I attended a Welsh church at Scranton, I was surprised at the nice appearance of the congregation, and I afterward inquired whether there were any miners there. But on my late visit I learned an almost invariable means of discovering who have worked in the coal mines. On the back of my host's hands were many blue spots, looking like faint tattooing. These were marks where he had been cut by the coal. Miners frequently have one or more of these blue scars upon the face. The coal-dust doubtless remains in the wounded place, like Indian ink in tattooing; and by these marks you can perceive that men have been miners, though their occupation now be quite different.

The Welsh have three suits of clothes, one for work, one for evening, and another for Sunday. Their children look very neat when going to church or Sunday-school. The Irish mother, too, loves to see her children look fine on these occasions, but she does not show so much taste. Both are much attached to their churches and Sunday-schools. The Germans are not so devotional.

The education of miners' sons is often much neglected. The law does not permit them to enter the public schools before the age of six; and although the Ventilation Act prevents children from working within the mines under twelve, yet no such prohibition exists as regards the breaker, or "cracker," above the mine. A superintendent says, "I have had them to come at six, and their mothers with them, to get them taken on."

Most of the recent Welsh emigrants, and those who are still poor and have large families, send their boys to work at the mine. But very few that have been in this country ten years are so poor as to be obliged to send them at an early age. We except those of dissipated habits, who spend their money in the saloons.

A German tells me that the children of German miners are generally sent to school, but so great is the demand for boys to pick slate in the breaker, that they generally go there at about eight or ten. Boys' wages in the breaker begin at thirty-five cents per day, and go up to seventy-five or eighty-five. A mule-driver gets from seventy-five cents to a dollar. Even the little boys in the breakers are proud to receive their month's wages, not to spend themselves, but to take home.

A friend says that as soon as the boy earns fifty cents at the mine, his sole ambition is to earn seventy-five, and then to be a driver. From driving one mule his desire is to drive a team, then to become a laborer, and then a full miner. To be a "boss," or superintendent, is a distant object of ambition, like being President—

"Alps on Alps arise."

Almost every one has to work for some time as a

laborer, loading coal, before he becomes a full miner. The sons of miners generally follow in their fathers' footsteps; but those who have been here many years often look higher for their boys, and give them trades. I met a lawyer, an intelligent young man, whose father is a miner.

For the benefit of the boys in the mines here, the Catholic Church has organized night schools, open during the six colder months of the year. The boys, if able, pay from twenty-five to fifty cents a month. A Catholic clergyman estimates that over two-thirds of the boys attend these schools. As a general thing, the use of the public school buildings has been granted them, but the rooms are often overcrowded. Though principally organized by the Catholic Church, none are refused on account of their belief. But after working all day, the boy cannot bring so much animation to the night-school as if he were not fatigued. The girls have better opportunities, but they are often put out to domestic service at twelve or fourteen.

The fare of the miner is from necessity simple, not luxurious. He breakfasts at about five or six o'clock on bread, butter, and tea. In a little tin can he carries his dinner of bread and cheese, perhaps with the addition of a bit of pie or cake, and in a tin bottle cold tea without milk. Even this simple luxury is sometimes discarded, and water taken in its place. The miner proper finishes his work about four o'clock, and finds his best meal at home, often a " good cooked meal" of meat, potatoes, etc. We may call this dinner, and the former meal lunch. A miner tells me, however, that he has often brought his food uneaten out of the mine from want of time; for he must have his car loaded when the driver comes for it, or lose one of the seven car-loads which form his daily work.

It is the Welshman who eats bread and cheese. His companion or laborer is generally Irish. He is detained longer in the mine, and wants meat for his noonday meal. Late in the fall, if the Irishman has not a pig, he generally buys from the country farmer a part of a beef, which he salts. Fresh meat from the stalls is too dear for him. When his beef runs out, he buys mess pork from the store; but I fear that he is not always able to take his bit of meat to the mine. Rather than cheese, he will take a couple of boiled eggs, for he is very fond of what he calls "a fresh egg." He carries milk in preference to tea, and he loves to own a cow. Cows are often seen pasturing upon the commons or the unfenced land belonging to the companies, the surface of which is not yet sold for building-lots. The Irishman is very fond of keeping geese and ducks. When he has a lot, he raises potatoes and cabbage, for here, or at home, he dearly loves cabbage with his boiled bacon.

The German takes for his lunch bread and butter, and perhaps a "chunk of sausage," and piece of pie or cake. His tin bottle holds coffee. The miner's dinner-kettle and bottle are slung on a rope over one shoulder, and on entering the passages of the mine are hung on one of the props that support the roof. The men often play jokes on each other by stealing pie or cake. Of course, the German makes sauerkraut. He keeps pigs, and sometimes buys a quarter of beef, which he smokes.

Great simplicity in food seems to exist among the

mining people in Wales, where it is said that they never think of eating butter and cheese at once; they would think it sinful. Mr. E——, of Scranton, says that he offered cold meat to an old Welsh lady who was visiting him, and she thanked him, but she had bread and butter. And Mr. J——, of Welsh birth, a miner from fourteen years to forty-six, tells me that if the streets were lined with meat, he could not eat it oftener than once a day, though he admits that he sometimes takes an egg or two for breakfast.

The Welsh miners who come to this country almost invariably bring one or two feather-beds. The German who can afford it sleeps in cold weather on one feather-bed and under another; if he cannot, he sleeps on straw and under feathers.

At his work the miner generally wears a woollen shirt, pantaloons of bed-ticking or stout linen, and heavy boots. I have seen the sole studded with iron lest the coal should cut the leather.

As to the number of miners who own their houses, I have heard various estimates for Scranton, as from one-third upward, the highest estimate being in one district seven out of ten of the married.

The German's house is a good one, painted or white-washed. Germans cultivate flowers and vegetable gardens, principally worked by the women, who carry produce in baskets for sale. The Welshman, too, when he has a home, has a comfortable one, looking quite pretty with its surroundings. But though the Irish often own their homes, these are of a ruder kind.

Has the miner aspirations? This question has been put, and I have been tempted to reply by another, Is he a man? Mr. L——, of Scranton, came to this country when about twenty. He worked a few months at Carbondale, in this Lackawanna region, and afterward in Ohio, mining bituminous coal by the bushel,—one hundred and twenty bushels a day, at two cents each. Here he laid by one hundred and thirty dollars, which he sent to Wales to bring his parents over. "I was," said he, "the only son they ever 'ad." At twenty-five he married, and soon after took a contract in a mine in Schuylkill County, Pennsylvania. Here the failure of his employer threw him into debt, from which he was not clear until about thirty. He took contracts on coal slopes, working always as a miner himself, but hiring hands to help him. For twenty years he was a foreman, a foreman's salary averaging twelve hundred dollars. He also went to California, and mined gold to profit. He bought, too, a farm in Pennsylvania for three thousand five hundred dollars, and tried farming himself for two years, but found it harder work than mining.

"Some eight of us," he says, "all miners, bought some years ago about five and a half acres of ground here for eight thousand and fifty dollars. We sold it out in building-lots, in about two months, for nearly the cost, and retained the mineral, which we value at twenty thousand dollars." By mineral is meant, of course, the coal, of which several valuable veins underlie Scranton at the point alluded to.

Mr. L—— continues: "Another company of us, all miners and all poor men originally, have bought a tract of four thousand acres of coal lands near the centre of

Alabama. I have been down twice to see it." He has now retired from active business, and lives in a neat house surrounded by a large garden, which he cultivates with pleasure and profit.

Another instance of success in a more intellectual field is Mr. ——, editor of a Welsh paper. When he was eight years old his mother was left a widow, with nine children, from three years of age to sixteen, and with nothing but a few household goods. By putting her children to work early at the mines she kept her family together. She herself spoke nothing but Welsh. Mr. —— was a precocious laborer, if I may use the expression, he being well grown, and becoming a driver at ten years, and a miner at sixteen. He never had but thirty-two days' schooling ; but having great delight in books, he got a Daboll's Arithmetic, and went through it twice, and found some one to set him copies for writing, making use afterward of copper-plates. One great advantage which he had was the leisure which the miner often enjoys. He says, " When I was working at Carbondale two years, I could generally get my day's work done by noon. When a miner, I wrote essays three times for the eisteddfod, and two of them drew prizes. These were each twenty-five dollars ; but the pecuniary reward was not what we aimed at,—it was the honor. I gave up mining in 1869, and have been connected with a newspaper ever since."

The miner occasionally attains to great wealth. Such, at least, was the case of Richard Care, of Minersville, of whom I hear that he came to this country a poor man, and died worth a million and a half.

But all these cases are exceptional. The chief ambition of the miners in general is plenty of work and good wages. "They're death on the wages," says one, "as the last suspension showed." As to their desiring to improve their condition, a German tells me that there is always such a desire among his people. "I can take you up," says he, "to Elmira, New York, and show you, I guess, a whole township of farmers who have been miners. The Germans who work here are very rarely from the mining districts of Germany, but from the agricultural. The German will take his boys into the mine to lay up a little capital, and having done this, he will buy a farm, or go into merchandise, or open a saloon."

What provision has the miner for times when he is out of work?

I might answer after the manner of another,—credit, credit, credit. The miner is paid monthly, but by the smaller companies not always so often. Could he once tide over the first month, and enter upon the cash system, he might be pecuniarily benefited by the change, but he seems wedded to the credit system. Should any trader advertise that he would sell goods for cash twenty per cent lower, I am told that the other store-keepers would throw their influence against him, and also that several cash stores have been tried in Scranton that did not succeed in the long-run. One of the main provisions against misfortune is the Beneficial Society. The miners do not, however, often join the Freemasons. Many of the Welsh belong to the following societies: Odd-Fellows, Foresters (a secret society of foreign origin), Ivorites (named for Ivor Hael, the Welsh founder), Red

Men, and the " Philanthropic Institution." There are other societies, Irish and German. As for the miner who does not belong to any of these, and who has no other means, if he meets with a serious accident or a protracted illness, he must go to the poor-house; but if I may credit good authority, he very rarely goes there.

Father —— says, " We need hardly use the word poor-house here, for I never knew a miner to get there. The Irish have a horror of it; but occasionally some aged, dependent person goes. The law here forbids out-door support for the poor." A young lawyer says, " No Welsh miner ever goes to the poor-house. He has a son or daughter, a brother or sister, a nephew or niece, who will not intrust him to the cold charities of the public. If his wife is industrious, she and the children can take care of him." Mr. L—— says, " Very seldom does a miner get to the poor-house, unless he be a drunkard; for if he be sober, his fellow-workmen in the mine, in case of accident or long sickness, make a collection for him." And Dr. H—— says, " A kinder set of men never walked the earth. When one of them meets with an accident in the mine, the men put in their hands and raise a little purse for him. They will divide their last dollar with a wounded comrade. The Irish extend their care to the widow of their unfortunate companion, whom they frequently set up in a little saloon, where she vends candy, pea-nuts, and various drinks." Since, however, the beneficial societies have become popular, there is not so much need of resorting to succor by sub-scription.

When urged to insure his life, the reply of the Irish-man almost invariably is, " What do I want to insure my life for my wife for? When I am dead, I don't want another man to spend my money."

In these dull times, when so many were out of work, I frequently saw quoit-pitching, which seemed to be a favorite amusement; some leap and some play marbles with the boys; but neither men nor boys spend their time in play. Some work for farmers, some pick berries, some "fuss about their gardens," or one, perhaps, has a sickly wife, and will stay at home and help. A young Cornish man whom I met was going to haul stone to build an addition to his house. I visited a young Scotchman, a foreman, who was employing himself in another manner. In the middle of his sitting-room stood a surveyor's compass upon its high tripod, and upon the table lay a book,—*A Conversation on Mines*, by William Hopton: Manchester and London. I said to him that he was differently situated from other miners, because he was interested in books, and could study in an idle time like the present. He replied that it was the fault of the others if they did not want to read and study; he had never heard of any one in any profession who could say that he had become perfect, and in his own case the more he learned, the more he found that there was to learn.

Among the Welsh, however, I learn that there is considerable culture besides that of which I have already spoken. In the Welsh Baptist church at Hyde Park a society meets once a week for reading and debating. They read the Bible and discuss its history and geography, for six months reading the Old Testament, and for six the New. In reading the Book of Samuel, the question arose, " Did the witch of Endor raise Samuel from the dead?" After some discussion the debate was found to take up too much time, and it was referred to disputants, two upon each side. The question brought up spiritualism, in which very few of the Welsh believe, but they love to discuss subjects of general interest. After an evening's debate, the chairman put the question, and it was decided that Samuel was not raised. With this decision the preacher does not agree.

About six years ago the same society argued the question whether the world was created in six days, and decided that the days were not periods of twenty-four hours. After the decision, they had a lecture upon geology from a former preacher, in which he took the same view.

The Welsh, without sectarian distinction, support the Philosophical Society at Hyde Park, its proceedings being in the Welsh language, and its meetings held every Saturday for eight months in the year. By voluntary contribution they are establishing a free library. Some of the Welsh miners also have considerable private libraries, of three hundred volumes and over.

The miners in this region are generally peaceable. Order is preserved in the mines by very strict rules. If one man strikes another, he is immediately discharged. If one insults another, the latter is to complain to the foreman, who acts as justice of the peace, and reports difficult cases to the general superintendent. Properly speaking, however, there are two foremen to a mine, one above and one below. On an average, there are about one hundred and fifty hands employed at each mine.

Even in idle times there is very little disorderly conduct. "The men," says R——, "will sometimes get tight, two or three of them, but as for getting up big rows, there is nothing of it. In the time of the great suspension there were threats of burning some buildings belonging to the Lackawanna Coal and Iron Company, and I went to guard one of them; but we never saw anybody."

To this general good order, however, there seems to be a notable exception. One evening my landlady sent her son to escort me with a lantern, the lamps along a principal street being "smashed." They had been broken, it appeared, for some time. I asked the boy why there was not a reward offered for the discovery of the persons who had done it. "Oh," said he, "the Molly Maguires will kill men!"

The Molly Maguires are the "Ancient Order of Hibernians," of whose doings in the coal regions dreadful stories have been told. Although when I was at Scranton it was said that the priests had broken up the society, yet I saw, one Sunday, members of the "ancient order" in handsome green and white or silver regalia, who seemed prepared to take part, with many other persons, in laying the corner-stone of a church near Scranton. Hence I inferred that the clergy had not broken up the society, but might have obliged them to give up their pledge of secrecy. After I left Scranton, however, a man was killed in that region, of whose murder I understand that the Molly Maguires were suspected. But so great at one time was the fear of the people at large of the Mollies, that two hundred or more revolvers were sold in one day.

There remains to be considered a subject of more general public interest than perhaps any other in which the miner is concerned, namely, strikes. " Suspension" is the genteel name among the men. In 1870 a great strike occurred here, which finally involved not only the whole of the anthracite, but a part of the bituminous region of Pennsylvania, which lasted near six months, bringing coal to an immense price in the market, and seriously embarrassing business, and which deserves the name of the great suspension. To make the matter perfectly clear, it is worth while to revert to the opening of our civil war in the year 1861.

The standard price paid to the miner in July, 1874, was ninety-three cents per car-load. At this rate he could make about three dollars and fifty cents per day for himself, and pay his assistant or laborer about two dollars and thirty-five cents. But before the breaking out of the rebellion the price of mining was as low as forty-five cents per car, or less than half the price in 1874.

During the war so great was the demand for iron, and consequently for coal, that prices had risen by 1864 to one dollar and sixty-eight cents per car, not very far from double the present price, but payable, as it will be remembered, in greatly depreciated paper money. In spite of this fact, this was the miners' flush time. I have been told that many were earning from one hundred and fifty to five hundred dollars a month, and that some of these bought homes, and afterward increased their landed property.

The manner in which this great advance in wages was obtained is especially worthy of note. The Miners' Union, or Working-Men's Beneficial Association,—the

W. B. A.,—began here, during the war, among the employés of the three great mining companies, the Delaware, Lackawanna and Western Railroad Company ; the Delaware and Hudson Canal Company ; and the Pennsylvania Coal Company. At the time the W. B. A. was organized, coal was rising in price, but the companies were not raising the men's wages. The miners felt themselves entitled to a share, the tenth or twelfth part of the advanced price, but they did not receive it until they called a convention. This, as I understand, was thus organized : The hands in each mine formed a branch of the W. B. A., and each branch was entitled to send two delegates to local conventions, and these in their turn appointed delegates to a general convention when one was held.

In order to obtain an advance in wages, the men appointed at their conventions committees to wait upon the general agent of each company, and to make the same demand upon the same day, and it was always granted, until the price had risen, as I have already stated, in 1864, to one dollar and sixty-eight cents, its greatest height. In September of that year, when the war was drawing to a close, and the price of coal had begun to decline, the wages of the miners were reduced eight and a half per cent., without causing any disturbance. By July of 1865 gradual reductions had brought wages down from one dollar and sixty-eight cents per car-load to one dollar and nine cents. On this decline there was a strike among the miners in the Scranton and Wilkesbarre region.

In the preceding May a convention had been called at Scranton to take action on the fall in wages. Many were opposed to striking. But in July another convention was called, and on the 15th the hands of the three great companies struck, from Wilkesbarre to Carbondale, and "stayed out" eleven weeks. The companies did not raise their wages before they resumed work, but they began again with the understanding that their pay would be raised, and an advance of five cents per carload was made in a few days, bringing the price up to one dollar and fourteen cents.

After this the men were quiet for over three years, but as wages declined, by January, 1869, great discontent was felt among the miners. There was no outbreak, however, until April, when the men of the two greatest mining companies suspended. These companies, the Delaware, Lackawanna and Western; and the Delaware and Hudson, when in full operation, sent at that time one hundred and eighteen thousand tons of coal weekly to market. The withdrawal of a mass like this must, of course, influence the price, and the Pennsylvania Coal Company (the third in size here, and employing about one-sixth of the hands) profited by the withdrawal of the other companies, and, figuratively speaking, made hay while the sun shone. The Miners' Union could not have been strong then, or the men of this company would not have worked while the others were out. It has been remarked that while prices continued to rise, the miners were delighted with the Union, but when wages began to fall, their interest in it fell too. However this may have been, the Pennsylvania Coal Company, in the strike of 1869, continued to work, and raised the men's wages about once a month, until they amounted to one dollar and thirty-one cents the car-load.

The two other companies probably tired, if corporations can be said to tire, of seeing the Pennsylvania Coal Company carrying on business thus, and it seems that hints were conveyed to the outstanding men by agents of their employers that they had made no organized application to the companies, informing them of their wishes. At length committees from the men called upon the agents of the companies, and offered to go to work at the rate at which the other men were working. To these the agents answered, " We are always ready to pay what our neighbors are paying ;" and the men went to work at one dollar and thirty-one cents. This was not a long-protracted strike, and the men were successful in obtaining nearly all which they demanded.

These good prices continued for over a year, partly it seems, for a reason to me unexplained, and in part because the price at which the men went to work, although a high one, was actually not so high as the companies could then afford to pay, so greatly was the stock of coal reduced and the market-price raised.

Wages continued then at one dollar and thirty-one cents, when, in November, 1870, the three companies united in notifying the men that in one month there would be a reduction to eighty-six cents. This decline was an immense one, over thirty per cent., and the news came upon the miners like a thunderbolt. It would have been much better policy for the employers to reduce the price gradually as coal declined in market.

This state of things may indicate that there is not much sympathy between the miners and the corporations, and I am told that the men feel bitter toward their employers from their showing so little respect for their manhood as not to be willing to consult with them. These are tender points with some in the Scranton region. You will find the foremen not very anxious to talk about them, but you will be able to obtain the admission from some here that the men feel their interest to be at variance with their employers'.

When the end of the month of notification arrived, the men declined to take the sum offered, and suspended. They claimed that the matter of wages should be determined by a sliding-scale, adjusted to the price of coal in the market, and this they called a basis. They also desired to have an agent to examine the books of the companies, and to see what their profits really were. The first demand is so reasonable that we can scarcely see why it should be refused, and it is granted in the Schuylkill County region.

This sliding-scale, or the basis, became a rallying-cry during the long and trying conflict which followed. And they stuck to this until they were starved out.

On their side, the companies thought that strikes were coming too often (the interval having been about sixteen or eighteen months); and now, as we have said, the three companies were united.

The miners, however, had not all been in favor of suspending work. Some of the leading Welshmen would have preferred to compromise by offering to go on at a reduction less than that demanded by the companies, but these were overborne by others, who were very violent in the meetings of the W. B. A., crying out, " Strike! strike!" until, I was told, it was as much as a man's life was worth to oppose them. So the pacific or conservative Welshmen were outvoted by the more reckless of their own nation and the rest. But once engaged, the Welsh were the most determined, being unwilling to yield until they had effected something. Says one, " I believe they would have held out to this day;" and another, "I believe they would have emigrated: they had strong talk of going out West in squads." As it happened, if we may call it chance, the only blood shed in the struggle was that of two Welshmen.

The Miners' Union did not anticipate that the companies would hold out as long as they did; but they seem to have been firmly banded, like the men, and they had the power of capital on their side. " It was like a big war," says an acquaintance,—" a six months' war."

It seems to the writer that in this contest, however, the men were struggling against fate; for as paper money advanced in value and approached to gold, so, as a general rule, must the price of everything decline that was paid for in that paper money, including wages, the price of labor.

The men were not literally starved out, it seems; for one interested says, " I heard of no miners that were suffering for provisions, though some of them were pretty hard up. The store-keepers took the miners' side, because it was their interest to do so. The bigger pay the miner got, the more he had to spend in the stores."

Of course the time must have come when the tradesmen could no longer give credit, and we readily infer that that point must have been nearly or entirely reached when the men had been out near six months.

During this period families were, of course, much restricted. They could probably get along with no new clothing, or but little; and the store-keepers trusted them for flour, tea, sugar, tobacco, and the other little *necessaries* of life. Such, too, as had lots, could raise potatoes, cabbage, etc., but some of them became deeply involved in debt.

However, the times had been so good that probably at least half the men had means to support themselves for a little time, and they grasped at any work they could find anywhere. As the strike began in December, however, the amount of work must have been small. Had not the other anthracite regions become involved, their comrades might have sent them funds, or given them a share of work; but this was impossible. The funds of the Miners' Union, the W. B. A., were very small. They were unable to support the men in such a time. Nor were they supported by the public. Says a friend, " Not one miner in this region went to the poorhouse, nor do I believe that one applied to the commissioners of the poor for out-door assistance. They would not have thought of such a thing, for they believed that the sympathies of the commissioners were with their employers."

About once a month a committee would call upon Mr. ——, the agent of the —— Company (and doubtless upon the agents of the others also) and inquire whether the company would grant them a basis on the former prices, but they effected nothing.

The Irishmen were poorer, and they were sooner ready to yield. At length a gentleman of Scranton induced thirty men to " break away from the Union," and to go to work in a mine belonging to a company smaller than the three mentioned. These men were almost entirely Irish. They went to work daily about seven in the morning, returning about five in the evening, carrying arms, and were accompanied by soldiers, and led by their employer.

When the news spread among the miners that a body of men had gone to work in a certain spot, the miners would gather upon the way to see who these were, and the on-looking crowd was swelled by boys, and perhaps by women. As the men who had yielded made their appearance, the cry arose among the spectators, " Here come the blacklegs!"—*i.e.*, the turncoats or traitors. One evening as these men were thus returning along the street in Hyde Park, it is said that a boy on the street threw a stone. One of the men attacked turned round, and, discharging his musket, shot two men through the body with the same ball, and killed them instantly.

At least one of these men was a miner, and was or had been a Methodist local preacher; the other was going to get medicine for a sick child. Both were Welshmen. There was immediately an immense excitement. While the man who fired the shot was being taken to the magistrates, some one cried out, " Kill him !" but others waved them back, saying, " Let the law do him justice."

The magistrate, a Welshman, committed him to jail at Wilkesbarre, whence he was bailed out, and when brought to trial was defended by the companies, was acquitted, and lives peaceably in the neighborhood now. I tell the tale as it was told to me.

So the men gave in. This bloody scene and the ensuing funerals probably broke the doughty spirit of the

Welshmen. They gave in and went to work in the latter part of May, not entirely six months from the outbreak of the contest. They began at eighty-six cents, the price which the companies had fixed ; but on the 1st of June their pay was raised to ninety-three cents.

Can strikes be prevented ? In speaking to a miner about the great suspension, I asked whether it would not be better for the company and the men to meet and settle these matters.

" It could not be done," he answered. The miners do not seem to have any desire to buy into the stock of the companies. Is it for fear that, as a miner's wife said, " the big fishes would eat the little fishes up ?"

But if the miner does not thus co-operate with his employers, or in the manner that the poorest sailor on a whaling vessel once did with the owners, the principle of joint-stock is not unknown to them. An intelligent man, once a miner, tells me that all working men are now aspiring to form co-operative associations for the purpose of carrying on mining and iron-works themselves. There are iron-mills on this system, he said, at Danville, and a number of furnaces and rolling-mills in Ohio. These are on the same plan as the renowned works at Rochdale, England, that have been in successful operation for many years.

There is, too, a co-operative store at Hyde Park, Scranton. This store has been in operation for several years, and pays stockholders from twelve to fifteen per cent. on stock and purchase. The majority of the stockholders are Welsh, and nearly all are miners.

IRISH FARMERS.

In 1881 I spent four weeks in Ireland, principally in the south, in the county Cork. Desiring to learn the condition of the farmer who himself follows the plough, I inquired among various classes of people. I boarded four days with a farmer, and about as long at a castle; down in the southwest I talked with a citizen who had been boycotted; travelling third-class on railways, I conversed with other passengers; in Dublin with fellow-boarders; in London with a prominent Irish politician. Of these interviews I took notes, so that I am not obliged to depend alone on memory for my simple story. I try to give conversations, but must allow the reader to draw inferences.

For many years I have known farmers living in comfort and accumulating property by the labor of their own hands upon their own soil. Such are Quaker farmers in Chester County and "Pennsylvania Dutch" in Lancaster. In Ireland I wished to visit a similar class. But I found no one who owns the land he ploughs, or ploughs that which he owns.

I was assured in Philadelphia by persons knowing Ireland that I could not find the house of a working farmer in which I would be willing to live. This discouraged me, but by means of introductions from two or three young women living at domestic service, I obtained a good opening into the land. One gave me a letter to her confessor in Cork, whom we will call the "Riverend Lawrence O'Byrne." I found him intelligent and genial; in person rather tall and thin but with a color in his cheek. He was at a loss to recommend me to any working farmer's house, saying that I should live on potatoes and skimmed milk; but I thought that I could live so for some days if those people did all their lives.

In further conversation, Mr. O'Byrne lamented the degradation caused by liquor, and declared that the bulk of the Irish people cannot be induced to take any interest in lyceums or intellectual culture.

Nearly thus he described to me the aim of the farmers in the present agitation. It is fifty years or more since Griffith, an agent of the English government, made a valuation of Irish lands. Since then rents have risen in some cases one hundred per cent., and the Land League is trying to reduce them to Griffith's valuation.

When tenants are evicted, others are forbidden to take them at the price demanded, and the evicted are supported by contributions to the Land League. I myself call it an agricultural strike.

Mr. O'Byrne says that there is much competition in renting farms, no other business being open to the people. This confirms the opinion of a publisher in Philadelphia, who had attributed the state of Irish affairs to the want of manufactures.

Mr. O'Byrne kindly made inquiry for me, and I found

a farmer willing to take a boarder. To see him I went by rail to a certain station. Near by I entered a humble dwelling, where a man was working at his trade, besides being a petty government officer. He talked pleasantly on Irish affairs, and said that some landlords have granted a reduction in rent of twenty-five per cent. I repeated what an editor in New York had said of the present condition of Irish affairs,—that bad harvests, the competition of American beef and mutton, and the consequent decrease in the value of real estate had made the farmers unable to pay their rent.

The Irishman admitted that American meat is much cheaper than theirs, but said that it had not brought down the price of their own. He said that four or five landlords and agents had been killed; at this a woman present smiled; and a man added that it is a pity there were not more. This was the only sanguinary remark that I heard a poor Irishman make.

At the railroad station the train from the west was behind time, and the agent suspected disturbances. When it came it was mostly filled with soldiers, who called out for water; but who reported no immediate disturbance. At this station I was met by the farmer and his wife with whom I was to lodge, who took me home in their cart. I call him Maurice Collins. He was not very poor for an Irish cultivator. He was doubtless considered quite fortunate in owning a horse and cart, even if the cart had no box and no seats, but was simply a bed or frame. Upon it lay a great bag of corn-meal, upon which sat Mrs. Collins and myself. I steadied myself down-hill with one arm at her waist, while my right hand grasped a projection of the cart. I expressed surprise at the number of ruined and abandoned dwellings, for we were within ten miles of one of the largest towns in Ireland. Collins said that farms once separate have been thrown together. When the population of a country falls thirty-seven per cent. in about thirty-four years, or from over eight millions to about five, it is not strange that abandoned houses are found when built like these, of stone. Dwellings of mud and straw are more readily demolished. Collins's house was on rather a sterile hill. To reach it we rose above the lower and more fertile ground. On our arrival a chair was brought out to enable us to alight from the cart. On entering the house we were followed by a young man, who staggered under the weight of the great five-bushel sack on which we had sat in the wagon.

There were twelve in the family,—six boys, one girl at home and one away, the old aunt, and the domestic. The living room had an uneven floor of earth. Within the front door stood the slop-barrel. A dresser of dishes stood on the left, and beyond it there was a red-painted, two-storied hen-coop. A hen and chickens occupied the lower story, and a setting hen the upper one. A second door faced the front door. It generally stood open, discovering a little muddy yard. A great settle or couch of wood stood on the same side of the room. Beyond it, on a low seat, sat a little fair, weak-eyed old woman, the aunt. She sat beside a small fire on the hearth, holding the baby. With her left hand she turned a crank and wheel, which by some invisible agency created an underground draught to kindle the fire. The fire was generally of coals. It bore no proportion to the fireplace, which occupied a large part of the third side of the room.

I saw the girl hang over the fire a large Dutch oven, called here a bastible. It was a round iron vessel with a lid. On its top she kindled a fire of furze, and hung the bastible to bake the large cake within, made of flour not fully screened, sour milk, and soda.

At nightfall the barefooted little ones gathered to the blaze, although it was in the month of June. The babe in arms was Tim, the three-year-old Norah, and the five-year-old, in trousers surmounted by a red woollen frock and blue apron, was Dennis. At one end of the long fireplace stood the heavy cradle. A steep staircase, almost like a ladder with a railing, led to the rooms above, for this house, roofed with slate instead of thatch, had a loft with a board floor. Wet weather makes the uneven earthen floors inconvenient. The water gathers in little pools. The door to my room was at the foot of the staircase. There were only two apartments on the ground-floor.

The fourth side of the apartment was lighted by a small window and the doorway through which we entered the house. There were only two windows downstairs, one in this room and one in mine. They were little iron-barred windows. I thought that they might be taxed, but I was mistaken. Collins told me that the glass came from England. They used to have glass-manufactories in this country.

I had taken tea before my arrival, and Mrs. Collins gave me some milk. She and her husband had been to Cork, where, she said, they had a cup of tea and a penny bun at a baker's. (The penny is about two cents.) In the evening we had a good talk. I commented on the nice hen-house standing in the corner, and Mrs. Collins told me that they had lost several chickens by the fox. " And do you still have foxes in Ireland ?" I asked, in some surprise.

" We do," she replied.

" And that is what the gentlemen hunt ?"

" It is," she said.

" And can you kill the foxes ?" I inquired.

" No, ma'am," was the reply.

This I afterward thought must be an error, as foxes are vermin ; but a gentleman born in the north of Ireland has told me that they would be evicted for killing foxes. Sometimes hunting clubs pay for poultry killed by foxes.

In the evening I spoke of the sun's setting so late and our being so far north, and asked the eldest son, a youth of fourteen, whether he had studied geography. He said he had, but his mother told me that he had been obliged to leave school at eleven, and her manner seemed sad and disapproving. There are no free schools in Ireland like ours. The poorest citizens need not pay in the national schools, but others must. A gentleman in Dublin, who publishes a school journal, told me that he doubted whether these schools would ever become entirely free to the public, like those in my own State. He had never heard that such a movement was contemplated.

In further conversation Mrs. Collins told me that they had lost seven cows in eighteen months, and that they were nearly broken down. They had to incur some debt to replace them, and they must meet the rent or be thrown upon the world. Their lease would expire in about six years. Do not these misfortunes make them

14*

dwell very near to the Divine Father, in humble sub-
mission and prayer?

About ten o'clock in the evening the wooden table was
put before the fireplace. The old aunt had gone to bed.
Collins was in one end of the fireplace, a boy asleep in
the other, and the eldest slept on the settle. Mrs. Collins made tea and put a bowl of white sugar on the
table. She told me that sugar cost about five cents a
pound (two and a halfpence). They cut pieces off of the
great cake baked in the Dutch oven, and ate their supper without any of the precious butter, which must go
to market. Little Norah had given a low laugh when
her mother handed her a bit of warm cake without anything spread on it. Mr. and Mrs. Collins had milk in
their tea. The tea cost about forty cents a pound. Collins helped himself quite freely to the cheap and nutri-
tious sugar, one of the blessings which the poor man
owes to free trade.

Collins and his wife gave up their own room to me.
It was the other room on the ground-floor. It also had
an earthen floor, with perhaps the addition of a little
cement, but it was not level. There I slept, and here
were set my simple meals, more luxurious, however,
than their own. Some of the dishes were of china,
which belonged to Collins's grandmother. I had plenty
of milk, eggs, butter, tea, and baker's bread. They
gave me goat's milk, richer than cow's milk, for tea.
For me especially Mrs. Collins procured meat, a bit of
jowl, but I am not partial to it. They did not, however, go to the extravagance of eating it themselves. I
was told of a farmer's family who had jowl and cabbage for a Sunday dinner. A watch was set for the

agent, lest, seeing such evidences of prosperity, he might raise the rent. Collins and his wife seldom ate meat. He told me that he had two eggs in the morning and the mistress one. They raised turkeys. Twenty-four were running with one hen. The servant fed them with a mixture of nettles, corn mush, and thick milk, but she said they scarcely ever ate a turkey even at Christmas.

In the morning, at breakfast, Mrs. Collins had some cold mush or stirabout cut up and boiled in sheep's milk. This saved bread and tea. I observed one day within the back door, and by the chicken-coop, a little trough with corn-meal. There seemed to be always food there. The chickens came in and helped themselves. Seeing a fowl eating, I said to the aunt, " That rooster ought to be fat." She did not understand me, and I tried again :

" That cock ought to be fat, he eats so much."

" He do ate a dale, God bless him," she said. She meant " prosper him," I think. Some neighbors visited the family one morning, and from my room I heard earnest talk. They spoke of the rumored arrest of Father Murphy, which had caused much excitement. One man came in who was full of talk of the Cork races on the preceding day. At first, Mrs. Collins allowed him to think that they were present, but they went to sell butter, and did not go to the race-ground.

The girl swept the earthen floor with a bunch of twigs without a handle. I mention these little things to show the poverty of the country. They had no almanacs at Collins's and no clock, except a Connecticut one, which did not run. Collins once intimated that it was painful to have such a poor harness for his horse.

One day I walked over to the school. I passed a house licensed to sell beer and spirits to be drunk on the premises. It was whitewashed, and looked better than most of the farm-houses. The boys told me that tea and sugar could be bought there. Bread was sold, but I could buy no sticks of candy for the children. A carpenter-shop and a blacksmith's forge stood near this public-house, but I saw no country stores like ours at home.

The Collins family carried water some distance uphill from a spring. This part of the country is supplied from springs. They had excellent roads, apparently macadamized, and free from tolls. When I spoke in Cork of the great cost of such roads I was told that they were probably made after the famine, when the government gave laborers employment. The roads, however, seemed deserted. Once I saw a man on horseback, and occasionally market carts were seen, but of plain carriages, like those of the farmers in Eastern Pennsylvania, I remember none. Poverty hangs like a cloud over the land. Yet the people seem honest. The servant-girl at Collins's said to me, "Nothing do ever be taken." I wished to know whether it was safe to leave my towels to dry on furze bushes near the road. Afterward, in a gentleman's house,—a gentleman who lived in a disturbed section, and whose tenants were not paying rent, —I was told that they would not be afraid to have plate in the house; the people there were honest.

Collins and his wife were trying to better their condition by going to a market-town and buying butter, which she brought home and reworked and packed into firkins to sell in Cork. This consumed so much of their time

that it was hard for me to see much profit in it. They
may have received five dollars a week more than the butter
cost them. Mrs. Collins was pleased in telling me of one
firkin or tub that brought the highest market price.
But during their absence the elder boys were left alone
at the farm-work. Nor did I see the great pressure of
labor found among our Pennsylvania German farmers.
This may be in part owing to open winters in Ireland,
which enable the farmer to work the year round, in part
to the fact that the patient, ox-like labor of the German
is not a trait of the Irishman, and partly to a national
disregard of time, producing such a proverb as " Hours
were made for slaves." When I apologized for having
talked so long to a poor man and his wife, she answered,
" Sure, many a year we'll rest in the grave." Calling on
my friend Collins and his wife before I left the county, I
found they had gone with their horse to the funeral of
a much-respected neighbor, and as they were so long
absent, had doubtless accompanied the funeral to the
place of interment, twenty miles. A manufacturer in
the county Cork said that the Irish girls in the mills
are not greedy enough. They would rather have less
wages and more play. They were not indolent, but
a bit of fun would call them off. A Quaker lady
in Cork said to me, " None of the Irish are thrifty.
They do not value their time." And afterward, "They
are a thrifty people in the north. They make use
of their time." She herself was born in Ireland, but
when she spoke of the Irish she did not mean to
include herself. When any one called the Irish lazy,
I replied that they did not seem so in America. They
left their temperate climate, came to our country,

and constructed railroads under our broiling suns. I heard in Ireland that girls who go to America say, "If we had worked as hard in Ireland as we do in America, we would have been well off there."

I spoke of Mr. and Mrs. Collins's drinking tea at supper. Once when they were absent, Mary, the servant, came into my room to hide the teapot, lest the boys should want sugar and bread.

"What do you give them for dinner?" I asked.

"Stirabout and new milk," she replied.

"Potatoes?" I suggested.

"They do not care about potatoes," she said.

Our corn-meal, among its many other Irish uses, seems likely to supersede the national dish. What a change since 1847, the year of the potato famine! This family used Indian meal because it was cheaper than oatmeal, but they did not like it so well. As for the inferior animals, they occasionally give horses corn-meal, but generally feed them in winter on oats, turnips, bran, and hay. Indian meal and bran are fed to cows with young calves. To pigs corn-meal is given the year round, occasionally adding a few boiled potatoes, the sortings. They are fattened on meal and sour milk when it can be spared. Poultry abounds here, and Ireland exports large quantities of eggs. I never saw corn-meal at home stand so constantly in the chicken-trough as at Collins's.

I have said that the domestic came into my room to hide the teapot. The cup which cheers but not inebriates is in immense demand here. The old aunt wanted tea. The children worried the girl for tea. The beggar-woman insisted on tea. The three-year-old Norah says she has a pain and wants tea. It might be a very happy thing for Ireland if the people would confine themselves to such cups as these; but, while all other manufactures are languishing in the county Cork, malt liquor and whiskey distilleries are flourishing. (However, Scotland, a Quaker told me, excelled Ireland in regular drinking.) As to what constitutes moderate drinking, I was amused by the remarks of a girl in Cork. Speaking of young men, she said that she did not object to a bottle of porter at dinner and one in the evening, but seven or eight bottles a day she thought gluttony and a sin. Porter, however, is not dear. On draught it sells at about eight cents the quart imperial. Whiskey is quite another thing. I hear that the tax on a gallon is twelve shillings and ninepence, or about three dollars. It has been said that Ireland pays more for liquor than for rent; yet estimates given me show that while over nine millions of pounds sterling are spent yearly on intoxicating drink, the rent of the country amounts to thirteen million pounds. Let no one jump to the conclusion that it is the working farmers who expend this great amount, for doubtless the small landlords are great consumers.

Distillers and brewers are great men in such a country. I heard of several celebrated Protestant churches indebted to them for funds. A distiller gave twenty thousand pounds and a brewer ten thousand pounds to assist in building or renewing an Episcopal cathedral in Cork. It is said to have cost Guinness, the great brewer, two hundred thousand pounds to remodel St. Patrick's Episcopal Church in Dublin and to build the appurtenant houses. And a distiller gave a great sum to repair Christ Church in the same city.

To return to my farmer, Collins, in whose house I saw no intoxicating liquor drunk. He rented seventy acres, of which twenty were bog, nearly worthless; the peat for burning being all cut from the bog land in this neighborhood. (Nor is the county Cork, taken altogether, a rich agricultural tract. Lewis's Topographical Dictionary, 1837, gave the acreage at about one million seven hundred thousand, of which about seven hundred thousand acres were bog and mountain.)

Collins's lease was for thirty-one years, of which six remained. He has built the part of the house in which we live, having slate-roofed it. He has also built a stone stable and a small dairy, with slate roofs. The landlord gave him almost nothing toward these improvements, not even the flooring of the loft. The stone Collins got off the place. When he came here the walls of the fields were mostly of clay or mud, and he has built stone ones. In this neighborhood the walls are mostly built of stone. In some cases they are covered with earth, and grass and other plants are growing on them. "These walls," I said to him, "must take up a great deal of room. That one beside your house is a yard across the top."

I have given Collins's rent at about one hundred and seventy dollars for seventy acres. Land sold in fee simple, apparently a rare thing, generally brings twenty times the annual rental. Yet, as a lawyer in Cork informed me, the average value here now, under present depressing circumstances, is not over seventy-five dollars per acre.

I have spoken of some of Collins's land as of inferior quality. His report of its produce, I therefore infer, is above the average crop. He says that on this land wheat ought to bring fifteen hundred-weight per acre, the hundred-weight of one hundred and twelve pounds. (This is twenty-eight bushels, which would be considered a fair crop in the wheat-growing region of Pennsylvania.)

Collins says that on land of best quality in good years wheat is expected to bring twenty-five hundred-weight. On his own land oats frequently brings fourteen hundred-weight to the acre, or about forty-three bushels. This land produces about one and one-half tons of hay, and better land about two tons per acre. A patch of potatoes is called a potato-garden, even if it contain several acres. The manner in which potatoes are planted was strange to my eye. The land is laid out in beds about four feet wide. Between those beds are deep trenches one and a half feet wide. These beds or ridges are made by turning six sods in with the plough. There are four rows of potatoes to a bed. These are hand-weeded, and never hoed. The people manure as heavily as they can for potatoes; and then, without additional manure, put the land into wheat. Barn-yard, guano, and artificial manures are used. On Collins's soil potatoes turn out about five tons to the acre, or about one hundred and eighty-six bushels. Potatoes have degenerated in Ireland; but of late a new kind, the Champion, has encouraged the people much. At an exposition in Cork in 1880, some farmers claimed to have raised from thirteen to fifteen tons per acre, or about five hundred bushels. Turnips are manured, sowed in drills or rows in May and June, thinned, hoed, and hand-weeded. They turn out twelve tons to the acre. Two men can fork out an acre in a day, and two men can top an acre a day, leaving the tops on the ground.

Domestic animals sell high for food. Beeves sometimes weigh thirteen and fourteen hundred-weight, and bring about three pounds per hundred-weight. Good fat calves of three months sell for five pounds. Fat sheep, weighing dressed about one hundred and twenty pounds, will bring three pounds, or near fifteen dollars. Mrs. Collins had an exceptional pig, supposed to be a fine bacon pig, lean and fat well mixed, or a "ribbon" pig. (An Irishman is said to have fed his pig one day and starved him the next, that there might be a streak of fat and streak of lean.) That pig of Mrs. Collins's weighed when dressed one hundred and eighty-two pounds, and she got four pounds and ten shillings for it, or about twenty cents a pound. In view of such prices the saying of my Cork landlady is not strange: "May the Lord of heaven spare us the American meat! It keeps the market within our reach."

Fruit did not seem plentiful in the county Cork. "The children would pluck gooseberries," was a reason given for not having them. A certain priest was supposed to have strawberries and gooseberries in his garden, but probably fruit-loving children did not disturb those of his reverence. When a retired lawyer took me into his garden he unlocked the gate. He had cut down an old orchard and would not plant another, because the neighboring children would get at the fruit. Thus, the saying of the domestic, "Nothing do ever be taken," does not seem to apply to fruit.

I had several conversations with Collins. He freely

expressed his disapproval or dislike of the British government. Working farmers rarely or never subscribe for a paper, but often buy one at a market-town. Collins had got one in Cork, and wished me to see a speech in it. He said that it alluded to a manufacturer at Blarney who took a prize at our Centennial.

"What would you think," said Collins, "when people manufactured goods that they could not send them right off from here to market, but must send them to Liverpool, and have them unloaded and carted there, and then sent back, causing that expense? Would you think that was just?"

"That is not so now?" I asked.

"Indeed it is; that manufacturer's goods must all be sent that way; and would you think that was justice?"

"It is pretty hard on him," I answered.

"And is it justice?" he insisted. "You shall have the paper and read the speech."

In Cork I called to see Mr. Mahony, the manufacturer referred to, who told me that there is no government regulation to hamper their manufactures in any way. It is doubtless a matter of convenience to ship from a great port like Liverpool, vessels not caring to stop and take on small quantities at Queenstown.*

As Collins, his wife, and I were riding on the cart, going to the market-town for butter, I asked whether he expected that there would be a time when there would be no rents to pay. He answered that he did not.

---

* I received permission to use the name of Mr. Mahony, the manufacturer. His brother wrote "The Bells of Shandon." The other names used are substitutes.

"I understood you to say the other evening that you did," I continued.

"No," he replied; "there has been a proposition for the government to take the lands, and the people to pay rent for thirty years——"

"And then the land be theirs?" I interrupted.

"Yes," he answered; "but they will never grant that. More moderate things they have refused. All we want is reduced rents, as the people can no longer pay high ones."

On our return journey I had an admirable opportunity to talk with him as he walked by the wagon. I had called on a magistrate in the market-town, a Protestant gentleman, who had seemed very ignorant or uncommunicative. He had, however, suggested over-population as a reason for the condition of Irish affairs. This magistrate bore a military title. I handed to him the introduction given me at Cork by the "Riverend Lawrence O'Byrne." Collins had suggested an officer of the market as suitable to introduce me. But I was in haste, and carried the letter. The magistrate said that he did not know the person. "No," said Collins, on my return, "you were wrong in two things. You said you were from Philadelphia, and they are afraid of the Americans, or do not like them, and Father O'Byrne is not their kind of man."

I told Collins that some papers in America had said that their magistrates should be elected, as with us in some States. He replied that they are appointed from the aristocracy, the land-holding class, and, of course, in cases of dispute between landlords and tenants, their sympathies are with their own class.

"If you were in America we should say that your head is level," I said; but I had to interpret the slang.

"There has been a change in Ireland," he added, "within some years. Formerly the wealthy classes and the learned could make *jupes* of the Irish people, but of late years there has been more education, and the people see things differently. Ireland was a dark country before the Catholic emancipation. Before the passage of that act no Catholic could hold office in this country. Now many places are open to them in the excise and elsewhere."

Collins intimated that the English are wrong in fearing the Catholic priests, for they counsel the people to peaceful measures, and they are the only persons who have sufficient authority over them to quiet them down. I spoke of Father Murphy and of priests who had presided at Land-League meetings.

"Yes," said Collins, "when peaceful measures were advised."

I replied that the government would not trust them because it thought that the people might become excited and burst from the priests' control, and because they feared that the priests might deceive them. The remark did not please Collins. He said that the people were excited at the report of Father Murphy's arrest because they are so united to their priests. "One is already in prison," he said, "Father Sheehey; and many meetings have been held to petition the government to release him and other leaders of the Land-League movement."

In a disturbed region in another part of the county Cork I was told of a priest who had refused to join the

League. The members would not send their children to the national school under his supervision, and the people thus opposed to him did not call him Canon Desmond, but only Desmond. On the other hand, I was told of two influential priests lately sent out of Cork by the bishop for being too active in the Land League. They were placed in country curacies—promotion backward— on account of the influence of a wealthy Catholic clique, which does not in politics hold to the Conservative, late Lord Beaconsfield party, "like the Protestants," but holds to the Liberal party, which is midway between the Conservatives and Land-Leaguers. It was added that one of these priests had gone to Rome to lay his case before the pope, not having been able to get the archbishop to interfere. The archbishop did not think it prudent to entertain the complaint.

Another of Collins's remarks may seem unjust to the government. He said that men's constitutions have changed. They are no longer able to live on potatoes. They must have Indian meal and bread and tea. " I think I would have been dead," he said, " if I had been kept on potatoes; and when men's constitutions are altered, any laws the government can make cannot have effect." But it is free trade in Great Britain and Ireland that makes bread and tea cheap.

The great domestic manufactories of the people demand a word. Collins wore to market one day a gray frieze coat (there pronounced frize). Calling at the house, I found an old woman engaged in spinning wool for the boys' clothing,—wool that had been beautifully carded at a factory. Collins's coat seemed to be black and white wool mixed, but the frieze is often dyed blue or red, and is also used for women's petticoats. The question of the want of manufactures is a great and somewhat puzzling one. At Dublin it was surprising to find that even the matches in my chamber were marked London. The want of coal has been given as one reason of the want of manufactories, but there is great and abundant water-power. The want of capital is also given as a cause of the lack of manufactures, and if we look into this point we come to two of the open sores of Ireland,—absent capitalists and want of national unity. In Guy's Almanac may be found a list of landholders of one thousand acres and upwards in the county Cork, leaseholders of over ninety years being put down as absolute owners. There are three hundred and seventy-five of these landholders, of whom about two hundred have residences in the county, and the remainder are entirely non-resident,—nearly fifty per cent.! As regards the want of capital, I asked a Protestant banker why they did not combine and form companies to manufacture. He replied, " As soon as eight Irishmen combine to do a thing, nine will combine to oppose them." The want of unity is owing, at least in part, to their being still two nations, if I may be allowed to say so, the conquerors and the conquered. Methodists and Quakers born in Ireland may be heard speaking contemptuously of the Irish. A woman of Scotch Presbyterian origin remarked, " It's a common saying, it's a blessed land and a cursed people." A Friend in Dublin said to me that the Protestants of the North are as bitter as the Catholics, " and more blamable, as they have the Scriptures." And I find the statement in my note-book that those who desired to be

considered the " upper ten," and Protestants from country localities, speak very contemptuously of the Land
League. Finally, the laws are unequal, the qualification for voters being higher in Ireland than in England.

On manufactures an Irish gentleman said to me,
" There are lots of American shoes brought to Cork.
Blacksmith's tools, agricultural implements, and carpenter's tools are brought to this country from America.
There's a finish and a style about them that they don't
do here." A Catholic manufacturer attributed the want
of manufactures to the lack of skill and knowledge in
the people; but does this account for the decline in
manufactures? As lately as 1837 there were one hundred thousand hides tanned yearly at Cork. It had
seven iron-foundries, five factories of spades and shovels,
numerous and extensive paper-mills, and two large
houses making flint-glass.* But where are most of them
now? My sprightly little landlady at Cork, a Catholic,
expressed in very simple terms a natural reason for this
decline, saying, " We want energy, for there's not an
atom of trade that the English did not spoil. There was
a cotton-factory here in Cork, and the English sent their
goods in and sold them a half-penny lower. They put
their foot upon these things, bless them! They have
crushed us out of the market in various ways. There is
a little screed of linen manufacture in the North, but I
believe that they cannot make it as good in England."

However, Mr. Mahony, a successful manufacturer of
tweeds at Blarney, says that manufactures are reviving
in Ireland. He thinks that three hundred power-looms

---

* Lewis's Topographical Dictionary, County Cork.

have been established within fifteen years. There is also ship-building in the north.

I talked with another working farmer. He had a tidy place near Cork, perhaps the neatest farm-house I saw, although there was no floor and no window in the principal room. Two hearty children and a domestic were present. The wife had been confined that morning, and the husband's breath indicated potations. "Such," said my landlady, who accompanied me, "do not employ a physician, but a 'knowledgable woman.' She is not recommended for skill in her profession, but 'she is lucky.' Had we gone into the room where the baby was, it would have been insisted on that we should take a glass of punch or we'd take away the beauty of the baby."

Dan Donovan, the father, said that he had sixty-five acres, all tillable, for which he paid the landlord one hundred and forty-two pounds yearly. He was also obliged to pay twelve pounds a year to the widow of the man who rented the farm before him. His taxes amounted to about twenty-five pounds, if not more, making the whole outlay in money about eight hundred and fifty dollars a year for sixty-five acres. He had been there about four years, and was only a yearly tenant, but he had manured the farm and put it in heart. That he was one of the very thriving farmers was evidenced by his stock of eight cows, eight calves, a pair of horses and a foal, a pair of donkeys, and twelve pigs. He employed more hands than an American would employ on so small a farm,—four "boys" or laborers at six shillings a week and their diet and lodging, which cost him as much more. He told us that he could not get ahead at all. "I am in debt to my master. He's a very intelligent man and fond of me. When I paid last year's rent the landlord promised some abatement this year."

Donovan is a voter. To a person of experience I mentioned how many hands Donovan employed. He answered, "He cannot get along with less, as he hauls manure from the city and hand-weeds." The speaker himself has four persons hand-weeding grain-fields, "taking out thistles and dock-roots that a previous tenant left as a boon."

On another walk I saw two men beside the road, one of them a remarkably neat old man, a farmer. They confirmed what I had heard, that very few around there could afford to save their hay and straw and feed cattle during the winter to manure their farms. "How do they manage, then?" I asked.

"Like that man," pointing to a handsome field opposite; "let land at five pounds an acre to those who have manure-pits."

Such, I understand, are men who, having donkey-carts, go around Cork gathering from houses the offal and garbage to throw into these pits.

I have said that Donovan was a voter, and this brings up the most serious complaint that the Irish have against the British government,—the inequality of the suffrage. This inequality does not exist in country districts. In counties in both countries the payment of an annual rent of twelve pounds entitles a man to vote for members of Parliament. But as Ireland is much poorer, doubtless the number of these voters is less. The inequality spoken of exists in boroughs. In England those living in towns have household suffrage, and even the lodger franchise; but in Irish towns the parliamentary voter must pay four pounds rent.

I have seen an estimate that in England two men out of five are voters; and in Ireland only one out of five is a voter. As to the operation of this high property qualification, we may observe that the county of Cork, having a population in 1871 of over five hundred thousand, returns under fifteen thousand votes. The city, having within the parliamentary boundary nearly ninety-eight thousand, gives under five thousand votes! But here is an illustration of the old rotten borough system of England: The county of Cork, with over fourteen thousand voters, elects two members at large. The city of Cork, with over four thousand six hundred voters, elects two members, while four boroughs in the county elect each a member; Bandon having four hundred and thirty voters, Mallow two hundred and ninety-three, Youghal two hundred and eighty-nine, Kinsale one hundred and ninety-four.

If, now, we come to teachers as voters, I hear that of the teachers of Ireland not more than one-twentieth can vote for members. This probably refers to teachers of national schools, nearly resembling our public schools.

I boarded some days at a castle, the residence of a gentleman who formerly belonged to one of the learned professions. Had his tenants been paying rent, it is possible that I should not have been received as a boarder. To this castle I went by rail. On the way I saw soldiers, of course, but they were so common that I hardly noticed them. The castle was a handsome stone building in a grove. The wall of the old part measured six feet in the embrasures of the windows. The new part measured three feet. I was shown into a great parlor, barely furnished, with a turf fire in the grate. It was in June. I call my host Mr. Loftus. The family were Protestant and Conservative, holding to the Church of Ireland, as the Episcopal Church is called since its disestablishment.

The tenants of Mr. Loftus sent a delegation to him. They offered rent on the basis of Griffith's valuation, which Mr. Loftus declined. He offered to allow them about one-fourth of the proposed reduction, or over sixteen per cent. on the rate of rent. But they went away without accepting his offer. Not to receive his rents was inconvenient for him, to say the least, as he had annuities to pay and bills to meet. Here I may add that a lawyer in Cork told me that the present unsettled state of affairs puts everybody on his guard against spending money, and so the laborers suffer. Some landlords have gone without their rent for two years, perhaps longer. Thus the bottom seems to be dropping out of society.

Another peculiarity in Irish affairs is the subletting of land; thus I heard of a farmer who has three landlords above him. To begin at the top, Mr. Prior lets land to the Osbornes, who get it from him on a perpetual lease for two shillings and sixpence per acre. The Osbornes let land to Daniel McBride, who has bought out a lease, but who has to pay also ten shillings and three pence per acre. Daniel McBride has other occupations, and does not work the land himself, but rents to a farmer, who takes a portion of the land, and pays

McBride seventeen shillings per acre. As said farmer holds thirty-six acres, possibly he has one or two laborers' houses which he rents out to men who would thus have four landlords above them.

To return to Mr. Loftus, the gentleman with whom I boarded. He spoke to me of the condition of the laborers in this district, which is but a poor one. It is natural for the aristocracy to look at this point, when farmers who are refusing them rent are themselves receiving rent from laborers. "The farmers of this country," said Mr. Loftus, "are the worst in the world. They drive the laborers very hard, and treat them badly. Often they do not give them a house fit to put a pig into. The houses are roofed with sods, as they want the straw for farming purposes. Nearly all the poor people lie on straw beds, and it is hard to get straw from the farmers. They allow the laborer about one-fourth of an acre for his potato-patch, and charge him rent of from two pounds to four pounds, sometimes in advance. The laborer's wages may be counted at one shilling a day the year round, and as his wife works in harvest, we may reckon hers at sixpence a day for six months. I speak only of my own neighborhood. I do not know the rates in others. There is near here a cluster of about a dozen cabins, all upon one farm. They are mud-walled and wretchedly roofed. A quarter of an acre of miserable boggy land is set apart for each tenant, and there is a large pool of stagnant water opposite each house. The tenant pays in advance three pounds and ten shillings yearly. The farmer sometimes makes the whole rent of his farm by what he receives from these people. I think the place a nuisance, and liable to breed a fever. None of these houses have windows, and many have no doors, except bunches of furze. The walls are propped up on the outside with pieces of bogwood to keep them from tumbling down."

The laborer, having no outbuildings, must necessarily protect his precious domestic animals under his own roof. Most laborers have a goat, and the poorest have poultry, but since the potato famine pigs have not been kept as before. Sometimes, however, there is a donkey.

"The children of the laborer," said Mr. Loftus, "go to the national school until they are about twelve years old. In most cases they go winter and summer without shoes and stockings. The laborer takes great pride and pleasure in being able to send his children to school. Laborers go to mass on Sunday, and in the afternoon may often be seen in the house, or beside a ditch, reading a newspaper. After mass they play ball in parties against each other, or have a fiddler and dance on the green or under trees. And they play cards, especially in Dublin county, where you can see them on Sundays playing on the banks of the ditches,"—*i.e.*, under shelter of a wall.

"What games do they play?" I asked.

"Forty-five and spoil five," he replied.

The laborer has no political privileges. Unless he pays a rent of over five pounds he pays no poor-rates, and no other taxes except the county or grand jury cess, and for malicious injuries, such as burnings. He pays this tax, but is not allowed to vote. "Would you put us under the Papists?" once cried an Irish Protestant on the question of universal suffrage.

On one occasion, when Mr. Loftus's man was driving

for me, he spoke of the desire or the efforts of the laborer to keep his little family together, for in the unions or poor-houses the sexes are separated. Mr. Loftus pointed out to me a building which he called the curse of the country. It is a union. "Children," he said, "brought up there are well fed, and idle, and never want to work." The number of these houses and the amount of money paid to sustain them seem almost incredible. Mr. Loftus's district is very heavily taxed, about five shillings in the pound, or twenty-five per cent. on the valuation of a man's annual income. The farmer pays this rate, but the landlord allows him half. The county of Cork, with a population of about five hundred thousand, has sixteen poor-houses. The one in Mr. Loftus's district contains about four hundred inmates, and the one in Cork over one thousand. The Cork poor-rate amounts to from two and one-quarter to four shillings a pound annually on every pound valuation of houses and lands, but the valuation for taxes is only about sixty per cent. of the annual income.

When the country is poorest these taxes are heaviest. Very few who go into the unions ever get out, excepting children. Said a guardian of the poor, "What causes the immense number of paupers in Ireland is the able-bodied persons going away and leaving the old. All the lower classes here speak of America as their home or final place of settlement. When the people send part of the money for their children, the board of poor-law guardians will sometimes supplement it gratuitously and send the children out. And at their own expense the board sometimes sends out lots of young women that are in the unions."

The region in which Mr. Loftus lives is a disturbed one. On a recent Sunday a Land-League meeting was to be held in the town. It had been extensively advertised in the newspapers. On the day before the meeting was to be held the lord lieutenant issued a proclamation forbidding it. About two hundred dragoons and infantry and one hundred armed police arrived at the town, bringing with them provisions, as no farmer nor storekeeper would dare to sell any to them. One storekeeper had already been boycotted for not joining the Land League. On the appointed Sunday, after mass, or about one o'clock, some five or six thousand people came together, with bands of music. Five or six Roman Catholic clergymen were among them. The people desired still to hold the meeting by erecting a platform on some other spot. Two stipendiary, or salaried, magistrates were present, and with them the priests entered into an agreement that the soldiers and police should not interfere with the people if they listened to no speeches, but simply formed in an orderly procession and paraded in the town. The affair went off peaceably, and the people went quietly home, although feeling much discontent at the action of the priests. If they had not obeyed the contract, the priests would have retired and left them to the mercy of the armed men.

At dinner, one day, in the course of conversation, Mr. Loftus said, "The country is well enough if it was left alone."

"But," said I, "you approve perhaps of one agitator, O'Connell; you like the effects of Catholic emancipation?"

"O'Connell!" he cried; "the best man Ireland ever

produced; a clever man. Not such a fellow as this Parnell, that nobody knows where he sprung from ; not fit to *clane* O'Connell's shoes in cleverness. O'Connell never allowed any quarrelling or disturbance. He kept up the agitation, but the people were kept in order. The repeal collections were kept up, but there was nothing like the burning, wounding, and killing that is going on in these times."

I asked whether there might not be a home parliament for local affairs, and delegates to a general parliament. He answered that the people are so much given to contention that they could not carry on affairs. "If half a dozen of them," he added, "come together at a poor-law meeting, they can't behave themselves."

After my return to Cork, an acquaintance advised me to visit a town in the southwest, where manners are more primitive. Accordingly I travelled thither, where women in a shop may be heard talking the Irish language. I went third-class. The railway terminated at the town. Falling into conversation with an intelligent fellow-traveller, he said that he had many men constructing a road. He was a steward or overseer. Looking out at the country, I asked, " Why are there no barns?"

" They have nothing to put into barns," he replied. " They sell their hay in the fields, and thresh their grain and get it quickly into market. They even sell their straw sometimes to meet their rent. Then when spring comes the landlord endorses for them in the bank. This answers for one year. On the next year the farmer must go to a money-lender, to whom he signs a note for twenty-five pounds, receiving only twenty pounds."

An intelligent Protestant, to whom I read this statement, made some corrections. He said that the landlord would only endorse for the rent, and the money-lender would charge ten or fifteen per cent.

I cannot substitute a name for that of my next witness. It is too well known, having been mentioned in Parliament. John Coppithorne is a Methodist. In politics, a Conservative. He says that if poor Beaconsfield were in there would not be any of these disturbances. He has a shop. He is a dyer, coloring frieze for country-folks. He rents several acres of land, and, finally, unfortunately for him, he lets " cars," or keeps a small posting establishment. It is on account of letting vehicles to the police that he is boycotted. He has lived for fifty-two years in the town of Skibbereen, in the southwest, near Cape Clear. Skibbereen is the terminus of the railroad, but beyond lies Skull, the residence of Father Murphy. Father Murphy is a quiet Catholic priest. One day a police-officer went into his house to get him to use his influence with the people. But Father Sheehy was already in jail, and the people, seeing the policeman, flew to the idea that Father Murphy was to be apprehended. A riot impended, and a message was sent to Skibbereen for a reinforcement of police. Not many police-officers were there, but they sent as many as they thought they could spare, and unfortunate John Coppithorne let them have cars to convey them, having no idea that the people would break out as they did. Mrs. Coppithorne was extremely alarmed when the mob attacked their house. They began about nine P.M., and continued at intervals until daylight, or about half-past two. It was not alone the breaking of windows, doors, and shutters which was alarming, but the accompanying sounds. The women were dreadful, howling and laughing. They brought stones in their aprons and encouraged the men. Horns were blown all night on the surrounding hills,—conch-shells and cows' horns. The military arrived by special train at three A.M., "and their arrival was as grateful as at Lucknow," said Mrs. Coppithorne.

At an early hour of the night some of the mob suggested to the priest that if the armed police were withdrawn they themselves would disperse. The stipendiary magistrate agreed to the proposition. The stipendiary, or paid magistrate, commands the armed forces, soldiers and police, in case of riot. So the police withdrew to barracks, and the mob took the priest on their shoulders and carried him home. The magistrate retired to his hotel, and then the mob came back in double force. Having before confined their efforts to the upper windows, they now attacked the doors and shutters below, and plundered the shop.

After all it was a false alarm, as Father Murphy was not apprehended. Tears came into Coppithorne's eyes when I asked him the amount of his losses. I hear that he claims damages to the extent of eight hundred pounds. He says that his business, worth perhaps two hundred pounds a year, is almost entirely ruined. Sometimes the people will come creeping in, perhaps with a permit to get frieze left to be dyed before the riot. There was a man in the shop while I was there, who wanted some frieze which some one had left for a petticoat. He had lost the ticket. The clerk declined to let him have it. "Only that the book was torn," he said, " I could let you have it." So the inconvenience of tearing books is not all on one side.

John Coppithorne is familiar with the pecuniary condition of the farmer. We could hardly expect him to be prejudiced in the farmers' favor. It is therefore remarkable that he confirms the report of the desperate condition of many of them. Of working farmers around him, he estimates that ten per cent. have barns. About fifty per cent. sell their hay. Then horses and cows are fed in the winter on the young shoots of the furze, chopped up for the purpose. (It is like donkeys eating thistles.) Fifty per cent. of the farmers sell their straw, and buy guano and phosphates. These are the small, unthrifty farmers. The large ones buy these, and use barn-yard manure also. But about fifty per cent. are never forehanded enough to be able to make manure in the winter sufficient to keep their land up to the standard. Poor creatures that have only a few acres can be seen going security for each other in the spring to buy guano for their potato ground. They live on potatoes, fish, milk, and Indian meal gruel.

About the same percentage sell all their grain to meet their rent and pressing demands, and then buy, often on credit, to feed themselves and animals. They buy their seed grain on credit at a high rate, paying, if they pay at all, after the next harvest. Legal process is not infrequently used to oblige them to pay. If money had not been sent into Ireland, and relief afforded by benevolent persons, half of the farmers would not have had seed potatoes in the spring of 1880.

Others at Skibbereen said that the competition is too great when farms are to be rented, and some farms are entirely too small to support a family, even if they had them rent free. Near the sea-coast an existence can be eked out by fishing, but there are many in Ireland cultivating five acres or less.

During my visit to Skibbereen I saw a funeral. The corpse was followed by wailing women, for this old custom still prevails. They buried the body at the graveyard of the abbey, an old ruin, where the dead were buried coffinless during the famine. It was so desperate that these people, who have so great a regard for funeral observances, would bury their dead, in some cases, in fields near the houses, and the parish cart went round and took up dead bodies that were buried in trenches. This great famine was caused by the potato-rot. A gentleman told me that at that time nineteen-twentieths of the people rarely ate bread.

But whether Ireland has not long been subject to famines is to me a question. Within two or three years we have seen one averted by liberal contributions, and there was one in 1822, or twenty-five years before the great potato famine just mentioned.

While in the county Cork I met another person well qualified to speak of the condition of farmers. Michael McBride's occupations were multifarious. He kept a shop, and a public-house distinct from it. He farmed many acres of land in different tracts. He sold his cattle at the fair. A public-house is a drinking-place, but McBride said that he drank no liquor himself. He was not a member of the Land League. He turned out a tenant and suffered by the League. While we talked in a retired corner of his " public," he occasionally spoke

in a loud voice, as though for others to hear, in this
manner: "England is getting sixteen million pounds a
year out of this unfortunate country, and plunging people
into jail under the coercion act for saying nothing but
the truth."

McBride appointed an hour for me to call again.   In
the evening he had to go out and raise contributions for
the poor of the parish.   "A very wild summer, thank
God," he said, meaning a cold summer, unfavorable to
agriculture. ("We thank God for everything," said my
landlady; "good, bad, or indifferent.   One of my English cousins could not believe that there was any reality
in thanking God for bad things.")   McBride said that
he held much land.

"Of course you employ some one to work it for you?"
I asked.

"Oh, bedad, yes," he replied.

He said that there are men who sell their clover green
when in want of money, and who will even take off
two or three crops in the year and sell them green.

The poor farmer sells his hay, straw, and turnips to
pay his rent, and therefore cannot make barn-yard manure
in the winter.   Guano was selling at thirteen pounds the
ton.   "It is a great evil to rely on," said McBride.
"The poor farmer may sell his oats at the glut of the
market at five pounds a ton, and afterward buy Indian
meal at seven pounds to feed his animals and himself."

In February, McBride paid seven pounds per ton for
hay, but in the preceding summer at harvest the same
quality was less than two pounds per ton.   He showed
me a note which he had signed to prevent a small farmer
or poor man from being turned out.   Such must have

two endorsers; but McBride's signature was enough, because he was a man of means. At first he refused. The man cried, for he was to be served with a writ if he did not pay that day. The note runs in this manner:

"16th of June, 1881.

"On demand we jointly and severally, or any two of us, promise to pay Messrs. Kelly & Co., limited, Patrick Street, Cork, or order, the sum of £10, for value received.

"DAVID SMITH.
"MICHAEL McBRIDE."

McBride added that he supposed that he signed "a thousand a year," and lost as "often as I have hairs on my head." On the above note for ten pounds the borrower was to pay ten shillings interest and sixpence other charges for the use of the money for three months, which is over twenty per cent. annually.

He said that of private bankers and money-lenders at exorbitant rates there are twenty in Cork, some of them pawnbrokers. In various towns there are many poor people who pawn their clothing on Monday and redeem it on Saturday.

McBride said that the great cause of the present embarrassment is the three bad years of 1877, 1878, and 1879. Oats, wheat, barley, and potatoes were bad. Some oat-fields were never cut. McBride said that seventy per cent. of the farmers around Cork are unable to pay their debts, and would be bankrupt if forced to do so. They would need three good harvests to bring them up. "They will never pay the same rents again. Their condition is owing to high rents, bad harvests, and American competition."

After leaving the county Cork I spent a few days in Dublin. From persons on the train thither and in that city I obtained information concerning other portions of Ireland. To this I add the testimony of an Irish gentleman well known in politics, whom I met in London.

A young man from the county of Limerick said that that county is all pasture. Not more than forty per cent. of the farmers in his neighborhood could afford to save hay and straw and feed cattle in winter for manure. Farms average from forty to fifty acres, some being as small as ten. He knew one man who farmed over three hundred acres, and paid three pounds and five shillings per acre therefor. He had two or three acres in potatoes, and the same in oats, but all the rest in pasture.

"Can he make money?" I asked.

"Not these late years," he replied. "He is served with an ejectment because he can't pay his rent."

None of our farmers will be surprised that a man cannot make money on grass-land at a rent of about sixteen dollars per acre.

Another passenger, who was from Tipperary, said that, with few exceptions, the farmers of that county can keep cattle in winter and keep up their farms. Take the whole of Ireland, however, and farm-lands are deteriorating in value. In Tipperary and Limerick lies "the Golden Vale," celebrated for its fertility. I had an impression that Tipperary was wild and riotous. In London I spoke to the political gentleman above alluded to, who knew the county well. In politics he is not in unity with Parnell, and is opposed to the Land League; but not, if we may judge by his conversation, to sanguinary measures.

"Tipperary," said he, "has not of late suffered so much as some other districts. Thirty or forty years ago the farmers were entirely at the mercy of their landlords. They took the law into their own hands and fought for their farms, shooting down the landlords or their agents. Many of them were hanged or transported. The land bill of 1870," he continued, "extended to all Ireland, restrains the landlord from evicting tenants without leases, unless paying them for their improvements." He says that the present trouble is caused mainly by landlords demanding increased rents.

My intelligent fellow-traveller from the county Tipperary further said that the provisions of the proposed land bill, by which the tenant is to hold his land as long as he pays his rent, will do away with all abuses. The Three F's of the land bill are: First, Free sale,—that is, the tenant is to have the privilege of selling his right in the farm; second, Fixity of tenure; and, third, Fair rent, to be determined by a court.

I remarked that this third F is against the free operation of trade; that everything should be sold at its value in the market. "No one puts such restrictions upon trade as you Americans," he replied.

When I arrived at Dublin I lodged at two different temperance houses. In one I met a plain man from the county Galway, in the west. He kept a shop, and was a dealer in hides. He traded from town to town. He said that his priest and bishop were good men, and that young boys and girls were signing the pledge. Of the farmers of Galway he estimated that seventy per cent. are unable to pay their rent unless they sell horse, cow, and calves; and even then they would be left in debt to the shopkeeper. He complained greatly of the recent coercion act, under which, he says, worthy citizens are apprehended or are in danger.

One fellow-lodger was a Methodist minister from the county Fermanagh, in the north. He had been attending the Cork Conference. He complained of the increase of luxury among farmers in buying tea and bread and in the clothing of their daughters, and spoke of their spending two days a week at market, and five or six shillings each time in treating each other.

"But your congregations are not of this class?" I said.

"Indeed they are," he answered. "There are plenty in my congregation who come home tipsy every market night."

He afterward took out change and called for a bottle of ale. They sent out and got it for him.

I was much interested in the conversation of two men who were dining at the house. One of them, a young man, said that the three F's would not satisfy the Land-Leaguers. They wanted the extermination of the landlords and the possession of the land. The other did not agree with him. He said, "It would be a nice thing for you to be paying two pounds and ten shillings for land, and a Land-Leaguer over the fence be getting it for half the money. I am an Orangeman," he added, "and the son of an Orangeman, and the grandson of an Orangeman, yet I am greatly in sympathy with the poor, suffering tenantry of this country."

He said of himself that he had been in the army nine years; that he was a landlord in a small way, five or six hundred pounds a year; and that he was now lying out of rents. Rather than disturb tenants he had paid as high as ten per cent. for money, and "glad to get it at that." He was originally from the county Cavan, northwest of Dublin. He said that the average size of farms there is about twelve acres. Some have thirty. About twenty per cent. of the farmers own horses. Many keep donkeys, but these are unfit for farming. They put out manure with jennets, which are not fit for ploughing. The poor farmer must wait until the richer one has done ploughing so as to hire horses, and then the land is ploughed shallow and injured. Both speakers were agreed on the trouble of hiring horses. You must pay ten shillings a day for a pair, feed them and the ploughman, and give him several glasses of whiskey, added one. If you have cash in hand, you can get horses when you will; but the small farmer cannot pay until he has harvested his crop. He generally pays labor in exchange for horses.

A suggestion that the British government should buy the lands of Ireland, rent them for the space of thirty years, and that the people should then become possessors, met with some favor. The Irish politician whom I met in London found two objections to this plan: First, that it would take from the country the cultivated class; and, second, that for thirty years it would drain the country of money.

ENGLISH.

I spent a few weeks in England in 1881, and visited three agricultural regions in the east, the north, and the south. An article on the last is to appear in *Harpers' Magazine.* The following is drawn principally from my visit to the east. Some account of my stay in the north and of a few days in a manufacturing county may appear hereafter.

My authority for the statements in the following article is almost entirely notes taken at the time, assisted in a small degree by recollections. But it cannot be assumed that this essay is without faults.

With regard to another country, I was advised to tell what I saw and how it impressed my mind, and not to endeavor to draw conclusions. But what a traveller sees and hears is greatly influenced by his own opinions. He goes to a foreign land, and if of different religious institutions from his own, he inquires on this point; of a different form of government, he asks political questions. He notices, also, differences in dress, food, and manner of living.

The first family with whom I boarded in Huntingdonshire was that of Mr. Jackson, a carpenter, who, besides working at his trade, rented a few acres. His wife, who

344

was a farmer's daughter, had a small dairy of three cows. Jackson appeared to have a splendid constitution. He was short and somewhat thick-set. He began his trade at eighteen, and was an apprentice five years and a journeyman three, when, having put by some money, he married at twenty-six. His wife was near thirty. One of them said that they had prospered with the help of the Lord.

Mrs. Jackson also had been able to save something wherewith to furnish a house. She learned a trade, and was also companion or lady's-maid to sick ladies and those going to Brighton. One of them made her a wedding present of neat china.

Jackson and his wife have four children,—the eldest about six, or as she says, "Four little children, not one of them able to put on a shoe nor a stocking." She attends to her dairy, boards the apprentice, and has no servant.

Their children are sweet and clean. Three of them go to the public school in the village. It is called the national school. Mrs. Jackson gave the eldest three pence to pay for their instruction for a week; which is at the rate of about twenty-four cents a quarter for each of them. The penny is a trifle over two cents, the shilling a little under a quarter of a dollar; but in turning sterling money into our own, it will avoid repetition to consider the English penny as two cents, and four shillings as a dollar.

The Jacksons' house seemed a perfect palace compared to that of any working farmer that I saw in Ireland. Coming freshly from that country, I thought it must be the gem of the village, but I was mistaken.

The busy activity of the Jacksons, who have a young family to keep, was more like what I have seen at home than what I saw in Ireland.

The house has a peculiar name placed on the front, something like Hallelujah House. Doubtless it was built by a dissenter. I saw another bearing title Bunyan Lodge.

A lodging-room was assigned to me, and I ate by myself in one of the front rooms below. (Thus to take lodgings is very common in England.) Jackson and his wife ate in the kitchen. When they had finished, she gave the apprentice what she chose. My room had strips of carpet on the floor, neat white curtains at the window, a suitable toilet service, linen sheets and pillow-cases. There stood in it a neat red chest with iron bands at the corners, and a white fringed cloth covering the top. It was locked, expressive of thrifty housekeeping.

Jackson and his wife do not go to the gray Church of England, which, with its spire, overlooks the trees. They attend the brick chapel, being Independents.

After he had taken me to see his calves and pigs, I asked him what proportion of the farmers in the neighborhood belonged to the Church of England.

He answered, "About one-half. I think that is just about the proportion that voted last year."

This answer amused me much, but I feared that his wife would not understand why I laughed.

"You mean to say," I said, "that large landed proprietors expect those who rent from them to go to church?"

"Yes," he said, "or they would not rent to them."

"Of course," said I, "it is not put into the leases.

But how can they know how they vote now that you have the secret ballot?"

"They go round and ask them, and if they would not promise, they would lose their farms. Many a farmer has been turned out because he would not vote for his landlord's party."

On another occasion I spoke to him of the wars which England had lately waged in Asia and South Africa, and Jackson spoke of the deficit in the finances when the Liberals came in. He said that he believed their country has had to smart very severely for unnecessary wars and bloodshed, and added, " Because it was a smart little country, what business had we to go and say to other nations, ' You shall do as we please' ?"

I did not stay many days with the Jacksons. Mrs. J. considered the burden of a dairy and of young children to be enough without taking lodgers. I was recommended to the house of Mr. Benton, the principal farmer in the village, and a friend called with me and introduced me to Mrs. B., who after an interval for deliberation consented to take me as a boarder at their family table.

Benton farmed about seven hundred acres, but not all in one tract. He owned a small part, and rented from various persons. One large farm he had taken at a heavy rent, and he was worried in these hard times. He used to follow the plough when a boy, but he cannot now, having so much to do in walking around and superintending work.

Mr. and Mrs. Benton adhered to the Established Church. He began to attend Sunday-school early, perhaps at two years, and had attended ever since, he being fifty, and a teacher. He was church-warden, and the most considerable parishioner in attendance; but was not on equal visiting terms with the clergyman.

He was more reserved than his wife; he said that the English did not incline to make new friends. He seemed to hold to the same opinions that he cherished in early life; to be of warm and constant attachments, and not free from prejudice. He said that Ireland should be sunk for twenty-four hours and repeopled with English and Scotch; that the reason the poor-rates are so heavy in Ireland is that the people are so lazy. He declined to tell to which political party he held, saying that the ballot is secret. He remarked of ourselves that he wished "the Americans would let our things go in there free, same as we let their things."

The Bentons had seven children, five of them daughters. The eldest son was twenty-one, and was actively employed attending to farm operations. The girls had taken music lessons, and could play upon the piano. The eldest two were away learning dressmaking, and Mrs. Benton thought that she might be able to get a place as lady's-maid for one or more of her girls.

Mrs. Benton had a large house, kept in good order. She was tall, fair, good-looking, active, and sprightly. She said that she "would rather have a penny of her own *hearning* than tuppence that anybody should give her." She did her housework with the help of the young daughters left at home. She said that, as a general rule, the tenant farmers had brought up their children too high, had hired servants, and now that these hard times had come, they had failed.

But Mrs. Benton's housework is not like that of the wife of a large farmer in Pennsylvania. She does not board any of the farm hands ; the only thing of the kind that they do now is to give them their beer in " 'ay-time." She hires a woman to help wash. In summer they wash about once in eight weeks, and in winter more rarely, having plenty of clothes. The washing is done in two days, Saturday and Monday. Mrs. B. and her daughters do the ironing, though sometimes she puts out a frilled petticoat. They iron only the starched things ; the others are mangled.

Nor does Mrs. Benton have the labor of milking, for it is done by one of the hired men. In the care of poultry she has the assistance of the shepherd's wife, who raises chickens at their own house. Mrs. B. furnishes feed, and pays her eight cents for every fowl that she raises, and four for every twenty eggs that she brings her. She pays her own daughter a trifle for the eggs which she brings in at the home-place.

As regards the number of meals that she gave her family, we had four daily ; for, in addition to the after-noon tea, we had a late supper. I noted one. All the young children had gone to bed, for Mrs. Benton was an excellent house-mother. For supper, we had onions, soft cheese, bread, cold pork, stout for the mother to drink, and ale for the father. After supper, Benton read aloud a small portion of the New Testament ; the son of twenty-one before going to bed kissed his mother and bade his father good-night, and the daughter kissed both parents.

Mrs. Benton asked a blessing at meals : " For what we are about to receive may the Lord make us thankful, for

Jesus Christ's sake. Amen." Thanks were returned by the young children. One said, "Thank God, father and mother, for a very good tea. Amen."

Mrs. Benton delivers tracts. She takes them to dissenters' houses; for the plan on which "the church" acts seems to be that all these are only stray sheep from their fold. They are indeed parishioners. Jackson, the carpenter with whom I boarded, as he rented land, was obliged to pay tithes for the support of the clergyman, although he himself was an Independent or Congregationalist.

Though she is a church-woman, Mrs. Benton tells me that one of her uncles is a bitter dissenter. He would not open a prayer-book, and even objected to the repetition of the Lord's Prayer at the close of another supplication.

FARMS AND FARMERS.

This village where the Bentons lived closely adjoins the fenny or swampy land of the east of England. Said Benton, "Perhaps a hundred years ago the fens grew nothing but reeds and rushes and produced a quantity of wild fowl." "All the geese in Lincoln fens" I had before heard of. The water is now kept out of the fens by means of steam-engines. This level land is well fitted for tillage, but bad weather had been very unfortunate for the wheat farmer. He generally holds more land than the dairy farmer, but he had been suffering from a succession of wet harvests. Before the abolition of the corn laws, high prices were kept up by a duty on foreign grain, but now the farmer cannot compete with our Western grain. An experienced man told me that the man who held even as high as one thousand acres was going behind every year.

In the summer of 1881, before the harvest was gathered in, I was told that there had not been a dry harvest since 1874. Some idea of what an English summer can be was given to me by Benton, the farmer with whom I boarded. He said that in 1879, at a Royal Agricultural Show near London, the farm implements were up to the hub in mud, and boards were spread for people to walk upon. In meeting, some would get shoved off up to the knees in mud. Men did not go round offering to black shoes, but with pails of water to wash off the mud. Yet there were thousands there.

The average of wheat raised in England is much greater than ours. In this country we do not hoe wheat and then weed it. But the production of England is scarcely half the amount required for the population. In 1880 the amount raised was sixty-four millions of bushels; the amount needed, one hundred and seventy-six millions. In 1881 they hoped to get one hundred millions of their own produce. One of my friends said that they would have starved the last year or two but for America.

In considering the English climate it is well to remember the high northern latitude. There is no city on our continent, not even Quebec, which is so far north as Paris. London lies in the latitude of Newfoundland and Labrador. Whether wet climates like that of England and Ireland can successfully compete in wheat-raising in the long run with our drier ones may well be doubted.

Another acquaintance spoke to me of the depressed condition of this district. He said that within a radius of six miles, six large farmers, cultivating three or four hundred acres each, had failed since the last harvest. "For four years," he added, "the seasons have seemed to alter,— snow and rain fell in seed-time ; there was little or no sun to mature the grain at harvest. There were floods of water covering acres of ground, so that one farmer holding perhaps five hundred or more acres, that had also been been cultivated by his father and grandfather, lost in three years about twenty thousand dollars. Then he took his remaining capital and went into other business."

It was surprising to one accustomed to the small farms of the fertile district in which I live to find such large farmers as many of the English. Said one of my acquaintance in Huntingdonshire, "One who farms fifty acres is scarcely called a farmer. He farms a little land. In another county I know a farmer who holds fifteen hundred acres." The tendency of course is largely to increase the number of farm-laborers, while diminishing the number of those who farm themselves.

The farmer with whom I boarded employed a large number of hands, forty I think, in the spring. In July he had four men hoeing turnips, potatoes, "mangles" (mangel-wurzels ?), and kohl-rabi. He had also about eleven children pulling weeds out of wheat, barley, and oats.

He kept twenty working horses, and with them had eight or ten hands. In the earlier season he had twenty hands hoeing wheat, barley, oats, beans, and peas. He had a shepherd to look after about two hundred sheep. He employs some women, girls, and boys. In the early morning I heard a peculiar cry as of a boy calling the cows, but he was crying to keep away the birds that depredate on the wheat,—linnets, sparrows, and blackbirds in the hedges. Benton also employed hands to go over fields that were to be planted in potatoes, turnips, buckwheat, and to pick twitch out of them. This, he said, is a wild and very troublesome grass, that fills the ground with roots, so that nothing else can grow.

I have just mentioned buckwheat. Benton had about thirty acres in this grain. It is fed to pigs and other animals; he said that he had never heard of its being eaten by men.

One of the most surprising things to me was the short number of hours that the farm-laborers made. That men should quit farm-work in July at or before six in the evening was novel to me. But all the work that is possible Benton puts out by the piece.

The price of land in this arable region is differently reported. One told me that it can be bought in fee simple for from two to three hundred dollars per acre. Perhaps this is the fen land and more valuable. The village in which I boarded was at a small distance from the fens. Land around this village sells at from one hundred to five hundred dollars per acre, but the latter are nice bits around the village. Land can be rented in this or the fenny region for farming at about nine dollars per acre. The tenure on which lands are held it was hard for me to understand. For instance, I was told that copyhold is nearly as good as freehold. At some length a friend endeavored to explain to me copyhold fine arbitrary, and then said that copyhold fine certain is more desirable.

In the depressed condition of farming of which I have spoken, it has been found that grazing and dairy farms are more profitable than grain. The abolition of the corn laws, said a friend, made bread cheap and enabled the mechanic and manufacturer to live, and they can buy more meat than before, and grazing and dairy farms are very profitable. Grain, which can readily be transported by sea, comes more closely into competition with the English grain than meat does.

One of the persons whom I met in Huntingdonshire was a retired farmer, and must have been a successful one. When he began to farm the fen land, that which he held had lately been brought under complete drainage, and was comparatively new. About 1835, on twenty-four acres of land he had the exceptional crop of sixty-four bushels of wheat to the acre. He has often grown four hundred bushels of potatoes to the acre on twenty-five acres, and he thought that his average yield had been three hundred bushels. He has had potatoes growing to the height of three feet, level as a floor, and not a weed to be seen. "There should not be a weed seen in an acre. I have grown," he continued, "one hundred and twelve bushels of oats to the acre, and did not think that I had a crop under eighty-four. However, I did what none of you Americans do. In the latter part of my time, when I farmed only one hundred acres, I used six thousand dollars a year (twelve hundred pounds) in fertilizing my farm. Thus I bought six thousand dollars' worth of grain and fed animals, especially pigs. Further, I sold the best of my wheat, oats, and potatoes, and consumed all the rest of my produce on the farm. I find no one who has fed so much on one hundred acres."

Mrs. Benton took me one evening to see a steam-plough or cultivator at work. It did the ploughing well here when the weather was sufficiently dry. It was an immense affair. There were two steam-engines, one on each side of the field, sending the cultivator back and forth. The whole cost of the machine (including the van for the men to sleep in) was about ten thousand dollars. The charge for ploughing was three dollars per acre (twelve shillings), and the farmer furnished coal and perhaps also one hand. The men who brought the plough boarded themselves. They were making long days, from four in the morning to nine at night. By working until ten, they could cultivate twenty acres per day, and in these high northern latitudes summer days are very long.

During my short stay in the east I heard the price of a few articles, principally farm products. Mrs. Jackson, wife of the carpenter with whom I boarded, had prepared for me (in July) a very nice sparerib of pork, for which she paid eighteen cents per pound. She thought that no mutton could be bought under twenty. She had understood that meat was dearer than with us and clothing cheaper. Bread was cheap, she said. But I have before quoted the saying that they would have starved lately but for America.

"After midsummer is turned," said Mrs. Jackson, "butter grows dearer. The pasture is shorter, and milk will not keep." It was then selling at thirty-two cents the pound, but last summer it was dearer. At supper she and her husband had a large piece of good cheese. I heard that the best American was bringing sixteen cents (eight pence). Leicester cheese, which used to cost about twenty-four cents, no longer sells here.

Benton, the farmer, said that American hams are very poor. I endeavored to inform him how finely swine are fed on corn in Illinois, but he said that the difficulty is not in the feeding, but in the manner of curing the meat. For American bacon they thought that they paid thirteen cents.

In conversation, Benton spoke of eleven fat beasts (beeves) that would have brought two hundred and fifty dollars last year, but had sold much lower this year, on account of the American beef coming in.

As regards milk, a retired farmer told me that he used to sell it at about ten cents the imperial gallon in summer and twelve in winter, and he had to convey it five miles to the railroad station. It had now risen a penny the gallon.

THE CHURCH AND THE RECTOR.

Two adjacent villages formed here one parish, which may be called Haddenham cum Stonea, from said villages. The living was a good one, as the rector received his house and six thousand dollars a year. This income was principally drawn from tithes, which amounted to about two dollars per acre on the arable land in the parish, and to near five thousand five hundred dollars yearly. From glebe land he drew the remainder of his income. He was, however, bound to keep his house in repair, and for the last eighteen months he had not drawn his full income.

Benton was the principal parishioner in attendance at church. His family, however, did not associate on equal terms with that of Mr. Rounce, the rector. On the occasion of a wedding-breakfast, Mr. Rounce had taken a meal at the farmer's, and Benton had dined at the rectory on the occasion of a church meeting. But Mrs. Benton did not expect the rector and his daughters to associate with them equally. I heard an intimation that the rector was originally poor, but no one who attended the church was now on a social level with himself.

I attended one Sunday afternoon. The congregation was not large, and very few looked well-to-do. The number of communicants, I was told, was over sixty. One young man, who came into church, was showy in appearance. He was neatly dressed, with plenty of large, silvery-looking buttons. He was the rector's footman.

The church was a gray stone building. Though plain, its appearance over the level fields was agreeable. The curtains within were rather shabby. From one at the end the rector emerged, so I suppose it concealed the vestry-room. In appearance Mr. Rounce, the rector, was blustering and brawny. His lungs seemed brazen, but perhaps some of the congregation were deaf. He wore a white linen robe, and upon his shoulders behind lay a mantle or hood of black, faced with magenta color. The text of the sermon was, "Not slothful in business; fervent in spirit, serving the Lord." I took some brief notes, which I reproduce. They contained one very

16*

happy, and, as adapted to the congregation, one very unhappy, remark. He said that it is difficult to continue piety amidst the cares of daily business. " I was going to compare this to tar, to being surrounded by tar ; very dirty, very sticky.

"There are people who shut themselves up in cells with one small bed, a chair, and a candle. This is the way that many are taking to become fervent in spirit, forgetting the first part of the text, diligent in business. In my young days there were but six monasteries and nunneries in all England, Scotland, and Wales ; now they number over six hundred.

"There are some who think that their religious exercises should be confined to Sunday. There are various things that we shouldn't do on Sunday; it's quite right we shouldn't read newspapers on Sunday. But religion has thus been defined : it is the art of being and doing good."

As we left the church, I asked its age, and the rector said that it was of the time of Henry VII. (who died in 1509). What is old has a great attraction to the people of our new country, and I looked in the churchyard for interesting monumental stones. The oldest that could be deciphered bore date 1672, and seemed to be that of a great pugilist. The gravestones were not numerous and showy. Some one told me afterwards that those who attend the church are the poorest of the poor, and are generally buried without tombstones.

Concerning the rector, I ventured to draw some conclusions as follows : Mr. Rounce is a strict Sabbatarian, between two fires,—Dissent on the one hand and High-Churchdom and Papacy on the other. In the eyes of a zealous incumbent of the English Church, even of a zealous low-churchman, all the people living in the parish are his people. But many, very many of them, are like lost sheep wandering on the barren mountains of Dissent, and so long have they refused to hear even the church that they have become to him like heathen men and publicans, and with them he does not wish to hold intercourse. He employs members of his own church, however, to distribute tracts among them as regularly as among his chosen people, even although these dissenters are full communicants in their own " chapels."

I was allowed to visit the rectory grounds and afterward to see the house itself, through the courtesy of an assistant in the National school, who was also a servant in the rector's family. The house was not so much distinguished by the elegance of its carpets and other furniture as by the number and variety of its cabinets (among them I may reckon a great carved chest), by the quantity of china displayed, and to some extent by paintings and natural history collections. The ladies were absent, but I met the rector for a moment or two, and it seemed to me that he considered me to need pruning or cutting down. But he was kind enough to allow the lady's-maid who conducted me to find for me in the library one or two works which I wished to consult, and she was sufficiently intelligent to aid me, and obliging enough to do so.

When we walked through the garden I observed that a net was spread to protect cherries from the birds, and that currants were trained to the top of the wall, about eight feet.

Mrs. Benton, the farmer's wife, received a letter from

the former rector. She said that he had removed to the "'op" country, to Kent. She described him as a tiny little man, over eighty, a very stanch liberal in politics; a clever, very learned man.

While I was still in the village, Mr. Rounce's two daughters had a lawn-tennis party on their grounds, and the guests could be seen from the road. Three of the men appeared to be "in their shirt-sleeves." I learned at Mr. Benton's that the guests would be about fifty in number, the farmer's young daughters being permitted to look on. It was thought that the refreshments would be tea, coffee, and cakes, handed round,— Miss Rounce being a teetotaller.

DISSENTERS.

A rector of the Established Church, whom I met upon a railroad train, spoke to me of there being here one hundred and fifty different religious sects, but the number seemed incredible. Afterwards, however, an acquaintance pointed out to me the list in Whitaker's Almanac for 1881. This list is headed

"Religious sects. Places of Worship.

"Places of meeting for religious worship in England and Wales have been certified to the Registrar-General on behalf of persons described as follows."

And the list, instead of numbering one hundred and fifty only, goes up at least to one hundred and sixty-nine.

The dissenting chapel in the village which I am endeavoring to describe was a brick edifice, and the yard contained a number of conspicuous monumental stones.

Two prominent sects were united to compose the congregation, and the number of communicants was one hundred and thirty. I call the building a chapel, as the English do; nothing is a church, in fashionable speech, that does not belong to the establishment.

There was within the bounds of the parish a third "meeting-house," where the assembly is composed mainly of a few members of a religious body, generally respected, but declining in numbers. I had a letter of introduction to one of the members here, and when I spoke of her to Mrs. Jackson, the carpenter's wife, Mrs. J. told me that I might be able to receive an introduction to others by means of her to whom the letter was addressed, who was a person of education and the wife of a retired farmer.

"Now," I asked, "how likely shall I be to see the rector?"

"Oh, not at all!" There is such a strong feeling against dissenters is one reason why I should not meet him.

On the other hand, a dissenting minister, in speaking to me of the Established Church, remarked that the feeling against it is more political than religious. There is nothing, he added, in the doctrines of the Church of England that is repugnant to a vast number of people who attend dissenting churches; the objection is to a religious denomination which is elevated by the state over others, and consequently has greater social power and prestige.

But one whom I met at a neighboring town spoke more strongly. He was a retired farmer who had travelled in our country. He brought forward the following objections to an established church. The people have little or no choice as regards their own clergyman; they have no control over their own forms of worship; and all spiritual life is destroyed in the church.

In further conversation he said, "Can I forget that I am socially persecuted because I am a dissenter; that my father was commercially persecuted for being a dissenter, —he could not rent a farm on equal terms; that my grandfather was probably excluded from holding office for being a dissenter; and my great-grandfather, if a dissenter, would have been thrown into jail for attending a conventicle. But it may be said, 'Why rake up old sores?' Simply because the same persecuting spirit remains, and if the dissenters were not so strong in numbers, and consequently in political power and wealth, the same things would be done again." He added that no farmer should be a dissenter. He himself belonged to a Liberation society. He wondered at the apathy of the Americans in not sympathizing with them in their efforts against an established church. (I have given my friend's words from my notes, but I suspect that the date at which Quakers and others were imprisoned in England was not so recent as that of the gentleman's great-grandfather.)

The following anecdote was given to me by another person, also a retired farmer. It concerns a man of some distinction, now dead, and who did not bear the name which I assign him. This as well as others are substitutes. My friend told me that when Carter Gray rented a mill from Lady Letitia Robyn he also rented from her a large farm, which he conducted to much profit. He built schools in his neighborhood and also a dissenting chapel, and the clergy got at the Lady Letitia and induced her to take the farm from him. But she did not take away the mill. Carter Gray was so popular that although a dissenter he was appointed a magistrate. The lord lieutenant of the county has the recommendation for magistrates and had declared against a dissenter, but Lord John Russell is supposed to have been in Mr. Gray's favor. "Lord John was a great liberal," added my acquaintance. "Until his persevering action in Parliament the dissenters had a hard time of it."

In the English village I describe, I called at the modest residence of the dissenting minister. He had studied at the Baptist Theological Seminary in London. I found him to be interested in several of our home authors. Among his books were the complete works of Ralph Waldo Emerson (London: Bell & Daldy). He said that there is no one he honors more than Emerson, except, perhaps, their own Carlyle. He said that he had in his theological library Channing's works and another man's, Beecher,—Ward Beecher. "I have a great admiration for that man." He had Lowell's poems, and rejoiced in Lowell. He spoke of the "Biglow Papers," and of the pious editor's creed, repeating,

> "I du believe in principle,
> But oh! I du in interest."

TAXES AND TITHES.

The rates for the poor, for repair of roads, for police (for there is a policeman in every village), and for the county prison amounted in the parish I speak of to about two shillings and sixpence in the pound of the assessed annual value of the land. As the pound is twenty shillings, the assessment consequently is over twelve per cent.

The burden of supporting the poor, while much lighter than in Ireland, must be far heavier than in our country. Huntingdonshire is one of the smallest counties in England. In 1871 it contained less than seventy thousand people, and at the time of my visit had four unions or poor-houses. But this does not altogether represent the amount of poverty. In another farming region, I understood that the farm-laborer, even though he be sober, honest, and industrious, seldom or never lays by enough to support his family in his age, but becomes partially or entirely dependent on parish relief. But out-door relief in the parish I have been describing, and perhaps in England generally, is granted only to the aged ; young people must go into " The House." There they pick oakum and work garden ground. Children are put out at fourteen or earlier, if they have passed in the school " the fourth standard." No child is allowed during the period that school is open to go to work under the age of ten.

Tithes in this parish of Haddenham cum Stonea average about one dollar and eighty cents to the acre. If there were sufficient land attached to the rectory for the income to support Mr. Rounce there would be no tithes, but there are only sixty acres of glebe land, and the living is worth, as I have stated, about six thousand dollars yearly. The sixty acres of glebe land bring in about five hundred dollars, hence the remainder is to be raised by tithes.

I have spoken of Jackson, the carpenter with whom

I boarded. He was a dissenter, and they attended the chapel. He rented, however, six acres of land, and his tithes to the English Church were about ten dollars yearly.

Formerly Quakers resisted the payment of tithes. A friend told me that his father, uncle, and grandfather were imprisoned in the county jail for non-payment. When he himself farmed three hundred and twenty-two acres, he paid five hundred and twenty pounds rent and one hundred and twenty pounds for tithes. This money was generally seized from him. He had land in three parishes, and numerous warrants were out against him. The officers would come with cart or wagon, and seize his grain while he was threshing. In his father's time they would have green boughs, and stick one into every tenth shock of grain or hay. But Friends have now given up this contest, and pay tithes quietly. Apparently he did not think them burdensome.

Tolls on roads were abolished in England only a few years ago, and the expense now falls on the landholder. We do not often see in our country such a road as connects the two villages which I describe under the name Haddenham and Stonea. It is a highway in splendid form and order, with a wide grassy margin and a ditch on each side. On one is a wide, gravelled footpath, and fine green hedges separate the road from the fields.

SCHOOLS.

There are three schools in these two villages. One of them is a Dame school, or an unpretending private one, which I did not visit; but the two principal ones deserve attention from the students of our institutions and of English ones. They are public schools, although people pay for tuition. That in Haddenham is a National school, that in Stonea a British school. In the former, Mr. Rounce, the rector, is manager, and the doctrines of the Church of England are taught. The other, the British school, is under charge of a board, or of a committee, of which several members are dissenters.

I first visited the National or Church of England school. Eighty-one names were upon the roll and fifty in attendance at one of my visits. (Some little ones were at work in the fields, weeding, or perhaps haymaking.) Pupils may enter at two years. The printed form issued by government asks, " How many have you under three?" And by the obligatory law the schools can claim them at five.

Upon the walls of the school were several maps, a large printed copy of the Creed, large tablets of the Commandments, and little pictures from the Bible, with perhaps a few from natural history. The blackboard was an insignificant one, about four feet square. I observed the small amount of blackboard surface provided, and the youngest teacher said that in the British schools there is blackboard on the sides of the room.

There was in the school a little picture of the royal family. "We teach them loyalty to the queen," said one of the teachers.

Connected with the school was an infant department. Here the blackboard measured about one foot by eighteen inches. There were a few objects upon the walls, but there seemed to me a general bareness of appliances for instruction.

This school is an endowed one, having fourteen acres of land; it has always been a National school, or one where the principles of the Church of England are taught. Five years ago it became a government school,—*i.e.*, it has become an "efficient elementary school" under the government; it is examined by a government inspector, and for children coming up to the government standard the school receives a small sum in payment on each These "results," as they are called, all pass into the rector's hands, as manager of the school, to be appropriated either toward the payment of teachers or for school apparatus. Here all apparatus is paid for from this fund.

For instruction of children farmers pay four cents a week for each child; others two. The parish pays for pauper children. The amount of the endowment and the government grant are not even enough, I am told, to pay the principal; and the two assistants are paid by the rector.

National or, in other words, Church of England schools are also visited by a diocesan inspector, appointed by the bishop to report their progress in "Holy Scripture, Prayer-Book, and Catechism." This school having been reported very good last year, a gift of about seven dollars was made to the teacher and monitor.

Instruction must be given for four hundred sessions yearly, equivalent to two hundred days.

Some teachers in government schools receive pensions, but as the number of pensions in England and Scotland is limited to two hundred and seventy, there are not enough for all. Before leaving this school, I may mention that I made some inquiry about the chapel, which stood not far off. One of the teachers answered, " I know nothing about dissent; I never go into those places."

The school in the other village of Stonea (Haddenham cum Stonea) was called the British school, and was much larger, having one hundred and forty pupils. The room was large and well lighted, and there was an appearance of thrift and animation in the scholars. It is not under the control of the Church of England; neither are members of that church excluded from its management. It is managed by a committee of seven, of whom two or three are members of the church. The services of the committee, including the secretary, are gratuitous. The school has an income of three hundred dollars, drawn from a gift in land, made many years ago for the free education of village-born children. This sum is supplemented by subscription. This school also is visited by the government inspector, and a certain sum is paid, according to the attainments of the children, called, as I have said, " the results." The committee decides what shall be done with this sum.

The school funds are further supplemented thus: In the village the children pay two cents a week. Those out of the village pay, if laborers, four cents for the first child, and two for each of the others. Persons of means pay twelve cents a week, but there are very few such.

Members of the Society of Friends, " who have always been active in education," raised a general subscription for building a new school-house, and the government added a grant; " the government would always thus assist to build a public school."

Religious instruction is not obligatory here as in the National school; it is at the option of the committee, who have decided to have Bible instruction for the first hour in the morning. The government allows any one who brings a written request from his father to absent himself from this instruction. No such case has ever arisen here. It may in towns where there are Free-thinkers and Catholics.

This school is plentifully supplied with blackboards. The principal difference that I observed in instruction between this and some public ones I have known at home was in arithmetic. A series of six small practical arithmetics was in use. At the close of each were examination questions. Here is the last in Standard 6, the highest: "If 27 men build 54 roods of garden wall in 26 days, how many roods will 32 men, working equally well, build in 39 days?" Perhaps twice in a week they have mental arithmetic. Here is the last question in Standard 5, mental: "A yard at half a guinea an inch?"

These elementary schools in villages are mixed, or for both sexes; in towns they are not. By the act of 1870, a pupil must enter school at five (education being obligatory), and remain until thirteen. There are, however, six standards in the school, and a pupil who wishes to go to work sooner may demand a certificate if he has finished the fourth standard, and is not obliged to finish the term.

I asked of one of the teachers or monitors in this British school whether she had ever visited the other, the National school. She replied that she would not like to go there. She seemed to fear that she would be thought a spy. The rector does not visit this British school. "Unfortunately," said one to me, "in our country the Church of England people think themselves above everybody else, and unless they can have the management of affairs will have nothing to do with them. The rector feels that he ought to have the management of the school, and is sore on that point; but it has been a successful school for forty years, and nothing that the rector can do can injure it."

I asked, "Has the teacher of the National school ever visited this one?"

"No; where the rector does not go, his people may not. We have tried every means to unite with them, but without effect. All the exertions here are for the good of the school, but in the other village for the good of the church. They want a teacher who will serve them in the school, the Sunday-school, and the choir."

But on this parish controversy a few words were spoken to me by a diligent member of the Established Church. He said, "The rector thinks he ought to be one of the trustees of the British school, as a bequest upon which it is in part founded says that the clergyman of the parish shall be one of the trustees, but they say that they will wait until the trusteeship is vacant." The place was filled, I understood, by the former rector, who, as I have said, was described as a tiny little man; a clever, very learned man; a stanch liberal in politics, over eighty years of age.

Afterwards, in Manchester, I met a person who spoke further on the subject of public schools. I give what he said, as drawn from my notes, on his own authority; for although it does not especially concern the parish of Haddenham cum Stonea, yet it does the general subject of English schools.

He said that the members of the Church of England support National or Church of England schools. The Roman Catholics support their own. The dissenters support unsectarian British schools, which receive all denominations. There is yet another class of elementary ones, namely, School Board schools. These boards are elected by the rate- or tax-payers. The schools are established in districts where there are not enough others to educate the children. It not unfrequently happens that a Church school or a British one which is unable to support itself, in spite of the government assistance before described, is turned over by its conductors to the school board. In Manchester this board has now in its schools about two-fifths of the children.

If the board wishes to establish a new school it has first to obtain leave from the committee on education of the Privy Council, belonging to the general government or to the ministry for the time being. The policy of the government is to prevent school boards from supplanting the sectarian schools; they are only allowed to supplement them, and no matter how poor the sectarian school may be, there is no way of getting it closed so long as Her Majesty's inspector pronounces it efficient. The reports of the inspectors show that Board schools are improving more rapidly than others.

When by the act of 1870 these schools were first established they were regarded by the conductors of the others with contempt, especially by those of the Roman Catholic and Church schools; but such has been their progress within this brief period that they are now regarded with jealousy.

As to the prices charged by the Board schools, they must submit the payment of their proposed fees to the committee of Privy Council. The others mentioned may charge up to eighteen cents a week for instruction.

If a private school be inefficient, the school board may prosecute the parents of the children. But this applies to schools which teach pupils at less than eighteen cents per week; such as the old "Dame schools," now nearly extinct, at least in Manchester.

MISCELLANEOUS.

Ways of living in England differ from those I am accustomed to in points before mentioned, such as the large number of meals, and the short hours of farm labor. A Lancashire youth complained that they *clemmed* or starved him in America on three meals a day. In this rural region those who can afford it take four, tea being in the afternoon and supper before going to bed.

Of articles of furniture I especially noticed two. One of them, which is nearly universal in England and Ireland, is entirely out of date where I live. It is the old-fashioned dressing-glass, which swings in a frame and stands upon a table. I do not remember its absence in any house that could afford it. Another article that I saw more rarely, but in both England and Ireland, was the canopy over the head of the bed. Of one I saw the framework was of heavy wood, with curtains at the side running on rings. A straight piece of the same material hung down behind the head of the bed. At my hotel in Cork this canopy was of faded blue damask; at the carpenter's in the village, of faded red, and above trimmed with heavy woollen fringe. A handsomer one was on my bed in London. Perhaps this canopy is all that remains of curtains that formerly surrounded the bed.

I have spoken of mangling as used in England. Mrs. Jackson, the carpenter's wife, hired a woman to come to the house once a month to wash. It took them both two days to do it, and Mrs. Jackson paid regularly about twenty-four cents a day; or if the woman made a long day, twenty-eight. In harvest she must pay higher. (When Benton, the farmer with whom I boarded, heard me speak of our paying washer-women here seventy-five cents or a dollar, he said that before he would pay so much he would turn his shirt or throw it into a pool and give it a slop wash.)

After Mrs. Jackson's clothes were dried she took them to a neighbor's to be mangled. The mangle is not unlike a great wringer with rollers; and if the clothes are damp, it rolls them smooth. Mrs. Jackson's neighbor allowed people to do their own mangling at " tuppence ha'penny or thruppence," according to the size of the basket. This is a great saving of fuel, and Mrs. Jackson said that they look just as well.

Active sports seem to have more prominence in England than in our own country. At Haddenham I called toward evening at the teacher's, and found that he had gone to play cricket. And young Benton,

17

son of the farmer, had gone too. He seemed actively
engaged in business, but one morning he was up early,
as he wished to go that day to a cricket-match, eleven
miles distant. At Benton's, mention was made of one
of their relatives, who had been much given to cricket
and other sports, and who had gone to Canada. He
said that if he had worked as hard in England as he did
in America, he would have got on there.

Yet Benton, the farmer, thinks it strange that I do
not want to see the races in their county town.

Skating is a favorite amusement. On a meadow near
by, which is always covered with water in the winter,
they have skating-matches. On the fens are great
skaters, I hear, and people come from all parts to compete with them.

One of the strongest evidences of a higher state of
civilization than ours (and perhaps of a different climate)
is that Mrs. Benton, the farmer's wife, told me that she
had never seen a man without stockings in her life. All
the children in the British school (I think in both
schools) wore both shoes and stockings, and some woollen
stockings, though the month was July. However, the
teacher said that in the north of England children go
barefoot; and I had just come from Ireland, where I
had heard of laborers' children that passed the winter
without stockings or shoes.

In our own country I had read or heard of English
farmers who rode in handsome vehicles, who wore silk
hats, who occasionally drank champagne. But great
farmers, cultivating hundreds of acres, must be capital-

ists. Of course there will be less luxury in straitened times. I heard, however, that a respectable farmer would never go to church, or especially to a funeral, places where he wished to show respect, without a silk hat. At market he might wear one of felt or straw.

Other matters being equal, the retired farmer is more nearly one of the gentry than the retired tradesman. In the parish of Haddenham cum Stonea, where I dwelt, perhaps the only person that came within that charmed circle, the nobility and gentry, was the rector of the church, and he did not stand high in it. I heard of the daughters of one clergyman who invited another to dine, and told him that it would be a nice party, " nobody who did not keep a footman or lady's-maid." If a distinguished dissenting minister like Spurgeon should come to a country town to lecture, in all probability he would not be socially noticed by the nobility and gentry.

A young Englishwoman told me that her sister, who lived in our country, said that the Americans are more polite than the English ; and two Englishmen who had travelled here spoke of the many attentions which they had received.

In this region of eastern England villages are found bearing names derived from the Saxon. I have called this parish Haddenham cum Stonea. The syllable *ham* comes from the Saxon, and means a dwelling, hence our word home. The syllable *ea*, in Stonea, means water.

Said the dissenting minister, " There is no part of England where the people are freer and more independent in thought than in these eastern counties of Norfolk, Suffolk, Huntingdon, and parts of Cambridge

and Lincoln." And he inferred that from these counties our Pilgrim fathers must have sprung. About fifty
miles from the parish I describe lies the city of Boston,
from which came Mr. Cotton, the preacher in whose
honor our own city of Boston was named.

"The last struggles of the Anglo-Saxons against the
Normans were in these counties," said one. "At Ely,
then an island in the centre of the fens, Hereward forti-
fied himself for a while, and made the last struggles
against the Normans."

An acquaintance who had visited America remarked
to me that the district of Cambridgeshire and Huntingdonshire, where we were, is typically agricultural; that
there are very few resident gentry; therefore the social
life of this region more resembles that of the United
States than does that of most other sections of England.

In this county of Huntingdonshire was born Oliver
Cromwell, and at its town of St. Ives he lived. In this
section he probably raised his celebrated soldiers called
Ironsides. But the conservatives of England do not
admire Cromwell. About twenty years ago in his
native county it was found impossible to raise means to
erect his statue.*

On this side of the county are no county families
bearing the title Esquire. —— Farrar, Esq., north of
us, is a great landed proprietor, with an income of about
two hundred and twenty-five thousand dollars. The Earl

---

* One was erected a few years ago at Manchester, and I was
told there that the Queen and Prince of Wales had not visited the
town since.

of S. and the Duke of M. are also large landed proprietors. The Duke of Bedford owns an estate in Thorny Fen of perhaps ten to fifteen thousand acres. My friend who tells me this thinks that the estate, however, is in another county from this. He understands that the duke expects each tenant to take one thousand acres and to keep a hunter. The duke is a liberal in politics.

The subject of politics was alluded to in the opening of this article, in the remarks of Jackson, the carpenter. Another acquaintance said, " If you go to a nobleman or great landed proprietor to rent a farm, you must be deferential and, as a general thing, you must vote on his side. If a man is a liberal, he must go under a liberal landlord; and if a tory, under a tory. Perhaps one-third of the House of Lords are liberals," he added.

Benton, the farmer, did not tell me his political opinions. He said that the ballot is secret. But he added that a man's political opinions have not now anything to do with renting the land.

But a person whom I afterward met in Manchester said that the agricultural districts were in the main thoroughly tory, the farmers being dependent on the landlords. He added that the late Lord Derby used to say, " Tell me what the landlords are and I will tell you what the vote will be."

Haddenham cum Stonea has declined in population. In 1840 the parish had nearly one thousand four hundred inhabitants. It now has about one thousand. Many went to America; now many go north into the manufacturing regions. Nor are these two villages alone in this. Jackson, the carpenter, told me of one where he had lived which, at the last census, had three hundred and thirty people. Twenty years back, he said, it had over five hundred.

Public-houses are numerous in these villages. They are mostly simple ale-houses, with such titles as the Three Horse-Shoes, the Rose and Crown, the Three Jolly Butchers. I counted at least eleven in a village of less than seven hundred people.

The wages of a farm-laborer here are under two dollars and seventy-five cents a week, and he boards himself. The cottagers on the farm where I boarded got their houses free and a rood of ground in which to plant potatoes. While at Haddenham I visited a friend in a near village, who took me to ride upon the fens, and her husband particularly desired her to show me some cottages, or laborers' houses, that he had built. The point that I was especially to observe was the rooms provided for sleeping, there being a bedroom downstairs and two or more above. On this subject I spoke to Mrs. Benton, the farmer's wife, who said that the laborers here have generally a kitchen, I believe a better room, and two chambers. She admitted that the boys and girls have to sleep in the same room.

Mrs. Benton said that if the laborer's wife, who has a number of young children, is kind and considerate of her husband, she will try to provide him a bit of meat daily, but it will be but a little bit; and the children will not taste meat oftener than once a week.

As I have before intimated, hours of labor are easy,— farm hands getting half an hour for lunch, and an hour for dinner. (But I cannot say whether this lunch-time is allowed at other than harvest.) In hay and harvest they work overtime, and are paid for overwork.

Fruit-picking was going on while I was at Haddenham. In fruit-gathering times, when the wives and boys get out a little, meat may be more plentiful in laborers' houses. There is a great press at fruit-gathering. The people go out in gangs about six or seven o'clock, and return about seven. The wages are about thirty-two cents a day. A market for the fruit is furnished by the manufacturing regions, where farm produce is more scarce.

At Haddenham I heard that after harvest they have a thanksgiving festival. There is a village flower-show in the rectory grounds and a public tea. They deck the church with wheat, barley, oats, beans, grapes, apples, and pears, and have a service in the evening. A collection is taken up for the county hospital, which is supported almost entirely by voluntary subscription.

To return once more to education. It is now compulsory, as I have said; but a friend estimated that of the people over thirty, a large proportion could not read and write.

PECULIARITIES OF SPEECH.

To us that one by which the English drop the letter h where it belongs, and put it on where it does not, is one of the most striking; as, Harable land is 'eavier taxed; my huncle is not very 'ealthy.

Two ways of speaking that are called Yankee with us are found here; one is the sharp *ou.*

" Please tell me," I inquired, " where Mr. G.'s house is."

" It's the last hayoose in tayoon; a big hayoose," answered the boy.

The other " Yankee" peculiarity is dropping the letter r. School-children said 'osses for horses. Buttah was said for butter, and Hemmingford sounded like Emmenfauld. A woman spoke of a certain Mr. Halbut. I had thought that his name was Wiseman. Yes; Mr. Halbut (Albert) Wiseman.

Comin' I heard for coming; they used to say shayhouse for chaise-house; and I am told that in Norfolk they say *du* and *tu* for do and to.

The carpenter's wife said, " The bread is silly," meaning heavy.

A spinney is a grove.

Laboring men call a lunch a dockey; and in another neighborhood a beaver.

Said an innkeeper, " The people come to flit them,"— to help them move.

Frequently " I dare say" becomes *dessay,* or *I'd say.*

We say to-day; they also say to-year. And when it begins to thaw, they say the weather is ungiving, it ungives.

APPENDIX.

THE PENNSYLVANIA GERMAN DIALECT.

The "Pennsylvania Dutch," which is spoken over a large portion of our own State, and is also heard in Maryland, Virginia, Ohio, Indiana, and Illinois, is not divided into dialects as are the languages of many European countries, but seems to be nearly homogeneous. The following specimen was taken from the lips of a working-woman born in Cumberland County, Pennsylvania, of German descent, but who learned most of her "Dutch" in the State of Maryland. She now lives in Lancaster County, Pennsylvania. An English article was read to her; and with some little difficulty she turned it into the version given. This version was submitted to a learned gentleman born in the eastern part of this State, but now living in Lancaster, and he declared it to be a good specimen of Pennsylvania German. I have abbreviated it, and give the English first, so that the difficulty may be observed which the translator found in the version.

"At Millville, New Jersey, about noon, while everybody in town was going to dinner, a deer came dashing down through the main street, and right behind it followed a dozen dogs, barking the loudest they knew how. Every dog on the line of the chase joined in, so that when the edge of the town was reached there were nearly fifty dogs after the deer. One solitary horseman caught on to the procession before it left town, and he was soon followed by a score of others, and inside of half an hour there were only women and factory hands left in the town. The deer got into the woods and escaped. A hound, which a merchant sent to Philadelphia for on Thursday, brought the deer to bay, and the merchant's son fired the fatal shot."

"*An Millville, New Jersey, about Mitdog, wie all die Leit in der Stadt zu Mittag gange sin, en Hayrsch is darrich die main*"

Schtross schprunge, und recht hinne noch ein dutzet Hund noch schprunge, und hen so laut gejolt als sie hen könne. All die Hund in der Schtadt sind oof die Geschpoor und sin noch; so wie sie an die End von der Schtadt sin der ware about fufzig Hund am Hayrsch noch. Ein ehnzige Reiter ist noch eh sie aus der Schtadt kumme sind und es ware gly zwanzig meh, und in weniger als en Halb-stund da war Niemand meh in der Schtadt als Wipesleit und die factory Hendt. Der Hayrsch ist in der Busch kumme und sie hen ihn verlore. En Houns voo ein Merchant in Philadelphia geschickt hat dafore, hat den Hayrsch schtill schteh mache; und der Merchant sei Sohn hat ihn dote schosse.

But although the Pennsylvania German is not divided into the great number of dialects or varieties found in Europe (I hear that there are about fifty in little Switzerland), yet there are differences here in the spoken dialect. While visiting at the house of a gentleman born in Lehigh County, but living in Lebanon, the following were pointed out to me. In Lehigh a lantern is a *lutzer;* in Lebanon, *lattern.* In the former the word for orchard is *boongart;* in the latter, *bomegarte.* Meadow is *Schwamm* in the former, and *Viss* in the latter. The adverb *orrick (arg)* is very much used in Pennsylvania German; but a clergyman coming to live in Lebanon County was reproved by some of his plain friends for its use. Perhaps it is nearly synonymous with our *darned,—* "That's darned cheap." *Der Arge* in the Bible is the evil one.

Mr. Weiser, of the Reformed Church, finds differences in adjoining counties. Thus, in Berks a set of bars in a fence is *en Falder;* in Montgomery, *E'fahrt* (or a place to drive through). In Lehigh they say of a drunken man, "*Er hat e Kischt ah*" (he carries a chest); but this is not heard in the near parts of Montgomery. Tomatoes are sometimes, I think, called *Goomeranze* in Allentown, and in Bucks County *Boomeranze* (from *Pomeranze,* an orange); but this is not heard in Lancaster County.

A learned German in Philadelphia says that several different dialects have flowed like streams into Pennsylvania,—one the Palatinate, another the Suabian, a third Allemanian, a fourth Swiss; and Prof. Dubbs, of Franklin and Marshall College, Lancaster, but born in Allentown, finds in the region with which he is familiar, east of the Susquehanna, three plainly marked sub-dialects. The one east of the Schuylkill is marked by the diminutive *chen* in the place of *lein.* In that district a little pig is called *Säuche*, and west of the Schuylkill *Säulie* (for *Säulein*). A third sub-dialect, he says, is peculiar to some of the sects of Lancaster County. It is probably of Swiss origin, and is marked by a broad drawl. (The late Prof. Haldeman remarked that in our dialect the perfect is used for the imperfect tense, as in Swiss; so that for "ich sagte" (I said) we have "ich hab ksaat" (gesagt), and for "ich hatte" (I had) we have "ich hab kat" (gehabt)).

(The following excellent remarks on the Pennsylvania dialect are taken from an article in the *Mercersburg Review* by Prof. Stahr, now also of Franklin and Marshall College, Lancaster. I have made some trifling alterations, mostly in parenthesis.)

" It is of course impossible in our present limits to specify all the peculiarities of Pennsylvania German, so as to give an adequate idea of its form to those who are not familiar with it. We may, however, state a few general principles, which will enable any one conversant with High German to read and understand the dialect without difficulty. In the first place it must be borne in mind that the letters have the *South German* sound : *a* has the broad sound like the English *aw ; st* and *sp* whenever they occur sound broad, like *scht* and *schp*, etc. Secondly, letters are commuted or changed. Instead of the proper sound of the modified vowel or *Umlaut* ö, we find the sound of the German *ē* or the English *ā*, and instead of *ü* we find *ie* or *i*, equivalent to the English *i* in *machine*, or the same shortened as in pin. Instead of the proper sound of *eu*, we have the German *ei* or the English *ī*. Instead of *au*, particularly when it undergoes modification in inflections, we have broad *a* or *aa* in the unmodified, and *ä* or *ää* in the modified, form. Thus we have *Baam* for *Baum*, and *Bääm'* for *Baüme ; laafe'* for *laufen*, and *laaft* or *lääft* for *laüft.* The diphthong *ei* is often changed into long *e* or *ee*. Thus for *Stein* we have *Stee'* (pronounced Shtay), for *Bein, Bee',* for *Eid* we have *Eed*, for *Leid, Leed. A* is often changed into *o*, as *Johr* for *Jahr*, *Hoor* for *Haar ; i* is changed into *e*, as *werd* for *wird* (*Es wird Schlimm* is spoken *Schvate schlimm*), *Hert* for *Hirt*, etc. Consonants are also frequently changed ; *b* into *w* (*Bievel* is heard for *Bibel*), *p* into *b, t* into *d*, etc. Thirdly, words are shortened by dropping the terminations, especially *n* of the infinitive or generally after *e*. Prefixes are frequently contracted, so also compound words. Thus instead of *werden, folgen, fangen*, we have *werre', folge', fange'; einmal* becomes *emol ; nicht mehr, nimme,* etc. Fourthly, the Pennsylvania dialect uses High German words in a different sense. Thus for *Pferd,* horse, we have *Gaul,* which in High German means a heavy farm-horse or an old horse ; *gleiche,* from the High German *gleichen,* to resemble, means in the Pennsylvania dialect, to like ; *gucke',* from High German *gucken,* to peep, to pry, means to look. Finally, we find English words introduced in their full form, either with or without German prefixes and modifications ; e.g., *Store* (Schtore), *Rüles, Cäpers, Circumstänces, trävele, stärte, fixe, fighte.*

"Nouns have scarcely any changes of form, except to distinguish singular and plural. These, where they exist, are the same as in High German. One of the most striking peculiarities is this : the genitive case is never used to indicate possession, the dative is used in connection with a possessive pronoun. Thus instead of *Der Hut des Mannes* (the hat of the man) we find *Dem Mann sei' Hut* (to the man his hat). . . . The definite article is used for *dieser, diese, dieses* (this), and *seller, selle, sell,* for *jener, jene, jenes* (that). The adverb *wo* is used instead of the relatives *welcher, welche, welches.*

"In inflecting pronouns, *mir* is used instead of *wir* (us). The verb has no imperfect tense ; the perfect is always used for it in Pennsylvania German. (And it will be observed, I think, that those accustomed to speaking the dialect will use the perfect thus in English.)

"From *wollen* we have : *Ich will, du witt, er will, mir wolle', ihr wolle', sie wolle' ;* and from *haben : Ich hab, du hoscht, er hot, mir hen* (from han, haben), *ihr hen, sie hen.*"

The number of writers in the dialect is becoming numerous. There are Mr. Zimmermann and Dr. Bruner, of Berks County, Rev. F. J. F. Schantz, originally of Lehigh, and Rev. Eli Keller and Mr. Henninger of the same; also Miss Bahn and Mr. H. L. Fisher, of York County. The most popular writer is the late Henry Harbaugh, of the Reformed Church, whose poems are collected under the title *Harbaugh's Harfe.* Among them the favorite is *Das alt Schulhaus an der Krick.* (The old school-house on the creek.) In publishing this volume, the English words introduced after the manner of our Pennsylvania Germans have been generally replaced by German, so that it is not a perfect specimen of the spoken language. Here follow a few lines from Harbaugh's *Heimweh*, or Homesickness:

> " Wie gleich ich selle Babble-Beem !
>   Sie schtehn wie Brieder dar ;
>   Un uf'm Gippel—g'wiss ich leb !
>   Hock't alleweil 'n Schtaar !
>   'S Gippel biegt sich—guk, wie's gaunscht,
>   'R hebt sich awer fescht ;
>   Ich seh sei rothe Fliegte plehn
>   Wann er sei Feddere wescht ;
>   Will wette, dass sei Fraale hot
>   Uf sellem Baam 'n Nescht."

> How well I love those poplar-trees,
>   That stand like brothers there !
>   And on the top, as sure's I live,
>   A blackbird perches now.
>   The top is bending, how it swings !
>   But still the bird holds fast.
>   How plain I saw his scarlet wings
>   When he his feathers dressed !
>   I'll bet you on that very tree
>   His deary has a nest.

The most witty prose articles that I have met are some in Wollenweber's *Gemälde aus dem Pennsylvanischen Volkleben.* (Pictures of Pennsylvania Life.)

Mr. E. H. Rauch (Pit Schwefflebrenner) accommodates himself to the great number of our " Dutch" people who do not read German by writing the dialect phonetically, in this manner : " *Der klea meant mer awer, sei net recht g'sund for er kreisht ols so greisel-heftict orrick (arg) in der nacht. De olt Lawbucksy behawpt es is was mer aw gewocksa heast, un meant mer set braucha derfore. Se sawya es waer an olty fraw drivva im Lodwaerrick-shteddle de kennt's aw wocksa ferdreiv mit warta, un aw so a g'schmeer hut was se mocht mit gensfet.*" (The little one seems to me not to be quite well, for he cries so dreadfully in the night. Old Mrs. Lawbucks maintains that he is what we call grown (enlargement of the liver), and thinks that I should powwow for it. She says that there was an old woman in Applebutter town who knew how to drive away the growth with words, and who has too an ointment that she makes with goose-fat.)

I have already stated that our Pennsylvania dialect has been thought to be formed from different European sources; but Mr. H. L. Fisher, of York, has lately shown me a collection of Nadler's poems in the Palatinate dialect, which, he says, more nearly resemble our idiom than anything else which he has seen. Also at Allentown, Mr. Dubbs, of the Reformed Church, has mentioned a collection which he thinks resembles much our Pennsylvania German. It is the poems of Ludwig Schandein, in the Westrich dialect. These are both dialects of the Rhenish Palatinate, the former of the district on the Rhine, the latter of the western or more mountainous part. And as the Germans coming into Pennsylvania were at one time called Palatines, it is not remarkable that these Palatinate dialects resemble ours. Here is a specimen of the eastern or lowland dialect:

> "Yetz erscht waasz i's, yetz erscht glaaw i's,
>   Was mar in de Lieder singt;
> Yetz erscht glaaw i's, dann jetz waasz i's,
>   Dasz die Lieb aam Schmerze bringt.

> "Nachdigalle dhune schlage,
>   Dasz 's dorch Berg un Dhäler klingt;
> Unser Bawrebuwe awwer
>   Dasz aam's Herz im Leib verschpringt!"

> At last I know, at last believe it,
>   That what our poets sing is so;
> At last I think, yes, now I know it,
>   That love brings also pain and woe.

> The nightingales so sweetly warble,
>   Their notes through hill and dale do ring;
> But oh! the heart in the breast is riven
>   Whene'er our peasant boys do sing!

Here is a specimen from Schandein's poems in the Westrich dialect:

> "So lewe wul, ehr liewe Alte,
>   Do i's mei' Hann, Glick uf die Rês!
> De' liewe Herrgott losze walte,
>   Dann Er es wul am beschte wêsz;

> Un machen euch kê' Gram und Sorje
> Ya denken an ihn alle Dah :
> Er sorgt jo heut, er sorgt ah morje,
> Er sorgt ah in Amerika."

Dr. Dubbs, of Franklin and Marshall College, has kindly given me this verse from his own translation :

> "Farewell! and here's my hand, old neighbors!
>   May blessings on your journey rest!
> Leave God to order all the future,
>   For He alone knows what is best.
> And do not yield to grief or sorrow,
>   Trust in His mercy day by day ;
> He reigns to-day, he reigns to-morrow,
>   He reigns too in America."

Various estimates have been given me of the numbers speaking the dialect in different parts of our State. Thus a lawyer in York County, beyond the Susquehanna, says that there are still witnesses coming to court, natives of the county, who do not speak English, and whose testimony is translated by an interpreter. Crossing the Susquehanna easterly, we come to my own county, Lancaster. My own neighborhood, near the Pennsylvania Central Railway, is much Anglicized. The southern part of the county is greatly "English," but as I was riding lately in the north, on the railway which connects Reading in Berks, to Columbia in Lancaster, a conductor estimated that along the forty-six miles of the railway about nine out of ten of the travellers can speak German. In Reading I am told in a lawyer's office that three-fourths of the women who come in to do business speak "Pennsylvania Dutch." My tavern-keeper says that many come to his house, born in the county, who cannot speak English. Another lawyer estimates that of the country people born in Berks County, three-fourths would rather speak Pennsylvania German than English ; and another thinks that in the rural districts of the county from one-half to two-thirds prefer to speak the dialect, although perhaps half of these can talk English. Another person says that when there is a circus or county fair at Reading, which draws the farmers' families, you hardly hear English, for the storekeepers accommodate themselves to the visitors. One of my friends, born in Germany, says that she saw at a forge in Berks County colored people, men, women, and children, that could not speak English; they spoke Pennsylvania German. If, now, we pass northerly to Lehigh County, we come to "Pennsylvania Dutch" land *par excellence*, for in no other county of our State are the people so nearly of unmixed German origin. I am told of Allentown, the county seat, with a population of about nineteen thousand, that Pennsylvania German, "Dutch," is the prevailing language. A lawyer estimates that more than one-fourth of its inhabitants do not speak English if they can help it, and a considerable number in town, born in this region, do not speak English at all. Of the county, a physician says that three-fourths of the people speak Pennsylvania German more easily than English, and another that nearly all the country people would rather speak the dialect.

East of Lehigh lies another very German county, Northampton. The county town Easton is, however, connected with New Jersey by a bridge over the Delaware, and Easton is to a very considerable degree Anglicized. Easton is the seat of a great Presbyterian institution, Lafayette College; yet a professor tells me that the Presbyterian Church cannot overcome the Lutheran and Reformed element. The Lutheran Church, he says, is very strong. Of the same county I was told some years ago that the people generally spoke German, except along the New Jersey line, and that outside of Easton and Bethlehem three-fourths of the people are Reformed and Lutheran. At the same period, about nine years ago, a physician told me that the public-school teachers in the rural parts must necessarily speak German for the children to obtain ideas, or must interpret English to them. These counties, with Lebanon, six in number, are the great German ones, beginning with York on the southwest, and ending with Northampton on the northeast; but the Pennsylvania German population is by no means confined to these counties. It spreads along the cultivated soil like grass. Adjoining Berks and Lehigh is Montgomery, the northern part of which is very "Dutch." Here I visited a preacher of one of our plain sects, whose great-grandfather came from Germany. But he, himself, speaks very little or no English, and he employed the ticket-agent to answer an English letter. One son and his children live under the same roof, making six generations in Pennsylvania; but the whole household uses the German dialect.

It must not be supposed of a large part of the Pennsylvania Germans that they are unacquainted with pure German. A simple and pure German they find in the Bible and in their German newspapers, of which there are several, altogether enjoying a large circulation. Also, at least in the Reformed and Lutheran Churches, there are many ministers who preach in pure German. Yet, when the minister goes to dine with a parishioner, they generally speak the dialect. The minister who speaks this to his flock is more popular. They could understand the higher German; but they say of him when he speaks the dialect, "*Er iss en gemehner Mann*" (He is a common, plain man, or one who doesn't put on airs.)

A gentleman in Lebanon, born in Berks, told me that he should be pleased to speak German as it is in the Bible. "But," he added, "as soon as a person begins to use pure German here among his acquaintances the Pennsylvania Dutch will say, "*Des iss ane Fratz-Hans*," or a high-flown fellow; or, as it may be rendered, "He's full of conceit."

One of the most amusing things in the dialect is the adopting and transforming of English words, as "Ich habe en Prediger *entgetscht*,"—I have engaged a preacher; "Do hat der *Eirisch* gemehnt er wott *triede*,"—the Irishman thought he would treat; "Sie henn en guter *Tietscher* katt, der hot die Kinner vieler Leut *getietscht*,"—they had a good teacher, who taught the children of many people; "Ich will dir's *exsplehne*,"—I will explain it to you; "Er hat mich *inweitet*,"—he invited me; "Do hen sie anfange *ufzukotte* und zu lache,"—then they began to cut up and laugh. A workman who was tired of waiting for material said, "Sie hen us nau lang genug 'rum *gebaffelt*,"—they have baffled or disappointed us long enough.

On the amount of English that is sometimes introduced into the dialect, a lawyer in Lebanon says that of the Pennsylvania Dutch which he uses in his political speeches, or in his practice, fully one-third is English. This specimen was given to me by a lawyer in Allentown, as the opening of a political speech: "Ich bin desirous um euch zu explaine die prerogative powers fum President." And this a lawyer to his client: "Ich bin certain das die Opinion was ich den morge geexpress hab, correct war."

Before leaving the subject of the idiom, I give some of the peculiar expressions heard in speaking English. A neighbor told me of her daughter's being invited to a picnic, and added, "I don't know what I'll wear on her."

Said a tavern-keeper's wife, "Don't jine sweeping." "It's time to jine sweeping," was the reply.

A girl got into a car near Mauch Chunk, and had headache.

"Don't sit with your back to the engine," I suggested.

"Do you sink?" she asked me. (Do you think so?)

"I guess it will give a gust," is said in Lancaster County.

"Do you want butter-bread?" (or bread and butter.) "No, I'd rather have coffee-soup,"—*i.e.*, bread broken into coffee.

"Mary, come down to the woods." "I dassent." She does not mean that she is afraid, but that she is not permitted, like the German *durfen*.

"I'm perfectly used to travel every *wich* way."

"A body gets *dired* if they *dravel*."

"Mind Ressler? He was in Sprecher's still;" or, "Do you remember Ressler? He used to be employed in Sprecher's store."

"It's raining a'ready, mother;" or, "Where's Mrs. M.?" "She went to bed a'ready."

"I guess that Mrs. B. does not spend all her income."

"She didn't still."

"She'd rather be married to him *as* to keep house for him" (like the German *als*).

We think those very "Dutch" who say "Sess" for Seth, "bass-house" for bath-house. Thus it would be, Beslem is in Norsampton County.

"I'm fetching a pig. I had it bestowed."

"We're getting strangers, and I was fetched." (They are expecting company at our house, and they sent for me to come home.)

"Mrs. M., how does your garden grow?" "Just so middlin'."

"Your head is strubly," means that your hair is tumbled.

A scientific friend, wishing to examine a specimen, said, "Let me see it once."

Of the same kind are these: "When we get moved once," "You'll know what it is when you hain't got no father no more once." (This use of *once* has been alluded to in the text.)

"Mother, don't be so cross!" "I ought to be cross" (angry).

I do not know that it is "Dutch" to say, "Did you kiss your *poppy?*" or, "Barbara, where's your *pap?*" (for father).

" How are you, Chrissly ?" (diminutive of Christian.) " Oh ! I've got it so in the back."

Those who live among Pennsylvania Germans cannot fail to observe that when they, speaking English, make mention of a couple, as, " She gave me a couple of peaches," they do not generally mean two only. Couple has doubtless to them the same meaning as the German word *Paar*, which is defined by Whitney " a couple, two or three, a few, sundry."

I cannot tell the deviation of our interjection of pain, *Owtch !*

Ok ! is doubtless the German *Ach !* or is it Irish ?

And what is the derivation of " *Sahdie ?*" so much used by children for " Thank you."

There is a word neither of English nor German origin which is sometimes used as a salutation by Pennsylvania Germans. It is familiarly *Hottiay*. Few would divine to see it thus that it is the French adieu.

PROPER NAMES.

Changes equally remarkable are found in proper names. The family of my own neighbor Johns was originally Tschantz, as is more easily perceived by the pronunciation; Johns ending with the s sound and not the z. The important family in Lancaster County named Carpenter were Zimmerman when they came in, the name being translated. But of a family in Berks County, some are Hunter and some Yäger. Some persons named Bender, who have removed to California, are there called Painter.

It is surprising in Pennsylvania to hear of persons with Irish or Scottish names who can scarcely speak English. A gentleman in Harrisburg told me of one he knew in Dauphin County named Hamilton (whose father was born in Dublin), and of two others named Dougherty. I have met in Berks County a person with a purely Scottish name who spoke of Norsampton County, and of Souss Reading (not pronouncing the *th*). But his mother was of a German family, and " Pennsylvania Dutch" his mother-tongue.

A lawyer in York, with an English name, tells me that his ancestors came from New England, and settled first in the Wyoming Valley, but some moved southward, and by intermarriage, to use, I think, his own expression, became quite Dutchified. He himself can speak the dialect.

Several families with French names are now not to be distinguished from the Pennsylvania Germans among whom they live and intermarry. It is said that the Bushongs were once Beauchamp; then probably the Deshongs were Du Champ. The Shopells were Chapelle; the Levans perhaps Levin. Delaplaine is pronounced *Dillyplen.* There are still Bertolettes, De Bennevilles, De Turks, De Planks, Philippes, Philippis, and Philippys. Coquelin has become Cockley and Gockley. These families were perhaps French Huguenots who sought refuge in Germany, where so many went on the revocation of the edict of Nantes. From the Palatinate came very many of our Pennsylvania Germans, and that state is directly east of France.

But it is also probable that many French names were translated when their owners removed to Germany. One of my acquaintances in Philadelphia is a German, born in the Palatinate. She tells me that her grandfather left France during the revolution. He was a Mennonite, and named Coquerel; but this was translated into Hähnchen; so that my friend was a Miss Hähnchen. Coquerel, Hähnchen, and our English word cockerel are synonymous.

Changes in the names of persons of the same family in Pennsylvania will be observed. I know a gentleman in Lebanon County with an English name, who tells me that his mother's name was Besore; supposed to have been La Bessieur. The name has also been spelled Basore, Bashor, and Bayshore. The name Beinbrecht is said to have gone through these changes; in Philadelphia there is a Bonbright, in Chambersburg a Bonbrake, and there are Bonebreaks. In Lancaster County, I hear of a father who writes his name Bear; but one son is Barr, and another Bair. There is a large Reformed family in Pennsylvania named Wotring, now turned into the English Woodring, which was originally the French Voiturin. Probably within the Reformed German Church are more French Calvinistic families than in the Lutheran.

Of the Buchanans and Livingstones in our country we might assume the Scottish origin; but *Der Deutsche Pionier* tells us that the German name Buchenhain [meaning Beech grove] has been changed to Buchanan, and Löwenstein to Livingstone. A more grievous change is said to have befallen the name Hochmayer or Hochmier [high steward], for in Virginia it has become Hogmire!

POLITICS.

One of the most remarkable distinctions between our Pennsylvania Germans is that which ranges the counties and townships inhabited by the *wehrlos*, or peaceable sects, with one political party; and those where the Reformed and Lutherans are strongest with the other. We might once have thought that the Democratic party was the war party; but during the great rebellion the counties of Berks, Lehigh, and Northampton still remained adherents of the Democratic party in its opposition to the war. The county of Montgomery, in the eastern part of the State, is thus divided; the Mennonites, Schwenkfelders (with Quakers), are almost invariably Republican; while the strong Democratic townships are almost entirely Reformed and Lutheran. Of course there are in all such localities many who do not belong to any religious body.

A Democratic editor in the same county of Montgomery says that he does not know a Mennonite or Schwenkfelder who is not Republican; so also are the great majority of the German Methodists. He, however, added that the Reformed and Lutherans are nearly equally divided in politics. But every politician who knows the people must concede that the counties which are the stronghold of these two churches are an immense Democratic stronghold.

Mr. H., of Easton, tells me of a man who stood looking at a procession in honor of the funeral of Jackson, Harrison, or some other distinguished person. In the procession were Freemasons, Odd-Fellows, and other societies. " Oh," said he, "*des ish alle letz!* That is all wrong. There ought to be only two societies,— the Democrats and the Lutherans. If a man lives up to the principles of General Jackson and Martin Luther, that is enough." He took his boys to delegate or town-meetings. "Now, boys," he said, "are you going to vote the Democratic ticket as long as you live? Always stick to the Democratic party, and carry out the principles of General Jackson. If you intend to do this, you can vote for delegates." (This anecdote is a little injured by the introduction in the beginning of the name of Harrison, who was a Whig. But it was given to me by a person of a well-known Democratic and Lutheran family.)

A few years ago, in an adjoining county, an adherent of the Democratic party told me that the word democracy has a magic sound for the people of Lehigh. "A Democratic parade," he added, "can easily be got up in Allentown two miles in length, composed in a great measure of farmers on horseback; and in Presidential campaigns sometimes farmers' daughters also appear on horseback in the procession. A skilful speaker, generally a lawyer, who speaks the dialect, and who will frequently introduce the words democrat and democracy, can lead the crowd. Even if he do not speak the dialect, if he will introduce those words, he can bring out the applause of his hearers."

An acquaintance tells me of a political speaker in Berks County, that Democratic stronghold. He was telling of *die Demokratie*, which he said goes over hill and dale, over the sea, and strikes the seat from under kings. "And if you ask where that democracy comes from, they will tell you from Berks County."

YANKEES.

An acquaintance once explained to me the prejudice against Yankees by telling me how, about fifty years ago or longer, the tin-peddlers travelled among the innocent Dutch people, cheating the farmers and troubling the daughters. They were (says he) tricky, smart, and good-looking. They could tell a good yarn, and were very amusing, and the goodly hospitable farmers would take them into their houses and entertain them, and receive a little tin-ware in payment.

A lawyer in Easton, from the State of New York, says that he never saw so large a body of people so honestly inclined as the Pennsylvania Germans. He speaks from a knowledge of the people of Northampton and Lehigh. They have an especial dread of the people of New England and New York, from their having been so terribly victimized by patent-rights' men. He adds that they are not a reading people, but by their careful and slow manner of getting along they really accomplish more than the people of New England and New York, who, he says, make a great display, and then frequently compromise with their creditors by paying fifteen or twenty cents on the dollar. A person present added of these Pennsylvania Germans that they never headed any great moral reforms and never drowned witches.

Another thinks that in his youth the Yankee drovers in Lehigh County were respected for their acuteness. He adds, however, that when the "Dutch" call a man a Yankee, it is not near so opprobrious as to call him a Jew. "But," says another, "when a Yankee comes to Reading with patent rights and inventions they point and say, '*Do geht en Yoot.*'" (There goes a Jew.) Dr. L., of Lebanon County, says that the "Dutch" idea of a Yankee is not of one who starts out to cheat for the pleasure of cheating, but of one who prefers to make his living by his wits rather than by hard labor. He starts with the idea of making money easily, and does not care much finally about the honesty of his proceedings.

In the market at York a learned man of New England origin asked a farmer, "What is the price of your apples,—twenty-five cents?" "Yes, you can have them for that; but I wouldn't let Kochersperger have them for a quarter,—he's a Yankee."

THRIFT.

In his speech in Congress upon the death of John Covode, Simon Cameron declared that he honored Covode for his true courage when he proclaimed in Philadelphia what weaker men would have tried to suppress, giving as a reason for his hostility to every species of human bondage the fact that his father had been sold as a redemptionist near the spot where he was then speaking. "Scarcely a generation had passed away," adds Cameron, "before the hired servants began to buy their masters' lands, to marry their masters' daughters, and to make good their claim to full equality with those whose bondsmen they had been. For a time the Scotch-Irish made a sturdy stand for that supremacy and superiority which seem to be their peculiar inheritance, place them where you may. At length the thrift, the superior patience, and the perseverance of the German blood prevailed. They bought, and still possess, the old homesteads, and have furnished us with an array of distinguished men of whom every citizen of our State is justly proud." The superior patience, says Mr. Cameron. *Geduld ist das beste Kraut, das man in America baut,*— patience is the best plant grown in America,—is a saying I have heard in Lancaster County. But I must interrupt my regular course to explain the word redemptionist used by Mr. Cameron,

It was applied to persons coming here from Germany who were unable to pay the expenses of their passage, and who were sold or indentured for a term of years until that expense was paid. Minor children were bound out until of age.

Mr. Cameron also speaks of the Pennsylvania Germans dispossessing the Scotch-Irish, and plenty of corroborative evidence of this can be found. A learned gentleman has said to me that the Scotch-Irish element, which used to be the leading one in Franklin County, is in a great measure replaced by the Pennsylvania German. "As the Irish farmers got poor and sold their land it was bought by the Pennsylvania Germans, who then got rich by their extreme thrift or severe economy and great industry." A correspondent of the Philadelphia *Press*, in 1871, goes further, and writing from Brown's Mills in the same county, from "the fertile and picturesque Cumberland valley," speaks of the Pennsylvania Germans of that region as wearing the short gown and petticoat, the shad-belly coat, and broad-brimmed hat. The district, he says, was first settled by Scotch-Irish and Welsh, but these have mostly been replaced; a few families of Lutherans and German Reformed linger here, but their numbers annually grow less, and the difficulty of supporting their ministers is yearly more serious. Then, if we may trust this correspondent, it appears that the *wehrlos*, or defenceless men (who do not pay ministers), are gaining possession of that region. It was said of old time that the meek shall inherit the earth. Far east of Franklin County, in Montgomery, I was told of peacemen, the Schwenkfelders and Mennonites, that they buy good farms. "They don't buy the hilly, stony ones; and, at the same time, I don't know how it comes they can afford to pay for them."

The severe economy of the Pennsylvania Germans has been just mentioned. One New-Year's day I saw in a bank a young man who was asked to subscribe for something. He declined, and spoke of "our old Dutch rule that it is a bad plan to buy on New-Year's morning. Always get money in before you pay it out." In Northampton County an old resident is reported to have said, "Do you know the difference between a Yankee farmer and a Dutch one? When a Yankee farmer has apples, he sells the scrubby ones and eats the good ones at home; and a Dutch farmer picks out the scrubby ones to eat at home, and sells the good ones."

One of my Lancaster County neighbors has grain-bags that have been in use on the farm for about seventy years, and bid fair to last for twenty more. They were made from flax and hemp grown on the farm. A young member of the family says that their preservation not only shows the economy, but impresses him with proofs of the good judgment of those who made them, in selecting material, and in the thorough manner of their work. He adds, "All these characteristics were, I think, possessed in full measure by the people, somehow and somewhere misnamed Dutch, in whose hands the largest part of Lancaster County has become what it is."

CHARMS AND SUPERSTITIONS.

Mrs. G., born in Lebanon County, says that when they were children one would take a looking-glass and go down the cellar-stairs backward, in order to see therein the form of a future spouse. Another custom was to melt lead and pour it into a cup of cold water, expecting thence to discover some token of the occupation of the same interesting individual. A person in York also remembers that at Halloween her nurse would melt lead and pour it through the handle of the kitchen door-key. The figures were studied and supposed to resemble soldier-caps, books, horses, and so on. This nurse was Irish, but the other domestics were German. A laboring woman from Cumberland County, and afterward from a "Dutch" settlement in Maryland, says that she has heard of persons melting lead to see what trade their man would be of. My German friend before quoted says that in the Palatinate they melted the lead on New-Year's eve. In Nadler's poems in the Palatinate dialect, St. Andreas' night is the time spoken of for melting the lead. This is the 30th of November. Further, in a work called "The Festival Year" (*Das Festliche Yahr*), by Von Reinsberg-Düringsfeld, Leipsic, 1863, the custom of pouring lead through the beard, or wards, of a key is mentioned.

A lawyer, born in Franklin County, tells me that it is a common superstition among Pennsylvania Germans that persons born on Christmas night can see supernatural things and hear similar sounds. He adds that his mother told him of a person who was sceptical and ridiculed the idea, and was told to go out into his feeding-room and listen. He lay down on the hay, and while there one of the oxen said, "*Uebermorgen schieben mir unser Meschter auf den Kirch-hof.*" (Day after to-morrow we will haul our master to the graveyard.) And his funeral was on the day specified. My German friend before quoted says that in the Palatinate they believe that as it strikes twelve on Christmas eve, all animals talk together. She adds, " I think that idea is through Germany."

A gentleman connected with schools in Northampton County says that at Halloween his daughters meet their companions and melt lead into water to tell their fortunes. They also fill their mouths with water that they may not speak, as speaking would break the charm; and walk around a block of houses. The first name which they hear is that of their future spouse. Another practice, which, unlike the foregoing, may be tried at any time of year, is to take a large door-key and tie it within the leaves of a small Bible, the handle remaining out. Two girls rest the handle upon their fingers, and repeat some cabalistic verse; of which, he thinks, each line begins with a different letter, and the key will turn at the initials of the future spouse. These, he says, are the remnants of old superstitions, and he suspects that the human mind is naturally superstitious. He adds, " The population of Easton is mixed so that we cannot tell how many of these are purely German; but by going into the rural German districts of Northampton County you will find many strange ideas, such as that on a certain church festival, say Ascension day, you must not sweep your house, lest it become full of fleas."

A simple-minded woman in Lancaster County, who showed some regard for the Reformed Church, said that she had sat up late sewing the night before, so as not to sew on Ascension day. " My mother," she said, " knew a girl that sewed on Ascension day; and there came a gust and killed her."

One of my German acquaintances calls my attention to the salt-cake eaten in Lancaster. It is made extremely salt, and is eaten by girls, who then go to bed backward without speaking and without drinking; and he of whom they dream is to be their future husband. This, he says, is a custom also in Germany.

But the most universal ideas of this superstitious kind are those connected with the signs in the almanac. Baer's Almanac, published in Lancaster, still has the signs of the zodiac down the pages, like one shown to me in the Palatinate, where a man of some education said, " Here is where I see how to plant my garden." What, however, is very mysterious is that when our people tell you you must not plant now, for IT is in the Posy-woman (and the things will all run to blossom, and not bear fruit), they cannot tell *what* is in the Posy-woman, or Virgo. I infer, however, that it is the moon.

I have been shown a German Bible, which belonged to the grandfather of one of my neighbors, wherein the family births were entered in the German language. I endeavored to decipher one, as follows.

" 1797, *September den 9ten ist uns ein Sohn gebohren ihm Zeichen Witter, ehr ist ihn dem nehmlichen Mohnat ihm Herren entshlafen.*"

" On the 9th of September, 1797, a son is born to us in the sign of the Ram [Aries]. In the same month he fell asleep in the Lord."

The same neighbor who owns the old Bible just mentioned tells me that one of the Russian Mennonites showed him a pamphlet in the German language, which the man had brought from Europe; wherein was told what would be the fortune of a child born in each sign, his health, wealth, etc. ; but my neighbor says that he, himself, had no faith in it.

" Grain should be sowed in the up-going ; meat butchered in the down-going will shrink in the pot." But my worthy neighbors do not appear to know what it is that is going up and going down. I infer, of course, that it is the moon. Is it not remarkable that my neighbors should be so attached to book-farming ? I knew a woman, born among Friends, but in a Pennsylvania German set-tlement, who was lamenting the smallness of the piece of meat on the table. " What a little piece, and so big before it was cooked ! How it has shrunk ! It is in the down-going. And those straw-berries, too, that I preserved, that went away to so little ; they were done in the down-going." But one of her family spoke up, bravely, " Just so, mother ; that must be it. Now I know what's the matter with my portemonnaie, that it shrinks away so; it's the down-going."

These beliefs in the influence of the heavenly bodies must be the relics of astrology remaining in the almanacs, and never drawn now from actual observation of the weather and the planets.

Mrs. Nevin relates the following (Philadelphia *Press*, June 2, 1875): " There are several superstitions connected with death and funerals in the country, which are a strange blending of the ludicrous with the mournful. One is that if the mother of a family is dying, the vinegar-barrel must be shaken at the time to prevent the 'mother' in it from dying. Said a man once in sober earnest to me, 'I was so sorry Mr. D. was not in the room when his wife died.' 'Where was he?' 'Oh, in the cellar a-shaking the vinegar-barrel; but if he had just told me, I would have done it and let him been in the room to see her take her last breath.'"

Mrs. Nevin adds: "Another superstition is that the last person that goes out of a house at a funeral will be the next one to die, and as the audience begins to thin, you may see people slip very nimbly out of a back or kitchen door to avoid being that last one."

The belief in *spooks* or ghosts is not lost in "Pennsylvania Dutch" land. In some of his verses Mr. Schantz tells (Allentown *Friedensbote*) of an abandoned school-house standing near a sand-pit, beside some woods. He says,—

> ——*"kam mir zu Ohr*
> *Vom Sandloch Schuhlhaus am Kreuzweg*
> *Was Lesern ich nicht gern vorleg.*
> *S' hen Leut g'sad 'Am Sandloch spukts!'*
> *En mancher hot oft g'frogt, 'Wie guckt's?'*
> *Reiter sie sin schnell geridde!*
> *Laüfer nahme g'schwinde Schridde!"*

"About the sand-pit school-house, at the cross-roads, things were said that I do not like to tell. It was told that there were spooks at the sand-pit, and 'In what shape?' was asked. People riding by rode rapidly, and those on foot hurried swiftly by." There are stlll standing near the Conestoga, close to Lancaster, the remains of a building long and extensively known as "the spook house." It probably became unpopular from a suicide in it, or from having been built in a field where strangers were buried.

A Lutheran clergyman said lately, "I do not believe in *spooks* myself, but plenty of people do; and sad enough it is that there should be such superstition."

MEDICAL SUPERSTITIONS.

The peculiarities of a people are always best observed by those who do not live among them, or rather by those who visit them occasionally. Most of my notes on this subject are taken from the conversation of physicians born in other localities than those in which they practise. One in my own county mentions the "*apnehme*," or wasting away of children. He says that popular remedies are measuring the child and greasing it by certain old women. Another says that the "Pennsylvania Dutch" also measure for wild-fire or erysipelas, generally using a red silk string, and measuring about sundown. They blow across the affected part to blow the fire outside of the string, at the same time they "say words" or powwow. This physician says that the greasing above mentioned is for liver-grown children, and not for "abnehme" (as it is spelled). One class of powwowers do not interfere, he says, with regular practitioners; but one old woman in this county (who builds a fire in the brick oven, and says words over the coals) has been known to hide the prescriptions of regular physicians. He adds: "If a person is burned, recourse is sometimes had to a professional blower, who blows across the surface, saying words in the interval. Along the Pennsylvania Canal, on the Susquehanna, where ague prevails, the patient who has a chill is tied to a tree by a long string, and he runs around the tree until the string is exhausted, and then on to some distance. This is tying the chill to a tree. A ' Pennsylvania Dutch' remedy for whooping-cough, and one by which they bother the millers a good deal, is to put the child into a hopper with grain, and let the child remain until the grain is all ground out. Blood-stopping is very common in Pennsylvania. I saw a man with an artery cut, in whose case a blood-stopper was called in. The man pressed his hand on the bleeding part and repeated something, raising his eyes to heaven; but the artery was too powerful for him."

On the west side of the Susquehanna the only county that can distinctively be called Pennsylvania German is York. A physician in the borough says that town and county are full of superstitions. He says, "In case of hemorrhage from the nose, from a wound or from other cause, a common cure is to wrap a red woollen string round each finger; another is to lay an axe under the bed, edge upward; and you can't talk them out of it. I used to get angry when I first came here, but I found that it was of no use. These are not occasional things only, but I have seen them over and over again. Then there are prayers for stopping blood, always in 'Dutch.' They can't be sick in English, and the first question to me as a physician has been '*Kann er Deutsch ?*' (Do you speak German?) One of the prayers for stopping blood is, I understand, for human beings, and another for animals; and I think that the names of the persons of the Trinity are introduced. I have often asked, but they are not allowed to tell. Soon after I came here, I ordered some boneset tea for a patient, and the mother asked in 'Dutch' whether the leaves should be pulled upwards or downwards. 'Will it make any difference?' I asked. 'Oh, yes; if you pull them upwards, it will work upwards; and if you pull them downwards, it will work downwards.' [A valuable hint for a physician if the same plant can be used both as an emetic and a purgative.] Of the blood of a black fowl,—no other color will do,—three drops are given internally. I think this is for convulsions; but I hear so many of these things, and have heard them so many years, that they make no impression on my mind. These are pure 'Pennsylvania Dutch' peculiarities; I have found none or few of them among foreign Germans.''

I asked whether these ideas still continue or whether they are wearing out. "No," he said, "they don't wear out. I meet them every day. They still speak of horses and animals being bewitched (*verhext*). I have a story from good authority of a horse that was said to be *verhext*, and that turned out to have a nail in his hoof. That is a fact. What are you going to do about it?''

But to come to another county, Berks. I hear that in Reading there is a woman called the *Wurst-frau*, because her mother sold sausages and "puddings.'' This woman has a large office practice in salves and powwowing. In an adjoining county, Lehigh, I remember a few years ago to have seen the names of two persons put down in the directory as *powvowers;* the word being spelled as pronounced in "Dutch.''

Norristown, in Montgomery County, is greatly Anglicized; but a physician says that an idea exists of stopping blood by a religious lingo, into which come the words "*der Vater, Sohn, und heilig Geist.*'' "A certain man told me that he had never failed to arrest bleeding from wounds or even from the lungs, nor was it necessary to be upon the spot; he could go home and repeat his lingo. This was his only medical skill; he did not claim to be a doctor.''

In Norristown also I met a woman who had been quite ill; but I heard that when better she would not get up on Sunday, lest she should never get well, and Friday was as bad. Her little grandchild having a birth-mark, she passed the hand of a dead person over it to take it away, but was unsuccessful.

To return, however, to this county of Lancaster, which I know better. A physician says that he found a child very ill with membranous croup, for which he left powders to be administered every half-hour, saying that when he called again, if it seemed possible to dislodge the membrane he would give an emetic. When he called, he found a powwower sitting, who looked very smiling. The doctor went up to the little patient, and asked whether the mother had given the medicine. She had given only one dose; the man had said that it was not necessary to give any powders. "Don't you think the child is better?" the mother asked. On examination the doctor declared, "I am sorry to tell you that the child will not live two hours;" which caused the countenance of the powwower to fall. The child died, and this case caused the doctor to declare that he would not practise in conjunction with powwowers; and if they are now called in, it is done privately.

Although one physician spoke of not finding many of these ideas among foreign Germans, yet my friend, before mentioned, from the Palatinate says that when children have earache there, or *abnehme* (wasting away), or when persons are in the early stages of consumption, country people say, "*Lasz dir brauche*" (or, Consult a powwower); and a woman comes and whispers some words. "My father" (she adds that he was a Reformed preacher) "knew a blacksmith to whom children were brought, suffering with earache. The man would heat the big tongs, hold them close to their ears, and whisper something. My father asked him what he said. He answered, 'Nothing; but if he did not whisper, the people would not believe in him;' and my father told him that he ought not to impose upon them.''

HOLIDAYS—EASTER.

I live in the country, but on last Good-Friday was at Reading, and was surprised to see so many persons going to church. Easter is greatly observed by Reformed and Lutherans. It is the time of confirmation and administering the sacrament; and you may hear of churches in country localities having as high as six hundred communicants. At Easter, of course, eggs greatly abound. At a boarding-house at Allentown I heard of colored eggs being offered to callers or taken to friends. Fragments of egg and of colored shells may be seen on the pavements for about a week.

A little childish myth is found in these more eastern counties, of which I have heard very little in Lancaster County. It is that the rabbit lays the colored eggs. A young man in Reading says that when they were children they always made a nest the evening before Easter Sunday, of an old hat or something similar, which they set near the door for the rabbit to lay the colored eggs in. An old man in a tavern, however, says that it is foolishness, like *Bellschnickel*. At my own tavern the landlady was coloring eggs, and had bought some canton-flannel rabbits with which to dress the guests' tables at breakfast on Sunday morning.

In Lehigh County a lawyer says that when they were children they would take flax and each make his nest under a bush in the garden. On Easter Sunday morning they would run out and find three eggs of different colors in each nest. Literalness has gone so far in Allentown that I hear of cakes in a baker's window in the form of a rabbit laying eggs.

At Easton a lady spoke of making nests for her two boys by taking plates, ornamenting them with cut paper in the form of a nest, putting into each a large candy egg and colored eggs, and placing a rabbit in one and a chicken in the other, and hiding them for the boys to find.

This myth of the rabbits' eggs is very common among the Moravians. One of my "Dutch" acquaintances, born west of us in Cumberland County, and afterward living in Maryland, says that her mother told them when children to set their bonnets at Easter for nests for the rabbits' eggs.

This is an old German myth. A gentleman from Switzerland says that he heard the fable there, and he thinks that it prevails all over Germany. Many or most of our early German emigrants into Pennsylvania seem to have come from or through the Palatinate. My friend before mentioned, who was born there, thus describes the custom at her former home. If the children have no garden, they make nests in the wood-shed, barn, or house. They gather colored flowers for the rabbit to eat, that it may lay colored eggs. If there be a garden, the eggs are hidden singly in the green grass, box-wood, or elsewhere. On Easter Sunday morning they whistle for the rabbit, and the children imagine that they see him jump the fence. After church, on Easter Sunday morning, they hunt the eggs, and in the afternoon the boys go out in the meadows and crack eggs or play with them like marbles. Or sometimes children are invited to a neighbor's to hunt eggs.

Prof. Wackernagel, of Allentown, has kindly pointed out to me the antiquity of the myth. The old German goddess of spring was called Ostara (whence Easter). She rode over the fields in the spring in a wagon drawn by hares. (Our Pennsylvania rabbit is really a hare, as it does not burrow in the ground.) The egg is an emblem, says the professor, of the resurrection from the dead; so herein he finds heathenism and Christianity blended. However, the author of *Das Festliche Yahr* (Leipsic, 1863) considers the myth older than Christianity; for he says that in Thuringia, Hesse, Suabia, and Switzerland it is said now, as apparently in ante-Christian times, that the hare or Easter hare lays the eggs. Finally, one of my German friends finds the whole a myth of the renewal of life in the spring.

HALLOWEEN.

On the 30th of last October our farmer locked the gate on the road, lest it should be taken off. Therefore the Halloween visitors limited themselves to taking down bundles of corn-fodder in the field and building a fence across the road, and to propping up one end of the market-wagon on the fence. I am told of a person who once had his wagon taken apart, and the pieces put up into different trees, so that it was some time before all were found. In Lebanon County a similar custom is found. One of my acquaintances living in a small town says that they celebrate Halloween roughly,—hanging beets and cabbages at the doors, moving steps, taking gates from hinges, throwing corn. The speaker was born in Lehigh County, where nothing of this prevailed, and this fact constitutes one of the chief distinctions among our Pennsylvania Germans of Lancaster and Lebanon on one hand, and Lehigh, Berks, upper Montgomery, and probably Northampton on the other. In Montgomery a young "Dutchman" did not even know when Halloween is, and when I described our Lancaster County custom, said, "That ain't any use." Traces of similar observances of Halloween are found, however, in other regions. In Philadelphia the boys indulge in ringing front-door bells. In Harrisburg people who had wooden door-steps used to take them into the house, lest they should be carried off. Of Franklin County, beyond the Susquehanna, I am told that at Waynesboro' it has been a favorite amusement at Halloween to gather store-boxes and build a fortification around the town pump, and collect wheeled vehicles around the public square. At Lockhaven, up the West Branch of the Susquehanna, my landlady was anxious that her cabbage should be housed, for fear that it would be carried off on Halloween.

My German acquaintances, before quoted, born in the Palatinate, do not report to me anything of this kind as existing in Germany at Halloween. One of them says, however, that at the time of putting up string-beans (which are preserved like sour-krout), children throw the strings into front doors. And Mr. Wollenweber, of Reading, also a native of the Palatinate, says that when the farm-work was over in October, they used to practise tricks. He has helped to take a wagon to pieces, and put it together again in a stable or barn. "We troubled ourselves very much," he says. He adds that the boys were expected, when the fun was over, to come together and take it down again; but this is not the case in Lancaster County.

Can it be that some of these practices belong to the season of the year, and are a warning to the tardy to gather the fruits of the earth and their farm implements?

In his work called *Die Alte Zeite*, or Old Times, Mr. H. L. Fisher, of York, Pennsylvania, describes such pranks as played at weddings or home-comings "infares." The boys hid the bridegroom's horse in a quarry, and the young men's saddles and bridles were put upon trees, straw-stacks, etc.

In the text I have spoken of Bellschnickel, who in "Pennsylvania Dutch" land takes the part of Santa Claus, being in fact the same personage; Bellschnickel, or Peltz Nickel, being St. Nicholas in furs. St. Nicholas day is not, however, Christmas eve. It is the 6th of December; but it is in Advent. One of my German friends thus describes Peltz Nickel: "In the Palatinate at Christmas they have the Christ-kindchen, which is a little girl dressed in white and riding on a donkey. I often made one myself, dressed in my mother's wedding-veil. If you have no donkey, a boy is dressed to represent one and goes on all-fours. The Peltz Nickel is a boy leading; he is blackened, and has a beard and rattling chains. He gives a switch to the mother, which sticks behind the glass the whole year, if the children do not hide nor break it. This begins on the first Sunday of December, with Advent, and may be practised till Christmas. He carries apples and nuts. The children must kneel and say their prayers, and if they say them nicely they get some of these, and perhaps honey-cakes and candy, which the Christ-kindel and Peltz Nickel distribute; but they do not give the Christmas gifts." She adds, "We only went to one or two houses."

As regards the New Year, Mr. Wollenweber says that in Berks County, around Womelsdorf, a dozen boys or so will form a company, choose a captain, take a gun, and go around the neighborhood, calling on different persons and asking leave to wish them a New Year. If they obtain consent, they will form into a rank, and the captain will repeat the following verses:

> " Nau wunschen wir euch en Neues Yohr,
> En Bretzel wie en Scheuer Thor,
> En Brodwurst wie en Ofen Rohr,
> Und in der Midde-Stub en Tisch
> Oof yedem Eck en gebrodener Fisch,
> Und in der Mitt en Bottell Wein,
> Das soll unser Neu Yohr's Wunsch sein."

" Now we wish you a New Year; a pretzel like a barn-door; a fried sausage like a stove-pipe; and in the middle room a table, with a fried fish at each corner, and in the midst a bottle of wine, —that shall be our New Year's wish."

Then they fire off the gun, and are invited to come in and take a supper. Generally they go to farm-houses, where there are a number of daughters, and these daughters are usually prepared to give them a hospitable reception.

This custom, says Mr. Wollenweber, also prevails in the Palatinate.

I am also told that the custom of firing-in the New Year is found in Lehigh, Berks, and Lebanon Counties.

THE PLAINER SECTS.

Some of our Pennsylvania German Baptist sects cannot escape a suspicion of asceticism. I speak of them as Baptists, for not only the Dunkers who dip, but the Mennonites who pour, are Baptists, because they baptize on faith, adults or young persons, and not infants. At the time of the great Centennial Exposition one of our farmers told me that although their members were not forbidden to visit it, yet it had been recommended for them not to do so. He said that there were worldly things there, unnecessary things. Of the stricter sect of New Mennonites I heard that they were forbidden. But as these churches are of simple congregational form, this rule and this recommendation may have been local.

I met another farmer on a railway train, and asked about the Exposition. He answered, " I don't think the Lord has any love to them things. It's like those picnics and things ; those that will go to them will do anything." But his name was afterward connected with a more disreputable thing than a picnic.

In some things our New Mennonites are very strict. It is said that one was obliged to take down his front porch and another to cut down his evergreen-trees, apparently because they were suspected of being " proud." A woman inclined to the same sect cultivated no flowers. Yet it is surprising how showily the members allow their unbaptized children to dress, in which they are a great contrast to the Amish. It is the same New Mennonites who have so rigid a ban in the church of which I have spoken in the text. I have spoken of a father who did not come to the family table. A member of the church was kind enough to explain to me the cause. He gave way to a selfish spirit, found fault unnecessarily. The wife bore it a long time, and then complained to the meeting, whereupon he did not show a penitent spirit ; he was not willing to humble himself before her. So they continued to eat apart, to be separate. Our Old Mennonites confess their faults to each other in an open meeting of the members. If the same rule prevails among the New Mennonites, we can see that it would not be at all grateful to the pride of "the natural man" to apologize thus to a meeting of which the wife was a part.

As regards another sect, the River Brethren, an acquaintance tells me that he was expelled from them for voting at elections; but still some of the brethren will vote. But against him there were two other charges, namely, of having a melodeon in his house and having his property insured.

Another division of the Mennonites are the Amish, who are very simple in dress and habits, very recluse. I once called on a plain old Amish farmer in moderate circumstances. His clothing was long worn, but clean and well mended, and his bent form, silver beard and hair commanded regard. A neighbor was with him whom he called Chrissly, the nickname of Christian. In conversation I spoke of one of my relatives as a lawyer, and I saw that this had an immediate effect. The neighbor remarked that when Judge Jasper Yeates was growing old, he said that lawyers are like woollen yarn, they will stretch. The old man added, "I guess they must tell rather more than the truth when they *blead.*"

I said to the old man, "You all vote?"

"Yes; there's some of them a little conscientious; but if they are, they can just leave it alone. It may be I'm dumb; but I just think we must have government,—we have Scripture for it,—and if the good people—what I call the tame people—stays away and leaves it all to the rowdies, how would it be? We must *bray* for the government; do all we can. We mustn't go to pole-raisings. It oughtn't to be, but sometimes they will, you know."

"Do any of your young men learn trades?" I asked.

"Yes; some are carpenters or cabinet-makers."

"But you would rather have them farmers; why do you like that best?"

"I think if a man's a *Gristian*, that's the best thing he can undertake."

I have been told of an Amish farmer who was sitting at table with several young men who had lately joined the meeting, having been baptized. One of these was his hired man called Yoney (a nickname for Jonathan). The Amish here do not in general wear suspenders, and the old man, addressing Yoney, said, " *Was hasht du verschproke in der Gemeh ?*" (What did you promise in meeting ?) The young man looked at his clothes, and the elder pointed out the suspenders.

Yoney answered that he was allowed to wear the clothes that he already had until they were worn out.

" These look like new ones."

" They were my best ones," he answered, " and I have just begun to wear them every day."

A girl who has lived among the Amish has told me that they are obliged to give to beggars or " stragglers," or they would be turned out of meeting. She does not know indeed that they are obliged to give to those who are able to work ; but she did not believe that she ever saw them turn any away.

The impression prevails concerning the Amish that they endeavor to fulfil the saying, " Give to him that asketh of thee, and from him that would borrow of thee turn not thou away." When I turn my mind to these plain people, I sometimes recall the trailing arbutus, which is found partly buried under the leaves and clinging close to the surface of the ground, but which when drawn up displays, though sometimes disfigured with dead, brown leaves, such a delicate form and tint, and exhales so sweet a perfume.

And I also have recalled Pope's *Temple of Fame :*

> " Next came the smallest tribe I yet had seen,
> Plain was their dress and modest was their mien ;
> 'Great idol of mankind, we neither claim
> The praise of merit, nor aspire to fame !
> But safe in deserts from the applause of men
> Would die unheard of, as we lived unseen.'
>
>   *   *   *   *   *   *
>
> 'And live there men who slight immortal Fame,
> Who then with incense shall adore our name ?' "

Yet our Amish are not a highly-educated people. Some years ago I inquired of a neighbor (who did not speak English fluently) on the subject of education. He said that they were not opposed to school-learning, but to high learning. " To send children to school from ten to twenty-one, we would think was opposed to Holy Scripture. There are things taught in school that don't agree with Holy Scripture."

I asked whether he thought it was wrong to teach that the earth goes round the sun. "I don't know anything about it; but I am not in favor of teaching geography and grammar in the schools: it's worldly wisdom."

All these Baptist sects have an unpaid ministry. Dr. H., of Bucks County, had a patient who was a Mennonite preacher, and the doctor refused to receive payment, saying that his father had taught him never to take pay from ministers of the gospel. The preacher looked sober and worried, but left quietly, and not long after he came bringing oats and corn for the doctor's horse. Afterwards he would bring flour or buckwheat-meal and choice bits about butchering time. Thus he seems, without entering into argument, to have relieved conscientious scruples about taking pay for preaching.

The ceremonial of these plain German sects is not formal and stately, like that of the Romish Church. A Moravian of Bethlehem was amused with one of their ministers, who, in ordaining a preacher, said, "*Nau kannscht du taufe, und nau kannscht du copulire.*" (Now you can baptize, and now you can marry.) Then turning to a brother, "*Hab ich net ebbes vergesse? Oh, ya; nau kannscht du auch beim Abendmahl diene.*" (Haven't I forgotten something? Oh, yes; now too you can serve in the Supper.)

Perhaps I would better translate the foregoing, "Thou can serve in the Supper," for our Pennsylvania Germans generally use the pronouns thee and thou.

The Mennonites have not a great yearly meeting like that of the Dunkers. In 1874 a correspondent of one of our Lancaster papers spoke of a national meeting held in Illinois by the Dunkers. He said, "They had abundant provision for the comfort of the brethren. The tent held ten thousand people. Eighty beeves were on the ground for steaks and roasts, and one baker had orders for eleven thousand loaves of bread." This year I see a statement that the national Conference was held in Indiana, and that twenty thousand people were on the ground. Dr. Seidensticker (*Century Magazine*, December, 1881) states the number of the Dunkers in the United States at about two hundred thousand, with nearly two thousand ministers, none of whom receives a salary. They pay more attention to education than the Mennonites, having now three collegiate institutes.

Mennonites are still found in Europe; in Holland, Prussia, Switzerland, the Palatinate, etc. They are sometimes distinguished in Germany into Heftler and Knöpfler, or Hook men and Button men; whence it seems that one of the distinctions here is widespread and of former origin. In 1881 I visited a family in the Palatinate, where I was shown a black satin waistcoat which the father had once worn, with hooks and eyes down the front; but none of our Amish here would wear anything so showy as a black satin waistcoat.

In the same year, 1881, a Mennonite preacher in the Palatinate gave me a list of many of the European communities, with names of their officers, such as preachers, deacons, etc. Many of the same names are found in Lancaster County, though not generally spelled in the same way. Such are Frantz, Lichti, Landes, Lehmann, Bachmann, Oesch, Bähr and Bär, Zercher, Krehbiel, Neff, Binkele, Muselmann, Brubacher, Staehly, Wickert. The family of Stauffer, in my own immediate neighborhood, has possessed for several generations the given names John and Christian. On the European list I find two Christian Stauffers, and one marked Johann Stauffer II.

I met in the Palatinate one who had travelled in Switzerland, and who had seen Mennonites there. All that he met there were farmers, who sold milk when near towns, or made butter and cheese when at a distance. They were mostly Amish. One Amish family, who still wore hooks and eyes, were named Stauffer. Other families whom he knew or heard of were named Wenger, Schwartz, Rettiger, etc.

I find in the volume just mentioned a little description of a Mennonite congregation near Tilsit, in Prussia, which shows how closely agricultural the people are. There are altogether about eight hundred (five hundred and twenty being baptized). Seven hundred and seventy live in the country, in town thirty. Fifteen belong to the mercantile class, to mechanics twenty-four, to laborers seventy. The rest own or rent land (*sind Grundbesitzer und Rentier*).

From this volume, some of the Russian Mennonites appear to have adopted river-baptism. One body of Russians went to Taschkant in Middle Asia, and seem to have been quite unfortunate, as most of us would expect non-resistants to be among those nearly barbarians. And these emigrants were extremists, refusing obedience to worldly authorities; they were unwilling to plant forests in lieu of military service in Russia; the office of preacher they considered a human institution, and called themselves the spouse of the Lord. (*Brautgemeinde des Herrn.*)

I have received a copy of the Family Almanac for 1882, published by a Mennonite company in Indiana, which bears on the cover a little engraving of the sword being beaten into the ploughshare, and the motto above, "Glory to God in the highest, and on earth peace, good will toward men."

Within the almanac, among other matter, is the well-known engraving of a man surrounded by the twelve signs of the zodiac, and headed thus, "Anatomy of Man's Body as said to be governed by the Twelve Constellations." I find the words *said to be* significant,—perhaps the introduction of some scrupulous person. On the same page is the statement, "Jupiter is the ruling planet this year."

A meeting calendar at the close of the almanac gives forty-two meeting-houses in Lancaster County, and twenty-two others in this State. Also eleven in Indiana, one in Michigan, and seventeen in Virginia. There are many Mennonites in Ohio, but this list does not speak of them. Those meeting-houses mentioned make nearly one hundred; but probably the list contains none of the New or Reformed Mennonites, also none of the Amish, who almost invariably meet in private houses. A peculiarity of the Mennonite meetings in the list just spoken of is the long-interval between meetings, which is mostly two or four weeks, and in three cases eight weeks.

In the article in the text called Schwenkfelders a careful observer will note a discrepancy. The author speaks of their holding the Spirit above the Scriptures; but also quotes Schwenkfeld as speaking in substance of "the gifts of grace revealed by the Father; yet so that this revelation should unite with the witness of the Scriptures." The author has not read Schwenkfeld's works, but quotes from different sources.

Before closing these remarks on the plainer sects, I may add that they are all evangelical, at least there are no Socinian "Menists" here as in Holland in the time of William Penn. The Dunkers do not believe in eternal perdition.

Further as regards one of these plainer sects, I may ask, Are they degenerating physically? This must be the tendency, it would seem, in all small religious bodies, limited in marriage to their own membership; but this may be compensated for by simplicity and purity of life and freedom from agitation and pecuniary distress

THE PEOPLE CONTRASTED.

It will be seen that there are among the Pennsylvania Germans two classes who may be compared or contrasted. The one party may be called the people of Lancaster and Lebanon, the Baptist and peace; the other, the people of Berks, Lehigh, and Northampton, the Reformed and Lutheran party. There are, however, many Reformed and Lutherans in the former division, but extremely few of the peace people in the latter. In Bucks and Montgomery on the east, Cumberland and other counties on the west, the different classes are mingled with many "English." I have already pointed out that many of the peace people are of Swiss origin; of the other division, many or most appear to have been Palatines, and perhaps French refugees. I have already pointed out also how these two parties differ, the most astonishing difference being that of politics. During the civil war the one party opposed the government, which the other sustained. I find a surprising instance in my notes: A worthy Schwenkfelder told me of places in the northern part of Montgomery where party spirit seemed to have run riot, where vendue-criers would use such language as this. one held up an old scythe, and, as if to enhance its merits, said that it would do to cut old Lincoln's head off. The great contrast, however, in politics between the two districts alluded to may of course have had some other origin than the sectarian differences of the people. It must be remembered, however, in Germany, that for a long period the Reformed and Lutheran were state churches; and these other bodies that existed there were dissenters.

In language I have pointed out small differences. In holidays I have shown how Lancaster and Lebanon keep Halloween, in a manner unknown to the eastern counties. In the three "Dutch" counties of the east we have the rabbit myth more extensive than here in Lancaster. While those three have great agricultural county fairs, Lancaster has held none since before the war. I attribute this in a great measure to the opposition of our Baptist farmers to horse-racing and its concomitants.

A friend gives me another small point of difference. In Lancaster, at Christmas-time, is sold a cake called *Motzebom*, which is not seen in Eastern Pennsylvania. This, he adds, is from the Italian *marzepane*, or bread of St. Mark, which came from Italy into Germany; in England called marchpain.

MISCELLANEOUS.

Said a young man to us, "My daddy won't sit in no rocking-chair. He has a crutch agin' a rocking-chair." It appears that the same objection has been felt by other Pennsylvania Germans. Wollenweber gives us a farmer talking to his children in the spring, who says especially that none of the girls is to sit in a rocking-chair on a working-day. In sounding the praises of Womelsdorf, Berks County, the same author tells us that the women are never seen sitting in a rocking-chair.

We may sometimes judge of a person's character by hearing the arguments used to induce him to act. Thus does Wollenweber endeavor to induce the people of Womelsdorf to erect a monument to Conrad Weiser, who is buried near the town, and who was a distinguished German pioneer. Wollenweber encourages them to raise a subscription. Certainly, he says, the man who owns the place would not object to having a beautiful monument on his farm; and thousands would go to see it; so that the railroad company, the turnpike company, and all the tavern-keepers in the neighborhood would make a good thing of it. "Alas!" he adds, "most of the people who live round there do not know how to prize the treasure they possess."

These are rural similes used by Wollenweber, whose little volume is "in the idiom and manner of speech of the Pennsylvania Germans." It tells of girls who want to be English (who profess to talk English), but when some one from town talks to them, they stand like a hen who has dropped an egg. Again, we read that Weiser remonstrated with Stiegel on account of his extravagance, etc.; but he might as well have talked to a dead calf.

Perhaps the best article in the collection (which is indeed of very unequal merit) is the story of the dreadful noise that was heard just before daylight in Lancaster County, near Berks. The people went to Squire Reinhold's to talk about it, and the squire, who was very high learned, thought it must be the train of the wild huntsman, presaging war, pestilence, and scarcity. He had a German book that told about it. One stout young fellow, however, had a mind to see for himself; and he took with him an old shoemaker, who had fought in the Buckshot war, and who was fearfully full of courage when he had emptied a pint of whiskey, but whom anybody could chase away when he was sober. (The Buckshot war was a bloodless affair at Harrisburg, in 1838.)

This pair went to watch, and heard nothing for two or three nights, but at last about three in the morning a noise was heard as if every storm-wind had broken loose. The shoemaker was so frightened that he sank down at the foot of a tree and buried his head in the fallen leaves. But the young man discovered that the noise was caused by an immense flock of wild pigeons.

It has been hinted in the text that the Pennsylvania Germans are not refined. One of their preachers has told me of their being a gross, unrefined people, and of his being often obliged to see things that he would rather not. Another preacher gave me this anecdote: A man, speaking of his son, said, "I would rather have lost my best horse as Jake. He was such a fellow to work."

Of those who are yoked together in life and do not pull together, the "Dutch" of Berks and Lehigh say, " *Der ehne keht chee un der onnere keht haw.*" (One gees and the other haws.) It is applied also to others who do not agree, and is heard also thus, " *Ehnce will chee, oonce anner will ho.*"

Although our "Pennsylvania Dutch" are of undoubted German origin, yet in common speech they almost always speak of themselves as Dutch, which sounds much more like *Deutsch* than German does; and it is not a great length of time since Germans were so called. I think that it was in Miss Aiken's life of Elizabeth that I found the following. One of the suitors to the queen was brother to the emperor of Austria. The Earl of Sussex wrote to Elizabeth, "His highness, besides his natural language of Dutch, speaketh very well Spanish and Italian."

The following are from newspapers of different dates:

In 1869 a literary society in Lancaster County discussed the question, Resolved, that wealth exerts a greater influence than knowledge. The decision was in favor of the affirmative.

In 1872 a lyceum in the same county debated the subject that wealth has a greater influence on the people in general than education. The decision was in favor of education, "contrary to expectation."

In 1879, in another literary society in our county, this referred question was answered, Is laziness a habit, a disease, or a sin? If we only had the answer!

At a lyceum in Berks County in 1882 was discussed this subject, Resolved, that ambition is a greater evil than intemperance. The judges decided in favor of the affirmative; the house afterwards in the negative.

The following seems to be from a report in the Reading *Eagle:* Samuel J. and his wife returned from their wedding trip on Monday evening, when they were serenaded early by a band, and later Butcher arrived before the bride's house with the si-gike, followed by about one hundred little boys. After making the welkin ring for about one hour, Samuel handed over a V, and the band left in high glee.

At my own home I have heard the sound of these rough serenades, borne over the fields in notes by distance made less harsh. The instruments are pots and pans beaten, and a horse-fiddle, made by putting rosin on edges of a box, and drawing a rail over them. In my own neighborhood I hear that this rough play is going out of fashion as musical bands are coming in.

In the south of England I saw an aged pair who had received a rough serenade on account of conjugal disturbances.

A friend, born in the Palatinate, tells me that rough serenades were formerly practised there, and called *Katzen*-musik (cat music), or charivari. They were introduced on the occasion of disproportionate marriages. Thus,—

> " *Eine alte Frau und ein junger Mann*
> *Die müsse Charivari han.*"

" An old wife and a young husband must have a serenade."

In Berks County a young publisher told me that when visiting the country and asking his subscribers how they liked his paper, he received answer that it was " a very nice paper for the cupboard." Being a large-sized paper, it was a good one to spread upon shelves to keep them clean.

Lancaster County men connected with the press have had similar experiences. One canvassing for a paper to be published in a small town came across an old man and his wife tying covers on pots of apple-butter, and showed them a specimen copy. He was answered, " *Ich verlang's net. Es macht net vier Happe-deckel.*" (I don't want it. It won't make four pot-covers.)

When the *Lancaster County Farmer* was started it was in small pamphlet form. A person in the office showed it to a man, who took hold of it, opened it, and looked at the other side, but believed he would not take it: it was almost too small to tie apple-butter crocks with.

A man came into the office of the Lancaster *Express*, Republican, and wished to " pay his paper." I will call his post-office Blackburn. Considerable time was spent in looking over the list of the weekly paper and trying to find his name, and then he was asked whether it was not the daily. No, he did not think it was. And was he sure that he got it from Blackburn Post-Office "Yes."

"Well, maybe it's the *Intelligencer*."

"I guess maybe it is; it's a Democrat paper."

I have spoken of old apple-butter. The following is condensed from a Lancaster paper of 1874: "A gentleman handed us a few days since a bottle of apple-butter made in 1820, being fifty-three years old last fall. It is still good, and retains its original flavor. It was part of the 'housestire' of Mrs. R. of this county after her marriage." (*Haus steur* is the house-furnishing. Apple-butter kept so long dries away to a very small bulk, but can be renewed by boiling it with water.)

At a Quaker settlement in Lancaster County, nearly extinct among the "Dutch," a father urged his son to activity thus: "Let me see if thee'll go on and help me like a little Dutch boy would do, or whether thee'll linger and loiter about." When the boy had got into college he told of his neighbors' saying, "Too much eddication, you know, makes a man lazy." A neighboring farmer was inquiring for a person to help him in haying and harvest, and the lad spoke for himself, saying that some people thought he was lazy, but that he could work and was willing to work. "Still, you're a little lazy," answered the farmer.

Riding one evening we met an Amish farmer on horseback driving a very clean sow. We stopped, and I asked whether he had a certain book which contains a notice of the Amish. He answered that he did not have many books.

"My Bible and Testament's enough for me to read;" then, recollecting himself, "and the Martyr-Book, I have that."

"Does Mr. Kennel live here?" inquired a stranger of an Amish farmer.

"Joe Kennel lives here. I'm the man."

Mr. R. has told me that in 1853, at the age of six, he went to public school in this county. He had just learned to read, and was put into a class in the Testament. They read four to six times a day. It took them about three months to accomplish the Testament, and then the teacher put them into the Bible, which they completed, Mr. R. says, before he was eight years old, but under a succeeding teacher.

"We hadn't many books in those days," says Mr. R.; "I used to read the weekly *Tribune* down to the names of the Kansas settlers."

The custom of barring out the teacher at Christmas appears not yet to be extinct in Lancaster County.

The scholars demand a Christmas gift, but are not always successful. One teacher near here walked calmly home, and allowed the scholars to open the door at their leisure.

An acquaintance, born in Northampton County, tells me that at his native place the teacher was locked out not at Christmas, but on Shrove-Tuesday, and merely for sport.

That peculiarity of some Germans by which they pronounce Goble like Kopel is also found in Pennsylvania. A certain carpenter could not tell me whether his son's name was Beck or Peck. And an "English" boy supposed that a certain man had a hare-lip, as he heard him spoken of as Cutlip, but his name was Gottlieb.

A neighboring farmer came to our house with his little boy, about five years old. I handed the little fellow a penny, and he began to pull his father, who was talking.

"He gives it to you, does he?" I asked.

"Yes, to put into his box. He's got two full. I'll have to steal them some day, I guess," winking at me.

"That's the way you teach them to save?" said I.

"Yes, keep them till he gets big. Buy a horse and buggy with them, he says."

Then, with paternal pleasure, "He tells his mother he don't

want no hilly land." Strange for a family of Swiss descent? Their ancestors had enough hills in Switzerland. How they enjoy this level limestone land!

One of my acquaintances thinks that the reason these people or this class got the rich limestone land was that they were not afraid of the labor of cutting down the heavy timber which grew on it.

I have just told how the little fellow was saving his pennies to "buy a horse and buggy,"—the great pride of our farmer boy's heart. On a neighboring farm to ours lived the grandfather, who had his own plain carriage, the father with another, and two sons, aged about twenty-one, each with a buggy. This must be the great extravagance of our young farmers now. But having buggies they can take the girls to ride; and they can sometimes take others too. The other day a lad kindly took me up; an Amish boy, in a plain buggy, driving a pretty good horse. As our Amish so often drive in wagons, covered with light-colored oil-cloth, I made some remark about the buggy, and the lad answered that it was his. He is fourteen years old.

On the other hand, I have heard of a Miss K., who was considered a great catch, being thought rich by the young "Dutch fellows." Among the numerous young men who came to see her was one who drove two horses. Her father asked him what business he was in.

"Not in any just now."

"Then I don't see how you can keep two horses;" which remark was fully understood as putting an end to the young man's suit. He need i't come there no more!

The mania for a driving-team accounts for the occasional disappearance of harness when left unguarded.

A lawyer in Lancaster describes a peculiarity of our people. In most places, he says, a man comes in, tells you what he wants, and perhaps retains you in his case. But here there is first a conversation on diverse subjects.

Another says that the country people expect you to hear an

account of their ailings and those of their friends and the state of the crops before proceeding further.

A neighbor coming to our house to get a horse and vehicle, talked perhaps half an hour, as if on a friendly call, before she told her errand.

It is hard for some of our Pennsylvania Germans to write a letter in English. I wrote once to a preacher, who got the ticket-agent at the railroad to answer. The following was sent by a workingman:

" Dear A B Your man have pacts that Roof has left some stuff mite I have them to pact my slate roof the leeke I sought the might spile so I mite youse it as well as let the leek away ensur soon.   Yours   C D."

Which may be interpreted thus: " Your man has patched that roof, and has left some stuff. Might I have it to patch my slate-roof,—the leak? I thought it might spoil, so I might use it as well as let it leak away. Answer soon."

A young " English" girl was visiting a " Dutch" one, and the father of the latter, a substantial farmer, was kindly going to take the visitor part way home. The girls stayed talking above until the voice of the farmer was heard at the foot of the stairs, " Staytsch!" He was no more to be trifled with than the stage-driver.

Once when absent from home he bought a plaster cast of Canova's Three Graces. Such things are not seen in " Dutch" farm-houses, and ere long the Three Graces were provided with petti-coats of pink and blue tissue-paper.

An expression that is very offensive to our Pennsylvania Germans, when applied to them by " English" folks, is " dumb Dutch." Dumb is of course the German *dumm*, stupid, and it is familiarly used by our Pennsylvania Germans themselves. One of my friends said that she thought she could learn to use a sewing-machine,—" People as dumb as me has learned to use them."

A Lancaster gentleman gave me this little anecdote:

Old Mrs. H., anxious to see a baptism by immersion, proposed to her hired girl, Susan, to go across the fields to the place where there was to be baptism in the creek. Waymaking they were to cross the same creek by a log, but Mrs. H. fell in to her waist Wading back to the bank, Susan standing alarmed, Mrs. H. said, quietly and quickly, "*Suss, mir hens yetst g'seh; yetst welle mir hame geh;*" or, "Susy, we've seen it now; now let's go home."

A lawyer, Mr. W., who taught in Schuylkill County about fifteen or twenty years ago, has given me some of his recollections.

He said that among the mines in Schuylkill the population is English, that is, American, Welsh, Scotch, and Irish, but in the valleys there are "Dutch" farmers, mostly Lutherans, he thinks.

"The farmers lived well in the valleys of Schuylkill County; no danger of freezing in winter between two feather-beds;" and Mr. W. liked the fried *pawn-haus*, although he found it rather rich.

"In that county I had some of the pleasantest times. I was there as a teacher, and they immediately appropriated m I was not obliged to wait for the formality of an introduction in the German community. I could see, however, a tendency to mistrust the man of Yankee origin, and to combine against him; the young men fearing lest the teacher should cut them out with the girls. I was invited to go one evening on a sleighing-party. There were an equal number of young men and girls, and at a village we took in two fiddlers. We drove several miles to a stone tavern or farm-house (for the tavern-keeper is generally a farmer). The fiddlers sat in the window-seats, formed by the thick stone walls; and the dance was lively until the small hours. The dancers made a business of it, and went to work with a will. The dances were called 'straight eights,' forward and back, and mostly shuffles. Although at a tavern, none got drunk. Coming home, the driver increased the fun by upsetting the party in the snow.

"I taught public school, and on account of not speaking German I had much difficulty with the younger scholars, who, being under the care of their mothers, seldom heard the English language. The home talk was always in "Dutch," as they called it, though the fathers, when transacting business, were able to speak English.

"Even the larger pupils were not able to understand all of their lessons in English. Some of the farmers were rich. The 'Dutch' farmers were universally Democrats." So says Mr. W.

———————

Another lawyer, named H. (of Pennsylvania German origin), has given me some of his recollections of Berks County. Berks is that county concerning which it has been a standing joke that its people still voted for Andrew Jackson,—a well-worn joke.

"It must have been a select party," says Mr. H., "that W. was at, if none of them got drunk."

"The great dancing tunes in Berks are Fisher's Hornpipe, Washington's Grand March, Charlie over the Water, Yankee Doodle, Hail Columbia, and We won't go Home till Morning."

"The walls in the stone houses in Berks are generally two feet thick, built like forts, with plenty of room to sit in the window-seats, but usually the landlord had a long bar-room table, on which he put chairs for the fiddlers. About every third dance they must have a drink, which frequent potations sometimes brought them to the floor, unable to distinguish sounds." "The dancing they indulge in in Berks," says Mr. H., "is not the fashionable kind, but is more exhausting than mauling rails in August, or thrashing rye with a flail. The figures are called out by some skilful person; the dances are called straight fours or hoe-downs, the dancers being arranged in four rows, in a sort of double column on each side. After the inside couples have danced and all have changed places, the former are allowed to rest while the outside couples dance."

"The battalion (Pennsylvania Dutch, *Badolya?*) is an annual day of joy and festivity in Berks County. The annual training, which gave name to the day, has long been given up, but still just before hay-making the landlords of the country towns, such as Kutztown or Hamburg, will advertise that they will hold the annual battalion (without any soldiers). The peanut-venders, the men with flying-horses, and the others who expect to reap the harvest, come during the night before, and by six in the morning everything is ready, and about that hour the farmers begin to come in, wives, sons, daughters, hired men, and maids, even little children and quite small babies.

" The farmers patronize the landlords by dining and drinking. You can get a good dinner at Kutztown for less money than in any other town I know. As for drinking, bars have even been set up upon the second floor where the dancing took place.

" The old folks amuse themselves by talking together, looking on and seeing how well their sons and daughters can dance, the old men drinking a little whiskey, several times repeated, and perhaps treating their wives to some sarsaparilla. By evening the old folks will be at home; but the daughters, who could hardly expect the young men to walk home with them as long as the sun was shining, stay later, carrying gingerbread and peanuts home in their handkerchiefs.

" Roving gamblers also visit the battalion; and many an unwary youth has lost all his money, earned by hard work, and, after that was gone, has striven to better his fortune, but unsuccessfully, by giving up his watch."

The remark of the last speaker, that they still have the *badolya*, or annual training, in Berks without any soldiers, reminds me that they still have in Germany the *Kirch-weih*, church consecration, or saint's day, without going to any church at all, but dance and are merry after harvest.

I was told some years back of farmers in Berks " worth from thirty to eighty thousand dollars who never bring wheat bread to the table except at Christmas and New Year's. This is from their great economy and desire to sell the wheat."

Mrs. R., of Lehigh County, tells me that at her father's they baked wheat bread on Saturday, for Sunday, but during the week they ate rye.

When her brother-in-law returned from a visit to Ohio, he said, "*Daraus in Ohio, 's is so schane. Sie essen laute waytzbrod;*" or, " Out in Ohio it is so fine. They eat altogether wheat bread."

There is a part of the city of Lancaster which is called Germany. Here natives of that country buy house-lots, and send their children out to beg until they find they have a secure footing. Nor does the average citizen disapprove of this proceeding; although he is dissatisfied if a woman who owns two brick houses sends to the soup-house for a free lunch.

I was amused one day in Lancaster by a boy's asking, "Won't you give me a penny to save?" A pretty little girl, comfortably dressed and speaking German, came into one of the newspaper offices for help, the family having been unfortunate. When some one gave her a penny, she took from her pocket a purse and put her money away.

Three great waves of emigration, it may be said, early settled Pennsylvania. The Quakers settled in the southeast. I have travelled among Friends in several localities, but I never saw any other community so strongly Quaker as Chester County.

The German immigration mostly lay outside of this, on the north and west. West of Chester County lies Lancaster, settled in a great measure by German Baptists (Mennonites), and which is probably one of the strongest Baptist populations in the world. Farther west the Scotch-Irish element is very strong. In the west of the State I was surprised by hearing a physician (I will call his name McCalmont) say that the Scotch-Irish had been the making of Pennsylvania. It is this class, doubtless, who have caused the region around Pittsburgh to be called the backbone of Presbyterianism.

This volume does not endeavor to describe the manners and ways of living of all Pennsylvania Germans, but only of the majority. People of wealth and education resemble each other in most civilized lands. And although the Pennsylvania Germans are principally devoted to agriculture, yet about twenty per cent., as I estimate, have gone into cities and into other employments. Among those who have aided less or more in the publication of this volume are ministers, lawyers, physicians, editors, bankers, merchants, and teachers of Pennsylvania German origin. Many persons of note in Pennsylvania have been of German descent, from Peter Muhlenberg, a Lutheran preacher, who commanded a regiment in the Revolution, to a number of governors of this State,— Snyder, Hiester, Shulze, Wolf, Ritner, Shunk, and Hartranft. Governor Hartranft's ancestor, then called Hertteranfft, came in with the Schwenkfelders in 1734.

To these distinguished Pennsylvania Germans I may add Dr. Gross, the eminent surgeon. The German blood is also found in a great number of families in our country. It is stated that Simon Cameron is of Scottish descent on the father's side; and on the mother's is descended from Conrad Pfoutz. The Hon. Jeremiah S. Black and William D. Howells, the well-known author, have told me that they are partly of Pennsylvania German origin.

THE END.